RELIGION &
THE ORDER OF NATURE

RELIGION &
THE ORDER OF NATURE

*The 1994 Cadbury Lectures
at the University of Birmingham*

SEYYED HOSSEIN NASR

New York   Oxford
OXFORD UNIVERSITY PRESS
1996

Oxford University Press

Oxford   New York
Athens   Auckland   Bangkok   Bogota   Bombay
Buenos Aires   Calcutta   Cape Town   Dar es Salaam
Delhi   Florence   Hong Kong   Istanbul   Karachi
Kuala Lumpur   Madras   Madrid   Melbourne
Mexico City   Nairobi   Paris   Singapore
Taipei   Tokyo   Toronto

and associated companies in
Berlin   Ibadan

Published by Oxford University Press, Inc.
198 Madison Avenue, New York, New York 10016

Oxford is a registered trademark of Oxford University Press, Inc.

Library of Congress Cataloging-in-Publication Data
Nasr, Seyyed Hossein.
Religion and the order of nature / Seyyed Hossein Nasr.
    p.   cm.
"The 1994 Cadbury Lectures at the University of Birmingham."
Includes index.
ISBN 0-19-510274-6; ISBN 0-19-510823-X (pbk.)
1. Nature—Religious aspects.   2. Religion and science.   3. Holy, The.
4. Philosophy of nature.   5. Environmental ethics.   6. Human ecology—
Religious aspects.   I. Title.
BL65.N53N37   1996
291.2'4—dc20   95-31919

9 8 7 6 5 4 3 2 1

Printed in the United States of America
on acid-free paper

بِسْمِ اللهِ الرَّحْمَنِ الرَّحِيمِ

وَإِذْ قَالَ رَبُّكَ لِلْمَلَائِكَةِ إِنِّي جَاعِلٌ فِي
الْأَرْضِ خَلِيفَةً قَالُوا أَتَجْعَلُ فِيهَا مَنْ يُفْسِدُ فِيهَا
وَيَسْفِكُ الدِّمَاءَ وَنَحْنُ نُسَبِّحُ بِحَمْدِكَ
وَنُقَدِّسُ لَكَ قَالَ إِنِّي أَعْلَمُ مَا لَا تَعْلَمُونَ
سورة البقرة - ٣٠

Behold, Thy Lord said to the angels: "Verily I am about to establish on earth a vicegerent." They said, "Wilt Thou place therein one who will spread corruption thereon and shed blood, whilst it is we who celebrate Thy praises and glorify Thy holy Name? God answered, "Verily I know what ye know not."

The Noble Quran—*Sūrat al-Baqarah*, v. 30.

Contents

RELIGION &
THE ORDER OF NATURE

Introduction

The Earth is bleeding from wounds inflicted upon it by a humanity no longer in harmony with Heaven and therefore in constant strife with the terrestrial environment. The world of nature is being desecrated and destroyed in an unprecedented manner globally by both those who have secularized the world about them and developed a science and technology capable of destroying nature on an unimaginable scale and by those who still live within a religious universe, even if the mode of destruction of the order of nature by the two groups is both quantitatively and qualitatively different. The plight of the forests of the Northwest region of the United States, the Amazon, and the Himalayas, the pollution of air and water worldwide, especially in the former Soviet Union, and the constant extinction of more and more species are stark witnesses to this tragic fact. The environmental crisis now encompasses the entire Earth. Strangely enough, although the destruction of the sacred quality of nature by modern man dominated by a secularist perspective is directly responsible for this castastrophe, the vast majority of the human species, whether participating directly or indirectly in the havoc wreaked upon the natural environment, still lives within a worldview dominated by religion. The role of religion in the solution of the existing crisis between man and nature is therefore crucial. Furthermore, any discussion of religion and the order of nature, which is interested in healing the wounds of the Earth and ameliorating the existing crisis now threatening man's terrestrial existence, cannot but take place on a global scale.

A need exists to develop a path across religious frontiers without destroying the significance of religion itself and to carry out a comparative study of the "Earths" of various religions as has been carried out for their "Heavens," if these terms are understood in their traditional metaphysical and cosmological sense. But even if such a method is developed successfully and the religious understanding of the order of nature in each tradition is taken seriously as a religious matter and not just historically or anthropologically, the problem still exists of numerous schools within each religion from which one can draw. Therefore, the question of the principle of selection becomes important.

In the following chapters we have first sought to develop the means of crossing from one religious universe into another without destroying the religious perspective itself and reducing it to either mere historicism or a phenomenological study devoid of the sense of the sacred and divorced from the reality of faith. Our next task has been to delve into various religious traditions to select those schools of thought, or at least some of them, that have displayed special interest in the order of nature, our guiding principle of selection being precisely the centrality of religious perspectives that are concerned with the natural order and that bear upon the existing environmental crisis. Needless to say, each major tradition such as Hinduism, Buddhism, Judaism, Christianity, or Islam presents a rich variety of schools often in contention with each other concerning the world of nature and religion's relation to the natural order. Countless studies could be devoted to any single religion as far as this issue is concerned. Our selection is meant to bring out some of the deepest salient features of the views concerning nature in the religious traditions we have discussed without in any way claiming to be exhaustive or asserting that the views chosen are exclusive in their presentation of the religious understanding of the order of nature in the religious world in question. But what has been chosen is nevertheless significant within each tradition and also contains some of the profoundest views concerning the order of nature, views standing in contrast to the prevalent perspectives on nature and held by a world that has chosen to neglect the significance of the religious understanding of the cosmos.

And precisely because there exists such a world—namely the modern world, which had its exclusive home in the West until the last century but has now spread to other continents and which bears the primary responsibility for the global destruction of the environment—we have sought to delve into a historical study of both philosophy and science in the West that, beginning with views similar to the philosophies and sciences of other traditional civilizations, developed in what can only be called an anomalous manner from the sixteenth and seventeenth centuries onward. It moved away from the almost universally held view of the sacredness of nature to one that sees man as alienated from nature and nature itself as no longer the progenitor of life (the very root of nature being from the Latin *nascitura,* meaning to give birth), but rather as a lifeless mass, a machine to be dominated and manipulated by a purely earthly man. It also divorced, in a manner not to be seen in any other civilization, the laws of nature from moral laws and human ethics from the workings of the cosmos.

We have also turned to the study of the concept of man himself in the Renaissance and its aftermath. This period witnessed the rise of a secular humanism and the absolutization of earthly man with immeasurable consequences for both the world of nature and traditional civilizations conquered by this new type of man for whom there was no longer any religious restraint upon the domination of nature and its forces, whether for the purpose of subduing nature itself in order to gain wealth or of conquering other civilizations or both.

In any case, in the West during the seventeenth century, religion lost its claim to the cosmos, and religious knowledge of the order of nature ceased to possess any legitimacy in the new paradigm of science, which came to dominate the scene. Moreover, until quite recently many theologians considered it the great glory of Christianity that it alone among the world's religions had permitted a purely secular science to develop in a civilization in which it was the dominant religion. It is only the environmental crisis of recent decades exemplified by global warming, the destruction of the ozone zone, and the death of so many animals and plants, a crisis now threatening the very fabric of life, that has finally caused many Christian theologians to have second thoughts concerning the rapport between religion and the order of nature. Even champions of secularism now speak of how significant the role of religion can be in averting a major global environmental catastrophe resulting in the loss of many human lives.

Consequently, many Christian theologians and also Jewish thinkers in the West have sought in recent years to develop a theology of the natural environment or what some now call *eco-theology*. After several centuries of neglect of this subject by both Catholics and Protestants, there is now serious interest in this field across the religious spectrum. And yet, as our study shows, despite a few exceptions, the concern of most religious thinkers in the West is with the development of environmental ethics and not the reassertion of the religious view of the order of nature as a legitimate knowledge that corresponds to an aspect, and in fact the most important aspect, of cosmic reality. To use the categories of Islamic thought, there is currently interest in *al-'amal* or action without *al-'ilm* or knowledge, whereas traditional Islamic sources have always taught that *al-'ilm* and *al-'amal* must accompany each other. *Al-'ilm* without *al-'amal* is, according to the famous Arabic proverb, like a tree without fruit. And *al-'amal* without *al-'ilm* is chaotic action without principle and ultimately positive efficacy, and it is usually more destructive than no action at all.

Strangely enough, in recent years the non-Western religions, including in this case Islam—in which such knowledge has continued to be present this day at the center of the religious scene—rather than being relegated to an "occultist" margin, have been mostly following the example of the West in dealing primarily with ethics rather than with the reassertion of a sacred science of nature. Only in the Islamic world at least debate about an Islamic science of nature independent of modern science has been carried out seriously in the past two or three decades. In any case, the reason for this neglect of the dimension of knowledge by non-Western religions in their response to the environmental crisis is that these religions, cut off for the most part from the forces driving modern science and technology and the deeper issues involved in the crisis at hand, are only now becoming aware of what this tragedy really involves. Only now is it beginning to dawn upon them that the present predicament is primarily the consequence of the loss of a sapiental knowledge of nature and an inner spiritual crisis and not simply the result of bad engineering.

Our aim in this study is to negate the totalitarian claims of modern science and to open up a space for the assertion of the religious view of the order of nature that various traditions developed over the centuries in their cosmologies and sacred sciences. Only if life is *really* sacred can one talk of the sacredness of life in anything more than a journalistic sense. In a world in which the very catergory of "sacredness" as applied to nature is meaningless, to speak of the sacredness of life is little more than sentimental thinking or hypocrisy. The religious view of the order of nature must be reasserted on the metaphysical, philosophical, cosmological, and scientific levels as legitmate knowledge without necessarily denying modern scientific knowledge, as long as it is remembered that this latter science is the result of very particular questions posed to nature. The great tragedy that came about in this domain, as has been also observed by others, was that modern science began by posing particular questions to nature and ending up by claiming that these are the only questions worth posing and in fact possible to pose. Hence, the religious understanding of nature, including the physical body, which is a central issue in so much of the contemporary debate about man and nature and which remains central to the teachings of so many religions outside those dominant in the West, must be fully asserted in the context of each tradition, and on the basis of such knowledge the religious ethics of the environment propagated in such a way that it would possess meaning on a global scale. We have ourselves sought to provide a few glimpses into the traditional teachings concerning the human body to demonstrate how essential such teachings are for the understanding of the religious order of nature without again claiming in any way to do anything more than provide a few salient examples.

Each tradition has both a wealth of knowledge and experiences concerning the order of nature, which, once resuscitated, can bring about a situation in which religions all over the globe could mutually enrich each other and also cooperate to heal the wounds inflicted upon Earth on the basis of a shared perspective of the sacredness of nature. Despite differences in the understanding of the meaning of the sacred and its source in various religions, they still share a great deal more in common and with each other than they do with a worldview in which the sense of the sacred has disappeared completely. Furthermore, such a resuscitation would not only make possible the serious implementation of ethical principles concerning nature, but it would also affect deeply many in the modern secularized West who are searching desperately for a spiritual relation with nature and who, not discovering it in what is available to them in mainsteam religious organizations, turn to everything from serious Oriental teachings, to cosmologies of religions long dead, such as the Egyptian, to various cults and to the whole spectrum of phenomena now termed "New-Age" religions.

The crisis of the natural environment is an external reminder of the crisis within the souls of men and women who, having forsaken Heaven in the name of the Earth, are now in danger of destroying the Earth as well. The environmental crisis requires not simply rhetoric or cosmetic solutions but a death and rebirth of modern man and his worldview. Man need not be and in fact cannot be "reinvented" as some have claimed, but he must be reborn as traditional or pontifical man, a bridge between Heaven and Earth, and the world of nature must once again be conceived as it has always been—a sacred realm reflecting the divine creative energies. There must be the rebirth of the religious knowledge of nature, the traditional cosmologies and sacred sciences still preserved in many of the non-Western areas of the world, while the heritage of the Western tradition in this domain must itself be resuscitated in a serious manner.

Moreover, a nexus must be created in this realm among the traditions, as has been carried out by the traditional proponents of the perennial philosophy for understanding of the Divine Principle and its numerous manifestations in various religious universes. One might say that in the same way that there is a *philosophia perennis,* there is also a *cosmologia perennis,* which in fact constitutes one of its elements and which shines through the multifarious traditional sciences of the cosmos.

Without the rediscovery of this sacred science of the order of nature, its exposition in a contemporary medium without distortion or dilution and the formulation of the link between such a knowledge of the order of nature and the ethics of the enviroment, there is no doubt that what remains of order in the natural and human worlds will turn into further chaos, not in the currently discussed sense of this term as prelude to a new phase of order and an element in the process of creativity, but as chaos that can destroy all human life on Earth. To preserve the sanctity of life requires remembering once again the sacred quality of nature. It means the resacralization of nature, not in the sense of bestowing sacredness upon nature, which is beyond the power of man, but of lifting aside the veils of ignorance and pride that have hidden the sacredness of nature from the view of a whole segment of humanity.

The composition of this book is the result of the invitation extended to us to deliver the Edward Cadbury Lectures at the University of Birmingham in the fall of 1994. When given this great honor and opportunity, it became almost immediately evident that in light of the present intellectual and spiritual malaise and the severity of the environmental crisis that so many people discuss while shunning the deeper issues involved, it was imperative for us to turn to the question of religion in its relation to the order of the nature but treated on a global scale. In a sense, this work follows our book *Man and Nature,* which comprised the text of our 1966 Rockefeller Lectures at the University of Chicago and which was one of the first works to predict the environmental crisis, and our 1981 Gifford Lectures, *Knowledge and the Sacred,* which itself ws followed by *The Need for a Sacred Science.* It is our hope that the present work will be a further humble step in turning the attention of those truly concerned with the human condition, as well as the order of nature, to the deeper issues involved. This book thus extends further the concerns of the works cited above, which sought to bring into focus the religious and spiritual dimensions of the environmental crisis and the significance of the gulf between knowledge and the sacred in precipitating the chaos and upheavals of a spiritual and intellectual order of which the pollution and destruction of the natural order is a most visible consequence.

We wish to thank the authorities of the Faculty of Theology of the University of Birmingham and especially Professor Frances Young for the invitation to deliver the Cadbury Lectures. We are also grateful to Katherine O'Brien for reading the manuscript and making valuable suggestions and to Muzit Hailu for preparing it for publication.

Wa mā tawfīqī illā bi'Llāh
S. H. N.

Bethesda, Maryland
September 1994

Religion
and Religions

دین حق را نیست حدی در ظهور می درخشد بر من و تو هم چو هور

گه پدید آید به اشکال بتان گه تجلی میکند بر کوه نور

The One cannot in the many but appear,
In creation as in these sacred forms,
Which, diverse in their outwardness,
Manifest a single inner Light, eternal.
I gazed upon Thy countenance in singleness,
How bewildered I am to behold Thy many Faces now.

Throughout the ages human beings have lived upon an earth that was for them *the* Earth, even if it constituted but a part of the globe, and under a heaven that was for them Heaven as such symbolized by the vast azure vault of the sky stretching from east to west. They lived on the Earth as at once a reflection of Heaven, progenitor of life and the female consort of celestial realities, the ground from which life originates and the theater from which it finally departs on its ultimate journey to the heavenly climes. There were on the earth other "Earths" wed to other "Heavens" of which human beings remained impervious until recent times and of which many, as yet not totally affected by the secularizing tides of modernism, remain unaware in a fundamental manner to this day.

It is only in these chaotic and turbulent times—when men and women, under whichever Heaven they happen to live, join those who have rejected the very notion of Heaven in its metaphysical, cosmological, and theological sense in destroying the Earth—that it is becoming incumbent to turn one's attention fully to the other Heavens and Earths that have determined the matrices of human existence over the millennia. As man succeeds in destroying so much of the order of nature and even threatens cosmic chaos of unprecedented proportions hardly imaginable just a century ago, it becomes necessary to turn to the other "Heavens" and "Earths" that have defined over the ages the *modus vivendi* of the many "humanities" which to an ever-greater extent are now unifying their efforts in the destruction of the natural order.

Although the crisis of the relationship between man and the world of nature on the scale observable today first began in the West where modernism was born, it is now global and demands an inquiry beyond the borders of the Western tradition[1] and the history of the attack against that tradition in modern times. Any inquiry into the question of the relation between religion and the order of nature, one that wishes to address the crucial issues emanating from the present-day environmental crisis, needs to cross the frontiers of various spiritual universes and journey from the Heaven and Earth of a single human collectivity to the many Heavens and Earths of the several "humanities" constituting present-day global humanity as such.[2]

To understand the relation of religion to the order of nature on a global scale, rather than from the perspective of a single tradition, a task to which we address ourselves in this book, it is necessary to understand the meaning of the order of nature or the "Earth" in the context of various religions. And by virtue of the inalienable link between Earth and Heaven, it is essential to turn to sapiential and metaphysical teachings of the religions in question as contained in their traditional cosmologies. It is also necessary to comprehend the sense in which the many "Heavens" have crowned the cosmos of various humanities. One must understand the truth that various religions over the ages have encompassed both the Heaven and the Earth of the humanity for which these religions have been destined and have therefore determined the meaning of nature and the order pervading it for their followers. Any serious study of this question must therefore turn, before discussing the order of nature itself, to the crucial problem of how to study religion and religions in a world in which the reality of other religions must be taken seriously as never before.

Moreover, this condition holds true especially for studies carried out in those parts of the world that have become fully exposed to the rationalism, humanism, and relativism characteristic of modernism and postmodernism, such as the modern West on both sides of the Atlantic. Any study that does not consider seriously the truth claims of religions other than one's own or rejects all religious truth, including that of one's ancestral religion, on the basis of doubt and skepticism cannot claim to say much that is relevant, in the context of present-day environmental crisis, about the living relation between religion and the order of nature. Nor could a study that disregards the truth of religions on a global scale come to any conclusions that would have appreciable significance for the majority of human beings on the globe who still live within the matrix of a religious universe and yet are participating, usually in opposition to the teachings of their own traditions, in the destruction of nature and the disruption of the order that still continues to dominate over the world of nature in such a blinding fashion.[3]

Let us then turn before anything else to the question of how to study religions "religiously" and yet in a scholarly fashion, a task of utmost significance especially in Western academic circles where the study of religion during the past century has often been itself a highly unreligious, if not antireligious, activity. Needless to say, this vast question is a subject that needs to be treated separately in not one but many separate works, and in fact numerous voices in recent years have turned to it from different perspectives and with varying concerns.[4] Here, although we would wish to address ourselves to the major issues involved in this central question, it is necessary to confine our discussion in the light of our present subject to the order of nature and leave aside the vast ramifications and extensions of this question to other domains of religion.[5] We must seek to understand the Heaven of each spiritual universe along with its Earth in the light of our understanding of that Heaven.[6] How else can we grasp religiously the religious significance of the order of nature in a religious universe other than our own?

CROSSING RELIGIOUS FRONTIERS

The question of crossing religious frontiers without loss of orientation and with full awareness of the reality of the sacred, which cannot be reduced to any other category, is perhaps the most daunting of all religious and theological tasks today and the only really new challenge of significance in the world of religious discourse of contemporary man.[7] The modern mind, affected by the relativizing influence of secularism and rationalism, has only too often been presented with the plurality of religions as proof of their relativity. Until recently, few in the West had sought to develop a metaphysics and theology of comparative religion that would avoid the trap of either retreating into a provincialism that would accept only one's own religion as being true and believe all other religions to be simply historic and social systems devoid of any absolute truth and therefore ultimately false or irrelevant from the point of view of that Truth, which is none other than the Absolute Itself, or considering all religions to be false.

The various possibilities followed in the West during the past century in the study of religion in a multireligious universe began with either the reduction of all religious realities to phenomena to be studied "scientifically" and historically in the perspective of *Religionwissenschaft* without regard for either the question of theological truth or faith, or phenomenologically with little interest in the historical setting as well as disregard for the question of faith or metaphysical truth. Outside the secularized universities where these approaches were cultivated and continue to be so to a large extent even today, the seminaries did not cease to treat other religions as simply those of "heathens" or "pagans" to be studied so as to be refuted or to better prepare missionaries for combatting them. In the West only during the past generation have a number of Christian scholars and theologians, and also a number of Jewish scholars, sought to develop a means of studying other religions theologically and spiritually as committed Christians or Jews. Meanwhile, there have also been those who have accepted a sentimental unity of religions at the expense of overlooking their formal differences and belittling what they usually refer to in a derogatory manner as "theological dogmas."

Amidst this rather bewildering scene, one also finds the view of the propagators of the perennial philosophy, the *philosophia* or *sophia perennis,* expositors of tradition such as R. Guénon, A. K. Coomaraswamy, F. Schuon, T. Burckhardt, M. Lings, and M. Pallis, who have provided the metaphysical knowledge necessary for understanding the multiplicity of religions while doing full justice to the claim of absoluteness within each authentic religion and the irreducible sacred forms and doctrines they contain within themselves.[8] And yet their views have not been taken seriously in academic circles until quite recently[9] since their metaphysical teachings negate the very basis upon which modern rationalism and historicism rest and challenge the very legitimacy of the modern and what is now called by some the postmodern world. Still, it is only the universal doctrines of the perennial philosophy as interpreted traditionally that are able to provide the key for the penetration into diverse religious worlds or different "Earths" and "Heavens" without destroying the sense of the sacred or the absoluteness of each authentic religion, which in its essence is religion as such.

The traditional interpretation of the *philosophia perennis* sees a single Divine Reality as the origin of all the millennial religions that have governed human life over the ages and have created the traditional civilizations with their sacred laws, social institutions, arts, and sciences. This Divine Reality is beyond all conceptualization and all that can be said of It, and is referred to by such sacred formulae as the *Lā ilāha illa'Llāh* (There is no divinity but God) of Islam, *neti neti* (Not this, not that) of the Upanishads, the "Tao that can be named is not the Tao" of the Tao Te-Ching and also the "I am that I am" of the Bible if the meaning of this well-known dictum is understood on the highest level.

Other traditions, especially the primal ones, refer to It only through silence or indirect allusion, whereas certain esotericisms such as the Cabala refer to It by means of expositions of blinding clarity that only veil Its infinite darkness transcending the light of manifestation. Even Its Name remains veiled and unutterable in certain traditions such as Judaism, but Its Reality is the origin of all that is sacred and the source of the teachings of each authentic faith. Like a mighty spring gushing forth atop a mountain, It gives rise to cascades of water that descend with ever-greater dispersion from each side, each cascade symbolizing all the grades of reality and the levels of cosmic and, by transposition, metacosmic reality of a particular religious universe. Yet all the cascades issue from a single Spring and the substance of all is ultimately nothing but that water which flows from the Spring at the mountaintop, the Reality which is the alpha of all sacred worlds and also the omega to which all that is within their embrace returns.

This Ultimate Reality, the Name that cannot be named, is the Beyond-Being of which Being is the first auto-determination. Together they comprise the Divine Order and are the principle of cosmic manifestation, the instrument of this manifestation being the Logos, the Word, the *Fiat Lux*, which one might say is the isthmus between the Divine and the cosmic orders, there being both an unmanifested and a manifested Logos. The Divine Order may be thus said to be comprised of the Divinity Itself, at once unconditioned and conditioned, supra-ontological and ontological, *Gottheit* or Godhead and the personal God, Allah in His Essence as well as Names and Qualities, the *nirguṇa* and *saguṇa* Brahman, "the nameless," which was the beginning of Heaven and Earth and the "named," which is the mother of the myriad creatures. [10] But also in a certain sense the Logos *in divinis* may be said to belong to the Divine Order, and this truth is of the greatest significance for the understanding of the religious assertion that the root of the natural order resides in the Divine Order.

From this Divine Order issue forth the many cascades alluded to above, each with different forms and trajectories and with no two cascades being formally the same, although all consisting of water. There are those that gush forth over similar types of formations and terrains corresponding to similar human collectivities, and thus constitute members of a religious family, while others display greater diversity and are produced by yet other types of terrains. There are never exact repetitions but there are always correspondences. Nor is it impossible for a tributary of one cascade to flow into another, but all cascades originate from the Spring on the mountaintop and none from each other. Their similarities are basically due to the oneness of their Origin and resemblances in the rock beds, which receive the water through that original act of gushing forth into each cascade that is theologically called "revelation." Only at the Spring Itself are all the cascades one and nowhere else should complete unity be sought among them. To repeat the well-known Islamic saying, "Unity is unique" (*al-tawḥīdu wāḥid*); one might add that only in that Supreme Unity, which is unique, must ultimate unity be sought. That is why Frithjof Schuon, the foremost contemporary expositor of the *philosophia perennis* especially as it concerns religion, has referred to this unity as "the transcendent unity of religions,"[11] thereby emphasizing that, although there is such a transcendent unity, religions do not necessarily assert the same truths on the level of their external forms and dogmas; on the contrary, they have a distinct character of their own, each religious universe being a unique creation of the Divine Artisan.

By virtue of this metaphysical view of reality, which sees the origin of all authentic religions in the Divine Principle—which manifests Itself through what the Abrahamic religions call revelations according to laws and an order belonging to the Divine Realm Itself—the traditional interpretation of the perennial philosophy[12] stands opposed to other current interpretations of religious diversity in basic ways. It opposes historicism by emphasizing the Divine Origin of each tradition and the spiritual genius of each religion, which is original in the deepest sense in that it issues directly from the Origin. It does not deny historical borrowings whether they be of Christian images in Sufi poetry or Sufi symbolism in St. John of the Cross or Taoist influences in Chan Buddhism, but it considers such borrowings as secondary in comparison with the living body of an authentic religion that must of necessity originate from Heaven. In emphasizing the reality of revelation and taking seriously a view of reality in which revelation is both possible and necessary, it certainly does not try to explain away major elements of a religion by simple recourse to historical borrowing as we see in the treatment of Islamic esoterism in the form of Sufism by so many Western orientalists from the middle of the nineteenth century to our own day.

Perennial philosophy, as traditionally understood, also opposes the phenomenological approach to the study of religion as usually practiced in academic circles by emphasizing the significance of faith, the question of religious truth, major and minor manifestations of the Spirit, and the ineluctable relation between phenomena and noumena, the former being a gateway to the latter despite the disclaimers of Immanuel Kant and most of post-Kantian Western philosophy. There are of course those Western scholars of religion such as H. Corbin, A. M. Schimmel, E. Benz, and others whose interpretation of phenomenology is close to the traditional understanding of the relation between the phenomenon and the noumenon of which precisely the phenomenon is the phenomenon, but such scholars constitute the exception rather than the rule.[13] As for M. Eliade, the foremost expositor of the phenomenological method in recent decades in America, it must be remembered that early in his life he drank deeply from the teachings of Guénon and Coomaraswamy and, despite moving away from the traditional position in his later life, retained certain important elements of the traditional worldview in his erudite and all-encompassing studies of various religions, although he no longer associated himself with that perspective.

The traditionalists, of course, also oppose the thesis based on the sentimental embracing of all religions within a unity that some envisage as a least common denominator among religions and which they hope to achieve at the expense of casting aside sacred doctrines and forms of a particular religion that do not seem to accord on the formal plane with those of another religion. Much of present-day ecumenism in the West is in fact based upon such a view and is thereby opposed by the proponents of perennial philosophy as being damaging to the very forms of that reality with which there is the need to create accord. They insist that authentic ecumenism can only be esoteric and cannot be achieved on the formal plane if one absolutizes the formal and relative plane with disregard for the basic metaphysical truth that only the Absolute is absolute.[14] Schuon has said quite aptly apropos of this question that harmony among religions is possible only in the divine stratosphere and not in the human atmosphere.

Needless to say, proponents of traditional metaphysics and the perennial philosophy also oppose both the relativists—who consider all religions to be relative, products of particular human societies without a Divine Origin that bestows an absoluteness upon each religious universe—and those who would consider their own religion to be the only true one and all other religions to be false. At least the latter view has the virtue of incorporating a lesser truth, but nevertheless a truth that has efficacy for those still living within a homogeneous religious world; but with the loss of such homogeneity it too falls into the danger of being rejected and repudiated. There is many a soul who cannot retain faith in his or her own religion at the expense of considering the followers of all other religions as being damned and who is intelligent enough to detect in the sacred art, doctrines, and rites of other traditions the seal of the Divine.

The metaphysics that the perennial philosophy, as traditionally understood, expounds is based not only on the hierarchy of universal existence to which we have referred briefly, but also the distinction between the outward and the inward, external form and essence, form and meaning, or phenomonon and noumenon. Without the comprehension of these basic distinctions, one cannot understand the dialectic of the traditional writers nor in fact the message of the perennial philosophy throughout the ages, a message echoed in works of seers and sages of the East and the West over the millennia; hence the perennial nature and also the universality of the *philosophia perennis*.

THE OUTWARD AND THE INWARD IN THE COSMOS AND IN RELIGION

Traditional metaphysics sees the universe not as a multitude of facts or opaque objects each possessing a completely independent reality of its own, but as myriads of symbols reflecting higher realities. Before the Divine Reality nothing in fact can be said to exist; but on the plane of manifestation, the light of the intellect, sacred in its own essence and also sanctified by revelation, penetrates into what appears as fact to reach its inner significance and meaning so that opacity is transformed into transparency. Phenomena thus become transparent to realities that transcend them and that they reflect on their own existential level. Phenomena become gateways to noumenal realities. The universe, both religious and cosmic, is realized as being constituted of symbols reflecting the archetypes or supernal realities that belong to the Divine, and not simply the psychological order. [15] The language of symbolism is foundational to religions and is referred to in many sacred texts such as the Quran which explicitly states that all things glorify Him with praise, [16] meaning they symbolize the Divine Archetype in their very existential reality, and their very substance is ultimately nothing other than the coagulation of that Divine Substance the Sufis call the Breath of the Compassionate (*nafas al-Raḥmān*).

> The doctrine of symbolism may also be concluded from other verses in which the Quran affirms that every single thing on earth has been sent down in finite measure, sent down as a loan rather than a gift, for nothing herebelow can last, and everything must in the end revert to its Supreme Source. In other words, the Archetype is always the Heir who inherits back the symbol in which It manifested Itself. [17]

The world is thus a veil that at once hides and reveals the realities beyond, being at once the shutter that hides the light of the inner or noumenal world and the opening to that world thanks to its symbolic nature and the inner reality (*al-bāṭin* in Arabic) of which every outward reality (*al-ẓāhir*) is the outward. In other words, there is nothing that is simply an external and brute fact or phenomenon because the very notion of externality implies inwardness. To use the language of Rūmī, every form (*ṣūrat*) possesses an inner meaning (*ma'nā*) and leads to that inner meaning provided the beholder possesses a vision that has itself been cured of the ailment of seeing only the outward dimension. [18]

This structure pertains not only to that macrocosmic revelation, which is the cosmos in all its levels, but is to be found also and above all in religion, which marks the direct eruption of the Logos into the human order. Religion has an outward aspect concerning everyone destined to accept its teachings, but it also possesses an inner dimension accessible to the few who are able to penetrate from the realm of outwardness to the inward, who are constituted in such a way as to seek at all costs that pearl of great price which was forbidden by Christ from casting before swine. Herein lies the basic distinction between the exoteric and esoteric so much emphasized by the traditional proponents of the perennial philosophy and so much neglected in the modern West where even the official religious institutions marginalized the esoteric teachings of Christianity to such an extent in recent centuries that these teachings often ended up as some form of occultism, usually with dangerous consequences of both a religious and an intellectual nature.

The insistence upon the esoteric as the only means of penetrating beyond the veil of distinct formal worlds of various religions to the inner meaning or transcendent unity—binding them together, and wherein alone can religious harmony be found in the deepest sense—has in fact been one of the major impediments for a wider appreciation of the approach of the perennial philosophy to the study of religion in academic circles. The mainstream approaches to the study of religion in universities on both sides of the Atlantic have remained until quite recently opposed to the very category of esotericism, often confused with occultism, as have theological circles which have considered esotericism to be alien to the mainstream Christian perspectives. If during the past two decades the study of esotericism has gained some academic respect, especially in France and Germany,[19] it has been most of all thanks to the revival of tradition and the magisterial exposition of esotericism by the expositors of traditional doctrines.[20]

Esotericism, traditionally understood, does not negate the significance of the exoteric. On the contrary, it insists upon its importance, for it is only through forms that one can transcend the formal plane, and one cannot surely throw away what one does not possess. In direct contrast to pseudo-esotericism, which is so prevalent in such diverse forms in the West today, esotericism as traditionally understood not only comprehends the necessity of the exoteric but also insists upon the sacrosanct quality of religious forms even on the exoteric level and the fact that they are ordained by Heaven and cannot be rejected by those who have not even reached the state of accepting such forms. Esotericism emphasizes the basic distinction between transcending forms from above and rejecting forms by falling below them, thereby forfeiting the very possibility of ever reaching the world of the Formless. Much of the traditional study of religions is in fact precisely devoted to sacred forms and the meaning they convey as symbols and myths without denying their historical reality and significance.

The traditional interpretation of perennial philosophy, therefore, envisages a universe in which the outward is the gateway to the inward in both the domain of religion and the cosmos, the former being in fact the key for the understanding of the latter. There are symbols innate to the nature of things and there are those sanctified and given efficacy by a particular religion. There are rites, doctrines, sacred art, and practices on the formal plane in each religion that must be fully respected for what they are on their own formal level without any attempt of reducing them to some harmless historical borrowing or stigmatizing them by classifying them under pejorative categories such as animism, which for only too long was the favorite means used by an army of anthropologists and scholars of religion to draw a veil over the deeper significance of what they were studying. But the traditional study of religions sees beyond this vast and wondrous world of multiple sacred forms the one single Reality that is the origin of the cascades descending from the different sides of the mountain of existence. And it asserts that it is only authentic esotericism, or literally the inward dimension, that is able to grasp this inner Reality of diverse religious universes.

Lest some think that this is simply a modern construct alien to the traditions themselves, let us recall the poem of the Persian philosopher Nāsir-i Khusraw who a thousand years ago said,

> *Gaze upon the inner dimension of the world*
> *with the eye of inwardness,*
> *For with the outward eye,*
> *thou shalt not see the inward.*

به چشم نهان بین نهان جهان را   به چشم عیان بین نبینی نهان را

Applying the doctrine of form and meaning alluded to above to the realm of religion, Jalāl al-Dīn Rūmī was to sing over seven centuries ago,

> *The difference among creatures issues from forms* (sūrat),
> *When one reaches the world of meaning* (ma'nā) *there is peace.*
> *O pith of existence, it is as a result of the*
> *difference in perspective*
> *That contention has come about between Muslims,*
> *Zoroastrians, and Jews.*

اختلاف خلق از نام اوفتاد   چون به معنی رفت آرام اوفتاد

از نظر گاه است ای مغز وجود   اختلاف مؤمن و گبر و یهود

INNER UNITY AND OUTER MULTIPLICITY

The traditional doctrine of the inner unity and formal multiplicity of religions, far from being a modern invention like the other academic methods for the study of religions, is perennial and embedded in the traditions themselves. Only now it is formulated anew according to the dire needs of present-day humanity for religious understanding across the traditional frontiers that have separated one humanity from another over the centuries. Nor do the traditional expositors of the perennial philosophy have recourse to the language of only one tradition. Rather, they employ fully all the possibilities of the rich Western metaphysical tradition in addition to those of Islam, Hinduism, and other religions. Thus, they speak of essence and form, or substance and form, archetypes and theophanies, *Ātman* and *māyā*, manifestation (*ẓuhūr*) and veil (*ḥijāb*), etc. The principial realm is that of the essences, whereas the things of this world belong to the realm of forms. The Ultimate Reality is the Supreme Substance of which every other order of reality below is an accident. Archetypes contain the realities which through theophany are manifested in this world that per se is but a mirror reflecting forms of a celestial origin while being nothing in itself. Only *Ātman*, the Supreme Self, is Real and all else is a veil that is unreal in the ultimate sense but possesses a reality on its own level, as *māyā* is not simply illusion as usually understood but the creative power and *shakti*, or female consort, of *Ātman*. The Divine manifests Itself through Its Names and Qualities, and yet things that manifest the Names are also veils or *ḥijāb*, which hide the Face of the Beloved. For the Prophet has said, "Allah hath Seventy Thousand Veils of Light and Darkness: Were He to withdraw their curtain, then would the splendours of His Aspect surely consume everyone who apprehended Him with his sight."[21]

To see beyond the veil of multiplicity—especially in the domain of religion—that unity which is the origin of all sacred forms and at the same time be able to grasp the significance of the *meaning* of sacred forms within the religious universe to which they belong are the tasks that traditional perennial philosophy has set before itself. It is a task which can be realized solely through recourse to that metaphysics that provides knowledge of the hierarchic structure of existence, the levels of reality, the reflection of the higher realities upon the lower planes, and the inward in the outward. They are tasks realized only through recourse to that hermeneutics which is aware of the esoteric dimension, of the objective realities that the phenomena veil and unveil beyond all the psychological, historical, and linguistic entanglements that have imprisoned the very notion of hermeneutics in recent years. It is also a task whose goal is the discovery of the truth that shines forth within each authentic religious universe manifesting the Absolute within its own boundaries without which it would in fact not be an authentic religion at all.

This question of the sense of the Absolute in each religion is of central importance especially in the present work, which seeks to study the relation between religion and the order of nature across religious frontiers.[22] Were there not to be the sense of the Absolute in a religion, that religion would not be religion as usually understood nor would anyone follow it seriously. And yet the very multiplity of religions implies relativity if one accords truth to the message of religions other than one's own. One can in fact ask legitimately that if each religion claims to be absolute, how can one have a multiplicity of absolutes, an assertion that is metaphysically absurd, multiplicity implying by definition relativity. The Absolute must of necessity be One and, in fact, *the* One as asserted by so many metaphysicians over the ages.[23]

The answer to this dilemma is to be found in the distinction between the Absolute in Itself and what F. Schuon has referred to in many of his writings as "the relatively absolute." This term appears as being logically problematic. And yet it points to a most profound reality that allows one to understand why each religion is absolute and yet the Absolute in its ultimate sense is beyond any of the forms in which It manifests Itself in a particular religious universe. In each religious universe, the link connecting it to the Divine Order, whether it be called prophet, *avatāra,* incarnation, or some other divine entity, is absolute within the religious universe in which it is a center and yet it is not the Absolute as such. It might be said that each manifestation of the Divine Logos, to use the language of the Abrahamic religions, is for the world for which it is the center, *the* Logos as such.[24] It is the sun in that planetary system which comprises its religious universe. And yet each sun is in reality a star in a vast firmament in which there are also other stars, which, while being stars in the firmament, do not cease to be suns in their own planetary system.

Furthermore, by virtue of the presence of this "relatively absolute" reality in a particular religious universe, other elements in that universe partake of the character of absoluteness, from sacred laws, to rites, to the efficacy of sacralized symbols and myths, to the significance of cosmos and to the order of nature. The fact that these elements within a particular religious universe might differ from or even contradict elements belonging to another universe does not prove their falsity or destroy their absoluteness within the universe to which they belong. The art of being able to cross religious frontiers in a religious and not simply anthropological, linguistic, or historical manner consists precisely of being able to appreciate the meaning of sacred doctrines, rites, forms, and symbols in the new landscape over which one is traveling with the sense of absoluteness that they possess and yet remain aware of *the* Absolute beyond all formal universes.

This art, which is also a science of the highest order, necessitates gazing upon forms in the sense of *ṣūrat* according to Rūmī, and not to be confused with the form in its Platonic or archetypal sense, always in function of the essence or meaning (*ma'nā*) and seeing the world of *ma'nā* reflected through the variegated forms comprising different worlds of the sacred. What must be done is to see the *religio perennis* as embedded in the inward dimension of the revealed religious universes, each of which is distinct and most precious in all its sacred details, as long as it has been preserved intact and has not undergone decay or deviation, and yet through its distinctness leads to that Universal Reality which is beyond all forms.

THE MANIFESTATIONS OF THE ABSOLUTE

The Absolute does not, however, manifest Itself in the same manner in different religious universes. The Ultimate Reality manifests Itself in multifarious sacred worlds sometimes in mythical forms and at other times as "abstract" monotheism. Sometimes It manifests Its Names and Qualities in the sounds and forms of a sacred language and at other times as divinities symbolizing the various divine forces; hence the distinction between a polytheism aware of the Divine Unity transcending multiple sacred forms[25] and idolatry decried so strongly by Judaism and Islam. In an atmosphere as anti-idolatrous as that of Islam the fourteenth-century angelic poet Shaykh Maḥmūd Shabistarī could say,

بدانستی که دین در بت پرستی است   بدانستی که دین در بت پرستی   مسلمان گر بدانستی که بت چیست

Were a Muslim to know what is an "idol,"
He would know that religion is idol worship,[26]

thus evoking the long Sufi tradition of identifying the *but* or idol not with a divinity considered as an independent reality of its own as was done by the pre-Islamic Arabs, but as the locus of the manifestation of Divine Presence (*ḥuḍūr*). As asserted by so many Sufis, followers of divinely revealed religions—whether speaking of the fire-temple, the Three Persons of the Trinity, or the many faces of Brahman—are singing the praise of the One even if it be in the guise of the many.

The difference in the manner of manifestation of the Absolute is also to be seen in the different positions that the "relatively absolute" holds within each sacred universe. In Christianity, Christ remains the central reality as do the Torah and the Quran in Judaism and Islam, respectively, without the Hebrew prophets and the Prophet of Islam ceasing to be of the utmost significance. In Zoroastrianism the archangelic and angelic worlds play a central role cosmologically, ritually, and soteriologically different from their role in the Abrahamic world, without angels ceasing to be of great significance in the religious economy of the sacred universes of the monotheistic religions.

The Buddha image plays a salvific role in Buddhism different from the role of the icon in Christianity, and both religions differ in this matter from the aniconic worlds of Judaism and Islam. The cardinal directions have a central role in Native American cosmology and ritual not to be found in Christianity. One could go on indefinitely citing other examples to demonstrate how "the relatively absolute" is "situated" differently within each sacred universe, not to speak of the vertical levels of the manifestation of the Absolute from the Supreme Essence or Ultimate Reality, which is the Principle Itself, to Pure Being, the Logos, the archangelic, and angelic hierarchies. This universal hierarchy can in fact be understood fully only from the purely metaphysical and esoteric points of view[27] while it is symbolized in the religious language meant for a whole collectivity usually by the "heavens" to which the Quran refers so often almost as a refrain[28] and which concerns the vertical hierarchy within a single religious universe. This vertical multiplicity of heavens must, moreover, be distinguished from Heaven referred to at the beginning of this chapter as symbolizing the transcendent pole of each of the religious worlds existing "horizontally" and side by side with each other on neighboring "Earths."

THE ORDER OF NATURE IN DIFFERENT RELIGIOUS WORLDS

In the light of this analysis one can understand better the difference in the status of the order of nature in both senses of the natural domain and the order dominating over it in different religions. All religions of course must of necessity also embrace the cosmic domain and incorporate its significance in their teachings and practices. But the religious meaning of the order of nature, its spiritual role in human life, and its soteriological function are far from the same in all religions. What is important is not only to try to understand the meaning of the order of nature in relation to the basic structure of each religion (as we shall seek to do in the next chapter) but also to comprehend the significance of the order of nature in the historic development of a particular religion such as Christianity, which is of special concern to our study precisely because of its special relationship with that worldview which came to negate all religious significance of the order of nature. Without paying attention to the latter factor, we shall never understand why Christianity, which believes in the incarnation of the Divine Word as flesh and in the spatio-temporal sequence, should in its later history surrender the world of nature to a totally nonreligious perspective without many of its leading thinkers ever being concerned with the violation of the original Christian theology that such a surrender of the cosmos implied.

Let us turn briefly to these differences before embarking upon a comparative study of the relation between religion and the order of nature in different traditions, limiting ourselves, in pointing to these differences, to the living religions whose views on this matter are of existential significance in the current environmental crisis.[29] One of the ways of distinguishing between the views of various religions concerning the order of nature is to turn to their attitudes regarding the nature of time and becoming. The primal religions—which must include the Shamanic family of Siberian origin with its later ramifications in Japan and the Americas, sometimes referred to as "indigenous" religions and which still survive despite the massive displacement and destruction of indigenous people during the past few centuries since the European expansion over the globe—live essentially in space rather than time conceived as a moving arrow. For them the world of becoming and time manifest themselves as a cyclical phenomenon, and there is no linear movement to history in need of being redeemed in the Christian sense of the term. Nature expresses herself most of all through her rhythms and what has been called "the eternal return."[30]

In such religions nature is not only a symbol of spiritual realities but *is* those realities not by a reduction of the spiritual essences to material forms but by an inner identity among those who share the primordial perspective between the symbol and the symbolized. Hence, in such worlds nature herself is the supreme cathedral. Her order *is* the Divine Order and her laws divine laws without there being in any sense a naturalism or animism in the pejorative sense of these terms or as they appeared during Hellenistic decadence when Christianity first spread into the Mediterranean world.

Then there are religions such as the Iranian and Abrahamic in which both the process of becoming and the movement of the "arrow of time" gain a religious significance, and a distinction begins to be made between the Divine Order and the order of nature, which now reflects the Divine Order as there is also an ontological separation between the symbol and the symbolized transcended only in the esoteric dimension of these religions, whose proponents still see God everywhere. Among these religions, Islam, while participating in the Jewish and Christian understanding of the religious significance of the flow of time, marks in a sense a return to the primordial religion. This return to a primordial state, to the *dīn al-fiṭrah* to use the Quranic term, is seen in the Islamic concept of the cycles of prophecy reflecting the cyclical march of time[31] and the central role of nature in the Quranic revelation.[32]

Hinduism occupies a special position in this scheme of classification in that it is on the one hand a primordial religion reflecting most directly the early Indo-Iranian and Indo-European religious universe. And yet it has adopted itself to the later stages of cosmic history where historical time gains ever-greater significance. It therefore contains views above the order of nature resembling those of the primal religions and yet possesses an elaborate doctrine of cosmic cycles, the most elaborate of any of the religions, in which the gradual divorce between nature and her spiritual prototype—through the very process of becoming, leading finally to the dissolution of the present world at the end of this cosmic cycle—is fully explained.

What makes the study of the relation of religion to the order of nature more difficult is the presence of not one but several perspectives and doctrines concerning this issue in each of the major traditions. In Christianity the secularization of the cosmos in the sixteenth and seventeenth centuries resulted in the theological significance of nature and the necessisty to study it seriously from a theological point of view being pushed aside. In fact, the issue did not become central again until quite recently. But before the modern period, Christianity, like Judaism as it developed in the West and especially in the bosom of Islam in Spain, possessed several perspectives on the meaning of nature, all of which contained profound religious significance. One has only to mention the Victorines along with Albertus Magnus, Roger Bacon, and Raymond Lull, not to mention the purely mystical views of nature expressed in the poems of the Irish monks, the German visionary Hildegard of Bingen, as well as the canticles of St. Francis. A similar situation could be found in Judaism in the works of an Ibn Gabirol, Maimonides, and the Cabalists. They expressed differing perspectives concerning the order of nature within Judaism as those mentioned above had done within Christianity. But this situation was to disappear more or less after the Renaissance especially in the mainstream of Christianity and at least to some extent in European Judaism.

In Islam and Hinduism the presence of several perspectives located in a sapiental hierarchy has not ceased to exist to this day. When one asks what is the

Islamic or Hindu attitude toward the order of nature, does one only refer to the Quran and the Upanishads? Does one speak only of the jurists and legalists of the two traditions or of an Ibn Sab'īn or Śankara, who deny that anything can even possess reality other than the Ultimate Principle? And where does one locate the elaborate doctrines concerning nature in both traditions? It is precisely here that the question of being able to situate the role of the cosmos and its study in each tradition becomes central. As already stated, the understanding of the order of nature and its significance in the religious life is not the same across religious frontiers. Moreover, it is not even always the same within the various schools of a single religious universe.

The situation is further complicated by the fact that each tradition is like a tree with its roots sunk in the Divine Ground but its branches, which have grown over time, spreading to cover a particular cosmic space. Furthermore, some traditions have been confronted with and compromised by antitraditional forces, foremost among them Western Christianity, whereas others have not undergone the same historical experience of secularization and in a certain sense marginalization, thus affecting their view of the order of nature, at least not to the same extent. One cannot simply compare most nineteenth- or twentieth-century Christian theologians as far as views toward nature is concerned with a Hindu, Buddhist, or Muslim religious thinker of the same period unless one searches to find the few non-Western religious thinkers influenced by such modern ideas as secularism, progress, and evolution. But the latter remain to this day marginal in their traditions, whereas the modernized Christian theologians who have altered their view concerning the order of nature as a result of accepting the secularization of the cosmos, far from being marginal, have even triumphed to a large extent even within the more traditional forms of religion in the West.

Also, the role of both modern philosophy and science in affecting the understanding of the meaning of the order of nature in the West has not been equaled in any non-Western society as a whole, even in the highly technological world of modern Japan or Marxist China. In the future the impact of such forms of secularist thought may spread much more than now and one might address the issue of the relation between religion and the order of nature on a global scale by studying various existing forces and ideas in a parallel fashion across civilizational frontiers. For the moment, however, one must understand the deep difference between the attitude of a Malay, Indian, or Burmese, whether they be Muslim, Hindu, or Buddhist or, for that matter, an Ethiopian Christian, and let us say even a believing Belgian or American toward the religious significance of the order of nature. Even more important is the understanding of the theological and historical causes that have brought about that crisis between man and the natural order, which is on the one hand global and on the other brought about by the applications of science in the form of modern technology, which grew under special circumstances in only one part of the globe and has only begun to spread over the surface of the planet fairly recently.

It is in the light of this situation that we must be able to distinguish first of all the most profound and enduring teachings of each religion concerning the order of nature from the less essential and to analyze and explain them no matter how briefly.[33] Second, it is necessary to delve into the views of Western philosophy and science along with the humanism underlying them separately because of their momentous impact upon the understanding of the order of nature in the West, an impact that is obviously very different from that of, say, Islamic, Hindu, Buddhist, or Taoist and Confucian schools of thought upon the understanding of the order of nature in respective civilizations molded and created by these religions. In this way perhaps some light can be cast upon both diverging and complementary views of the various religions concerning the order of nature and a step be taken in creating accord, despite outward differences, among different religions concerning the order of nature at a time when both the religious view of nature and nature herself are threatened with unparalleled destruction by forces totally opposed to religion and yet blaming religion for what they have brought about through their very denial of the sacred basis of the natural order. This exercise might also help to make clear how Western Christianity, at least in its mainstream, separated itself so drastically in recent centuries from all the other religions in the understanding of the order of nature, with grave consequences for itself, for global religious accord, and for the preservation of the natural environment.

The study of the order of nature as envisaged in various religions, which display the infinite richness of the Divine Nature, reveals remarkable correspondences and similarities especially if one remains within the traditional world not yet adulterated by various forces of modernism that penetrated even into the realm of religion in the West and are now beginning to do so elsewhere. All religions in their deepest teachings, and despite important formal differences, relate the order of nature to the order within human beings and envisage both orders as bearing the imprint of the Divine Reality, which is the Origin of both man and nature. There are religions in which the Earth plays a more important role than in others and in which natural forms themselves fulfill the function of sacred objects of art created by human beings in other religions. The sun and the moon, the rivers and the mountains do not always speak with the same tongue nor is their eloquence heard in the same manner in all religious climes, especially since religions can decay or have certain of their teachings eclipsed or forgotten. Certainly Pizarro, who massacred so many of the Incas, did not hear the call of the Andean peaks as did the people whom he vanquished even though he knelt before the Cross, which symbolizes the Incarnation of the Word in the very stream of the flow of time and the world of becoming.

Still, the order of nature has recalled over the ages and across many religious frontiers the order both within us and beyond us. Nature has not only displayed the wisdom of God through her order and harmony but has also carried out incessantly a discourse about those spiritual realities that constitute the very substance of our existence. Her order has been nothing other than our order and her harmony that inner harmony which still chants the eternal melody at the center of our being despite the cacophany of our ego dispersed in its world of forgetfulness. The limbs of nature are our limbs, her life our life, and her destruction our destruction. It is this lesson that the religions have taught over the ages in a hundred languages and with many levels of profundity ranging from seeing in nature God's wisdom to seeing in her the direct reflection of that Divine Proto-type, which is also our Prototype, that Eternal Man or Universal Man (*al-insān al-kāmil*), to use the language of Sufism, who is at once the prototype of man and nature. It was to this reality that the English poet William Blake was referring when he wrote the following verse, in direct opposition to all the powerful currents of rationalism and secularism dominating the scene around him:

> *So man looks out in tree, herb, fish, beast,*
> *Collecting up the scatter'd portions of his immortal body . . .*
> *Wherever a grass grows*
> *Or a leaf buds, the Eternal Man is seen, is heard, is felt,*
> *And all his sorrows, till he re-assumes his ancient bliss.*
>
> (*The Four Zoas*, Night VIII)

And it is this supernal reality whose echoes we shall try to hear in varying tones on the many Earths and under the many Heavens through which we now hope to journey.

NOTES

1. Throughout this work, as in our other writings, we use the term "tradition" as encompassing principles and truths of a sacred origin along with their unfolding, applica-tion, and manifestation within a particular civilization, which by virtue of its link to these principles is called a traditional civilization. See S. H. Nasr, *Knowledge and the Sacred* (Albany: State University of New York Press, 1989), Chapter 2, "What Is Tradition?," pp. 65–92.

2. We do not wish to denigrate in any way the significance of studies of a theologi-cal, philosophical, scientific or, needless to say, metaphysical nature dealing with the question of the order of nature in the context of one particular religion such as Judaism, Christianity, and Islam, or non-Abrahamic religions whether they be Hinduism and Buddhism, or one of the primal or "indigenous" religions such as those of the Native American. Such studies are both necessary and of great value even for people belonging to another tradition. What we wish to emphasize is that it is also necessary to turn to more than one tradition to bring out an understanding of the rapport between religion and the order of nature on a global scale at a time when the threat to the natural order is also global.

As pointed out in the Introduction to this work, our aim here is not only academic, although we have tried to conform to strict academic and scholarly standards. It is also practical in the sense of trying to provide one key among others to understand better the deeper dimensions of the current environmental crisis and hence to seek a solution on a level where alone we believe solutions can be found. See in this context S. H. Nasr, *Man and Nature: The Spiritual Crisis of Modern Man* (London: HarperCollins, 1989).

3. For the moment we shall use "nature" in the ordinary sense of the term. In the later chapters, however, we shall discuss in a philosophical manner what we mean exactly

by nature in this study. Likewise, the term "order" will be discussed more fully in the next chapter.

4. For example, R. Otto, J. Wach, G. van der Leeuw, M. Eliade, W. C. Smith, N. Smart, J. Hick, G. Parrinder, and H. Smith just to name a few among academic figures, not to forget the traditionalists to whom we shall turn shortly.

5. We have dealt in a more general manner with the question of the study of religion in a multireligious universe in *Knowledge and the Sacred*, Chapter 9, "Principal Knowledge and the Multiplicity of Sacred Forms," pp. 280–308; and also in *Religion and Religions: The Challenge of Living in the Multireligious World*, The Loy H. Witherspoon Lectures in Religious Studies (Charlotte: The University of North Carolina Press, 1985). See also S. H. Nasr, *The Need for a Sacred Science* (Albany: State University of New York Press, 1993), Part 2, pp. 443ff.

6. The terms "Heaven" and "Earth" possess at once a metaphysical, cosmological, and theological symbolism that no amount of the secularization of the cosmos and the reducing of "Heaven" to an incandescent mass of gases or the Earth to various types of rocks and geological formations can destroy. And it is, needless to say, in their eminently symbolic meaning that we use the terms Heaven and Earth as well as other traditional metaphysical and cosmological concepts throughout this book.

7. See M. Pallis, "On Crossing Religious Frontiers," in his book *The Way and the Mountain* (London: Peter Owen Ltd., 1991), pp. 62–78; and Lord Northbourne, *Religion in the Modern World* (London: J. M. Dent & Sons Ltd., 1963), especially Chapter 1, "Religion," pp. 1–12.

8. We have dealt with these authors in *Knowledge and the Sacred*, pp. 100ff. As for their works dealing specifically with religion see Nasr, *The Need for a Sacred Science*, p. 67.

9. The work of F. Whaling (ed.), *The World's Religious Traditions: Current Perspectives in Religious Studies* (New York: Crossroad Publications, 1984), is perhaps the first academic work to take this perspective into consideration along with other academically better known ways of studying religions in their multiplicity. See also H. M. Vroom, *Religions and the Truth: Philosophical Reflections and Perspectives,* trans. J. W. Rehal (Amsterdam: Editions Rodopi, 1989). See also Nasr, *The Need for a Sacred Science,* Chapter 5, "The *Philosophia Perennis* and the Study of Religion," p. 53ff.

10. See the first lines of the first chapter of the Tao Te-ching to which we shall turn in the next chapter. Some of the primal religions refer to these levels of Divinity, respectively, as Grandfather and Father. On the levels of the Divine Order in various religions see also James B. Robinson, "Levels of Godhood in the World's Religions" (in press).

11. See Frithjof Schuon, *The Transcendent Unity of Religions,* trans. P. Townsend (Wheaton, Ill.: Theosophical Publishing House, 1993).

12. We keep emphasizing the traditional interpretation of perennial philosophy because there are now those who claim to accept the perennial philosophy but who espouse such theories as evolution, which is totally alien to the traditional point of view according to which cosmic forms, life and humanity in particular, have descended from the Divine Order and not ascended from matter. See Nasr, *Knowledge and the Sacred*, Chapter 7, "Eternity and the Temporal Order," pp. 221–252.

13. Corbin, with whom we were closely associated for two decades, used to translate phenomenology in a seminar we used to teach together at Tehran University to the Persian-speaking students as *kashf al-mahjūb,* literally "rending asunder of the veil to reveal the hidden essence," and considered his method of the study of religious texts and also rites to be spiritual hermeneutics (*al-ta'wīl*) as understood in classical Sufi and Shi'ite thought. See

D. Shayegan, *Henry Corbin: La Topographie spirituelle de l'Islam iranien* (Paris: Editions de la Difference, 1990).

14. See Frithjof Schuon, *Christianity/Islam: Essays on Esoteric Ecumenism,* trans. G. Polit (Bloomington, Ind.: World Wisdom Books, 1985).

15. This distinction needs to be made because of the psychological interpretation of archetypes that has become "popular" ever since the advent of Jungian psychology.

16. For example, the Quran asserts, "The seven Heavens and the earth and all that is therein glorify Him, nor is there anything but glorifieth Him with praise; yet ye understand not their glorification" (XVII: 44, trans. M. Lings).

17. M. Lings, *Symbol and Archetype: A Study of the Meaning of Existence* (Cambridge: Quinta Essentia, 1991), pp. 1–2. On the traditional understanding of symbols see R. Guénon, *The Fundamental Symbols of Sacred Science,* trans. A. Moore (Cambridge: Quinta Essentia, 1995). As for the centrality of symbolism in religious language, see Mircea Eliade, *Images and Symbols,* trans. Ph. Mairet (New York: Sheed and Ward, 1961).

18. See S. H. Nasr, *Islamic Art and Spirituality* (London: Golgonooza Press, 1987), pp. 89–90, 129–130.

19. The works of Gilbert Durant and Antoine Faivre are particularly significant in this respect. See Faivre, *Accès à l'ésotérisme occidentale* (Paris: Gallimard, 1986); and Durant, *Science de l'homme et tradition* (Paris: Berg International, 1979). See also Jean-Paul Corsetti, *Histoire de l'ésotérisme et des sciences occultes* (Paris: Larousse, 1992).

It is of some significance that a whole volume of *World Spirituality: An Encyclopedic History of the Religious Quest,* Vol. 21, is entitled *Modern Esoteric Spirituality* (New York: Crossroad Publications, 1993), (eds. A. Faivre and Jacob Needleman). The content of these works, especially those of Faivre and Corsetti, also reveals the rather loose and wide definition given to esotericism in such studies, a definition that differs in certain fundamental ways from the meaning of esotericism as understood by traditionalists, although there is a notable common ground between them.

20. The most important contemporary traditional work on this subject is F. Schuon, *Esoterism as Principle and as Way,* trans. W. Stoddart (Pates Manor, U.K.: Perennial Books, 1990); see also L. Benoist, *L'Ésotérisme* (Paris: Presses Universitaires de France, 1963).

21. This famous metaphysical and cosmological work is in fact a commentary upon the Light Verse (*āyat al-nūr*) of the Quran and this *ḥadīth.* For a translation of this work from the original Arabic and also from the traditional point of view, see Ghazâlî, *Le Tabernacle des Lumières Michkât Al-Anwâr,* trans. R. Deladrière (Paris: Seuil, 1981); see also W. H. T. Gairdner, *Al-Ghazzali's Mishkat al-Anwar* (Lahore: Sh. Muhammad Ashraf, 1952), pp. 76–77.

22. See F. Schuon, "The Sense of the Absolute in Religions," in his *Gnosis: Divine Wisdom,* trans. G. E. H. Palmer (Pates Manor, U.K.: Perennial Books, 1978), pp. 11–28.

23. This is especially true of Muslim sages such as Ṣadr al-Dīn Shīrāzī, who in numerous works has "proven" the oneness of God from His absoluteness and His absoluteness from His oneness.

24. It is this doctrine that was expounded in earlier days by ibn-'Arabi in his *Fuṣūṣ al-ḥikam.* On his "logos doctrine" see his *La Sagesse des prophètes,* trans. with commentary by T. Burckhardt (Paris; Albin Michel, 1955, trans. by A. Culme-Seymour as *The Wisdom of the Prophets,* Gloucestershire: Beshara Publications, 1975); see also W. Chittick, "A Sufi Approach to Religious Diversity, ibn al-'Arabi on the Metaphysics of Revelation," in S. H. Nasr and W. Stoddart (eds.), *Religion of the Heart: Essays Presented to Frithjof Schuon*

on His Eightieth Birthday (Washington, D.C.: Foundation for Traditional Studies, 1991), pp. 50–90.

25. On polytheism as not the negation of but polymorphous manifestation of the Divine Reality in the Hindu context, see A. Daniélou, *Hindu Polytheism* (New York: Pantheon Books, 1964), Bollingen Series LXXIII.

26. From the *Gulshan-i rāz,* ed. Javād Nūrbaksh (Tehran: Khāniqah-i Nimatullāhī, 1976), p. 56.

27. See Nasr, *Knowledge and the Sacred,* Chapter 5, *"Scientia Sacra,"* pp. 130ff.

28. We are referring to *al-samāwāt wa'l-arḍ,* literally "heavens and earth," which is repeated throughout the Sacred Text. It is of great significance for the explanation given above that *arḍ* or Earth is in the singular, symbolizing the last level of cosmic manifestation, and the heavens in the plural, referring to the many levels of reality separating the "Earth" from the Divine Realm.

29. Naturally, the views of such religions as that of the ancient Egyptians and Greeks are also important because of their influence upon later civilizations, particularly in the West, and also because of the innate interest of some of their doctrines, which contain profound teachings on these subjects that need to be recalled and resurrected.

30. This is the term used by Mircea Eliade in his well-known work *The Myth of the Eternal Return,* trans. W. Trask (New York: Pantheon Books, 1954). It must be added, however, that in traditional doctrines the return is to an analogical point, which is not simply the same point marking a repetition of cosmic history. The movement of history is, strictly speaking, helical rather than cyclical, but in any case it is not linear. On the traditional view of cosmic cycles see René Guénon, *Formes traditionnelles et cycles cosmiques* (Paris: Gallimard, 1970). See also Nasr, *The Need for a Sacred Science,* pp. 27ff.

31. See Abu Bakr Siraj ed-Din, "The Islamic and Christian Conceptions of the March of Time," *Islamic Quarterly* (Vol. 1, 1954), pp. 229–235.

32. On this question see Nasr, "The Cosmos and the Natural Order," in S. H. Nasr (ed.), *Islamic Spirituality: Foundations,* Vol. 19 of *World Spirituality: An Encyclopedic History of the Religious Quest* (New York: Crossroad Publications, 1987), pp. 345–357.

33. One of the difficult tasks in such a study is to distinguish within each religion what are the most central attitudes and doctrines concerning the order of nature even though some of these doctrines may have developed later than the period of foundation and incubation of the religion in question. In the case of Christianity this task is made even more difficult in the present work because we are dealing with philosophy in the next chapter, which includes not only antireligious philosophy in the West but also Christian philosophy. In this case we shall confine ourselves in the discussion of the Christian attitude to the order of nature mostly to St. Augustine and St. Maximus the Confessor, who is accepted as a saint by both the Catholic and Orthodox churches, and we shall deal with the views of some of the later major Christian thinkers in the chapter on philosophy. Such a treatment will not be followed for other religions because of the obvious difference between the role of the philosophical understanding of the order of nature in relation to the religious view in the West and other traditions.

2

The Order of Nature

نظم این گیتی خدایا از کجاست   حکمت جاری این عالم کراست

در عجب هستم ولی دانم همی   پادشاهی جهان حق را سزاست

I observe in things the order prevalent,
From the lowly dust to the firmament,
Yet whence cometh this order, I know not,
Save there is certitude, He is the Lord of all.

Our existential situation here on Earth leads us directly to the experience of order. In fact, the Greek word for order, *cosmos,* is still used to refer to that totality of external reality which is perceptible and that naturalistic philosophers identify with reality as such, while religions and religious philosophers consider it to be all that is other than the Divine Principle, which in Arabic is called *mā siwa'Llāh,* literally "that which is other than Allah." Creation itself is envisaged in most sacred cosmogonies as the imposition of order upon chaos or the generation of order itself as observed in the opening verses of Genesis to which Milton refers in his famous verse,

Till at his second bidding darkness fled
Light shone, and order from disorder sprung.

(*Paradise Lost,* III, 713)

Religions have sought to explain this order in religious terms, philosophers in philosophic ones, and, more recently, science according to the parameters of modern scientific thought. Even if the study of chaos has recently become a favorite subject of discourse,[1] and some scientists have sought to free the order of nature from the deterministic manner in which it has been envisaged in classical physics and have spoken of the emergence of order from chaos on the basic of spontaneous creativity, it is still essentially order that is the subject of scientific inquiry while cosmic order continues to be of central significance in most religions.[2] In this chapter our goal is to examine the meaning of order *in* nature, and of necessity the order *of* nature, not according to the modern scientific view but as treated by various religious traditions that have not only created a human society but also a cosmic ambience imbued with religious significance.[3]

Before delving into this vast subject, however, it is necessary to ask ourselves what we mean by order. The *Oxford Dictionary* defines order as the "formal disposition or any regular, methodical, or harmonious arrangement in the position of things contained in any space or area, or composing any group or body" and also "the conditon in which everything is in its proper place, and performs its proper function." Moreover, order refers to "a class, group, kind, or sort of persons, beings, or things, having its rank in a scale of being, excellence, or importance, or distinguished from others by nature or character." It is according to the first two of these definitions that we shall try to understand the religious meaning of the order of nature—that is, in the sense of order and its functioning observable in the processes of the natural world—and according to the third meaning that we shall seek to comprehend the order of nature as contrasted, let us say, with the Divine or human orders. Although our concern is primarily with the meaning of the order of nature in the light of the first two definitions given above, we must of necessity also delve to some extent into the religious significance of the order of nature according to the third definition even though our aim in this book is not primarily the religious view of nature in relation to the universal hierarchy of existence but of order in nature, while being aware that such a concern cannot be separated from the consideration of nature as a distinct realm in that hierarchy and hence a recognizable order.[4]

A difficulty that besets such a study is the definition as to what we mean by each "religion" whose view of the order of nature we intend to study. Do we mean the scriptures or myths of each religion or its later developments? And then in the case of such religions as Christianity how do we distinguish between the religious view and the view of its religious philosophers since we intend to deal with Western philosophy separately in the next chapter? These are questions not having a clear and definite answer if one limits oneself to a purely historical perspective. But from the point of view of the *philosophia perennis,* with whose aid we seek to study the heart and archetypal reality of each religion along with its later unfolding on the basis of that archetype, it is possible to discover perspectives essential to a particular religion, even if they have become crystallized later in time, and seek to study that religion's views concerning the order of nature through those perspectives. Success in such an endeavor depends upon the extent to which one is able to identify such archetypal realities and major perspectives within various religions.

Moreover, some religions possess several basic perspectives conerning the order of nature and have developed over the ages philosophies and theologies of nature different from what existed earlier in their history, as can be seen so clearly in Christianity when one studies the views of an Origen, a St. Augustine, and a St. Thomas Aquinas as they relate to this subject.[5] In this vast and bewildering ocean of possibilities we have sought to select perspectives, essential to the religion in question, that have dealt with the order of nature and that have had an abiding influence upon the tradition in question. In such cases as Hinduism, Buddhism, Judaism, Christianity, and Islam we have not been able to speak of all the perspectives, schools, and interpretations relevant to this issue, but we have chosen from among the most essential aspects of each religion's understanding of the order of nature. It is hoped that in this way we can come to comprehend better the religious sense of the order of nature across many religious boundaries and, on a global scale, a sense of order against which the modern philosophic and scientific revolt took place in the West over four centuries ago, an order being challenged through much of the rest of the world with the global spread of modernism some two centuries ago, but an order that is still living and far from being of only historical interest.

THE PRIMAL OR INDIGENOUS RELIGIONS

Several hundred million followers of primal religions, which are branches of the archaic and primordial religions of humanity, still survive in the Americas, Africa, the Polynesian islands, Australia, India, New Zealand, and elsewhere even after their decimation in recent centuries, especially as a result of the European colonization of much of the globe. Despite great differences in their myths and practices, these religions present a remarkable morphological resemblance as far as their relation to nature or the Earth is concerned. They have been for millennia the guardians of the natural environment with an ear finely tuned to the message of the Earth, and they possess views concerning the order of nature that are of profound significance as far as the question of the preservation of the natural environment is concerned. In fact, the acute environmental crisis now threatening human existence itself has caused many people, whose ancestors dismissed the views of primal religions as simple animism, fetishism, etc., to reexamine what these guardians of the Earth have to say about the meaning of the order of nature. In any case, the view of the primal religions concerning the order of nature forms an important strand in the contemporary tapestry in which elements from various traditions are being woven together to resuscitate a spiritual view of nature before the crass marterialism of the modern world destroys the very fabric of life that has made this materialism possible for a fleeting movement in human history.

SHAMANISM AND THE NORTH AMERICAN TRADITIONS

Shamanism, which was the ancient religion of the center and east of Asia and which is related to the ancient Tibetan Po religion, to Shintoism in Japan, and to the North American religions along with other important religious currents, presents a primordial view of the order of nature and man's rapport with the natural world, a view that has gained much attention recently.[6] The basic structure of the Shamanic universe is founded upon the three tiers of the upper, middle, and lower worlds, or the sky, the earth, and the underworld connected by a central axis, the *axis mundi,* which the Mongols called the "Golden Pillar."[7] This pillar corresponds to the cosmic mountain that appears in various religions under different names such as Mt. Meru of the Indians, the Haraberezaiti or Alborz of the ancient Iranians, and Himingbjörg of the ancient Germans.[8] The Pole Star is fastened to the top of the cosmic mountain, and it was through this star that in the days of old all human beings could ascend to the regions above, a feat that can be performed only by the Shaman today. The sacred mountain is complemented by the world tree, which is "a Tree that *lives and gives life"*[9] as the axis of the cosmos, all parts of which are also alive and conscious according to a "hylozoism" or what some call "panpsychism" so characteristic of the Shamanic religions. It is this cosmic life and awareness that dominate over the whole of nature and are the source and cause of what we observe as order in the natural realm.[10]

The Shamanic view of the cosmos can be summarized as follows:

> The universe is multi-layered or stratified, with an Underworld below and an Upperworld above as principal divisions. Underworld, and Upperworld are usually further divided into several levels, each with its respective spirit rulers and other supernatural denizens. There are also gods of the principal world directions or quarters, and supreme brings that rule respectively over the celestial and chthonic spheres (for example, sky gods, lords of the dead, etc.) . . .
>
>   The several levels of the universe are interconnected by a central axis (*axis mundi*) which merges conceptually with the Shaman's "sky ladder" and world tree.[11]

The world of the Shaman is one in which the sacred dominates at once over the world of nature and of human beings, and a single order relates the human and the cosmic worlds in an inseparable bi-unity. The Shaman is able to go beyond the cosmos through the Pole Star, but he must respect the order and harmony of the cosmos without which he would not be able to make his meta-cosmic journey. There is in this primordial perspective no clear separation between the sacred and the natural nor does a rational system of concepts intervene between the Shaman and the world of nature with which he is in contact in a most intimate manner.

Shintoism

One of the important branches of Shamanism—not only because of its innate characteristics but also owing to the fact that it has remained to this day the foundation of Japanese culture and society despite Japan's rapid modernization— is Shintoism. Originally the religion had no name, but in confrontation with Buddhism the word *shintō*—meaning "the way of the *Kami"*—came to be used as distinct from *Budsudō* ("the way of the Buddha"). There also developed a Buddhist Shinto that identified the *Kami* ("spirits" or "power of harmony" of Shintoism) with the *avatāras* of Buddhism and a Confucian Shintoism that interpreted Shintoism according to the neo-Confucianism of Chu Hsi and Wang Yang-ming. In the seventeenth century during the early Edo period, Shintoism was revived by Motoori Norinaga and others, and opposition arose against these earlier forms of syncretism. [12]

Shintoism is based upon the *Kami,* spirits governing the world of nature as well as that of the soul and which must be understood more than anything else as spirits responsible for the harmony of creation, being themselves powers of harmony and order. Shinto cosmology, following Shamanism in general, distinguishes among three vertical planes of reality: Takamanohara ("plain of high heaven"), which is the abode of the gods; Nakatsukuni ("middle land"), which is the human world including the natural ambience surrounding man; and Yomi ("the underworld"), which is the land of death. According to Shintoism the history of Japan itself begins in Takamanohara, or Heaven, and the natural features of the Japanese islands are related to the theophanies of Shinto deities and the *Kami,* which govern all things. Moreover, Shintoism emphasizes the mystical significance of beauty in nature and identifies the order and harmony of nature with the beauty that the natural world displays everywhere. [13] The identification of the order of nature with beauty and the close link between the rites of religion and natural phenomena and features of the land and sea are among the chief characteristics of Shintoism, which has manifested itself throughout Japanese history and revealed itself, as has Zen, in forms of art of unparalleled "natural"— and at the same time spiritual—beauty.

The North American Native Traditions

Despite the tragic decimation of their habitat, cultures, and social life, the traditions of the North American natives or so-called Indians have survived to this day as major branches of the family of Shamanic religions. Moreover, these religions, especially those of the Great Plains, have preserved something of their primordial character, which is of remarkable beauty and majesty. Aware of at once the transcendent and immanent nature of the Spirit within the forms of nature and yet beyond all forms, the Native Americans have preserved a sacral view of nature in which the order of nature, of human beings both individually and collectively, and the sacred are bound in an organic unity that is itself sacred. Virgin nature was the cathedral of the Native Americans and the forms of nature at once theophanies and objective counterparts to the various forces and powers within the human soul. [14]

The cosmology of the Native American traditions resembles for the most part that of Shamanism in general as outlined above. For example, according to the Ojibway the universe is multilayered with *flat-earth* located between the cosmic regions identified as Heaven or Sky and Earth, each region being further divided into sublayers with its own dominating spirits responsible for its order. [15] The entire universe is alive and connected by the cosmic axis traversing all the layers. More specifically, the universe is ordered and governed by the spirit power called *manitou.* These powers existed before the creation of *flat-earth* and govern over the realm of human existence, while other *manitou* are the life forces and principle of order of the creatures of the natural world, what we would call both animate and inanimate beings.[16] Thus, the *manitou* have both cosmic and human qualities and also act as bridges between various levels of the cosmos. They bestow order upon the many levels of existence and bind man and nature in a unity that both underlies and transcends the domain of multiplicity.

Among the Sioux, emphasis is placed especially upon the Great Spirit of *Wakan-tanka,* which is both the cause of all transformations and the order we observe in nature. Among the Lakota the presence of the Great Spirit is called *Taku Skanskan* or simply *Skan.* Its role in the order of nature is made clear by the discourse between an old Lakota priest and an American scholar on the subject of *Skan.* The sage asks:

> "What causes the stars to fall?" "*Taku Skanskan.* . . . He causes everything that falls to fall, and He causes everything to move that moves." "When you move, what causes you to move?" "*Skan.*" "If an arrow is shot from a bow what causes it to move through the air?" "*Skan.* . . . *Taku Skanskan* gives the spirit to the bow, and He causes it to send the arrow from it." "What causes the clouds to move over the world?" "*Skan.*" "Lakota have told me that *Skan* is the sky. Is that so?" "Yes. *Skan* is a Spirit and all that mankind can see of Him is the blue of the sky; but He is everywhere!" "Is *Skan Wakan-Tanka?*" "Yes!"[17]

The great twentieth-century Sioux medicine man Black Elk emphasized this truth himself and spoke of the transcendent as well as immanent nature of the Great Spirit, pointing to a "polysynthetic animism" that is at the same time "monotheistic" and that comes from their awareness that natural beings are coagulations of the Divine Substance, which is at the same time transcendent vis-à-vis all its coagulations—hence what has been aptly called the "spiritual naturalism" of the Native Americans and their refusal to separate the human order from the order of nature.[18] This "spiritual naturalism" also implies that everything in the universe is alive and given order and harmony by the Spirit. It means "in principle and metaphysically, that, whatever be the object envisaged, there springs from its existential center an ontological ray, made up of 'being,' 'consciousness' and 'life,' to its luminous and celestial prototype; from this it follows that in principle it is possible for us to attain the heavenly Essences by taking anything whatever as starting point."[19]

The Great Spirit gives order to the whole of the cosmos starting with the cardinal points, which are its most direct manifestations and which bestow order upon space and all that is therein.[20] Furthermore, the Great Spirit manifests itself, by virtue of its very transcendence, through the Sky and the Earth, the plants and the animals. Symbolically speaking, all these multiple manifestations of the Great Spirit are none other than the Great Spirit. "Things are not mysterious themselves, but manifestations of mysteries, and the Great Spirit, or the Great Mystery, synthesizes them in Its transcendent Unity."[21] The order of nature veils and reveals a reality beyond and yet immanent within nature, an order inseparable from the order prevailing within man himself.

The views of the Native Americans concerning the order of nature indicate not only the perspective of one of the best kept branches of primordial Shamanism toward the natural world, but are also at once a powerful challenge and a stark contrast to the mechanistic view of the order of nature underlying the modern technological worldview and the attitude toward nature of that civilization which conquered and crushed the Native American world. Paradoxically, this primordial attitude made possible the preservation of a whole continent in the state of an almost Edenic perfection before the advent of the Europeans and the gradual destruction of the natural environment, with an accelerated pace ever since. It is not accidental that with greater awareness of the environmental crisis the white man's view of the Native Americans' understanding of nature has gone from its earlier total rejection as "animism," "totemism," or "pantheism" understood in their most pejorative sense, to praise and adoration in many circles today. In any case the Native American understanding of the meaning of the order of nature is a most important and precious element in the current global religious response to the acute crisis between man and the natural environment.

African Religions

Countless studies have been made of the African religions ever since the European colonization of the African continent—studies mostly driven by either missionary zeal or scientism, both of which remained impervious to the nature and state of the religions being studied. When religions are considered as untrue or the whole question of truth is considered to be an irrelevant category in the study of religion, then one can hardly expect a distinction to be made between religions that have remained intact and those that have undergone a process of decay and degeneration. This indiscriminate study of the "phenomena" of religions is also to be seen in the Americas and Polynesia, but is especially evident in Africa where the most crass religious beliefs and teachings ranging over the whole gamut of veritable animism, ancestor worship, sorcery, and the like have been considered along with intact doctrines as general attributes of African religions. Only in recent times have a number of perceptive Western scholars been able to gain knowledge of oral teachings and have also been willing to apply more suitable methods and concepts to the subject of their study, while at the same time some of the authentic African followers of the still surviving primal religions have begun to express their teachings through Western languages. As a result, gradually a deeper insight is being gained of these religions as closely tied to the world of nature and yet anchored in the Spirit and the Transcendent of which nature is a manifestation or presence. In fact, as far as the order of nature is concerned, the views of those African religions that have preserved their integral traditions are not very different from those of other primal religions.[22]

Among African religions that have survived in a relatively intact manner to this day, one of the most remarkable is the religion of the Bambara, whose esoteric teachings reveal clearly the outlines of a primordial cosmology akin in many ways to that of Shamanism.[23] According to these teachings, there is a World Tree that joins Heaven and Earth, and in their initiation rites the Bambara learn 240 symbols that "are suspended" from this tree.[24] The universe itself is generated by the Word as one observes also in both the Abrahamic and Indian cosmologies.

As for the Bambara, "The heart of the esoteric teaching consists of the mysteries surrounding the Word. All of the universe is generated by the primal (and still continuing) vibrations that make up the Word. Out of this primal energy, matter and finally form are condensed. The vibrations marked out the cardinal points, and up and down, in [their] oscillations. It produced from the center the seed of all things. . . ."[25]

When these vibrations double back on themselves in thought, consciousness is established. This doubling back also establishes the elemental order in the preexisting flux and is the origin of order in the cosmos. According to one observer: "The source of the structured universe, then, is *Yo,* thought or will. *Yo* is the silent word that 'speaks' all that we know and can detect in the world. According to the Bambara, *Yo* comes from itself, is known by itself, departs out of itself, from the nothingness that is itself."[26]

Beyond the noise of the world lies that silence or *Yo,* which is also the harmony and order underlying all outer discord, while man himself is the image of *Yo* and contains this primordial harmony and order within himself.

Lest one should think that the remarkable teachings of the Bambara, which are so reminiscent of traditional metaphysics and cosmology found in so many other climes, is an exception, let us turn to another African religion, that of the Diola.[27] According to Diola cosmology, there is a pyramid of cosmic beings always in a state of harmony and equilibrium. Above human beings are located the spirits and finally God (*Ata Emit* or *Emitay*), the creator of the cosmos and all the diversity within it.[28] Everything receives its energy from *Ata Emit,* the supreme Force and Energy or God. Furthermore, there is an equilibrium, order, and harmony in the hierarchical cosmos created by God. Yet, within this order there are dynamic and vital currents so that one must conceive of the order of nature to be at once static and dynamic, hierarchical and vital. And here, as in the Shamanic religions, the order and harmony of the cosmos include and embrace man, who must live according to the order pervading all things.

The followers of the primal or indigenous religions, of which a few examples have been mentioned here, have been for millennia the witnesses as well as guardians of the Earth, her rhythms and harmony. Their religions, both conceptually and in the practical domain, contain teachings of great significance for our contemporary understanding of the relation between man and the order of nature. In any case, their views constitute an important element in the contemporary religious landscape as far as the religious significance of the order of nature is concerned and are a precious reminiscence of an "Edenic experience" of the natural world so much forgotten in the artificial urban ambience in which so many human beings live today.

THE EGYPTIAN RELIGION

All sacred lands reflect on Earth a celestial archetype, and this is particularly true of Egypt, the abode of one of the world's most hieratic and immutable sacred traditions. It was, in fact, a common refrain in the ancient period that "Egypt is made in the image of Heaven."[29] The Egyptian tradition dealt on the deepest level with the order of time, space, and forms and left an indelible mark upon much of later Mediterranean thought including central elements of Greek philosophy and science, where its influence was complemented by that of Mesopotamia. The greatest influence of the Egyptian heritage is to be found in Hermeticism, with which we shall deal in the next chapter, but also through the cults of Isis and Osiris many in the Roman Empire fell under the sway of the Egyptian religion, including such major figures as Plutarch, and many came to identify Dionysius, so central to Greek mystical teachings, with Osiris.[30]

Egyptian cosmology and theology represent on the surface great local variations and display a lack of cohesion commented upon by many of its students, a characteristic that Henri Frankfurt called "mythopoeic" to distinguish it from the need for a single rational explanation by the Greeks.[31] But despite these outward variations, deeper principles dominate over the whole of the tradition and unify it, principles reflected on the observable plane by the remarkable formal unity of the Egyptian tradition especially as mirrored in its art.

As far as written accounts of cosmology and theology are concerned, one of the most relevant to the subject of our inquiry is what has come to be known as "Memphite theology," according to which the Divinity Ptah contains the creation in his heart and creates beings through his tongue, that is, by the Word. The ninefold cosmic realities called the Ennead, and including Atum (the primordial Adam), are created by Ptah by simply pronouncing them.[32] The world created by Ptah includes the Sky goddess Nut, the Earth god Geb, and their separation by the Air god Shu,[33] while in the Ptolemaic period the hieroglyph designating Ptah is itself composed of Sky and Earth with the androgynic Ptah in between, implying that Ptah is also the link between the various cosmic elements such as Heaven and Earth, known together as the Ennead.[34] The order of the cosmos is thus both generated and sustained by the Divinity.

It is true that there is a cycle of worship from Horus to Re to Osiris during the long history of the Egyptian religion, but there are basic principles concerning the order of nature that continue through these transformations, such as the identification of cosmic elements with real divinities possessing a personal existence.[35] Most important of these principles for the understanding of the order of nature is the *Neter,* which has received many interpretations, some even equating it with the Hebrew *El.*[36] The *Neter* is a principle conveyed by a sign, the hieroglyph being itself called *Medu-Neteru.* It is the Idea of which a material object is the crystallization.

> In the pharaonic sense, the natural thing or being is none other than the materialization of the Idea of which it is the symbol. The bird living in the

air has an aerial nature; through its habits (life, nourishment, method of hunting, affinities and enmities, character, mode of assimilation, etc.) it becomes the *incarnation* of a function, of a stage in the universal genesis, and finally, of an Idea. Thus every natural thing is the incarnation of a principle; it is the principle's symbol.[37]

The order of nature is the reflection of the order that belongs to the realm of the principles or *Neteru,* which man also carries within his being as a consequence of his central position in the cosmic order. "Every natural type is a revelation of one of the natures and abstract functions that rule the world, a verb of the divine language—that is, the entities or fully realized Principles (Neteru). They are fully realized in the sense that they are types or definite stages in the cosmic embryology of man."[38]

The Egyptian tradition has remained even beyond its historical life span as a testimony to a view of the natural order in which the divine and cosmic domains remain inwardly linked through principles that also govern the human order. There is no separation of the divine and natural orders nor of the cosmic and the human. The Egyptian religion created a remarkable civilization based on the ever-living presence of the *Neteru* in the human world and brought into being works of art depicting forms of nature through which divine ideas seem almost to manifest themselves as external forms.

The Egyptians also recorded the order of time by creating a remarkable calendar based upon the *Sothic* year determined by the periodic return of the heliacal rising of Sirius, thus creating a fixed year, which was called the *year of God.* Moreover, they applied principles of sacred geometry to the ordering of space as well, according to that enduring harmony which characterizes Egyptian architecture, an architecture which succeeds in an unparalleled fashion to create within the bosom of the changing world of nature a reflection of the immutability of the Eternal Order.

THE FAR EASTERN TRADITIONS: TAOISM AND CONFUCIANISM

The religious landscape of the Far Eastern world, comprising China, Korea, and to a certain degree Japan and what was known until fairly recently as Indo-China, has been dominated for millennia by the primordial Chinese tradition incorporated to some extent in the *I-Ching* and its bifurcation into Taoism and Confucianism, to which one must add both indigenous Shamanic elements and in later centuries Buddhism and even Islam.[39] The Chinese religions and their extension into Korea and Japan have been based from the beginning on direct concern for nature and its order, which is also the order of the human world, and these traditions have produced some of the most profound doctrines concerning the order of nature.

Already in the *I-Ching,* this oldest text of Chinese metaphysics and cosmology attributed to King Wen and Duke Chou, the main concern is with the domain of change and the order pervading it, the title of the work itself meaning *The Book of Change*.[40] It seeks to explain the Ultimate Cause and the manner in which change and transformation are related to It. "There is T'ai Chi—the Universal Principle, the Ultimate Cause, the Absolute, the Eternal, the Never-Changing, the Ever Changing, the One, the All."[41] *I*, or change, characterizes the world of nature and all its forms but it occurs according to an order and set of principles with which the *I-Ching* deals. *T'ai Chi* leads to the two complementary principles *Yin* and *Yang* from whose interactions all change and becoming take place.

T'ai Chi

Yang   (Heaven, active, male   *Yin*   (Earth, passive, female,
          strong, light)   weak, dark)[42]

The process of change involves going from the One through the primal polarity of *Yin* and *Yang* to the many, and therefore the *I-Ching* enumerates eight trigrams and their combination, resulting in sixty-four hexagrams combined of the symbols of *Yin* and *Yang* in different permutations and combinations. It is said that these trigrams, each consisting of three broken or unbroken lines such as ☰ ☷ ☳ etc., were first drawn by the mythical emperor Fu Hsi[43] and were originally used for divination. But they were also cosmological symbols explaining the structure of the cosmos and its order.[44] Later Chinese cosmological thought was to draw constantly from these ideas, especially the *Yin-Yang* doctrine. In fact, in the former Han Dynasty there developed the *Yin-Yang* school with an elaborate cosmology based "on the correlations made between the Five Elements, four compass points (plus the center as a fifth direction), the four seasons, the five notes of the scale, the twelve months, the twelve pitch-pipes, the ten 'heavenly stems', the twelve 'earthly branches', and various other numerical categories."[45] The basic concepts of *T'ai Chi, Yin* and *Yang* along with the *Tao*—which is also used in the *I-Ching* sometimes as being synonymous with *T'ai Chi* and at other times as its dynamic aspect associated with the way or the path—have constituted over the ages the principles by which both Taoism and Confucianism have sought to understand the order of nature.

Taoism

Scholars have debated as to what is meant exactly by Taoism; some have referred to Lao-Tze and Chuang-Tzu as constituting the sources of Taoism, whereas others have spoken of attachment to the way of the Celestial Master in the second century A.D. as that which constitutes this religion. Be that as it may, there is no doubt that there is such a thing as a Taoist reality in the Chinese world dating back to Lao-Tze and that this tradition has been especially concerned with the world of nature as can be seen in the Tao Te Ching. The Taoists have spoken in many ways of the order of nature and have also sought to transcend "nature" through "nature" and thereby to gain immortality, which is the goal of Chinese alchemy.[46]

Without doubt the Tao is the most celebrated of all concepts and realities in the Chinese religious traditions. At once the Principle and the way to the Principle, that which governs and bestows order upon all things and also the root of that order itself, "Tao makes things what they are, but is not itself a thing. Nothing can produce Tao, yet everything has Tao within it."[47] Tao, at once infinite and "nameless" and the "ontological" principle or named, is that from which Heaven and Earth and the myriad of beings between them originate. As the opening of the Tao Te Ching asserts,

> *The Tao that can be expressed is not the eternal Tao;*
> *The name that can be defined is not the unchanging name.*
> *Non-existence is called the antecedent of heaven and earth;*
> *Existence is the mother of all things.*[48]

The Tao is the principle of all order and harmony, the unchanging principle of all that changes.[49] The process of change itself is, however, understood in Taoism as in the *I-Ching* in terms of the *Yin-Yang* principles. *Yin* is the chaos from which rises order and form or *Yang* and hence she is the "great mother" of all things on the cosmic level, being herself of course derived from the *Tao*. *Yin* corresponds to the Earth, the Moon, coagulation, and the esoteric; *Yang* to Heaven, the Sun, solution, and the exoteric. From those two "essences" all transformations are born, and they are responsible for the harmony pervading all things that exist and become according to their *Tao* and ultimately *the Tao*. As Chuang-Tzu has said, "The perfect negative principle is majestically passive. The perfect positive is powerfully active . . . the interaction of the two results in that harmony by which all things are produced."[50]

Taoism emphasizes that the harmony and order of nature does not come from an imposition from without but issues from the inner nature of things that exist and function by virtue of the *Tao*. Furthermore, the harmony and order of the cosmos also dominate over human existence, and Taoism, like Zen, emphasizes the significance of "naturalness" as the means to regain that harmony pervading all things. The order of nature is inextricably related to order within human beings; the Taoist sages, who retired to mountains and forests to contemplate nature, were also meditating upon the harmony and order within themselves, thus discovering the Tao and living according to Its tenets.

Confucianism

Although from the beginning Confucianism emphasized the importance of man and his society being in harmony with the harmony of Heaven and Earth, it is especially in neo-Confucianism, which flourished in what corresponds to the European Middle Ages, that one can discover the most profound expositions of Confucianism concerning the order of nature. In neo-Confucianism, as in the *I-Ching, T'ai Chi,* the Great Ultimate, is also considered as the origin of the universe. As the eleventh-century neo-Confucian scholar Chou Tun-i observed,

> The Great Ultimate [*T'ai-Chi*] through movement generates *yang*. When its activity reaches its limit, it becomes tranquil. Through tranquility the Great Ultimate generates *yin*. When tranquility reaches its limit, activity begins again.
>
> By the transformation of *yang* and its union with *yin,* the Five Agents of Water, Fire, Wood, Metal and Earth arise. When these five material forces [*ch'i*] are distributed in harmonious order, the four seasons run their course. . . .[51]

In neo-Confucianism there is a rise of the importance of the concepts of *ch'i* and *li,* the first signifying "ether," "breath," "matter/energy," "material force" or "vital force" and the second principle, pattern or law.[52] The Ch'eng brothers, also eleventh-century philosophers, emphasized *li* and *ch'i* as the fundamental constitutive elements of all things, even eclipsing *T'ai Chi. Li* was considered as the "principle of nature" that governed all things, the universal order in the dynamic creative process and the source of all other principles of order. It was considered as at once the universal ontological principle and the *ontic* principle of each particular thing. Hence, neo-Confucianism came to be known as the "School of Nature and Principle."[53]

The attempt to synthesize the two trends to emphasize *li* and *ch'i* was made in the twelfth century by Chu Hsi for whom *li* is the nature or order of a thing and makes a thing be what it is, whereas *ch'i* is the physical object itself ordered and structured according to *li.*[54] Furthermore, *T'ai chi* is "not only the principle of all things, but the principle of each and everything. In other words, *T'ai-chi* is not only the *li* of the universe, but, at the same time, the *li* which is inherent in a particular individuality."[55]

A point emphasized greatly in both Chinese and the later Korean neo-Confucianism is the interrelation and, in fact, unity between the human order and the order of nature. The eleventh-century Chinese sage Chou Tun-i stated:

> The Sage with respect to Heaven and Earth is at one with their character, with respect to the sun and the moon is at one with their brilliance, with respect to the four seasons is at one with their order and with respect to the spirits is at one with the good fortune and the misfortune [which they mediate].[56]

This truth was also to be emphasized by the sixteenth-century Korean neo-Confucian Yi Hwang, also known as T'oegye, who spoke constantly of the unity of the order of the cosmos and of human nature. His commentaries upon the Western Inscription of the eleventh-century Chinese sage Chang-Tsai is a testament to his insistence upon this unity.

> *Chi'en* [Heaven] is called the father and *K'un* [Earth] is called the mother. I, this tiny being, am commingled in their midst; therefore what fills up all

between Heaven and Earth, that is my body, and that which directs Heaven and Earth is my nature.[57]

Chu Hsi was to comment that the principle *li* is one while its manifestations are diverse. T'oegye adds by way of commentary to this idea, "In terms of principle, there certainly is no distinction between the self and things, the internal and the external, the subtle and the coarse. . . ."[58] Such neo-Confucian figures as Chang-Tsai and the Ch'eng brothers also spoke firmly of the universe being a single body, each person and each creature being a member of a family that is the universe governed by the same order and harmony. Chu Hsi summarized this view while identifying the force of love as that which attaches *Jen* or humanity to the cosmos: "If one is impartial, then he looks upon the Heaven and Earth and all the creatures as forming a single body and there is nothing he does not love."[59]

The Far Eastern traditions present us with some of the most profound meditations upon the meaning of the order of nature as it is related to the order that should dominate over human life. They present several grand interpretations of the doctrine of the interrelatedness between human and natural order, and the link which binds principles governing human beings and those governing nature into a unity whose negation is the origin of all discord and disorder.

THE INDO-IRANIAN AND EUROPEAN RELIGIONS

The people who came to occupy lands as far apart as India and northern Europe, who gave their name to countries as distant as Iran and Ireland and who have usually been known as Aryans, not only possess tongues with linguistic affinities but over the centuries they practiced religions which belong to the same family and demonstrate family resemblances. These religions range from those of India such as Hinduism, Buddhism, and Jainism to the religions of Iran such as Mithraism, Zoroastrianism, and Manichaeism to the religions of the Greeks, Romans, ancient Germans, and Celts. Most of these religions have disappeared, and among them only Hinduism, Buddhism, and Zoroastrianism still survive as living religions. It is therefore to these religions and their understanding of the order of nature that we shall turn. But in the discussion of this family we must make an exception and also include the Greek religion because of its great significance in the rise of the Western philosophical and scientific understanding of nature and also the challenge it indirectly posed to the Christian formulation of the philosophy and theology of nature in the West.

Hinduism

In its multifarious developments over the millennia and the presence within it of diverse schools of metaphysical and religious interpretation or *darśanas*, Hinduism offers many paths for the understanding of the order of nature. Although certain of its schools such as the *Vedānta* and *Mādhyamika* do not display great interest in this question, others such as the *Sāṃkhya* present extensive teachings concerning nature. The *Sāṃkhya* is in fact the most important of the *darśanas* for the understanding of the Hindu view of nature.[60] But before the formation of the different schools of thought or the *darśanas*, already in the Vedas are to be found the most profound prinicples of the Hindu understanding of the order of nature. The Vedas are not only the source of knowledge of the universe, but according to the Hindu view they are the origin of the universe itself, for the Veda is "the Eternal as word." The whole universe, including the divine powers, are said to emanate from it.[61]

The Ṛg-Veda speaks of *Puruṣa*, the primordial cosmic being and celestial prototype of man,[62] and his sacrifice as the cause of the genesis of the universe, *Puruṣa* being at once the source of the physical universe and its order and the social order, which are inseparable from each other.[63] The order in nature derives from the reality of *Puruṣa* for everything in the universe is related bodily to its Divine Source. The celebrated hymn of *Puruṣa* in the Ṛg-Veda (10.90) explains in a poetic and lucid manner this relationship:

Thousand-headed is Man [Puruṣa]
With a thousand eyes and feet.
He envelopes the whole earth
Of him all the worlds are only one-fourth,
Three-fourths are immortal in Heaven. . . .
When with Man [Puruṣa] as their offering
The Gods performed the sacrifice,
Spring was the oil they took
Autumn the offering and summer the fuel. . . .
From that cosmic sacrifice,
Drops of oil were collected,
Beasts of the wing were born,
And animals wild and tame. . . .
When they dismembered Man,
Into how many parts did they separate him?
What was his mouth, what his anus,
What did they call his thighs and feet?
The Brahman was his mouth;
The Rajanya (Princes) became his arms;
His thighs produced the Vaiśya (professions and
*   merchants)*
His feet gave birth to the Śudra (laborer).
The moon was born from his mind;
His eyes gave birth to the sun;
And Vāyū (the wind) from his breath was born.
From his navel the midair rose;
The sky arose from his head;
From feet, the earth; from ears, the directions.
Thus they found the worlds.[64]

The myth of the sacrifice of primordial Man or *Puruṣa* reveals the inalienable nexus among the individual human order, the social order, and the order of nature, a view that has been dominant in Hinduism over the ages.

There are, however, other Hindu cosmogonic myths including the creation of the world from the primordial sound associated with the sacred mantra *Aum,* with the consequent result that a single energy (*prāṇa*) pervades all levels of the cosmos and relates the order of nature to its Divine Source. There is also the famous myth of the "egg of Brahman" mentioned in the Chāndogya Upanishad (III, 19, 1–2):

> The Sun is *Brahman*—this is the teaching. An explanation thereof [is this].
> In the beginning this [world] was non-existent. It became existent. It grew.
> It turned into an egg. It lay for the period of a year. It burst open. Then
> came out of the eggshell, two parts, one of silver, the other of gold.
>
> That which was of silver is this earth; that which was of gold is the sky.
> What was the outer membrane is the mountains; that which was the inner
> membrane is the mist with the clouds. What were the veins were the rivers.
> What was the fluid within is the ocean.[65]

Here again the myth alludes to a reality of Divine Origin that contains all the possibilities of manifestation of a particular cosmic cycle. All that unfolds in the life of that cycle is in accordance with the order contained in the original cosmic "egg" or *brahmāṇḍa,* which "grows" and bursts forth to include both the world of nature or the cosmos and man.

These various myths all point to a principle fundamental to the Hindu understanding of nature as being sacred,[66] a doctrine that has led many to conclude incorrectly that the Hindu view of nature is pantheistic. Whatever may have resulted from decadence in popular practice or belief, there is no doubt whatsoever that the metaphysical and cosmological doctrines of Hinduism are not pantheistic. The hymn of the *Ṛg-Veda* dedicated to *Puruṣa* states clearly that only one-fourth constitutes all the worlds, thereby denying explicitly the equivalence between Divinity and the cosmos, which constitutes pantheism as usually understood.

With this very important reservation and the constant remembrance of the Unconditioned Brahman, which is the Absolute Reality, beyond all cosmic levels of existence, it must nevertheless be emphasized that much of Hinduism identifies the cosmos with "the body of the Divinity" and sees the order of nature as a direct manifestation of the Divine Order. The Mūṇḍāka Upanishad (I.i.7), in fact, states, "As a spider sends forth and draws in its threads, as herbs grow on the earth, as the hair grows on the head and the body of a living person, so from the Imperishable arises here the universe."[67] This truth is also expressed explicitly in that sublime synthesis of Hinduism that is the Bhaghavad-Gita where the Lord Kṛṣṇa (Krishna) sings,

> *I am the birth of this cosmos:*
> *Its dissolution also.*
> *I am He who causes:*

No other beside me.
Upon me, these worlds are held
Like pearls strung on a thread.
I am the essence of the waters,
The shining of the sun and the moon:
Om in all the Vedas,
The word that is God.
It is I who resound in the ether
And am potent in man.
I am the sacred smell of the earth,
The light of the fire,
Life of all lives,
Austerity of ascetics. . . .
You must know that whatever belongs to the states of sattwa,
rajas and tamas proceeds from me.
They are contained in me,
but I am not in them. . . .[68]

The cosmos is thus the raiment of the *avatāra*, and the cause of all events in nature, the tendencies that, according to Hindu doctrines, govern the world of nature are to be found in him; and yet he is beyond all cosmic determinations. This view must not, however, belittle the significance of law or *rta*, which even precedes the gods in the Vedas. The two basic Hindu concepts related to cosmic as well as human law are *rta* and *dharma*, the former being Vedic and the latter post-Vedic, and as we shall see shortly also of cardinal importance to Buddhism.[69] These terms imply both cosmic and ethical law and have at once religious and "natural" dimensions. As found in other traditions discussed above, so in Hinduism the two are never separated from each other. Hinduism is itself called eternal law or *sanātanadharma*. The Upanishads identify *dharma* with *Ātman* or the Essence of the soul, and the *Laws of Manu* with the principles governing human society in conformity with cosmic laws, while the Gita mentions *dharma* as flowing from the Divine Nature Itself. There is a single law rooted in the Divine Order that determines at once the order of nature and the human world that are inalienably bound together.

Precisely because it functions according to *dharma*, nature can act as a spiritual guide or *guru* in its own right as asserted by the *Bhāgavata-Purāna*. The Lord of the universe, according to *Pañcadasī*, is the "bliss-sheath" who is the carrier of all the *vāsanās* (or potential developments and natural laws contained in *māyā*).[70] He is the "Inner Ruler of the Universe" and "the world (*jagat*) remains 'implicate' in the Lord. He creates it according to the *karmas* of living beings.[71] Man can learn from nature about the laws that are ultimately those governing his own being and be led to the "Inner Ruler of the Universe," hence deliverance. Knowledge of nature can lead ultimately to freedom in the Hindu sense of deliverance from all limitation by virtue of the principles manifested in nature and yet transcending nature. The knowledge of nature, moreover, is not of only one level and must not be confused with empiricism. There are modes of knowing nature in accordance with the mode of consciousness of the knower and there are levels of order in nature, both exoteric and esoteric, all of which are real on their own level and which can be known by a transformation of the consciousness of the knower while this knowledge itself also brings with it such a transformation. Knowledge of the order of nature thereby leads to awareness of the reality of the cosmos as the raiment of the Divinity and laws that have their roots in the Divine Order.

Before leaving this brief discussion of Hinduism, a word must also be said about the order of time or the historic unfolding of the cosmic cycles discussed in greater detail in this religion than in any other. The religious understanding of the order of nature encompasses not only this order in space but also in time. Hinduism envisages vast cosmic cycles, discussed in such texts as the *Purāṇas,* in which cosmic rhythms are examined and the laws of unfolding of various states of the cycles comprising the *kalpas, manvantaras,* and *yugas* elucidated in the light of their spiritual, social, and natural consequences.

Although it is not possible here to deal with what Hinduism states about these cycles, it is essential to mention them as the most explicit example of the religious concern with the temporal order of nature, one that is also found among the Egyptians and Babylonians with their sacred calendars, the ancient Persians with their division of the history of the world into twelve periods, the Muslims with their doctrines of cycles of prophecy determining both human and cosmic history, as well as among others. But in Hinduism this religious significance of the temporal order of nature and the unfolding of cosmic cycles and subcycles is expounded in unparalleled detail and hence needs to be mentioned here as a most important element in the general religious understanding of the order of nature, even if this doctrine has not been expounded in the same manner or to the same extent in other religions or is even rejected or passed over in certain traditions. What is significant to note in the context of the present study is the existence of a temporal dimension to the religious understanding of the order of nature in general.

Buddhism

One might think that in a religion such as Buddhism, in which emphasis is placed upon overcoming the suffering inherent in *saṃsāric* existence and reaching *nirvāṇa* without wasting human life "so difficult to attain" on trying to understand the nature of things, there is no room for a doctrine concerning the order of nature. This is true only if one seeks elaborate cosmologies as one finds elsewhere, although of course even this is not absent from later developments of Buddhism as one finds in Tibet or among certain Chinese and Japanese schools. But if one wishes to understand in the most fundamental manner the meaning of the order of nature in a Buddhist context, one can find important indications which lie at the heart of Buddhism even before the development of its later philosophical and comological elaborations.

First of all, according to the Buddhists the Buddha was one of those rare beings who are Tāthagata, that is, those who have realized the nature of things or their "suchness" (*tathatā*). Second, they have discovered that it is *dharma* which constitutes the nature of all things, and *dharma* is both religion and the universal order or "natural law" by which the world or *saṃsāra* functions.[72] This *dharma* according to Buddhism, however, has no cause or originator. The Buddha did not create or originate *dharma* but discovered and revealed it.

Dharma or *dhamma* in Pali has always meant "principle" and "law," the law that dominates over the universe, bestowing order upon it, and that the Buddha taught. In Pali texts *dhamma* means the interpreted order of the world.

> That which the Buddha preached . . . was the order of law of the universe, immanent, eternal, uncreated, not as interpreted by him only, much less invited or decreed by him, but intelligible to a mind of his range and by him made so to mankind as bodhi: revelation, awakening. The Buddha is a discoverer of this order of Dhamma, this universal logic, philosophy or righteousness ("Norm"), in which the rational and ethical elements are fused into one.[73]

In later schools the concept of *dharma* received extensive elaboration. In Mahāyāna, *dharma* came to signify both the immanent and transcendent reality of all things and the Buddha's teachings, elucidating the universal order of nature as well as the path toward deliverance from *saṃsāric* existence. In the Sarvāstivāda School the doctrine of *dharma,* conceived of as at once truth, knowledge, duty, and morality, became expounded in a particularly systematic way.[74] According to this school, objects have no substance but only modalities, and the world is not constituted of a series of substances but is a flux of *dharmas.* This flux, however, is not chaotic or incoherent but follows strictly the law of "dependent origination" (*pratīya-samutpāda*). Furthermore, the moral law of *karman* is imposed upon this strict causal law governing both the animate and inanimate worlds.

There are seventy-two *dharmas* comprising all the elements of phenomenal existence. These are conditioned because they follow the law of causality, but three of these *dharmas* are unconditioned and not bound by causal laws. This *dharma* theory "propounds an explanation of how the universe functions within the context of a sentient life, particularly a human flux, for it is human life that Buddhism is concerned with."[75] Some of these *dharmas* are associated with the world of bodies, not as substances by sense-data, and there are elaborate classifications of them always in relation to cognition. The Sarvāstivāda School considers these *dharmas* to be real, coming into being and passing away according to the laws of *karman,* but other schools such as the Lokottaravāda consider all the conditioned *dharmas* to be unreal and only the unconditioned to be real. As for the Mahāyāna, it considers even the *dharmas* to be "empty" and part of *saṃsāric* flux. Therefore, it does away with the *dharmas* altogether and emphasizes instead *Dharma* as Ultimate Reality symbolized by the eternal body (*Dharmakāya*) of the Buddha.[76]

Later schools of Buddhism, especially those in Japan, present striking developments of these cardianl ideas in understanding the domain of nature as one sees so clearly in Zen and the works of Dōgen. But even at the beginning of Japanese Buddhism one observes particular attention paid to the understanding of Buddhism in connection with the sacredness of nature so much emphasized by Shintoism, which teachings had permeated Japanese society for so many centuries before the spread of Buddhism in that land. Kūkai, who was the first to bring the teachings of the Buddha to Japan, understood ultimate Buddha as "Buddha— nature that shines like a great light within all things."[77] The Shinto *Kamis* became the *Gohoshin,* the god guardians of *dharma,* and became included in the Japanese pantheon. In the context of Japan, Buddhism was in fact not world- denying but manifested itself in the world of nature, and some Japanese scholars have spoken of the soteriological function of nature.[78] In any case, there is no doubt that there existed a tendency in Buddhism, which led during the later period of Buddhist history, to the discussion of the Buddhahood of the elements of nature such as plants and trees in East Asia and especially Japan, where in the case of a sage as a Saigyo the greater significance accorded to nature led through a hermeneutic process to the attribution of a basic soteric role to the world of nature. The "suchness" of things came to be realized within the very forms of the natural world.

In Buddhism as elsewhere and despite the very different climate from both Hinduism and the Abrahamic religions and therefore a denial of the Source of *dharma* in the sense of its Originator, there remains the emphasis upon the existence of an order of nature possessing religious significance, an order insepara- ble from the moral order, dominating human life and inextricably related to it. The *dharmas* of the natural world and that of human beings are not alien or distinct realities but belong to the same understanding of the meaning of *dharma,* at once truth, principle, law, and our duty to act and live according to the law.

Zoroastrianism

Of the Iranian religions, Mithraism and Manichaeism are no longer extant while Zoroastrianism has a small number of followers located for the most part in Persia (Iran) and India. Yet, the historical role of these religions in the general religious and philosophical life of western Asia and the Mediterranean world has been immense, and therefore something needs to be said here at least about the most important of the Iranian religions, namely Zoroastrianism. The significance of the other members of this family, especially Mithraism and Manichaeism— particularly as far as the domain of cosmology is concerned—must be kept in mind, however, and one needs to remember the extensive spread of Mithraism, with its emphasis upon the divine nature of the stars and astrology in general within the Roman Empire[79] and the challenge Manichaeism posed to Chris- tianity, playing an important role in the life of no lesser a figure than St. Augustine.[80] As for Zoroastrianism, besides its impact upon both Greek philo- sophy and the Abrahamic religions, its founder became associated in the esoteric Western tradition with the cosmological sciences, and scientific treatises came to be attributed to him. In any case, the Zoroastrian view of the order of nature is of great significance both in itself and because of its impact on many later schools of religious and philosophical thought in both the Islamic world and the West.

Zoroastrianism establishes a direct relationship with the world of nature and cosmic elements through a liturgy that incorporates this relationship in the rituals of the religion and not only in its doctrines. Concerning the ritual of the 28th day of the month, the sacred scripture of Zoroastrianism asserts, "We are celebrating this liturgy in honor of the Earth, which is an Angel."[81] In this perspective, Earth itself is seen as part of the hierarchy of angels so central to Zoroastrianism, and the question is not what is the Earth but who is the Earth. In the words of Henry Corbin: "We have to capture here the phenomenon of the Earth as an angelophany."[82] The cosmology and physics of such an Earth possess a structure that contains the response to the question "Who?" and not only "What?"

Mazdaean cosmology, which is the foundation for its understanding of the order of nature, is based upon the well-known ontological distinction between the two principles of Ohrmazd (Ahura Mazda), the "infinite height of Light," and Ahriman (Angra Mainyu), "the unfathomable abyss of Darkness."[83] Hence, the attribution of dualism to Zoroastrianism, which is strongly rejected by Zoroastrians today who consider themselves monotheists. In any case, the genesis of the cosmos, and the order pervading it and its laws, are at once existential and ethical. Earth and in fact the whole of Creation is the battleground of the forces of Light and Darkness until the apokatastasis, when the mixture (*gumēzishn*) of these forces or elements, which constitutes the very texture of the cosmos, is brought to an end through their separation (*wizārishn*), marking the end of cosmic history.[84] Cosmic history is thereby marked by the three fundamental points of creation, mixture, and separation. The cosmos has an origin and an end and is also governed by a strict law or *Asha,* which is at once cosmic and ethical and which is the celestial and cosmic representative of Divine Justice. *Asha* is the principle of all order in nature as well as human life, resembling the *Tao* of the Chinese tradition, *r̥ta* and *dharma* in Hinduism, and to a large extent the Greek *Dike.*[85]

The universe is governed from on high by the seven "Holy Immortals" (*Amesha Spenta*) consisting of Ahura Mazda and the six archangels, which together comprise the primordial heptadic archetype of all Creation. Their energies, as described in *Yasht XIX* of the Avesta, activate and pervade all things. Three of the archangels are masculine and three feminine, while Ahura Mazda unites their nature within Itself. Beings in this world are created by liturgical acts, each angel or power of light bringing into being a part of Creation through its flowing energy, this part being the personal "hierurgy" of the angel in question. Thus did the archangel *Vohu Mana* (Bahman) generate the animal creation, *Spenta Armaiti* (*Isfand-ārmuz*), translated by Plutarch as Sophia, the Earth, etc.[86] These angels are assisted by another host of angels, the *Yazatas* (*Īzads*), meaning literally the Adorable Ones. Among them is to be counted Zamyāt, the feminine angel of the Earth, or to quote Henry Corbin *Dea Terrestis,* the telluric (terrestrial) glory who cooperates with the archangel *Amertāt* (*Murdād*) in governing the world of nature.[87] Furthermore, there are the feminine celestial entities, the *Fravarti,* those who have chosen to fight on the side of Ahura-Mazda and who are the heavenly archetypes of individual beings and their tutelary angels.

Zoroastrian cosmology also emphasizes the distinction between *gētīk,* the earthly, and *mēnōk,* the heavenly. Each earthly being has a celestial or *mēnōk* counterpart, or, to put it another way, everything possesses two levels of existence—the spiritual or celestial, and the physical or earthly. Moreover, the spiritual has an embryonic and seminal relation to the physical, and one might say that what we observe as the *gētīk* of things is a development here below of their *mēnōk* reality. One cannot, however, perceive the *mēnōk* of things or the Earth itself as a whole as an angel by ordinary perception. What is needed is the transformation of the mind and the imagination and the attainment of what Corbin calls *Imaginatio vera.*[88] This transformation cannot come about save with the help of that celestial light which Zoroastrianism calls *Xvarnah* (*khurrah*) or "Light of Glory."

This light has been in operation in the world from the beginning as the sacral light, which bestows order and coherence upon things and ensures the final victory of the light of beings over their darkness. It also possesses an important eschatological function and is depicted in art as a luminous halo. The *Bundahishn* identifies it with the very essence of the soul, and it is through this *Xvarnah* of the soul that the transformation of the perception of Earth from simply a physical object to an angel is made possible. With the help of this light one can gain a profound knowledge of the order of nature and of the Earth, which in contrast to ordinary geology we may call with Henry Corbin a *geosophy.*[89]

Zoroastrianism also possesses important doctrines concerning the sacrifice of the original bull and the primordial man (Gayōmard), which present striking resemblances with, as well as certain differences from, corresponding Hindu doctrines and which are of significance for the understanding of the Zoroastrian view of the order of nature. But the most important of all Zoroastrian doctrines is that of the angels, which govern and bestow order upon all cosmic beings, and the struggle between the forces of light and darkness, which is also the battle between good and evil—hence the ethical significance of the order and processes of nature and its laws. To perceive of the Earth as an angel is not only of great poetic beauty but also expresses a profound cosmological and religious truth whose forgetting in the modern world is far from being irrelevant both to the desecration, combined with the destruction, of the natural order and of the Earth that modern man has been carrying out so systematically and successfully during the past few centuries.

The Greek Religions

The various strands of Greek religion, or one could say different Greek religions, chthonian as well as Olympian, which were closely interrelated at earlier times,[90] and the Dionysian–Orphic tradition, have all disappeared from the face of the Earth. Yet the treatment of their understanding of the order of nature is essential, not only because the metaphysical schools of Greek thought such as Platonism were closely related to them and their gradual weakening and demise gave rise indirectly to the birth of both Greek philosophy and science, but also as a result of the fact that it was Greek paganism which during the Renaissance succeeded in killing medieval Christian civilization and was directly instrumental in the rise of Renaissance humanism and indirectly in the advent of modern philosophy and science. The rebellion in the West against the Christian—and, more generally speaking, religious—understanding of the order of nature is closely wed to that transformation of the Greek religious worldview, which for the first time permitted the separation of religion from both intellection and *mythos*[91] and the treatment of the world of nature as a reality depleted of the presence of the Divine[92]; hence, the great significance for us in this study of the views of Greek religion toward nature and the cosmos.[93]

The Greek term for the world of nature in its vastest sense, that is, *cosmos,* is most revealing as far as the Greek conception of the world is concerned. Although this term has remained in European languages to this day, it does not by any means possess the same range of connotations in these languages as it had for the Greek mind. Most of its current users are not in fact even aware of its primary meaning as order. For the Greeks the term had "the highest religious dignity."[94] It meant not only order but also beauty, harmony, and intelligibility. It was never a bland word like "world" in English whose original meaning as the "great man" corresponding to *Puruṣa* or *al-insān al-kāmil* has been totally lost.[95] For the Greeks to call the universe cosmos meant that the universe was a perfect exemplar of order, both beautiful and intelligible, or according to Plato the highest sensible being, "in very truth a living creature with soul and intellect."[96] That is why this order was to be imitated by human beings,[97] and the order of nature remained inseparable from the moral order as asserted already by Hesiod.

Cosmos was born out of the primordial Chaos or void as asserted in the *Theogony* of Hesiod: "First of all, the Void (*Chaos*) came into being, next broadbosomed Earth, the solid and eternal home of all."[98] The Earth itself was divine, the progenitor of life and mother of the gods as asserted in the following Homeric hymn:

> I will sing the well-founded Earth, mother of all, eldest of all things. She feeds all creatures that are in the world, all that go upon the goodly land, and all that are in the paths of the seas, and all that fly. . . .
>
>   Hail, Mother of the gods, wife of starry Heaven; freely bestow upon me for this my song substance that sheers the heart![99]

For Homer, *Moira*—that is, Fate or Destiny—antecedes and is above the gods. It is *Moira,* at once cosmic and moral decree, that causes the division of the Earth and in fact the world as a whole among the gods as asseted by Hesiod:

> Earth (*Gaia*) first of all gave being to one equal to herself, the starry Heaven (*Ouranos*), that he might enfold her all round, that there might be for the blessed Gods a seat secure for ever. And she brought forth the high mountains wherein the Gods delight to inhabit. And she gave birth also to the waste Ocean, swelling with rage, the sea (*Pontos*).[100]

In this primary cosmogonic process the world is divided into three portions (*moirai*), and order is imposed by the principle of Destiny or *Moira* to which the gods as well as the elements are subjugated. It is only later in the history of Greek religion that the will of the gods replaces *Moira* as the source for the order in nature, and the apportioning of various domains of nature to the different gods becomes the result of legislation by Zeus. The allotting of the universe by *Moira* was called *nomothesia*—that is, the process of laying down or fixing of *nomoi* or laws pertaining to each domain of nature, the key Greek term *nomos* or law being related to the verb *nemein* (to distribute). Order governed nature according to the law dominating over the different allotments of the domains of nature, an order that was at once necessary and just, cosmic and moral. [101]

It was the abandonment of the world by the gods that prepared the ground for Anaximander's replacing of the gods with natural cause, or eternal motion, which is in a sense closer to the concept of *Moira* than is the will of the gods but is nevertheless already removed from the *Weltanschauung* of traditional Greek religion. The very concept of the order of nature in both senses of the term entered Greek philosophy and science not as a result of the observation of nature but primarily from Greek religion. [102] Consequently, some of the early Greek religious ideas such as the moral character of the laws of nature continued to persist as an accepted principle in the West until the complete secularization of the sciences of nature in modern times.

Greek religion was not confined, however, to the Olympian religion; it became integrated with the chthonian cults, with the central conception of *Moira* dominating over its view of the order of nature. There is also the mystical religion of the Greeks associated with Dionysius and Orpheus in which the element of time and direct contact with the Divine were central, [103] and where *Dike* (righteousness) replaces *Moira* as the principle of order, *Dike* itself carrying also the meaning of "the course of nature." [104] *Dike,* as already mentioned, bears much resemblance to such principles as *Tao, ṛta,* and *Asha* in Taoism, Hinduism, and Zoroastrianism, respectively, and the latter may have actually influenced Orphism and Pythagoreanism, [105] for it is the principle that bestows order upon things, turning chaos to cosmos.

The Orphic hymns have been lost, but their influence is detected in many strands of Greek thought. There is no doubt that Orphism possessed ideas of great cosmological significance especially as far as it concerned music and the relation between musical harmony and the order of the cosmos. [106] It was this aspect of Orphism and the esoteric dimension of Greek religion in general that was to become crystallized later along with Egyptian elements in Pythagoreanism. Since in a sense Pythagoras marks, along with the Ionians, the beginning of Greek philosophy, we shall turn to Pythagoreanism in the next chapter and simply emphasize here the significance of the esoteric currents of Greek religious thought for the understanding of certain important dimensions of the Greek conception of the order of nature.

The same holds true for Hermeticism, that esoteric current which from the beginning displayed a great concern for the study of nature and from which grew a philosophy of nature that influenced European thought well into the eighteenth and nineteenth centuries. Hermeticism, at once a child of Egyptian and Greek religions, is also a philosophy in the time-honored sense of the term and was in fact identified during the Renaissance with the original expression of the *philosophia perennis,* which was also considered to be the *philosophia priscorium.* [107] Therefore, we shall also deal with it in Chapter 3.

Before leaving the discussion of Greek religion a word must be said about Gnosticism, which some relate to Iranian dualism and others even see as an outgrowth of Christianity, [108] but which in any event was an important current in the late Hellenistic world, with its influence spreading to religions as diverse as Christianity and Buddhism. [109] Gnosticism, which must be distinguished from gnosis, as illuminative knowledge corresponding to *jñāna* in Sanskrit and *al-ma'rifah* in Arabic, [110] represents a most complex set of religious phenomena with far-reaching ramifications. It did possess a view concerning the order of nature, [111] but because of the (theologically speaking) negative attitude toward the governance of the world and its fragmented character and diverse forms in which it manifested itself, it cannot be treated in the present context without taking us too far away from our central concern. Its significance must nevertheless be mentioned not because of its transient character as a Christian heresy, but because of its influence upon certain aspects of later Western thought. [112] Had Gnosticism persisted as a religion, its views of the order of nature, even if for the most part the reverse of what one finds in nearly all other traditions, would have had to be considered as would the views of Manichaeism, which also had a fairly transient existence but more enduring influence. But considering the nature of the historic manifestation of Gnosticism, we must be content in this study simply to mention it without delving into its cosmology and views concerning the order of nature. [113]

THE ABRAHAMIC RELIGIONS

The Abrahamic monotheisms—that is, Judaism, Christianity, and Islam— belong to the same spiritual universe, with belief in the one God who, while being transcendent, not only has created but also governs the world according to an order that issues from his Wisdom as well as his Will. And yet, the conception of the order of nature in these three religions is hardly the same. There are important differences as well as remarkable similarities of both morphological and historical origin. Moreover, all three religions developed elaborate theologies and philosophies over time, often influenced by developments in one of the other sister religions as well as Greek philosophy. It is therefore necessary to treat them separately and at the same time be judicious in the choice of what we consider to be the view of these religions and what developed later in their various philosophical schools, which were all based in one way or another on their basic religious teachings. This problem is especially acute for Christianity, which not only developed numerous philosophical schools concerned with the order of nature but also served as the background for modern Western philosophy, many of whose schools have refuted altogether the religious understanding of the order of nature.

Judaism

When we ask where we should seek for the Jewish understanding of the order of nature, naturally the Torah and the Talmud come to mind, but the first has been interpreted differently by various schools, whereas the second is concerned most of all with the questions of law and the religious life. However, there is an early rabbinic *midrash* of the fourth century dealing with Creation and commentary upon the Book of Genesis, the part of the Torah that is most crucial for this question. There are those, moreover, who claim that one should turn to Philo with his doctrine of the Logos containing the archetypes of Creation and being the source for the order of nature.[114] Some of these scholars, in fact, consider Jewish philosophy as a *midrash* and assert that such *midrashim* "antedate even the earliest rabbinic *midrashim.*"[115]

As far as the earliest verses of the Torah concerning Creation and the bringing into being of order are concerned, there have remained profound differences over the ages among Jewish Talmudic scholars and philosophers as to even the meaning of *creatio ex nihilo* (creation from nothing). Scholars have debated as to what views Philo and Maimonides held concerning *ex nihilo,* while the medieval Jewish philosopher Gersonides in *The Wars of the Lord* developed fully the doctrine of Creation from an eternal formless matter, drawing from the apocryphal *Wisdom of Solomon,* thus opposing the prevalent medieval view as well as the view held by Talmudic scholars.[116]

It is of interest to recall that in the Talmudic period *Ma'aseh Bereshit* ("Act of Creation") was considered as belonging to esoteric lore, and the *Mishnah* (Hag. 2:1) states that it should "not be expounded before two people."[117] It was only later in Jewish history that it became the subject of public discourse, but the true understanding of it and therefore the deepest meaning of the order of nature still has to be sought in Jewish esotericism especially in such Cabalistic works as *Sefer Yezirah,* where it has been expounded systematically.[118]

According to the Cabala, the Divine Reality or *Ein-Sof* is also present in God's Creation, which serves as the means of knowing Him, and the ten *Sefiroth* are the direct principles of cosmic order. Creation occurs from within God, an esoteric doctrine to be found also in Christianity and Islam, and to which we shall turn again shortly, and the *ex nihilo* of the beginning of Genesis is identified with *ayin* (nothingness), which is the first step in the manifestation of *Ein-Sof.*[119] God "withdraws" from Himself unto Himself in order to allow for the creation of the cosmos:

> The God who is all can have no other. Here the divine light has to hide itself that it might be revealed. It withdraws itself from being in order that it might be seen, in order to allow for us to exist as "other," so that we might

see and bear witness to it. This paradox of divine self-withdrawal is what the sages call *tsumtsum*.[120]

Through this beautiful and profound doctrine the Cabala explains the origin of the order of nature in a "nothingness" that is none other than the self-negation of the Divine Reality. As for the process of Creation, the myth of the "breaking of the vessels" or cosmic catastrophe links the very substance of the cosmos to the Divine Order. According to this myth, Divine Light struck the six lower *Sefiroth*, from *Ḥesed* to *Yesod*, all at once causing them to break. The vessel of the last *Sefiroth*, *Malkhut*, also cracked but did not break to the same extent. Much of the light of the cracked vessels were hurled down with the vessels themselves, thus forming the cosmos, the shards of these vessels or *Kelippot* becoming the sources of gross matter.[121] The very substance of the cosmos is therefore related to the coagulation of a reality that ultimately belongs to the Divine Order, whereas the order of nature is due to the laws governing all things, even this cosmic catastrophe, for this catastrophe was not chaotic but occurred according to clear internal laws.

The Cabalists as well as the followers of medieval Hassidism were also fully aware that all the order of this world derives from the archetypal realities (*demuth*), which all things, both animate and inanimate, possess. Moses was in fact shown these archetypes by God.[122] The process of Creation outlined in the *Zohar* involves this nexus between the archetypal realities and outer worlds:

> The process of creation, too, has taken place on two planes, one above and one below, and for this reason the Torah begins with the letter "Beth," the numerical value of which is two. The lower occurrence corresponds to the higher; one produced the upper world (of the Sefiroth), the other the nether world (of the visible creation).[123]

The Divine Life is manifested in Creation, and all the order of nature derives from this ever-renewed creativity. Moreover, the vestiges of this inner divine creativity is manifest throughout the cosmos: "On every plane—in the world of the Merkabah and the angels, which is below the Sefiroth, in the various heavens, and in the world of the four elements—creation mirrors the inner movement of the divine life."[124] The laws of nature are inseparable from the laws of the archetypal world and the Divine Wisdom and Will governing all Creation.

Not all dimensions of the Jewish religion have shared in the depth of the wisdom unveiled by the Cabalistic and Hassidic sages, and most, like the majority of Christians and Muslims, have remained satisfied with simply accepting the order of nature as being based upon the Will of God, the Creator, and therefore sharing in the moral character of the laws that also govern human society. The unity that binds the order of nature and human order and religious and cosmic laws together remained over the ages part and parcel of the traditional Jewish worldview, even if not all believing Jews were able to share in that vision of nature being immersed in Divine Life as expounded by the sages and seers of the Cabala and Hassidism through the centuries.

Christianity

When we turn to Christianity, which being the main religion of the West is also inextricably related to most Western schools of thought concerning nature over the centuries, it is difficult to select the appropriate sources to bring out the Christian view of the order of nature. There are the long Catholic and Orthodox traditions as well as the smaller Eastern churches. And then there is Protestantism, which, despite what some have called its acosmic theology, is of great significance if only because of its role even if it be indirect in many of the philosophies of nature that have developed since the sixteenth century.[125] Furthermore, we shall deal in the next chapter with some of the most important Christian philosophers of nature including St. Thomas, whom we shall therefore not discuss here. In this survey, we will limit ourselves to a few comments upon the Gospels and the early figures and then turn to two of the most important and influential personages of Catholic and Orthodox Christianity, St. Augustine and St. Maximus the Confessor, respectively, while remembering constantly the view of God as the creator and sustainer of the order of the cosmos as a contingent domain of reality that these and other voices of Christianity share with Judaism and Islam.

Already the opening verses of the Gospel of John, "In the beginning was the Word" (1:1), in a sense defines the deepest Christian understanding of the order of nature. It must be remembered that the Word here is the translation of *logos*, which in Greek also means "harmony." One could therefore say that at the beginning was the Logos, which was also the eternal harmony, and that it is as a result of this harmony, which accompanies the very meaning of Logos, that order and harmony dominate over the world. The Christian view of the incarnation of the Logos implies also the incarnation of harmony within all things, for "It was by the Word [Logos—Harmony] that all things were made." This view was followed by many Christian contemplatives and mystical theologians over the ages. But even for those who did not associate the idea of the *logos* with harmony, it was in the Logos or Christ that the order and harmony of creation was to be ultimately sought as the very concept of Christ as *axis-mundi* indicates.

The early Christians still believed in demons occupying the Earth, but these demons were conquered by Christ and were no longer intermediaries between God and man.[126] The early Christians also believed that the *pneuma*, which is "the fragrance of God," fills the cosmos, for as the Bible states "the spirit of the Lord hath filled the whole world" (Wisdom 7:22–23). This spirit is "the ordering and formative power" of all things or, as St. Augustine states, "As the creative will of a sculptor hovers over a piece of wood, or as the spiritual soul spreads through all the limbs of the body; thus it is with the Holy Ghost; it hovers over all things with a creative and formative power."[127] The same view is held by many of the early fathers and theologians, and even St. Jerome, who was not given to ecstatic utterances, speaks of the *pneuma* that penetrates the world as well as the soul.[128]

The meaning of the order of nature was pursued in greater detail by St. Augustine (354–430), who was deeply attracted to the significance of the world of nature and stated, despite his belief in the effect of the Fall of Man upon the natural world, "The whole of the world in its infinite variety is a divine creation."[129] St. Augustine believed that "Nature [*natura*] means nothing else than that which anything is conceived of as being in its own kind: and that every nature, as far as it is nature, is good."[130] This good Augustine identifies with measure, form, and order present in all things but more in some things than in others. But because only God is good, perfect goodness is only to be found in God, nature participating in the good, which means also order to the extent that it exists. Needless to say, Augustine rejected Aristotelian naturalism and saw the end of the world as being beyond the world and the order in nature as issuing from beyond nature.[131]

Especially sensitive to the challenge of Manichaean doctrines, Augustine insisted upon *creatio ex nihilo* and rejected the idea of Creation in God. God created the world because He is the Good, and it is in the nature of the Good to give and generate beyond itself.[132] Moreover, "God produced the world according to number" (Isaias 40:26) and "Thou hast ordered all things in measure and number and weight" (Wisdom 11:21), which points to the order bestowed by God upon His Creation according to His infinite knowledge, which can encompass infinite numbers and is beyond the ken of human understanding.[133] For Augustine, "In the beginning (*in principio*) God made the heaven and the earth" means not in time but in the Logos and instantly including the heavens, the angels, and earth and material formlessness correponding to the "boundless waters."

As for how this formlessness was transformed into the formal and ordered world of nature, according to St. Augustine this came from the "Ideas" of God in the Platonic sense, which were imposed upon formlessness, Ideas he usually renders as *ratio*. For St. Augustine the Ideas are "principle forms or stable and unchangeable essences of things. They are themselves not formed, and they are eternal and always in the same state because they are contained in God's intelligence. They neither come into being nor do they pass away, but everything that can or does come into being and passes away is formed in accordance with them."[134]

Furthermore, St. Augustine distinguishes between creatures that are fixed in their form from the act of Creation and those created only as a germ that develops later, as in the case of plants, animals, and Adam's body. These germs he calls *rationes causalis* or *rationes seminales* with which God's Creation is pregnant. These "seminal reasons" possess the principle of activity, are governed by numbers, and do not imply later additions to Creation, for from the beginning Creation was complete "wherein all things were made together (*ubi facta sunt omnia simul*).[135] God preserves the order of Creation and commands the growth of the germs or seeds that He created in order to enable them to reach the full stage of development envisaged by His Wisdom. Therefore, while there is growth in Creation, it is according to order, and the *rationes seminales* are agents of stability rather than haphazard change. All creatures grow and function according to God's creative power. And yet, as mentioned above, nature has participated in Adam's Fall, for "after such disorders, what remains of the nature fashioned by God? Evil was only the evil of sin in Adam, but in its propagation down to our own day it became the evil of nature. A vitiated and vicious nature took the place of a good nature thenceforth."[136]

This thesis of the most influential of the early Catholic theologians was to have a profound effect upon certain elements of Christian thought in the West, both Catholic and Protestant, as far as the attitude toward nature was concerned. Long after the doctrine of the *rationes seminales* was forgotten—or worse yet came to be interpreted in evolutionary terms—the idea of nature as darkened by the effect of the Fall of Man draw a heavy curtain between the supernatural and the natural and veiled the spiritual significance of the order of nature and the Divine Origin of this order from many eyes, although dissenting Christian voices over the centuries asserted more strongly the spiritual character of nature and the order that pervades over her multifarious domains.

Orthodox theology of the early centuries followed a somewhat different path, as can be seen in the works of one of its greatest representatives, St. Maximus the Confessor, who died a martyr's death on the coast of the Black Sea in 662. For St. Maximus, and following Dionysius, categories of order (*taxis*) in nature are established by God and denote God's active care for his Creation.[137] The principles of Creation in its differentiated forms exist already in God. They are the *lógoi*, which are also Divine Wills or Intentions. The *lógoi* of various beings are held together in the Logos, which expresses the unifying factor in Creation whose purpose is a living relationship with God. Moreover, St. Maximus emphasizes that Creation is not only the act of the Father but of all the Trinity.

Already in the second century, Origen had developed the idea of the *lógoi* being present as ideas in Christ as wisdom, adopting the Greek and more specifically Stoic idea of *logos spermatikós* to Christian cosmology as St. Augustine was to do in a different fashion after him. St. Maximus also adopted this idea but placed much greater emphasis upon the *lógoi* being held together in the Logos. For him the *logoi* define not only the essence but also the coming into existence of things.[138] On the one hand the *lógoi* are fixed, preexisting in God. On the other hand there is motion and freedom to change in the created world. God has allowed creatures to be or not to be in harmony with their *logos*. Only when they are in harmony, however, do they fulfill God's purpose.

Because all *lógoi* exist in the Logos and have their unity in Him, and the Logos is incarnated in the *lógoi*, the Christian can contemplate the Logos in the *lógoi*. "The *logoi* of intelligible beings may be understood as the blood of the Logos, and the *logoi* of sensible things as the flesh of the Logos, through which those who are worthy are allowed to have spiritual communion with God."[139] The Logos is not only incarnated in the flesh in Christ but also in the *lógoi* of all things as well as in the letters of the Scripture. The Logos holds together Creation, revelation, and salvation; and as a result of the order established in nature through the incarnation of the Logos in the *lógoi*, natural law, written law, and the law of grace are interconnected. All of Creation possesses a *télos*, which is reflected in its order and harmony, and "the ultimate end of the whole of creation must be that for which all things are, and which itself is caused by nothing, that which is its own end, i.e., God."[140]

Through this incarnationist view of nature according to which the Logos is incarnated in the very ideas or forms of nature, called by St. Maximus the *lógoi,* a Christian view of the order and harmony of nature is presented, which is of great metaphysical depth and which could not be as easily desacralized as the mainstream Catholic views of nature at the end of the Middle Ages. Western Christianity was, however, far from being bereft of similar visions and expositions of the Divine Roots of nature, as we see in the remarkable hymn of the twelfth-century German mystic Hildegard of Bingen that was dedicated to the *spiritus creator:*

> *I am the supreme fiery force*
> *That kindles every spark of life;*
> *What I have breathed on will never die,*
> *I order the cycle of things in being:*
> *Hovering round in sublime flight,*
> *Wisdom lends it rhythmic beauty.*
>
> *I am divine fiery life*
> *Blazing over the full-repined grain;*
> *I gleam in the reflection of the waters,*
> *I burn in the sun and moon and stars,*
> *In the breeze I have secret life*
> *Animating all things and lending them cohesion.*
>
> *I am life in all its abundance,*
> *For I was not released from the rock of the ages*
> *Nor did I bud from a branch*
> *Nor spring from man's begetting:*
> *In me is the root of life.*
> *Spirit is the root which buds in the word*
> *And God is the intelligible spirit.*[141]

It was this vision of the order of nature, as both the natural order and the origin of order in nature, that was to be challenged in the later history of Western thought, bringing about that radical transformation of the understanding of the meaning of the order of nature whose consequences are visible everywhere in the present-day environmental crisis. And yet for centuries Christians have repeated in the Mass *Sanctus, sanctus, sanctus, Domine Deus Sabaoth. Pleni sunt coeli et terra gloria eius* (Holy, holy, holy, Lord God of hosts, heaven and earth are full of His glory), and continue to do so today although usually not in Latin, using the text taken from the prophet Isaiah's vision of the seraphim encircling the Divine Throne. Christians continue to attest to the wedding of Heaven and Earth in bearing witness to God's Glory, despite the eclipse of this perspective in much of Western civilization and the separation in the secularist culture, which grew in opposition to Christianity, of the order of nature from the Divine and the sacred.[142]

Islam

Our account of the meaning of the order of nature in various religions concludes with Islam, the last of the Abrahamic monotheisms, which often appears as an embarrassing postscript when the history of religion is treated in a historical manner leading up to Christianity. And yet the Islamic view of the order of nature is of special interest in the context of this present study, which aims to understand how and why the religious view of the order of nature was transformed in the modern world, with the catastrophic consequences it bears for man's relation with the natural environment. The reason is that Islam also knew the Greco-Alexandrian antiquity and developed a vast scientific tradition based to a large extent upon that of the ancient world, a science of nature that itself played a crucial role in the history of Western science.

However, Islam, heir like Judaism and Christianity to the spiritual universe of Abraham, did not reject its religious understanding of the order of nature while cultivating the natural sciences.[143] And it has not done so to a large extent even today despite the spread of modernism into the Islamic world during the past century and more recent views of all kinds of "reformists" and so-called fundamentalists equating the Islamic view of nature with that of modern science.[144] In any case our concern here is with traditional Islam, which has been the Islamic norm for fourteen centuries and still determines the worldview of the great majority of Muslims.

Of course, Islam, like Judaism, Christianity, Hinduism, and many other religions, has developed numerous schools of thought, theological, philosophical, scientific, and mystical, dealing with the order of nature. These have ranged from the views of the Peripatetic and Ismāʿīlī philosophers of the early centuries such as Ibn Sīnā and Nāṣir-i Khusraw, to those of the later philosophers such as Suhrawardī and Mullā Ṣadrā, to the theologians such as al-Ghazzālī and Khwājah Naṣīr al-Dīn al-Ṭūsī, to numerous scientists such as al-Bīrūnī, to the Sufis such as Ibn ʿArabī, all of whom have written extensively on this question.[145] Furthermore, there have been those such as al-Ashʿarī who have denied all reality to the order of nature, which they have equated plainly and simply with the effect of the Divine Will. Here, we shall concern ourselves mostly with the views contained in the Quran and *Ḥadīth* while making reference, when necessary, to the development of doctrines contained in these twin sources of all things Islamic in the works of later traditional authorities.

The order of nature is seen in the Islamic perspective to derive according to Divine Wisdom from the prototype of all existence in the Divine Order, the prototype which is identified according to the language of Quranic cosmology with the Pen (*al-Qalam*) and the Guarded Tablet (*al-Lawḥ al-maḥfūẓ*).[146] God wrote by means of the Pen, which symbolizes the active principle of Creation, the realities of all things,[147] upon the Guarded Tablet, which remains eternally with Him, while through the cosmogenic act, the realities written upon the Tablet were made to descend to lower levels of existence and finally to the world of nature. The order of nature, therefore, reflects and issues from the order that exists in the Divine Realm. This thesis is confirmed by the insistence of the Quran, reaffirming the Book of Wisdom, that everything is created according to measure, or to quote the Quranic verse, "Everything with Him has its measure (*miqdār*)" (13:8). It is important to note that the root of the Arabic word for "measure," namely *miqdār*, is related to *qudrah* or power. God as the All-Powerful (al-Qādir) has determined the "measure" of all of Creation. Furthermore, the Noble Quran, which is esoterically the archetype of Creation and whose structure parallels that of the created order was first revealed during the *laylat al-qadr* or "Night of Power." The very Power that created the world of nature and revealed the Quran is therefore the origin of the order and harmony perceived throughout Creation, the order or measure (*miqdār*) of things deriving from His Power or *qudrah*, which is never whimsical, ad hoc, and disorderly but is inalienably related to the very source of order, for in the world of the Divine Names and Qualities ultimately all the Names are one. *Qudrah* or Divine Power is none other than *Ḥikmah* or Divine Wisdom, or to express it somewhat differently—God as the Powerful (al-Qādir) is also God the Wise (al-Ḥakīm). The very act of the creation of nature implies the imposition of an order inseparable from the Creative Power that has created the universe.[148]

The Quran states, "In Whose Hand is the dominion (*malakūt*) of all things" (23:88). This verse not only implies the governance of all things by God but also the existence of the metaphysical root of all things in God's "Hand." The term *malakūt* means at once the spiritual state of existence transcending the physical world (*al-mulk*) and also the spiritual principle of beings constituting the world of nature.[149] This Quranic verse therefore implies that nature is not an independent domain of reality with its own independent order, but that its principle resides in another realm of reality, which is Divine. God is at once the ruler of the world of nature over which He has dominion and holds in "His Hands" the principles of the world of nature from which derive that order and harmony that are observable throughout Creation and to which the Quran points constantly as outward proofs of God, His Wisdom and His Power.

Later Islamic metaphysics elaborated the Quranic teachings concerning God's Names and Qualities to make more evident the link between the natural and Divine Orders and esoterically the very extension of the Divine Order into what constitutes outwardly the order of nature. All cosmic reality consists of reflections of combinations of the theophanies (*tajalliyyāt*) of various Divine Names and Qualities that are the roots (*aṣl*) or support (*mustanad*) of all the realities or phenomena of this world, which exist and function as a result of being supported (*istinād*) by the Divine Names. According to Ibn 'Arabī, "There is no property in the cosmos without a divine support and a lordly attribute."[150] The Divine Names are the principles of the immutable archetypes (*al-aʿyān al-thābitah*), which are the "Ideas" of all cosmic manifestation contained in the Divine Intellect.[151] God "breathes" upon these archetypes, and thus the cosmos comes into being. The very substance of the cosmos is the "Breath of the Compassionate" (*nafas al-Raḥmān*) while cosmic forms and all that constitutes the order of nature emanate from the archetypal realities and ultimately the Divine Essence Itself.[152]

The doctrine of the "Breath of the Compassionate" is also related to the Sufi doctrine of the dilation of the cosmos according to what is called "the renewal of creation at each instant (*tajdīd al-khalq bi'l-anfās*).[153] At every moment the universe is absorbed in the Divine Center and manifested anew in a rhythm of contraction (*qabḍ*) and expansion (*basṭ*), which the rhythm of human breathing resembles. This doctrine, like that of the transcendent unity of being (*waḥdat al-wujūd*—which considers only the Divine Principle to be Real and negates reality from everything else from the point of view of the Divine Truth (*al-Ḥaqq*)—only emphasizes the utter reliance of all things upon the Divine Principle. It removes from the world of nature any illusion of independence and permanence and thereby relates by implication the order of nature in the deepest sense to the Divine Order. The order of nature reflects and has its roots in the Divine Order, and the order *in* nature is a reflection of the order of the archetypes and ultimately the possibilities within the Divine Itself.

On a more profound level, one can say that the order of nature is nothing but the Divine Reality manifesting itself on the plane of phenomenal existence. It is to this essential reality that the Quran refers when it asserts, "Withersoever ye turn, there is the Face of God" (II:115), an utterance to which the numerous Sufi treatises on *waḥdat al-wujūd* are so many commentaries.

The traditional Islamic cosmos is filled with angels and *jinn,* those psychic beings mentioned explicitly in the Quran, as well as the stars and mountains, the plants and animals, and, finally, human beings. The order of this vast complex of creatures is of course based on the Divine Will but is maintained and carried out by the vast army of angelic beings. Islamic cosmology, like other traditional cosmologies, is inseparable from angelology on both the intellectual level and in the everyday life of the believers. The presence of these hosts of nonmaterial beings carrying out their functions according to the duties assigned to them only emphasizes in the traditional Islamic cosmos the reliance of the order that one observes in nature upon the spiritual world and ultimately upon the Supreme Divine Principle.

Likewise, in Islam, as in other religions already mentioned, the laws governing nature are not separable from those governing human society. The term *al-Sharī'ah* or Divine Law, which governs Islamic society, is also applied to other creatures. The birds and the flowers also have their own *sharā'i'* (pl. of *sharī'ah*), which, because of their perfect obedience and submission to God, they follow without deviation. It is their obedience to the Divine Will that constitutes for us the laws of nature that certain Islamic thinkers such as the Ash'arites have in fact denied by relying solely upon the Divine Will in a voluntarism that removes the "nature" of things from them. The Quran and most later schools of Islamic thought speak distinctly of an order to be observed and also contemplated in nature. In fact, the Quranic term *sunnat Allāh,* which is described as being unchanging,[154] is interpreted by many traditional commentators to apply to the cosmos as well as to the world of men. It might be said that in a sense while the *sunnah* or wonts of the Prophet are for human beings, the *sunnah* of Allah is for all creatures. In any case, there is no complete dichotomy between laws governing human society and possessing a moral character and those governing nature. Both issue from the Divine Reality whose Wisdom and Power are reflected in the order of nature and also in the human order as long as humans abide by the Divine Law that, in contrast to nature, they have the freedom to obey or disobey.

Creation in God

On the level of theological and exoteric formulations, the three Abrahamic religions assert the fundamental truth of *creatio ex nihilo* as a means of negating all reality independent of God; additionally, the esotericism of these faiths speak not only of creation *by* God but also *in* God. *Nihilo* is thus identified not with the ordinary sense of nothingness but as that principial archetypal reality before it was existentiated through the *fiat lux* or the Quranic Be! (*kun*). The most profound expressions of this esoteric truth are to be found in the Cabala, in the writings of such Christian metaphysicians as Johannes Scotus Erigena, to whom we shall turn in the next chapter, and in the works of numerous Sufis such as Ibn 'Arabī.[155] What they express in essence is that the root of cosmic reality must exist already in the Divine Reality without which the world could not have come into being.

From this esoteric point of view, which in fact joins certain doctrines of non-Abrahamic origin, the universe is generated by the Divine Principle, without this implying pantheism, which means equating God with the universe, or denying divine Transcendence. The physical cosmos does not of course exist *qua* physical cosmos in the Divine Reality, but it has its ontological principle in that Reality and is linked through the hierarchy of cosmic manifestation to the Divine Principle. Far from being opposed to each other, creationism and the idea of manifestation or emanationism, if correctly understood, represent the same metaphysical truth. While rejecting the kind of emanationism that would deny Divine Transcendence, monotheistic esoterisms emphasize the basic truth that, although God transcends all limitation, the cosmos is, symbolically speaking, like "His garment," which at once veils and reveals His Reality. The order of nature is not only created by God through His Will, but derives from the Divine Substance. The root of the order of nature is to be sought in the Divine Order, and the order of nature *is* none other than the Divine Order manifested upon the particular level of cosmic existence that we identify as nature.

CONCLUDING REMARKS

In this rapid journey through different religious climates in quest of the meaning of the order of nature, it has been necessary to leave aside many questions of great theological and metaphysical significance, questions that are worthy of the most acute attention but that need to be dealt with separately to do them justice and that at the same time are not central to the main concern of this book. There is, for example, the question of the different levels of the meaning of order, understood not only empirically and mathematically where one can distinguish between order on the subatomic level as well as within snow crystals and the order of visible nature as a whole, but also from the religious point of view where one must make a distinction between exoteric and esoteric order. Then there is the whole question of causality, which is so closely related to the question of the origin and meaning of order. Here the whole issue of vertical and horizontal causality, as well as the denial of horizontal causality even in certain religious climates, comes into play and leads to vast philosophical discussions that have filled many tomes in both Eastern and Western religions and even in antireligious philosophies.

In certain religious climates such as those of Abrahamic monotheisms there arises also the question of the contingent nature of the world in contrast to God, who is the necessary Being, and also determinism versus free will in relation to the order of nature and our rapport with it. In such climates there have been interpretations ranging all the way from the denial of both human free will and the order of nature, possessing its own specific laws in favor of complete determinism and the substitution of the Will of God for the laws of the natural order, to the assertion of both human free will and the order of nature as an order of reality created by God but possessing its own laws that determine its order.

Then there are the interpretations of scholars of religion and philosophy in the modern West according to which the religious understanding of the order of nature has evolved, in the sense of progressed, from preanimism to animism to the rational understanding of natural phenomena. To such categories of classification are added interpretations of the meaning of nature as being pantheistic, panpsychic, totemic, and so forth among the followers of older religions, all of which have been transcended through the gradual evolution of man's understanding of the order of nature into the positivism that so dominates the modern worldview. Needless to say, we reject any such evolutionary interpretation categorically, but would need to deal with each view separately in order to present reasons for its rejection if such an undertaking were not to take us too far away from the purpose of this chapter, which is to bring out some of the quintessential teachings of the religions under consideration concerning the meaning of the order of nature.[156]

Of much greater significance for the relationship between man and the natural environment and the role of religion in this relation in the context of the current global environmental crisis is the accord concerning several major doctrines among religions of very distinct structures and belonging to different climes and times. The first is that the order of nature is related to an order "beyond" itself, to what we might call "spiritual principles." Traditional religions agree that the reality of nature has a significance beyond its appearance, that there is a "sacred" quality within nature, however we understand the term "sacred" and its formal manifestations in different religious worlds. Second, the order of nature has a purpose, a meaning, and this meaning has spiritual and moral significance for human beings. Third, the human and natural orders are intertwined in a bi-unity in such a way that their destinies are interrelated not only here and now but even in that ultimate state that is eschatological.[157] Fourth, the laws of man and the laws of nature are not totally distinct but are again closely interrelated and in some traditions the same, as seen in such key concepts as *Tao, rta, dharma, Dyke, al-Shari'ah*, and *sunnah*.

Finally, Earth is man's teacher and man can learn from the order of nature not only quantitatively but also morally, intellectually, and spiritually. The order of nature speaks to human beings' deepest needs and their final end, even if this end transcends the outward forms of nature, and the message of different religions concerning that order only enriches the message that is to be heard and results in the recollection of forgotten truths by a particular human collectivity. Even if destined for the invisible world of the Spirit, human beings need to learn from the order of nature, or as certain Sufis have said, the cosmos itself can assist man to transcend the cosmos. [158]

This universal heritage of the religious view of the order of nature, which is in a sense an aspect of what we might call a *cosmologia perennis*, [159] was to be challenged by modern Western philosophy and science and replaced by another view of nature divorced both from man's final end and the Divine Principle, a view that, having undergone its incubation and growth in the West, has now spread over much of the globe and has resulted in a crisis of unprecedented proportions for both human life and the natural environment. It is for us to examine in future chapters the process by which this transformation took place, then to delve into its consequences and to search for means of curing the ailment it has caused, an ailment that becomes ever more difficult to treat with the passage of each day. Meanwhile, the religious understanding of the order of nature continues to possess its validity for those with eyes to see and ears to hear despite what appearances may dictate to the contrary, for it corresponds to a truth that is in the very nature of things.

جامد، افسرده بود ای اوستاد   عالم افسرده است و نام او جماد

تا ببینی جنبش جسم جهان   باش تا خورشید حشر آید عیان

خاکها را جملگی شاید شناخت   پاره خاك تو را چون مرد ساخت

خامش اینجا، و آن طرف گوینده اند   مرده زین سوی اند و آن سوزانده اند

با شما نا محرمان ما خامشیم   ما سمیعیم و بصیریم و خوشیم

The world is frozen; its name is jamād (*inanimate*): jāmid *means "frozen," O master.*

Wait till the rising sun of Resurrection that thou mayest see the movement of the world's body.

Since God hath made Man from dust, it behooves thee to recognize the real nature of every particle of the universe,

That while from this aspect they are dead, from that aspect they are living: silent
    here, but speaking Yonder. . . .
They all cry, "We are hearing and seeing and responsive, though to you, the
    uninitiated, we are mute."[160]

(Rūmī)

NOTES

1. See James Gleick, *Chaos: Making a New Science* (New York: Viking Press, 1987).

2. See the works of Ilya Perogine, especially his *Order Out of Chaos: Man's New Dialogue with Nature* (with Isabelle Stengers) (New York: Bantam, 1984), where he speaks of spontaneous creativity in nature, the reversal of the flow from order to chaos according to the law of entropy, and the "re-enchantment of nature." We shall deal with his views in Chapter 4.

3. Obviously it is not possible to deal with all religions. Our principle of selection has been based on the goal of this work, which is the study of the importance of the religious view of the order of nature in the light of the present-day environmental crisis, which is the result of the destruction of so much of nature by modern man. We have therefore chosen the major living religions such as the Abrahamic faiths, Hinduism, Buddhism, Taoism, and Confucianism, and some of the primal and Shamanistic religions along with certain religions such as the Egyptian and Greek, which are no longer living, and Zoroastrianism, which still possesses a small following. All of these have played an important historical role in the formulation of attitudes toward nature in later schools of thought.

4. The concept of order with its wide range of meanings from law to intelligibility to pattern along with those mentioned above is, moreover, used in different senses in various fields as far apart as mathematics and ethics, taxonomy and music, physics and politics. Its relation to its opposite term "chaos" has also been envisaged in terms as different as those of Genesis and modern thermodynamics. In the present work, in the context of the meanings of order mentioned above, our understanding of order will be the traditional one that relates it to principle, intelligibility, law, purpose, and also inevitably hierarchy. The specific meaning of order in different religions as well as in philosophical and scientific schools of thought will become clearer in the individual context in which this basic concept is discussed.

Thomas Aquinas was to give one of the best and earliest philosophical definitions of order when he said,

The terms "before" and "after" are attributed according to the relation of some principle. Now order includes some mode of "before" and "after." Hence, wherever there is a principle, it is necessary that there be also an order of some kind. [*Summa Theologica*, 2a2ae, 26.1] quoted in P. Kuntz, "Order" in the *New Catholic Encyclopedia* (London and New York: McGraw-Hill, Vol. 10, 1967), pp. 720ff.

For a general discussion of the meaning of order especially as understood by various modern scholars and philosophies see Paul Kuntz (ed.), *The Concept of Order* (Seattle and London: University of Washington Press, 1968); and Hermann Krings, *Ordo:*

Philosophische-historische Grundlegung einer abendländischen Idee (Halle: M. Niemeyer, 1941).

5. One detects *mutatis mutandis* a similar situation in the Hindu *darśanas* and later development of Hinduism or in Buddhism of the Theravada, Vajrāyana, and Mahāyana schools.

6. See, for example, Mircea Eliade, *Shamanism, Archaic Techniques of Ecstasy*, trans. W. R. Trask (New York: Pantheon Books, 1964); Roger N. Walsh, *The Spirit of Shamanism* (Los Angeles: Jeremy P. Tarcher, 1990); Douglas Sharon, *Wizard of the Four Winds: A Shaman's Story* (London: Collier Macmillan Publishers, 1978); and Michael Ripinsky Naxon, *The Nature of Shamanism* (Albany: State University of New York Press, 1993), p. 105, "The Psychotropic Universe: Cosmology of the Spirit World." But besides these and many other recent scholarly works, there is also the "practical" interest in America among many "New Age" seekers and others in Shamanic practices as seen in the popularity of the works of Carlos Castaneda and "weekend Shamanic workshops" on the American West Coast against which authentic Native Americans continue to protest.

7. See Eliade, *Shamanism*, p. 260, and Walsh, *Spirit of Shamanism*, p. 114.

8. The symbol of the cosmos as a sacred mountain is universal and is even to be seen in sacred architecture ranging from ziggurats in Babylonia to Buddhist temples. Perhaps the greatest of all Buddhist temples, Borobodur, was in fact constructed as a cosmic mountain, showing the correspondence between the order of nature and sacred architecture. See Paul Mus, *Barabuḍur. Esquisse d'une histoire du Bouddhisme fondée sur la critique archéologique des textes*, Vol. 1 (Hanoi: Imprimerie d'Extrême-Orient, 1935), p. 356.

On the relation between order in the cosmos and order in sacred architecture mostly in the context of the Indian traditions, see Adrian Snodgrass, *Architecture, Time and Eternity*, 2 vols. (New Delhi: Aditya Prakashan, Śata-Piḳata Series, Vol. 356, 1990).

9. Eliade, *Shamanism*, p. 272.

10. Walsh, *Spirit of Shamanism*, pp. 114–117.

11. Peter T. Furst, "The Roots and Continuities of Shamanism," *Arts-Canada* (December 1973/January 1974), p. 40, quoted in D. Sharon, *Wizard of the Four Winds*, pp. 184–187.

12. On Shintoism and its role in Japanese religion see Joseph Kitagawa, *Religion in Japanese History* (New York and London: Columbia University Press, 1966); Hirai Naofusa, "Shintō," in the *Encyclopedia of Religion*, p. 282; and Tsunetsugu Muraoka, *Studies in Shintō Thought*, trans. Delmer M. Brown and James T. Araki (Tokyo: Japanese National Commission for UNESCO, 1964), especially Chapter 1, "Characteristic Features of Japanese Shinto: Japan's Uniqueness in Oriental Thought," pp. 1–50. See also Carmen Blacker, *The Catalpa Bow: A Study of Shamanistic Practices in Japan* (London: Allen & Unwin, 1975).

13. "Shrine worship is closely associated with a keen sense of the beautiful, a mystic sense of nature which plays an important part in leading the mind of man from the mundane to the higher and deeper world of the divine." Cited in Sokyo Ono, *Shinto: The Kami Way* (Rutland, Vt., and Tokyo: Charles Tuttle, 1962), p. 97.

14. See Joseph E. Brown, *Animals of the Soul* (Rockport, Mass.: Element Books, 1992), in which the author outlines the relation between the various animals and the facets and powers of the human soul according to the Lakota. See especially pages 6–7 where the Lakota worldview based upon the unity underlying the diversity of the forms of nature and of man is outlined.

15. See John A. Grim, *The Shaman: Patterns of Siberian and Ojibway Healing* (Norman: University of Oklahoma Press, 1983), especially Chapter 4, pp. 74–92, on cosmology.

16. Ibid., pp. 82–83.

17. The conversation between the Lakota priest Finger and J. R. Walker quoted in *The Sun Dance . . . of the Teton Lakota* cited in Joseph E. Brown (ed.), *The Sacred Pipe: Black Elk's Account of the Seven Rites of the Oglala Sioux* (Norman: University of Oklahoma Press, 1953), p. 65.

18. See Frithjof Schuon, *The Feathered Sun: Plains Indians in Art and Philosophy* (Bloomington, Ind.: World Wisdom Books, 1990), pp. 30–31. As Schuon writes, "The Indians possess a 'polysynthesism' which is the consciousness of the profound homogeneity of the created order and the sense of universal solidarity which results therefrom." Ibid., p. 20. See the whole of Chapter 2 of Schuon's work, "A Metaphysics of Virgin Nature," for a masterly treatment of the Plains Indians' view of the order of nature.

19. Ibid., pp. 30–31.

20. Ibid., pp. 31ff.

21. Ibid., pp. 18–19.

22. Many African religions refer explicitly to the Almighty or Supreme God in their theologies, whereas others refer to the Supreme Being only indirectly. A case of the former is *Olódùmarè,* or Almighty God, in the Yoruba religion. See Wande Abimbola, "Yoruba Traditional Religion," in Yusuf Ibish and Peter L. Wilson (eds.), *Traditional Modes of Contemplation and Action* (Tehran: Imperial Iranian Academy of Philosophy, 1977), p. 186.

23. See Evan M. Zvesse, *Ritual Cosmos: The Sanctification of Life in African Religions* (Columbus: Ohio University Press, 1979), especially Chapter 7, "Initiation and the Meaning of Knowledge." On the Bambara see also the well-known studies of Marcel Griaule such as his *Conversations with Ogotemmêli* (New York and London: Oxford University Press, 1965); also Marcel Griaule and Germaine Dieterlen, *Le Renard pâle, Travaux et Mémoires,* 72 (Paris: Institut d'Ethnologie, 1965).

24. See Zvesse, *Ritual Cosmos,* p. 153.

25. Ibid., p. 153.

26. Germaine Dieterlen, *Essai sur la religion Bambara* (Paris: Presses Universitaires de France, 1951), p. 5. Quoted by Zvesse, *Ritual Cosmos,* p. 154.

27. See L. V. Thomas, "Brève esquisse sur la pensée cosmologique du Dida," in Meyer Fortes and Germaine Dieterlen, *African Systems of Thought* (New York and London: Oxford University Press, 1965), pp. 366–382.

28. Ibid., p. 370.

29. R. A. Schwaller de Lubicz, *Sacred Science: The King of Pharaonic Theocracy,* trans. André and Goldian Vanden Broeck (New York: Inner Traditions International, 1982), p. 169. The works of this author are particularly pertinent in revealing the inner meaning of Egyptian myths and symbols without falling into either a crass naturalism or a vague occultism so characteristic of so many studies in this field. See especially de Lubicz's *Le Temple de l'Homme,* 3 vols. (Paris: Caractères, 1957). The interpretations of Schwaller de Lubicz differ markedly from those of official well-known Egyptologists who, basing themselves on naturalistic and evolutionary foundations, have refused to delve into the inner meaning of the material with which they have dealt so masterfully on the external plane. For an example of the latter see James Henry Breast (ed.), *Development of Religion and Thought in Ancient Egypt* (New York and Evanston, Ill.: Harper & Row, 1959), pp. 3ff.

30. See Jean Hani, *Le Religion égyptienne dans la pensée de Plutarque* (Paris: Societé d'Edition "Les Belles Lettres," 1976).

31. See Henri Frankfurt, *Ancient Egyptian Religion* (New York: Harper & Row, 1948), p. 4; see also Frankfurt's, *The Intellectual Adventure of Ancient Man* (Chicago: University of Chicago Press, 1946).

32. See Byron E. Shafer (ed.), *Religion in Ancient Egypt: Gods, Myths and Personal Practice* (London and Ithaca, N.Y.: Cornell University Press, 1991), pp. 95ff. How similar is this to the Christian and Islamic doctrine of the creation of the world by the Divine Word!

33. On the separation of Heaven and Earth, see R. T. Rundle Clark, *Myth and Symbol in Ancient Egypt* (New York: Grove Press, 1960), p. 250.

34. Shafer, *Religion in Ancient Egypt*, pp. 121–122.

35. Cosmic deities such as "heaven, earth, sun and moon, air and water (Nile) did have the rank of real gods with a personal existence." Siegfried Morenz, *Egyptian Religion*, trans. Ann E. Keep (Ithaca, N.Y.: Cornell University Press, 1973), p. 30.

36. See Earnest A. Wallis Budge, *The Gods of the Egyptians or Studies in Egyptian Mythology*, Vol. 1 (New York: Dover, 1969), p. 67.

37. R. A. Schwaller de Lubicz, *The Temple in Man: Sacred Architecture and the Perfect Man*, trans. Robert and Deborah Lawlor (New York: Inner Traditions International, 1977), p. 31.

38. R. A. Schwaller de Lubicz, *Symbol and the Symbolic: Ancient Egypt, Science and the Evolution of Consciousness*, trans. Robert and Deborah Lawlor (Rochester, Vt.: Inner Traditions International, 1978), p. 85.

39. We have already dealt with Shamanism and will turn to Buddhism and Islam shortly. In dealing here with the Far Eastern traditions, we shall limit ourselves to Taoism and Confucianism and their common ground in the original Chinese tradition.

40. See John Blofeld (ed. and trans.), *I Ching: The Book of Change* (New York: E. P. Dutton, 1968).

41. Ibid., p. 39.

42. These qualities must not be taken in a negative or pejorative sense but are as necessary in the order of things as their opposites.

43. See Fung Yu-lan, *A History of Chinese Philosophy*, Vol. 1, trans. Derk Bodde (Princeton, N.J.: Princeton University Press, 1973), p. 378.

44. "The objects symbolized by the eight trigrams are thus made the basic constituents of the universe." Ibid., p. 382. For example, the *ch'ien* trigram (☰) symbolized Heaven, the *k'un* trigram (☷) Earth, etc.

45. Ibid., Vol. 2, p. 11. Beginning on page 11 of Fung Yu-lan's book, one finds an elaborate account of these cosmological, calendrical, astrological, and musical correspondences in the *Yin-Yang* School attesting fully to the centrality of the *Yin-Yang* doctrine in elaborating the order of nature in the Chinese tradition while this school sought to integrate the tradition of the Five Elements and the eight trigrams. It needs to be pointed out also that in this and in many other Chinese schools of thought the order of nature has been understood in both time and space so that the understanding of the temporal order has been as much of concern as the "spatial" one. The detailed ordering of time in calendrical elaborations in both China and ancient Egypt and the doctrine of the cycles in Hinduism are directly related to this question. There is in every tradition a concern for the order of nature as it manifests itself in time as well as in space along with form, energy, and "matter."

46. On the history of Taoism, see Isabelle Robinet, *Histoire du taoisme des origines au XIme siècle* (Paris: Les Editions du Cerf, 1991).

Chinese alchemy, associated with Taoism, is itself a vast subject of great significance for the Chinese understanding of nature and her inner forces, but cannot unfortunately be treated here, needing a separate study to do justice to its depth and also its rich history. On Chinese alchemy see Michel Strickmann, "On the Alchemy of T'ao Hung-ching," in Holmes Welch and Anna Seidel (eds.), *Facets of Taoism: Essays in Chinese Religion* (London and New Haven, Conn.: Yale University Press, 1979), pp. 123–192; Nathan Sivin, *Chinese Alchemy: Preliminary Studies* (Cambridge, Mass.: Harvard University Press, 1968); J. R. Ware, *Alchemy, Medicine and Religion in the China of 320 A.D.* (Cambridge, Mass.: Harvard University Press, 1961); and the still interesting but to some extent superseded study of Arthur Waley, "Notes on Chinese Alchemy," *Bulletin of the School of Oriental Studies* (Vol. 6, no. 14, 1930), pp. 1–24.

In his monumental study *Science and Civilization in China,* Vol. 5 (Cambridge: Cambridge University Press, 1974), Joseph Needham has also dealt extensively with Chinese alchemy but mostly as chemistry and not as a symbolic and cosmological science. See Needham's work (p. xxiv) where he criticizes our views on the traditional sciences such as alchemy and their significance.

47. *Chuang-Tzŭ,* trans. Herbert A Giles (London: B. Quaritch, 1926), XXII.

48. Tao Tê-ching, trans. Chu'u Ta-Kao (London: Unwin Paperbacks, 1982), p. 17.

49. "[Tao is] the Mother of all things, the principal creative cause, the self-existent source, the unconditioned by which all things are conditioned, for although it does not create it is the source of all creation, the animating principle of the universe; it is 'the unchanging principle which supports the shifting multiplicity.'" J. C. Cooper, *Taoism: The Way of the Mystic* (Wellingborough, Northamptonshire: Aquarian Press, 1990), p. 14.

On the Taoist philosophy of nature see also Livia Kohn, *Taoist Mystical Philosophy: The Scripture of Western Ascension* (Albany: State University of New York Press, 1991), p. 83.

50. *Chuang-Tzŭ,* XXI.

51. Wing-tsit Chan, *A Source Book in Chinese Philosophy* (Princeton, N.J.: Princeton University Press, 1963), p. 465. See also Michael C. Katon (trans. and ed.), *To Become a Sage: The Ten Diagrams on Sage Learning by Yi T'oegye* (New York: Columbia University Press, 1988), p. 37; and Tu Wei-Ming, "The Continuity of Being: Chinese Visions of Nature," in his *Confucian Thought: Selfhood as Creative Transformation* (Albany: State University of New York Press, 1985), pp. 35–50, where he speaks of the "continuity of being" between man and nature and *ch'i* as the foundation for an integral cosmology. We shall return to his views in Chapter 6.

52. See Ro Young-chan, *The Korean Neo-Confucianism of Yi Yulgok* (Albany: State University of New York Press, 1989), pp. 17ff.

53. Ibid., p. 22. Not all neo-Confucians, however, emphasized *li* to the extent of implicitly identifying it with *T'ai chi.* Some considered *ch'i* to be more important.

54. "A significant effort to understand *T'ai-chi* in a 'cosmo-ontologic' way was then made by Chu Hsi, who tried to synthesize neo-Confucian cosmology and ontology by explaining Chou Tun-i's cosmology through the Ch'engs' ontological notions of *li* and *ch'i.*" Ibid., p. 24. In the words of Chu Hsi himself,

> Throughout Heaven and Earth there is *Li* and there is *Chhi. Li* is the Tao [organizing] all forms from above, and the not from which all things are produced. *Chhi* is the instrument [composing] all forms from below, and the tools

and raw material with which all things are made." Quoted in Colin A. Ronan, *The Shorter Science and Civilization in China: An Abridgement of Joseph Needham's Original Text,* Vol. 1 (Cambridge and New York: Cambridge University Press, 1978), p. 239.

Also, to quote Chu Hsi again,

Take, for example, the Yin and the Yang and the Five Elements; the reason why they do not make mistakes in their counting, and do not lose the threads of their meaning [i.e., do not fall into immediable disorder], is because of *Li.*" Ibid., p. 241.

Needham prefers to render *Li* as pattern rather than law in the sense of the juridical sense of law, which is closer to the Chinese *Fa.* But if we understand by law principle or order in a cosmic as well as human sense, then *Li* could also be rendered as law despite the major differences in the Chinese and Western understanding of law. See Ronan, *Shorter Science,* p. 276. We shall deal with this subject in Chapter 4.

55. Ro Young-chan, *Korean Neo-Confucianism,* p. 26.

56. Quoted in Katon (ed.), *To Become a Sage,* p. 38.

57. Ibid., p. 51.

58. Ibid., p. 94.

59. Ibid., p. 152.

60. See Sarvepalli Radhakrishnan and Charles A. Moore, *A Source Book in Indian Philosophy* (Princeton, N.J.: Princeton University Press, 1973), Chapter 12, pp. 424ff. Also Surendranath Dasgupta, *A History of Indian Philosophy,* Vol. 1 (Cambridge: Cambridge University Press, 1969), Chapter 7, p. 208; and Gerald J. Larson and Ram Shankar Bhattacharya (eds.), *Encyclopedia of Indian Philosophies: Vol. 4. Sāṃkhya: A Dualist Tradition in Indian Philosophy* (Delhi: Motilal Banarsidass, 1987).

61. Jan Gonda, *Change and Continuity in Indian Religion* (London: Mouton, 1965), p. 7.

62. *Puruṣa* corresponds to *al-insān al-kāmil* of Islamic esotericism and must not be interpreted simply anthropomorphically. See René Guénon, *Man and His Becoming According to the Vedanta,* trans. Richard C. Nicholson (London: Luzac, 1945), Chapter 4, pp. 46ff. On the significance of sacrifice in Hinduism as it pertains to both man and the cosmos as well as Vedic rites, see Ananda K. Coomaraswamy, "Ātmayajña: Self-Sacrifice," *Harvard Journal of Asian Studies* (Vol. 6, 1941), pp. 358–398; Bruce Lincoln, *Myth, Cosmos, and Society: Indo-European Themes of Creation and Destruction* (Cambridge, Mass.: Harvard University Press, 1986); Brian K. Smith, *Reflections on Resemblance, Ritual, and Religion* (London and New York: Oxford University Press, 1989); Jan Gonda, *The Haviryajñāḥ Somāḥ: The Interrelations of the Vedic Solemn Sacrifices. Sankhāyana Śrauta Sūtra, 14, 1–13* (Amsterdam: North-Holland, 1982); and Alain Daniélou, *Hindu Polytheism* (New York: Pantheon Books, 1964), pp. 63ff.

63. See Klaus K. Klostermaier, "Spirituality and Nature," in Krishna Sivaraman (ed.), *Hindu Spirituality: Vedas Through Vedanta* (New York: Crossroad Publications, 1989), pp. 319ff.

64. Antonio T. de Nicolás, *Meditations Through the Ṛg Veda: Four-Dimensional Man* (Boulder, Colo., and London: Shambhala, 1978), pp. 71–72; for the translation of Edward J. Thomas of the same hymn, see Radhakrishnan and Moore, *Source Book in Indian Philosophy,* pp. 19–20.

65. Mircea Eliade, *Gods, Goddesses and Myths of Creation: A Thematic Source Book of*

the History of Religions, Part I: From Primitives to Zen (New York: Harper & Row, 1974), p. 114.

66. "Everything in the whole of the cosmos is sacred." Rani Ravindra and Priscilla Murray, "The Indian View of Nature," in Rani Ravindra (ed.), *Spirit and Nature* (New York: Paragon Press, 1991), p. 48.

67. Quoted in Ravindra, *Spirit and Nature,* p. 48.

68. *The Song of God: Bhaghavad-Gita,* trans. Swami Prabhavananda and Christopher Isherwood (New York: New American Library, 1972), pp. 70–71.

69. *Dharma* (from the Sanskrit root *dhr* meaning to hold or sustain), translated here as law, also means principle, duty, correct way, and other related concepts. It is, therefore, one of the most difficult of Sanskrit terms to render into English. Although it also pertains to nature, *dharma* must not, however, be equated with "law of nature" as this term came to be understood in seventeenth-century Western science.

70. Klostermaier, "Spirituality and Nature," p. 325.

71. Ibid., p. 326.

72. For the Buddhist meaning of *dharma,* which the Buddha took from Hinduism, see Helmuth von Glasenapp, "Zur Geschichte der buddhistischen Dharma Theorie," in *Zeitschrift der Deutschen Morgenlandischen Gesellschaft,* Vol. 92 (1938), pp. 383–420; and Theodore Stcherbatsky (Fedore Ippolitovich Shcherbatskii), *The General Conception of Buddhism and the Meaning of the Word "Dharma"* (London: Royal Asiatic Society, 1923).

For Buddhism in general, especially as it concerns the doctrine of *dharma,* see Edward Conze, *Buddhist Thought in India: Three Phases of Buddhist Philosophy* (Ann Arbor: University of Michigan Press, 1967). The different meanings of *dharma* in early Buddhist texts have been assembled and discussed by Magdalene and Wilhelm Geiger in *Pali Dhamma vornehmlich in der kanonischen Literatur* (Munich: Abhandlungen der bayrischen Akademie der Wissenschaften Philosophische—Historische Klasse, vol. 31, No. 1, 1920).

73. From *Pali-English Dictionary,* T. W. Rhys Davids and W. Stede (eds.) (London: Pali Text Society, 1921), p. 171, quoted in Edward Conze, "Dharma as a Spiritual, Social, and Cosmic Force," in P. Kuntz (ed.), *The Concept of Order,* p. 240.

74. See Tadeusz Skorupski, "Dharma: Buddhist Dharma and Dharmas," *The Encyclopedia of Religion* (New York: Macmillan, 1987), Vol. 4, pp. 332–338.

75. Ibid., p. 334.

76. See Frithjof Schuon, *Treasures of Buddhism,* trans. Marco Pallis (Bloomington, Ind.: World Wisdom Books, 1993), Chapter 10, "The Mystery of the Bodhisattva," p. 107.

77. David E. Shaner, "The Japanese Experience of Nature," in J. Baird Callicott and Roger T. Ames (eds.), *Nature in Asian Traditions of Thought: Essays in Environmental Philosophy* (Albany: State University of New York Press, 1989), p. 167. Shaner adds, "In other words, the pervasive infinite character of *Mahavairocana (Dharmakaya)* was likened to the *Dainichi* (Great Sun), which not only shined over the entire universe but also, in the sense of *Amaterasu,* shared the same heritage with all other natural phenomena—that is, as the offspring of *Izana-gi* and *Izana-mi. Just as Amaterasu* participates and shares the same reality as that upon which she shines, *Dainichi Nyorai,* as the anthropomorphization of the *Dharmakaya,* permeates all things," p. 167.

78. See William LaFleur, "Saigyo and the Buddhist Value of Nature," in Callicott and Ames, *Nature in Asian Traditions,* pp. 183–208. In this essay he make a case study of the twelfth-century Buddhist sage Saigyo about whom he says, "What saved Saigyo was the Tathagata-which-is-Nature," p. 208.

79. In recent years some Western scholars have sought to find a Roman rather than

Iranian origin for Mithraism counter to the views of the older scholars such as Franz Cumont. Irrespective of their revisionist history, however, the significance of Mithra, the god of the old Iranian pantheon, can hardly be denied, and the religion remains a member of the Iranian family of religions despite its Romanization as it spread within the Roman Empire.

80. On Manichaean cosmology, which is, needless to say, closely related in many ways to Gnosticism, see Hans Jonas, *The Gnostic Religion* (Boston: Beacon Press, 1963), pp. 209ff.

81. Henry Corbin, *Spiritual Body and Celestial Earth: From Mazdean Iran to Shīʿite Iran*, trans. Mancy Pearson (Princeton, N.J.: Princeton University Press, 1977), p. 3, quoting from *Le Zend-Avesta*, trans. James Darmsteter, 3 vols. (Paris: Leroux [Annales du Musée Guimet, 21–22, 24] 1892–1893, Sīrōzā, I, pp. 296–322, Sīrōzā II, pp. 323–330).

82. Corbin, *Spiritual Body*, p. 5.

83. On Zoroastrian cosmology see H. S. Nyberg, "Questions de cosmogonie et de cosmologie mazdéennes," *Journal Asiatique* (1929), pp. 193–310; (1931), pp. 1–134, and 193–244; Marjan Molé, *Culture, mythe et cosmologie dans l'Iran ancien* (Paris: Presses Universitaires de France [Annales du Musée Guimet, Vol. 69], 1963; and S. H. Nasr, *Cosmology in pre-Islamic and Islamic Persia* (Tehran: Tehran University Press, 1971).

84. It needs to be mentioned that most Zoroastrian cosmological texts belong to the Pahlavi period and are much later than the Avesta, especially the major text, the *Bundahishn,* meaning literally "Creation."

85. See Francis M. Cornford, *From Religion to Philosophy: A Study in the Origins of Western Speculation* (Atlantic Highlands, N.J.: Humanities Press, 1980), pp. 172ff.

86. For the detail of this schema see Corbin, *Spiritual Body,* pp. 8–9, as well as the other works cited in note 80.

87. Corbin, *Spiritual Body,* p. 9.

88. Needless to say, this meaning of imagination used also extensively in Islamic metaphysics must not be confused with the modern term, which has the pejorative connotation of unreality. On the traditional meaning of *imaginatio/khayāl* see Henry Corbin, *Creative Imagination in the Sufism of Ibn 'Arabi,* trans. Ralph Manheim (Princeton, N.J.: Princeton University Press, Bollingen Series XCI, 1969), Part 2, pp. 179ff.

89. "In what here is the *principium relationis* we can perceive something like a Mazdean *sacramentum Terrae;* in its essence, and from the very name Spenta Armaiti Sophia, it can be described as a geosophy, that is to say as being the *Sophianic* mystery of the Earth, whose consumation will be its eschatological Transfiguration (*Frashkart*)." In Corbin, *Spiritual Body,* pp. 15–16.

90. See William K. C. Guthrie, *The Greeks and Their Gods* (Boston: Beacon Press, 1955), especially Chapter 9, "The *Chthonioi,*" pp. 217–253, where he discusses the significance of the earth gods or *chthonioi* for the Greek conception of nature.

91. We do not use intellect here as the equivalent of reason and try to juxtapose *logos* to *mythos.* Rather, we use intellect or *nous,* in its Platonic sense, which must not be confused with reason or *ratio,* and which is far from being opposed to *mythos* as the Platonic dialogues themselves demonstrate.

92. A number of works written during the past few decades have shown the clear link between Greek religion as it decayed and the rise of both Greek philosophy and science. Among these the pioneering works of Francis M. Cornford still stand out. See Cornford's *From Religion to Philosophy* and also *Principium sapientiae: The Origins of Greek Philosophical Thought* (Gloucester, Mass.: P. Smith, 1971).

93. On Greek religion see Herbert J. Rose, *Ancient Greek Religion* (London and New

York: Hutchinson's University Library, 1948); Alain Hus, *Greek and Roman Religion* (New York: Hawthorn Books, 1962); William K. C. Guthrie, *Greeks and Their Gods;* Karl Kerenyi, *The Religions of the Greeks and Romans,* trans. Christopher Holme (New York: E. P. Dutton, 1962); and Ulrich von Wilamowitz-Moellendorff, *Der Glaube der Hellenen,* 2 vols. (Basel: Benno Schwabe & Co., Verlag, 1956), especially Vol. 1, "Homerische Götter," pp. 31ff.; Vol. 2, "Weltgeltung und der Niedergang des Hellenentumes," pp. 258ff.

For a summary of the Greek view of the cosmos see David C. Lindberg, *The Beginnings of Western Science* (Chicago and London: University of Chicago Press, 1992), Chapter 2, pp. 21ff.

94. Hans Jonas, *Gnostic Religion,* p. 241. On the Greek conception of *cosmos* see also Ernst Cassirer, *Logos, Dike, Kosmos in der Entwicklung der griechischen Philosophie* (Göteberg: Elanders Boktryckkeri Aktiebolag, 1941); and Werner Jaeger, *Paideia: The Ideal of Greek Culture,* Vol. 1, trans. G. Highet (New York: Oxford University Press, 1945).

95. The term *world* "comes from the Old English *weorold,* which probably stems from *wer* 'man' (the term is still found in *werwolf,* man-wolf) and *ald* meaning full grown, big (hence *old*). The world is a dead giant or god." Elémire Zolla, "Traditional Methods of Contemplation and Action," in Yusuf Ibish and Peter Lamborn Wilson (eds.), *Traditional Modes of Contemplation and Action* (Tehran: Imperial Iranian Academy of Philosophy, 1977), p. 60.

96. *Timaeus,* 30B: 34A.

97. Cicero, *Cato Major,* XXI, 77, quoted in Jonas, *Gnostic Religion.* The Stoics in fact identified the cosmos with God and believed that its wisdom was revealed "by perfect order of the whole." Jonas, ibid., p. 246.

98. *Theogony,* 116, quoted in Eliade, *Gods, Goddesses and Myths of Creation,* p. 115.

99. *The Homeric Hymns,* XXX, quoted in Eliade, *Gods, Goddesses and Myths of Creation,* p. 55.

100. *Theogony,* 116, quoted in Cornford, *From Religion to Philosophy,* p. 17.

101. "The most significant truth about the universe is that it is portioned out into a general scheme of allotted provinces or spheres of power. . . . The world, in fact, was from the very early times regarded as the kingdom of Destiny and of Law. Necessity and Justice—'must' and 'ought'—meet together in this primary notion of Order." Cornford, *From Religion to Philosophy,* p. 40.

102. We do not wish to deny by this statement the significance of the Babylonian and especially Egyptian traditions in the genesis of Greek science and philosophy. On the contrary, in contrast to the revisionist history created by the Renaissance and later periods, which in glorifying the Greeks sought to belittle their Oriental and African predecessors, we consider the role of Babylonian and Egyptian teachings to be of great importance in the rise of Greek philosophy and science, even if the sacerdotal perspective of those traditions became eclipsed by Greek rationalism and naturalism. Nevertheless, the background from which the Greek scientific and, to a large extent, philosophical conceptions of nature grew is Greek religion and its allotment of domains of reality according to *Moira.*

103. On the mystery of Dionysius, see André Jean Festugière, "Les mystères de Dionysos," in *Études de religion grecque et hellénistique* (Paris: Librairie Philosophique J. Vrin, 1972), pp. 13–63.

104. See Cornford, *From Religion to Philosophy,* Chapter 6, "The Mystical Tradition," pp. 160ff.

105. Ibid., pp. 172–177.

106. "And Orpheus in his left hand lifted up his lyre and made trial of his song. He sang how the earth, heaven and sea, which were formerly joined together in one form, were separated from each other after deadly strife. He sang of how stars and the moon and the paths of the sun always hold a fixed place in the sky." From Apollonius Rhodinus, *Argonautica*, I, 494–511, quoted in David G. Rice and John E. Stambaugh, *Sources for the Study of Greek Religion* (Missoula, Mont.: Scholars Press, 1979), pp. 39–40. Furthermore, according to Orphism, music itself was instrumental in this process of turning chaos into order, and the lyre of Orpheus could produce melodies that affected the order of nature. See Jocelyn Godwin, *Harmonies of Heaven and Earth: The Spiritual Dimensions of Music* (Rochester, Vt.: Inner Traditions International, 1987), pp. 16ff.

107. See Charles B. Schmitt, "Perennial Philosophy: Steuco to Leibnitz," in his *Studies in Renaissance Philosophy and Science* (London: Variorum Reprints, 1981), I, pp. 505–532; also in the same volume "Prisca theologia e philosophia perennis: Due temi del Rinascimento italiano e la loro fortuna," II, pp. 211–236.

108. This is the thesis presented by Simone Petrement in her book *A Separate God: The Christian Origin of Gnosticism*, trans. Carol Harrison (London: Longman and Todd, 1991).

109. On Gnosticism see *Studies in the History of Religion XII: Le Origini dello gnosticismo. The Origins of Gnosticism* (Leiden: E. J. Brill, 1967); Kurt Rudolph, *Gnosis: The Nature and History of Gnosticism*, trans. and ed. Robert Mc. Wilson (New York: Harper & Row, 1983); Giovanni Filoramo, *A History of Gnosticism*, trans. Anthony Alcock (Oxford: Basil Blackwell, 1990); Gilles Quispel, *Gnosis als Weltreligion: die Bedeutung der Gnosis in Antike* (Zurich: Origo Verlag, 1972); and Elaine H. Pagels, *The Gnostic Gospels* (New York: Random House, 1979).

110. The distinction between gnosis and Gnosticism has come to be recognized by many scholars despite confusions that still reign in this field. According to the colloquium held in Messina, Italy, in 1966 on Gnosticism, it was agreed that "In order to avoid an indifferentiated usage of the terms *gnosis* and *Gnosticism*, it seems that there is every reason to identify through the cooperation of historical and typological methods a determined fact, that is, 'Gnosticism,' beginning methodologically with a group of systems of the second century A.D. On the contrary, 'gnosis' is conceived as the knowledge of divine mysteries reserved for an elite." *Le Origine dello gnosticismo*, Colloquio de Messina (Leiden: E. J. Brill, 1970), p. XXIII (translation ours). See also Christian Jambet, *La Logique des Orientaux: Henry Corbin et la science des formes* (Paris: Editions du Seuil, 1983), especially Part 2, Chapter 1, "Le sentiment gnostique de la vie," pp. 147–176, where the above decision of the Messina Colloquium is also quoted (p. 171). We mention this distinction here because of its significance throughout this study and in our other writings where we distinguish clearly between gnosis and Gnosticism.

111. For the view of Gnosticism toward nature see Hans Jonas, *Gnostic Religion*, pp. 241ff.; see also his *Gnosis und spätantiker Geist* (Göttingen: Vandenhoecf & Ruprecht, 1964); Rudolph, "Cosmology and Cosmogony," *Gnosis*, pp. 67–87; and the section "Gnosticismo, Giudaismo e Cristiànesimo: Tipologie particolari," in *Studies in the History of Religions XII*, pp. 429ff., which includes the essay of Jean Daniélou, "Le mauvais gouvernement du monde d'après le gnosticisme," pp. 448–459.

112. Hans Jonas in his *Von der Mythologie zur mystischen Philosophie* (Göttingen: Vandenhoecf & Ruprecht, 1966) deals with the influence of Gnosticism on such figures as Origen. Henri C. Puech has also dealt in depth with this subject as well as the deepest aspects of Gnosticism in his numerous studies, such as *En quête de la gnose*, 2 vols.

(Paris: Gallimard, 1978); see also his *Sur le manichéisme et autres essais* (Paris: Flammarion, 1979).

113. We need to repeat that the goal of this chapter is not to outline the view of every religion concerning nature but only those that are of significance in one way or another in the religious views of the order of nature held by various parts of humanity today. Therefore, we have left both Gnosticism and Manichaeism aside without in any way denying that their negative attitude toward the Creation and the order of nature was itself of some significance in the rise of that dualism in the modern world, which was to sever radically the spiritual link between mankind and nature.

114. On the Philonic Logos doctrine see Harry A. Wolfson, *Philo-Foundations of Religious Philosophy in Judaism, Christianity and Islam,* Vol. 1 (Cambridge, Mass.: Harvard University Press, 1947), Chapters 4–6, pp. 200ff., especially pp. 325ff. where Wolfson speaks of the immanent Logos as the origin of the order and laws of nature. The Philonic doctrine of the Logos is, naturally, of great significance for later schools of Christian as well as Jewish and Islamic thought, especially as it concerns the question of the relation between the Platonic Ideas and the Logos and the role of the Logos in the ordering of the cosmos. It is only the limitation of space that has prevented us from dealing with Wolfson more extensively. On the significance of the Philonic Logos in the order of nature, see also, besides the majesterial study of Wolfson, Georgios D. Farandos, *Kosmos und Logos nach Philon von Alexandria* (Amsterdam: Editions Rodopi N.V., 1976), which contains a detailed account of Philo's cosmology in relation to the role of the Logos; and Emile Brehier, *Les Idées philosophiques et religieuses de Philon d'Alexandrie* (Paris: J. Vrin, 1950), Book II, pp. 67ff., especially Chapters 2 and 4 where he speaks about the Logos and its role in the cosmos, discussing also the influence of Stoic cosmology upon him, especially the doctrine of the sympathy of all parts of the Universe for each other.

115. Seymour Feldman, "In the Beginning God Created: A Philosophical Midrash," in David B. Burrell and Bernard McGinn (eds.), *God and Creation: An Ecumenical Symposium* (Notre Dame, Ind.: University of Notre Dame Press, 1990), p. 3.

116. See Jacob Staub, *The Creation of the World According to Gersonides* (Chico, Calif.: Scholars Press, 1982).

117. Shalom M. Paul et al., "Creation and Cosmogony," in *Encyclopedia Judaica* (Jerusalem: Keter Publishing House), p. 1063.

118. On Jewish esotericism see Gershom G. Scholem, *Major Trends in Jewish Mysticism* (New York: Schocken Books, 1977); Leo Schaya, *The Universal Meaning of the Kabbala,* trans. N. Pearson (London: Allen & Unwin, 1971); and the Introduction of Paul Vuillaud to Ibn Gabirol, *La Couronne royale (Kether malcouth)* (Paris: Dervy Livres, 1953).

119. Lurian Cabala speaks of the doctrine of *Tsimtsum* as the "withdrawal" of God from being so as to make manifestation or Creation possible. See Scholem, *Major Trends,* p. 260.

120. Rabbi Arthur Green, *Seek My Face, Speak My Name: A Contemporary Jewish Theology* (London and Northvale, N.J.: Jason Aronson, 1992), p. 65.

121. See Paul et al., "Creation and Cosmogony," in *Encyclopedia Judaica.*

122. Scholem, *Major Trends,* p. 118.

123. Quoted by Scholem in *Major Trends,* p. 222.

124. Ibid., p. 223. In a contemporary context the Jewish perspective on nature has been summarized as follows: "The Jewish worldview holds that nature has a value independent of human interests, as an expression of the creative power of God." Eric Katz, "Judaism and the Ecological Crisis," in Mary E. Tucker and John A. Grim (eds.),

Worldviews and Ecology (Lewisburg, Pa.: Bucknell University Press, and London: Associated University Presses, 1993), pp. 67–68.

125. As a result of the environmental crisis, there has been a greater interest in recent years in the Protestant view of the order of nature and the natural sciences. See in this context John Dillenberger, *Protestant Thought and Natural Science* (Notre Dame, Ind.: University of Notre Dame Press, 1993). There is no doubt that Protestantism, for the most part, joined Catholicism after the trial of Galileo in abandoning the domain of nature to the scrutiny of a totally secularized science.

To quote a contemporary Protestant theologian, "Many nineteenth- and twentieth-century Protestant thinkers came to view nature no longer as a theatre of God's glory and power in which humanity is essentially embodied as it was for the Reformers; even less as a grand symphonic, albeit finite realization of divine goodness, as it was for Bonaventure and Augustine; still less a world of friends and fellow travelers, as it was for [St.] Francis. Nature now was approached as a self-enclosed, machinelike structure without any value or life of its own before God, set apart from both God and humanity. We may legitimately speak of the secularization of nature in the Reformation tradition in the nineteenth and twentieth centuries." H. Paul Santmire, *The Travail of Nature: The Ambiguous Ecological Promise of Christian Theology* (Philadelphia: Fortress Press, 1985), p. 133.

126. See Hugo Rahner, "Earth Spirit and Divine Spirit," in Joseph Campbell (ed.), *Spirit and Nature: Papers from the Eranos Yearbooks,* trans. Ralph Manheim and R. F. C. Hull (Princeton, N.J.: Princeton University Press, Bollingen Series XXX:1, 1982), pp. 122–148.

For the views of the early Christian Church concerning nature, see Charles C. Raven, *Natural Religion and Christian Theology* (Cambridge: Cambridge University Press, 1953), First Series, Chapters 2 and 3, pp. 21ff.

127. *De genesi ad litteram,* IV, 16, quoted in Rahner, "Earth Spirit and Divine Spirit," p. 139.

128. This doctrine echoed through the Middle Ages in the works of such figures as Hildegard of Bingen and the Victorines. Adam of St. Victor, echoing St. Augustine some seven centuries after him, wrote in one of his liturgical poems:

> *Love of Father, Son, together,*
> *Equal of them both, with either*
> *One, the same in every part!*
> *All thou fillest, all Thou lovest,*
> *Stars Thou rulest, heaven Thou movest,*
> *Though immovable Thou art.*

The Liturgical Poetry of Adam of St. Victor, Vol. 1 (London: Kegan Paul, Trench & Co., 1881), p. 100, quoted in Rahner, "Earth Spirit and Divine Spirit," p. 140.

129. Jeroslav Pelikan, *The Mystery of Continuity: Time and History, Memory and Eternity in the Thought of St. Augustine* (Charlottesville: University of Virginia Press, 1986), p. 73, quoting from *On the Morals of the Catholic Church,* 10.16. Augustine was much interested in the philosophical meaning of order in general to which he devoted his *De ordine.*

130. Pelikan, *Mystery of Continuity,* p. 71.

131. "[St. Augustine] refuse l'autarchie du monde naturel, éternel et autosuffisant, et rejette, dès lors, le naturalisme et la métaphysique d'Aristote-construite, comme sa morale, pour un monde qui a son but en lui-même. . . ." Michele F. Sciacca, *Saint Augustin et le néoplatonisme* (Paris: Éditions Béatrice—Nauwelaerts, 1956), p. 47. On

Augustine's view of Creation in relation to God, see also Battista Mondin, *Il Pensiero di Agostino* (Rome: Citta Nuova Editrice, 1988), Chapter 8, pp. 198–208; and Etienne Gilson, *The Christian Philosophy of St. Augustine,* trans. L. E. M. Lynch (New York: Random House, 1960).

132. St. Augustine alludes to Plato's confirmation of this doctrine in the *Timaeus.* We shall turn to the Platonic understanding of the order of nature in the next chapter.

133. Gilson, *Christian Philosophy of St. Augustine,* pp. 189ff.

134. Ibid., p. 19, summarizing sections of Part 1, Chapter 5 of the *Confessions.*

135. Ibid., p. 207.

136. From *De Div. Quaest. ad. imp.,* I, i, ii, quoted by Gilson, *Christian Philosophy of St. Augustine,* p. 151.

137. This analysis of St. Maximus's theses is based primarily upon Lars Thunburg, *Microcosm and Mediator: The Theological Anthropology of Maximos the Confessor* (Lund: C. W. K. Gleerup Lund, 1965), especially Chapter 2, "The Cosmological Context," pp. 51ff. See also Philip Sherrard, *Human Image: World Image—The Death and Resurrection of Sacred Cosmology* (Ipswich, U.K.: Golgonooza Press, 1992), much of which is based on the view of St. Maximus and other masters of Orthodox theology concerning sacred cosmology.

138. Thunburg, *Microcosm and Mediator,* p. 78.

139. Ibid., p. 81.

140. Ibid., p. 95.

141. Walter Wili, "The History of the Spirit in Antiquity," in Campbell (ed.), *Spirit and Nature,* p. 104 (last verse of translation slightly modified).

142. It is of symbolic significance that one of the greatest fugues composed by Johann Sebastian Bach is the *sanctus* of the B-minor Mass especially the *Pleni sunt coeli,* which contains some of his most dense contrapuntal compositions in which Heaven and Earth seem to have become wed in a perfect spiritual unity. One still experiences the marriage between Heaven and Earth in this work composed in the middle of a century when the wedding was becoming unravelled so rapidly in philosophy and science.

143. We have dealt extensively with this issue in many of our own works, including *Science and Civilization in Islam* (Cambridge: Islamic Text Society, 1987), Introduction; and our "Islamic Science, Western Science—Common Heritage, Diverse Destinies," in S. H. Nasr and Katherine O'Brien (eds.), *In Quest of the Sacred* (Oakton, Va.: Foundation for Traditional Studies, 1994), pp. 161–175.

144. Scientism is one of the most important points that most modernists and "fundamentalists" in the Islamic world share in common. See S. H. Nasr, *Traditional Islam in the Modern World* (London: KPI, 1989), pp. 18ff.

145. See "The Meaning of Nature in Various Perspectives in Islam," in S. H. Nasr, *Islamic Life and Thought* (Albany: State University of New York Press, 1981), p. 96.

146. Reference to the Pen and the Tablet is found in the Quran (such as LXVIII:1 and LXXXV:22).

147. There are *ḥadīths* of the Prophet stating that the first thing which God created was the Intellect (*al-'aql*) or the Word (*al-kalimah*) or light (*al-nūr*). The Pen can be considered to symbolize this reality, which is at once the Intellect, the Word (Logos), and Light by which all things were made, while Islam rejects any connotation of incarnation in its understanding of the function of the Logos in the generation of the world.

148. One hardly needs to mention that Islam, like Judaism and Christianity, believes in God creating the world *ex nihilo* (*min al-'adam* or *'udum*) and has also produced numerous interpretations of the meaning of *'adam* as we see in the case of *ex nihilo* referred

to above. See Frithjof Schuon, *The Play of Masks* (Bloomington, Ind.: World Wisdom Books, 1992), *Ex Nihilo, Deo,* p. 37.

149. Later Sufi cosmology was to interpret *al-malakūt* as one state among several that separate *al-mulk* from the Divine Essence, the others being *al-jabarūt* (the archangelic world) and *al-lāhūt* (the world of the Divine Names and Qualities). See Frithjof Schuon, "The Five Divine Presences," in Schuon, *Dimensions of Islam,* trans. Peter Townsend (London: Allen & Unwin, 1970), pp. 142ff.

150. *Al-Futūḥāt al-makkiyyah,* IV, 231.21, quoted in William Chittick, *The Sufi Path of Knowledge* (Albany: State University of New York Press, 1989), p. 38. Chittick, commenting upon Ibn 'Arabī's doctrine of the Divine Names, writes, "Everything in the cosmos can be traced back to the divine realities or names. Hence Ibn al-'Arabī often refers to reality as a 'root' (*aṣl*) or 'support' (*mustanad*) and speaks of the phenomena of this world as being 'supported' (*istinād*) by the Names." Ibid., p. 37.

151. See Titus Burckhardt, *Introduction to Sufism: The Mystical Dimension of Islam,* trans. D. M. Matheson (Wellingborough, U.K.: Aquarian Press, 1990), Chapter 9, "The Archetypes," p. 62.

152. On the "Breath of the Compassionate" and the "breathing upon the archetypes," see Burckhardt, *Introduction to Sufism,* Chapter 10, pp. 65ff. On the gnostic (*'irfānī*) view of Creation and the order of nature see Nasr, *Science and Civilization in Islam,* Chapter 13, pp. 337ff.

153. See Burckhardt, *Introduction to Sufism,* Chapter 10, "The Renewing of Creation at Each Instant," pp. 65ff, and Toshihiko Izutsu, *Unicité de l'existence et création perpetuelle en mystique islamique,* trans. Marie-Charlotte Grandry (Paris: Les Deux Océans, 1980), especially Chapters 3 and 4, pp. 85ff. Part of this study appeared originally in the *Philosophical Forum* (Vol. 4, no. 1, Fall 1972), pp. 124–140, as "Creation and the Timeless Order of Things: A Study in the Mystical Philosophy of 'Ayn al-Quḍāt."

154. For example, the verse "Thou wilt not find for the wont of Allah [*sunnat Allāh*] aught of power to change" (48:23).

155. This subject has been dealt with at length by Leo Schaya in his *La Création en Dieu à la lumière du Judaisme, du Christianisme et de l'Islam* (Paris: Dervy Livres, 1983).

156. We have dealt with the question of evolution in our *Knowledge and the Sacred* (Albany: State University Press of New York, 1989), Chapter 7.

157. The eschatological significance of the order of nature that has been discussed among certain early Muslim as well as Jewish and Christian theologians is now being used by certain contemporary Christian theologians to develop a Christian theology of the environment. See, for example, John F. Haught, *The Promise of Nature: Ecology and Cosmic Purpose* (New York: Paulist Press, 1993).

158. See S. H. Nasr, *An Introduction to Islamic Cosmological Doctrines* (Albany: State University of New York Press, 1993), Chapter 15, pp. 263ff.

159. This term has already been used by Titus Burckhardt and might be considered as a dimension of the *philosophia perennis.* See his book *Mirror of the Intellect,* trans. W. Stoddart (Albany: State University of New York Press, 1987), Chapter 2, p. 17ff., "*Cosmologia perennis.*" This thesis does not claim that the various traditional cosmologies are the same on the formal level, but that certain universal and perennial principles are common to traditional cosmologies that are, after all, extensions of metaphysics and gnosis and therefore share in the supraformal unity of the latter.

160. From the *Mathnawī* (III:1008–1117). Translated by Reynold A. Nicholson in *Rumi-Poet and Mystic* (London: Mandala Books, Unwin Paperbacks, 1978), p. 119.

3

Philosophy and
the Misdeeds of Philosophy

چیست حکمت راز حق آموختن   شك و تردید تفکر سوختن

باطن از ظاهر مجرد ساختن   شعلهٔ علم کیان افروختن

Wisdom is possession of that Truth whose radiance
Crowns our life, our knowledge, our existence,
Its love, true philosophy as it has always been,
Casting the light of certitude upon earthly doubts.
How strange that the hate of that sophia, divine,
Neglect of her beauty and Truth Itself,
Also parade as philosophy in these days,
Forgetful of all that is within, yet claiming to be
Our guide in this our earthly journey.
And we in need of that light supernal,
Shining forth from the Source of all reality,
Above, and within the substance of our being.

It is now for us to consider the role of philosophy in the understanding of the order of nature. Our comments in this chapter will be limited to the West because it was here that a rebellion took place against traditional philosophy, which had remained inalienably linked to religion everywhere and in all stages of premodern history save for a brief period in Greco-Roman antiquity. This rebellion resulted in a new chapter in the history of Western philosophy wherein much of philosophy set itself against the very principles of religion and even wisdom. Only in the West did a philosophy develop that was not only no longer the love of wisdom but went so far as to deny the very category of wisdom as a legitimate form of knowledge. The result was a hatred of wisdom that should more appropriately be called "misosophy" (literally hatred of *sophia*, wisdom) rather than philosophy.

In both Greek antiquity and the European Middle Ages, Western philosophy possessed schools that could be compared with the great intellectual traditions of China and India, not to speak of the Islamic world, which shared much of the heritage of antiquity with the West. It is only in the postmedieval period that the mainstream of Western philosophy turned against both revelation and noesis or intellection as sources of knowledge, and limited itself to empiricism or rationalism, with results that were catastrophic for the unity of Western civilization as far as the relation between faith and reason was concerned.[1] Other religions, whose views concerning the order of nature were discussed in the previous chapter, created civilizations in which schools of philosophy were cultivated in the traditional sense of the term; however, none of them paralleled the development of postmedieval Western philosophy, at least not until the nineteenth century. That is why a number of scholars with some justification have refused to apply the very term "philosophy" to Oriental doctrines because one cannot call, let us say, the *Sāṃkhya* and Kantianism, philosophy unless philosophy is taken to possess a distinct meaning in each of the cases in question. However, one could quite legitimately call Pythagorianism and *ishraqī* doctrines[2] or neo-Confucianism philosophy and have a clear understanding, based upon principles, of what is meant by philosophy, which must, nevertheless, be endowed with a definition universal enough to embrace expressions of traditional philosophy as different as Pythagoreanism and neo-Confucianism.[3]

In any case our task in this chapter is to deal precisely with this transformation in the understanding of the meaning, role, and methods of philosophy as far as the order of nature is concerned. It is to examine how Western philosophy from its inception in Greece to its transformation during the Renaissance and finally up to the contemporary period has dealt with the order of nature and how changes came about in the philosophical understanding of that order, which were both affected by the religious understanding of the natural order and later combatted, opposed, and influenced that understanding. The full grasp of the current religious and also antireligious understanding of the order of nature and its consequences for the environmental crisis, which is the final goal of this study, cannot be achieved without dealing, in addition to religion, with both Western philosophy and science.[4]

GREEK PHILOSOPHY

Both Greek philosophy and science were born in the wake of the weakening of the Greek religions and came to fill the vacuum resulting from the retraction of the religious *Weltanschauung* as already discussed in the previous chapter.[5] But the general characteristics of the Universe as a domain of order and intelligibility governed by an intelligible principle persisted even as different schools of Greek philosophy arose.[6] The Universe was an order or cosmos; it possessed life and moved in an orderly manner. It was, therefore, an intelligent animal whose parts participated in the life and intelligibility of the whole. Different schools were to interpret this order in different ways, but most remained faithful to these principles, which were intimately linked to the Greek religious view of the Universe. That is why the Greek philosophical explanations of the order of nature did not cease to possess a religious significance and could for that very reason be integrated by the schools of philosophy within the Abrahamic monotheisms, especially as far as the major schools of antiquity such as Pythagoreanism, Platonism, and Aristotelianism were concerned.

The first Greek philosophers, the Ionians, were already keenly interested in the order of nature and were in fact called by Aristotle "theorists of nature" (*physiologoi*).[7] They were all attracted to the study of *physis* (that "something" in things which made them behave as they did), and many treatises were written during the sixth century B.C. bearing the title *Concerning Nature (Perí phýseos)*.[8] It was to discover the real nature of *physis* that Thales was inspired to speak of water as the universal substance while Anaximander identified universal substance with the Boundless, which he identified with God as the immanent Divine Principle. He already gave an outline of a cosmology that refers to the order and structure of the cosmos, which for him, as for other Milesians, was alive and "ensouled"; hence, the reference to the view of the Milesians as hylozoism. Another Ionian, Anaximenes, considered air to be the universal substance, which was divine. Eternal rotary motion of the cosmos caused air or vapor to become differentiated and segmented into various substances. Anaximenes began to turn from the question of what is the basic substance of which other substances are made, a question that had remained the basis for Ionian natural philosophy, to the question of the structure or form of things, which was to characterize the school of Pythagoras.

The Ionians realized three basic points about nature that were to have far-reaching repercussions into even modern science:

1. that there are realities which are "natural" things;
2. that "natural things" together constitute a single reality, which is "the world of nature";
3. that what is common to all "natural things" is their being constituted of a single "substance" or material.[9]

Although the early speculations of the Ionians concerning nature are of great significance for understanding the origin of both Greek philosophy and science, it is the Pythagorean school, heir to the esoteric dimension of the Greek religion, that is of central importance for the understanding of a certain view of the meaning of order that has persisted over the ages and that has had profound influence on both religious philosophies and science in both the West and the Islamic world. It was this school that was especially concerned with order in the cosmos. In fact, "the centerpiece of Pythagoras's thought is the idea of order: musical order, mathematical order."[10]

The Pythagorean concept of the order of nature is one of the most profound links between religion and traditional science in Western intellectual history, bringing about that wedding between the religious vision of the Universe and a science of the cosmos that one discovers in a medieval cathedral such as Chartres. Although Aristotle remains one of the most important sources for the knowledge of Pythagoras and his school (especially in *Metaphysics*, I, 5, 985b), he was actually impervious to the musical dimension underlying the whole Pythagorean concept of mathematics. It was not mathematics as ordinarily understood that characterizes Pythagoreanism but a mathematics at once qualitative and quantitative, at once music and geometry or arithmetic. The Pythagorean number is not only a quantity but also a "state of being," an intelligible idea[11] whose qualitative dimension is revealed through the musical melodies generated according to mathematical laws and presenting another aspect of that reality whose quantitative aspect we study in geometry or arithmetic. Pythagoras sought to understand the pattern of nature through mathematics, but a mathematics that was symbolic and intimately bound to musical harmony. He related numbers to the archetypal realities as well as harmony and at the same time musical harmony with the order of the cosmos.[12]

Pythagoras not only believed firmly in the existence of order in nature as did other Greek philosophers but he also sought to explain this order not by asking what is the nature of the constitutive substance of the cosmos, but what is its pattern. His response to this question was mathematical structures that constitute the forms of things and by virtue of which things are what they are and are distinguished from each other. It is the mathemtical structure of things that makes them be what they are and not their matter. The cosmos is mathematically intelligible, but on the condition that mathematics be understood in its qualitative as well as quantitative sense and be seen symbolically. It is precisely this aspect of mathematics that was denied by those in the sixteenth and seventeenth centuries who evoked the name of Pythagoras in seeking to mathematicize physics and reduce the science of nature to the study of pure quantity, with results that from the spiritual point of view can only be called catastrophic, for what is not symbolic (from the Greek verb *symballein,* meaning to unite) cannot but be diabolic (from another Greek verb *diaballein,* meaning to divide). Pythagorean mathematics was a means of uniting rather than dividing, and Pythagorean numbers and geometric patterns are so many reflections of Unity, of the number one or the geometric point, which echo Unity but somehow never break away from It.

According to the Pythagoreans, what provided order in the realm of nature was not just any mathematical pattern but patterns based on harmony or, more precisely, on musical harmony. The Pythagorean table, rediscovered by Albert von Thimus in the nineteenth century,[13] relates the ratio of small whole numbers to musical tones, and the Pythagoreans claimed that various natural beings from minerals to animals to the stars were constructed and moved according to an order that was, musically speaking, harmonious. This was also true of sacred works of art and architecture that emulated the cosmic order. It is this truth that those who have spoken over the ages of the music of the spheres had in mind as did Goethe when he referred to traditional architecture as frozen music.[14]

The idea that the order of nature is not only mathematical but also musical and that mathematics itself is at once qualitative and quantitative is the most important heritage that Pythagoreanism bequeathed upon both Western and Islamic civilizations.[15] Without doubt drawing from Egyptian sources,[16] Pythagoras opened a new chapter in both Greek philosophy and science in the sixth century B.C. by emphasizing the meaning of the order of nature as being related not to the nature of the "stuff" of the Universe but to patterns hierarchical and mathematical, whereas mathematics itself, far from being pure quantity, is of a symbolic and also qualitative nature. Moreover, it is this musical harmony that holds the key to the understanding of the harmony and order of the world of nature and that makes the cosmos precisely *cosmos* or order. For the next 2,500 years wherever the question of the religious and philosophical significance of the order of nature has been discussed, the spirit of Pythagoras has been present and his heritage has not completely died out even in the modern West. In fact, today a number of those who are trying to rediscover the religious and metaphysical significance of the order of nature are turning to Pythagoreanism once again.[17]

Although he criticized some aspects of Pythagorean thought, Plato may be said to be the most significant expositor of the teachings of Pythagoras, emphasizing like the master the significance of order and pattern and especially geometry, without which knowledge no one could enter the Platonic Academy, and identifying mathematical forms with the intelligible archetypes or ideas. Plato's works are in fact interspersed with mathematical allegories that can only be understood musically[18] and, as is well known, music played a major role in his educational scheme. For him as for Pythagoras, mathematics, music, and the order of nature are interconnected through an unbreachable bond. In the *Epinomis* Plato observed:

> To the man who pursues his studies in the proper way, all geometric constructions, all systems of numbers, all duly constituted melodic progressions, the single ordered scheme of all celestial revolutions, should disclose themselves . . . [by]the revelation of a single bond of natural interconnection.[19]

Plato provided the metaphysical foundation implicit in the Pythagorean doctrine of numbers and geometric forms, for the Platonic ideas are nothing other than the realities that the numbers and figures of Pythagorean mathematics symbolize and with which they are identified in essence. This can be seen in the clearest fashion in the *Timaeus,* that most Pythagorean of Plato's dialogues. There, Plato argues, as he had done in *Philebus,* that whatever becomes must have a maker and cause, which in the case of the cosmos is the Demiurge, whom he likens to a craftsman, a cause that "is said to be Intelligence, the King of Heaven and Earth."[20] The visible world is the working of Divine Intelligence and an image of the Real or Archetypal World. As for the motif for the generation of the world by the Demiurge from chaos to cosmos, Plato states:

> Let us, then, state for what reason becoming and this universe were framed by him who framed them. He was good; and in the good no jealousy in any matter can ever arise. So, being without jealousy, he desired that all things should come as near as possible to being like himself. That this is the supremely valid principle of becoming and of the order of the world, we shall most surely be right to accept from men of understanding.[21]

Whether we interpret the Demiurge as a myth in the veritable sense of the term or in its negative sense—both views having been held by scholars of Platonism—this statement of the *Timaeus* states clearly the cause for the order of the world and its generation, those being first the goodness of the Divine Principle and second the creation of this world in accordance with and in imitation of the World of Ideas whose eternal order is therefore reflected in the world of becoming. Creation for Plato is precisely the bestowing of order in accordance with the reality of the Archetypal World, which is beyond the creative act of the Demiurge and is without temporal origin.

In the *Timaeus* Plato seems to speak of two kinds of order, the first being the order imparted by Creation and the second the order that unfolds in the creative activity of the objects that have been created. Plato is furthermore also concerned with the question of disorder, which also exists in the world. This disorder is the result of both the multiplicity of Forms and the degree of intensity of the images of the Ideas. Both of these factors are related to space, which Plato calls "the matrix of change" and "mother of all becoming," space being the receptacle of Forms but not Form itself and hence not order since all order comes from Forms.[22] One might say that the Divine Intellect cannot completely overcome the "unpurposive aspect of things" in the cosmos and that matter remains somewhat recalcitrant against the action of the Demiurge. This recalcitrance is also observable in the monstrosities one observes in nature, but by and large intelligibility dominates completely over unintelligibility and order over disorder. The good that is identified by Plato with intelligibility far outweighs evil and is in fact the very nature of reality since the source of reality is the Supreme Good or *tò Agathón*. Despite the presence of partial disorder, therefore, the Demiurge remains successful in imposing order and creating the cosmos in which order far outweighs disorder.

The world created by the Demiurge is not only an order or cosmos but a living order directed to the good and teleological in nature. The body of the world possesses a soul, the World Soul, and within the Soul resides the Intellect or *Noūs*. Plato asked:

> What was the living creature in whose likeness he framed the world? We must not suppose that it was any creature that ranks only as a species; for no copy of that which is incomplete can ever be good. Let us rather say that the world is like, above all things, to that Living Creature of which all other living creatures, severally and in their families, are parts.[23]

That Living Creature is itself a Form containing the Form of all species and therefore the source of the order observable in all the species in this world of shadows, which imitate and also participate in the World of Forms.

Opposed to the views of the skeptics and materialists of his day, Plato further insisted that the order of the world is not by chance, and he therefore asserted emphatically that the World Soul precedes the body of the world and contains within itself the order manifested in the world. The World Soul—composed of existence, sameness, and difference—is divided harmonically by the Demiurge according to the number series 1 2 3 4 8 9 27, which according to the Platonic philosopher Crantor was divided as

and later scholars have debated as to the validity of each scheme. A Pythagorean analysis of the number series reveals, however, that "both arrangements lead tonally to equivalent solutions, although their arithmetic appearances are different."[24] The World Soul contains harmony, in the musical sense, within its very structure, a harmony then transmitted to the visible world. "Plato's 'World Soul' proves to be a cosmological model in smallest integers for all possible systems definable by old-fashioned Pythagorean theory."[25]

Whatever interpretation is given to the significance of the number series connected with the structure of the Soul, there is no doubt that it implies the existence of harmony in the Pythagorean sense within the World Soul, which in turn is the source of order and harmony in the world. The harmony of the World Soul is also related to the harmonic proportions of the regular solids that are key to understanding the structure of the world of the elements and the harmony governing the movement of the heavens.[26] Through this Platonic exposition, as well as from other sources, the Pythagorean conception of order was to become a major strand in Western intellectual history, with profound ramifications in the realms of both religious philosophy and science.

To understand fully the Platonic doctrine of the order of nature, it is necessary to delve somewhat further into the meaning of the Platonic Idea or Form. Form is what is real, whereas all becoming involves entities that imitate the Forms and are only real to the degree that they participate in them.[27] Forms are not perceptible in themselves but only intelligible, and they constitute in their plurality the intelligible world (*noetos tepos,* or the *mundus intelligibilis* of medieval philosophy). Forms are real because they are totally themselves, and there is nothing in them save themselves, in contrast to natural objects, which are always becoming. They "are" only to the extent that they participate in the Forms. Because Forms and only Forms are completely intelligible, to the extent that an object becomes physical, it is removed from the realm of intelligibility, although the Forms, while being transcendent as Plato insists in the *Symposium* and *Phaedo,* are also immanent so that intelligibility can also be found in the world of change in the reflection of the Forms in that world. The science of nature, however, can only be a science of the formal structure of the world from whence comes the order of nature. The structure of natural things is in fact not the Forms of those things in themselves but the tendency within those things to approximate pure Forms. Plato's interest in the order of nature in a cosmos made by God and at once a living organism and intelligible is not in the matter of the objects of nature but the

Forms that are reflected therein. It is the Forms that bestow order upon nature through the World Soul, which pervades the entire body of the cosmos.

The order of nature is, therefore, ultimately a reflection of the Divine Order, and Plato expresses in a philosophical language a truth which is none other than that held with certain variations by the several religions mentioned in the preceding chapter. Furthermore, Plato relates, as do so many of the religious doctrines discussed already, the principles governing human society to those ruling over the cosmos, the cosmic order being an image of the moral order.[28] No wonder then that he was so readily integrated into the religious universes of the Abrahamic monotheisms and that St. Augustine claimed Plato to have been a Christian before Christ, while some of the greatest of Islamic sages and saints such as Ibn 'Arabī were called the Platos of their day.

Plato's foremost student and the father of Greek natural philosophy, Aristotle, did not reject the doctrine of Platonic Forms or Ideas, as some have claimed, but he did refuse to accept their reality independent of matter. For him, in contrast to Plato, the process of the world is self-causing; it is a self-existing process and intelligibility is *within,* changing things themselves. Within everything resides a nature (*physis*) that is its source of movement, and things possess the principle of growth and organization within themselves.[29] But all growth and change occur according to an order that, as in the case of Plato, is related to the Form of things. Matter is simply potentiality and the *terminus quo* of the cosmic process and plays a more passive role than it does in the Platonic understanding of it. It cannot be known in itself; rather, it is the Form of things that can be known and that is intelligible. Form constitutes the structure of a thing and is "just that by virtue of which it moves, grows, and alters, and comes to rest when it has reached the terminus of its movement."[30]

There is within all things, which consist of Form and matter, a movement from potentiality to activity, there being no pure matter since "matter is the unrealizedness of unrealized potentiality."[31] All natural processes occur according to an order based upon the movement from potentiality to actuality, for there is in every potentiality a nisus (or impulse) by virtue of which it is moving toward actuality. For Aristotle the final and efficient causes of things are the same, for he develops the idea of an ultimate immaterial efficient cause. Forms themselves act as efficient causes in the world of nature and are the objects of desire of things, which in his scheme possess souls and *can* desire. As Aristotle states in the *Metaphysics,* "Desire of the material thing is a desire to embody this form in its own matter, to conform itself to it and to imitate it, as well as possible, in that matter."[32]

One can say that the Aristotelian Forms are God's "thought" and reveal the way God "thinks." In contrast to Plato, for whom God is the efficient cause of the world of nature and the Forms the final cause, Aristotle identifies God ultimately with the Forms. There is one single Unmoved Mover in the ultimate sense with self-knowledge who contemplates Himself, Forms being the categories of this contemplation. This is the highest activity which inspires the whole of nature with the desire for it and provides the nisus toward reproducing it.

Aristotle also states that the love (*eros*) of God pervades the whole of nature and that the processes of nature are produced by the love of God. Even "inert" impulses of nature move toward God by virtue of this love, which pervades all things. It might, in fact, be said that in Aristotle's cosmology the love of God is the source of order in the world of nature. There is, however, a hierarchy in this order and the ends toward which things move, only the ultimate end being God. There are many secondary unmoved movers, the supreme one being God whose activity is pure intellection (*nómos noéseos*) emulated by the perfect circular motion of the *primum mobile* whose soul is directly activated by the love of God.

While God contemplates Himself, other Intelligences contemplate Him. They thus share in God's life but in a limited sense. That is why the other planets directed by these Intelligences move in curves that are modifications of the perfect circle, nearly circular but not exactly so. The planets imitate the Intelligences but not God directly, and the comtemplation of the Intelligences is imperfect. Hence the imperfection of their orbits. There exists a complex society of Intelligences forming an eternal and immaterial model for all cosmic movement. It might thus be said that despite his differences with Plato, "Aristotle is repeating in his own way the doctrine of the *Timaeus,* that in making the material or temporal world God modeled it upon an eternal pattern—viz. the immaterial or eternal world of forms."[33] It is the Intelligences that govern the order of nature and even determine principally the differentiation of nature's activities. According to Aristotle, there are no individual transcendent Forms as found in Platonic metaphysics; the Forms are immanent to things. But there are the Intelligences, which are the models for the movement of the cosmos.

It must also be mentioned that Aristotle conceives all change in the world to be not only according to order but also teleological and not blind as claimed by the atomists. "For Aristotle all conformity to law is teleological, like that displayed in the artist's creation. The regular recurrence of natural phenomena is the manifestation of this type of law in which both plan and purpose are evident."[34] There is thus a purposeful order to the processes of nature in a well-ordered cosmos made intelligible by the Unmoved Mover and permeated by a love that the most Christian of poets, Dante, was to interpret as the "Love that moves the Sun and the Stars." But in comparison with that of Plato, the Aristotelian understanding of the order of nature is less directly identifiable with the good, and teleology does not play the same irreducible role as it does in Platonism. In fact, a number of interpreters of Aristotle have claimed that by weakening the necessity of teleology for the explanation of natural phenomena and relating it simply to the regularity of change as claimed also by atomists, Aristotelianism opened the way for the rejection by modern Newtonians of teleology as being scientifically relevant.[35]

And yet, the Aristotelian view of the order of nature, while differing in many ways from the Platonic, still preserved, despite Aristotle's empirical epistemology, a metaphysical foundation that made it possible to become integrated, as did Platonism, into the religious intellectual universe of the Abrahamic religions and to be transformed by figures such as Ibn Sīnā (Avicenna), Maimonides, and St. Thomas Aquinas into a vision of the order of nature that conformed to the religious view of the cosmos as it had been revealed and developed within Judaism, Christianity, and Islam.

The major manifestations of Greek philosophical speculation did not exhaust themselves with Aristotle, although the Pythagorean–Platonic and Aristotelian schools were the most influential ones of Greek philosophy. An important new school that appeared upon the scene shortly after Aristotle and whose views of the order of nature are of great significance, both in themselves and because of their later influence, is Stoicism, especially early Stoicism, for the later Stoics of Rome did not display much interest in cosmology except perhaps for Seneca in his *Letters to Lucilius* and *Natural Questions.*

The Stoics emphasized the significance of the order of nature to the extent that they considered the goal of life to be to live in harmony with that order and with *physis* itself, some referring to Zeus as the universal law pervading all things. Hence their emphasis upon the study of physics as a part of the education necessary for virtuous behavior. *Physis* for the Stoics was seen as at once the force generating the Universe, holding it together and imposing order upon it, *physis* being equivalent to the "true order" of the cosmos.[36] The contemplation of this order remained central to the Stoic way of life and the main concern of Stoic physics and cosmology.

This cosmology owed much to the pre-Socratics, Plato, and Aristotle as well as the Greek medical tradition. For the early Stoics, as for most of their predecessors, the Universe was a living being, a *zōon,* and behaved as a living creature. It arose out of an original substance (*ousia*) and would dissolve into it again. Two principles (*archai*) interacted with each other in the genesis of the cosmos: the active principle (*poioun*) and the passive one (*paschon*), the first identified with *theos* (and later in Latin Zeus), which was almost interchangeable with *physis,* and the second with *hylé,* which the Stoics took from Aristotle. For the Stoics, in contrast to Plato and Aristotle, however, God is immanent in the cosmos and not transcendent. The Divinity is like the Platonic Demiurge, which is itself the Forms and origin of patterns of the Universe while being immanent within it.[37] The active principle is also identified by the Stoics as the hot fiery principle that Diogenes Laertius calls "the seminal reason" of the Universe,[38] and that must be distinguished from the element fire. According to all the early Stoics such as Zeno, Cleanthes, and Chrysippus, it is this active principle, or *theos,* that, acting upon the *hylé,* causes the generation of the four cosmological elements (fire, air, water, and earth) from which the sublunar world is made, whereas the heavens are made of ether.

One cannot understand the Stoic view of the order of nature without turning to the concept of *pneuma* and its role in Stoic cosmology. Aristotle had already spoken of the existence of an inner *pneuma* within bodies as distinct from *psyche,* but the early Stoic Zeno identified the two, and with Chrysippus the doctrine of *pneuma* became central. According to Chrysippus, *pneuma* penetrates all bodies and accounts for all bodily phenomena. Furthermore, this is also true for the cosmos as a whole. For Chrysippus there is a cosmic *pneuma* that is the equivalent of God or the Divine Intellect (*noūs, lógos*) in some texts replacing the creative fire or active principle.[39] Its pervading of the cosmos in varying degrees of strength and weakness is responsible for the shapes and order of things. Diogenes Laertius, quoting Chrysippus, observed:

> This mind pervades every part of it, just as the soul does in our bodies. But through some parts it pervades more, through others less. Through some parts it passes as a "hold" or "grip," functioning as the bones and sinews in our bodies; it pervades other parts as mind, functioning as the command center in our bodies.[40]

The cosmic *pneuma* is the source of order, a divine power that causes a body to be in a particular state and also links bodies to each other in a causal chain.[41] Creating a continuum spatially and materially, the *pneuma*, which has its "command center" in the Sun or, according to some, in the purest part of ether, brings about that strict chain of cause and effect to which Stoics referred to as the chain of fate, with fate being a "pneumatic force."[42] The *pneuma*, pervading the entire Universe, also causes an affinity or *sympatheia* among all its parts that together constitute a unified structure of the whole, which fortified further the Aristotelian concept of order. According to Cleomedes in his *De motu circulari*, the first two attributes of nature are the order of its parts and the order of its occurrence, the third being "the mutual interaction (sympathy) of its parts."[43] This *sympatheia* caused by the *pneuma* was to be seen everywhere, and some Stoics like Cicero pointed to the influence of the moon upon the tides as an evident example of it.

The Stoic theory of the *pneuma*, which brings about pneumatic tension and sympathy throughout the cosmos, gradually changed the conception of the order of nature by emphasizing the following principles: The same laws prevail throughout the cosmos ruled by a single *pneuma*; a "universal gravitation" attracts all things to each other as the idea of *hexis* or the physical state of the body suggests; and the cosmos is a closed whole not affected by the void outside it, for within it there is no void but only a continuum. Such ideas were not only important philosophically but were also of much significance for the later study of physics.[44] As explained by Sambursky, they posited such ideas of major significance for physics as fields of force, the epistemology of causal nexus, and the continuum.

Still, Stoic cosmology did not depart completely from the metaphysical and religious understanding of the order of nature. That is why, although its doctrine of the burning and purification by fire (*ekpyrōsis*) and its limiting the Divine to Its immanent aspect were criticized by Christian thinkers, Stoicism exercised some influence upon the philosophies developed both in the Islamic world and the West. Strangely enough, later Islamic philosophers came to identify the Stoics (*al-riwāqiyyūn*) with the Illuminationists (*al-ishrāqiyyūn*), who were as far removed as possible from the transcendence-denying Stoicism of the late Roman Empire. As for Greco-Roman antiquity, the interest in nature and cosmology nearly disappeared from late Stoicism, and this aspect of Stoic philosophy was left for poets rather than philosophers to discuss and contemplate as we see in the *Astronomica* of the poet Manilius:

For I shall sing of God, mighty through the silent mind of nature
And infused in the heavens, in earth and the seas,
Governing the universe mass with a measured bond;
(And I shall sing) that the entire universe
Through its alternating sympathy is alive,
And is driven by the movement of reason,
Since one pneuma *inhabits all its parts,*
And, pervading all things, strengthens the spherical world
And assumes the likeness of an animate body.[45]

Although many have celebrated the Stoic vision of nature as a declaration of independence from the religious perspective, it is not difficult to see in the words of this poem, reflecting the principles of Stoic cosmology, the link that still survives between the Stoic view of the order of nature and the religious and even mystical view of this order.

The full exposition of the metaphysical significance of the order of nature in relation to both the transcendent and immanent aspects of the Divine was to come during the waning period of Stoicism in the third century A.D. with the rise of Neoplatonism and especially in the works of its founder Plotinus. In reemphasizing the religious significance of the order of nature and outlining a philosophy of nature totally integrated into metaphysics, Plotinus created a philosophy that became easily absorbed into later schools of religious thought, leaving a profound mark upon both the Jewish and Christian as well as certain dimensions of the Islamic intellectual tradition, where although not known by name and confused with Aristotle, Plotinus was nevertheless called the "spiritual teacher of the Greeks" (*shaykh al-yūnāniyyīn*).[46]

Nature (*physis*) for Plotinus is the active faculty of the World Soul and that which bestows substantiality upon matter, which in itself is nothing but an abstraction signifying the receptivity to Forms. Nature is the lowest of the spiritual beings standing below the One, the Intellect and the Soul, and all that is below Nature is merely a shadow or copy of reality. All the activities of Nature come from the World Soul, which creates the sensible world through Nature, resulting in the four elements and their mixtures. As Plotinus states, "The sensible world is a reflexion of the spiritual world in the mirror of matter."[47] As for the Forms or patterns in the world, they issue from the creative powers (*lógoi*), which are "thoughts" of the Soul and flow ultimately from the Intellect or Spirit.[48] The *lógoi* present in the sensible world unfold and actualize the possibilities within them without this unfolding implying in any way an evolution of Forms.[49]

Nature then is a spiritual principle derived from the World Soul and is itself the expression of perfect intelligence and a vision of the higher levels of reality contained within itself. It is the World Soul that originates the order of nature and the human soul that, thanks to the Spirit present in it, discovers this order and comes to know of the order of the spatio-temporal domain, as the Spirit itself within us perceives the order of the spiritual world (*cosmos noetós*). The order and regularity observed in nature are the result of the *táxis* or order imposed by the World Soul upon this world, and they are inseparable from the laws of the world of the Spirit they of necessity emulate. In the *Enneads* III, 8, Nature herself speaks in these words in answer to the question of why it brings forth its works:

> It would have been more becoming to put no question but to learn in silence just as I myself am silent and make no habit of talking. And what is your lesson? This; that whatsoever comes into being is my vision, seen in my silence, the vision that belongs to my character who, sprung from vision, am vision-loving and create vision by the vision-seeing faculty within me. The mathematicians from their vision draw their figures: but I draw nothing: I gaze and the figures of the material world take being as if they fell from my contemplation. As with my mother (the All-Soul) [or the World Soul] and the Beings that begot me so it is with me: they are born of a Contemplation and my birth is from them, not by act but by their Being; they are the loftier Reason-Principles, they contemplate themselves and I am born.[50]

Nature created by contemplation also generates by vision of the higher worlds and acts as the means whereby intelligibility and hence order, which belongs ultimately to these higher worlds, is imposed upon the sensible world.

One of the most important elements in Plotinian cosmology is the unity of the cosmos and its order. To quote the *Enneads* again,

> But if we remember that we posited that the universe is a single living thing, and that since it is so it was absolutely necessary for it to have an internal and self-communication of its experiences [*sympathes*]; and we remember further that the process of its life must be rational and all in tune [*symphonos*] with itself, and that there is nothing casual in its life but a single melody and order [*harmonia kai táxis*], and that the celestial arrangements are rational, and each individual part moves by numbers, as do the dancing parts of the living being; we must admit that both are the activity of the All . . . and that this is the way the All lives.[51]

The natural Universe is therefore an organic whole with sympathy between its parts and possessing a Divine Presence that we can detect by virtue of the presence of the Divine within us.[52] All parts of the visible Universe act reciprocally upon each other as a consequence of being parts of the one living All and being bound by sympathy for each other.[53] Furthermore, the wholeness and perfection of the universe depend upon the unity-in-diversity of the Intellect, or *Noũs*, for, as already mentioned, the sensible world is formed by Nature as an agent of the World Soul on the model of the intelligible world. The World Soul makes "preparatory sketches" of the patterns of the visible world and individual souls work and produce according to "these sketches." In the *Treatise on Providence* the Logos in a sense takes the place of the World Soul and becomes the means whereby the *Noũs* is made present in the sensible world without the World Soul being denied. Here Plotinus also emphasizes the profoundly moral character of the order of the world that the Logos brings about.[54] The Logos thereby discharges

the duties assigned earlier to the World Soul, being at once unifier and harmo-
nizer of the world. In a sense it unifies the two hypostases, that is, the World Soul
and Nature unto itself, being directly in contact with matter and bringing about
the harmony and sympathy pervading all things. Plotinus once again defends in a
most emphatic manner the goodness and justice of the order of the cosmos and the
moral as well as spiritual character of this order.

The grand synthesis created by Plotinus from the metaphysical strands of
earlier Greek thought and especially Platonism resulted in the creation of several
branches of Neoplatonism with different emphases as one finds in the varying
interpretations of the School of Athens and Syria, and it produced such major
figures as Proclus and Iamblichus, who along with Plotinus left a profound mark
upon many of the more esoteric strands of Western thought throughout the
centuries. Furthermore, Neoplatonism was certainly the most important of the
later schools of Greco-Alexandrian philosophy. But its domination was far from
being complete. Besides the antimetaphysical currents of later Greek and Roman
philosophy, there appeared another school of great metaphysical and cosmological
importance that vied with Neoplatonism in spreading its influence and that in
later centuries was adopted as a complement to Neoplatonism that some even
associated with it. This school came to be known as Hermeticism, named after its
mythical founder Hermes but based on texts in Greek that appeared in Alexandria
at the beginning of the Christian era and that contain Egyptian as well as Greek
elements, Hermes being a wedding between an Egyptian and a Greek deity cum
archetype of sage.[55]

The Hermetic writings, including the *Corpus Hermeticum* and the *Tabula
Smaragdina* or *Emerald Table,* which have been attributed to Hermes by both
Islamic and Greek sources,[56] became disseminated in the Islamic world in the
ninth century and also in the West from the eleventh century onward. But it was
especially during the Renaissance that the Hermetic corpus became widely read,
many considering Hermes to have been much more ancient than the Greek
philosophers, and he was referred to as the Egyptian Moses. Hermetic philosophy,
"exteriorized" and made more public after the Middle Ages and henceforth concerned primarily with nature, wielded wide influence upon numerous schools and
figures ranging from Paracelsus, Giordano Bruno, and the Cambridge Platonists
to the young Goethe.[57] In fact, the Hermetic philosophy of nature and its understanding of the natural order, which was opposed to the mechanistic views of
modern science, became nearly synonymous with the understanding of the order
of nature among the more esoteric schools of Western thought until the nineteenth century and has witnessed a major revival of interest in our own day, not
only in occult circles but even among "mainstream" scholars seeking to resuscitate
Hermetic philosophy as a way of looking at the world.[58] Thus, it is important to
turn to the Hermetic understanding of the order of nature not only as an important strand in the tapestry of Greek philosophy, but also as a major intellectual
influence upon later European history.

The Hermetic view of the order of nature is reflected in the twelve sayings or
principles of the secret practices of Hermes (*Verba secretorium Hermetis Tris-*

megisti), these sayings having been considered for centuries as the very essence of Hermetic philosophy by both Muslim and Western alchemists:[59]

> In truth, certainly and without doubt, whatever is below is like that which is above, and whatever is above is like that which is below, to accomplish the miracles of one thing.
>
> Just as all things proceed from One alone by meditation on One alone, so also they are born from this one thing by adaptation.
>
> Its father is the sun and its mother is the moon. The wind has borne it in its body. Its nurse is the earth.
>
> It is the father of every miraculous work in the whole world.
>
> Its power is perfect if it is converted into earth.
>
> Separate the earth from the fire and the subtle from the gross, softly and with great prudence.
>
> It rises from earth to heaven and comes down again from heaven to earth, and thus acquires the power of the realities above and the realities below. In this way you will acquire the glory of the whole world, and all darkness will leave you.
>
> This is the power of all powers, for it conquers everything subtle and penetrates everything solid.
>
> Thus the little world is created according to the prototype of the great world.
>
> From this and in this way, marvellous applications are made.
>
> For this reason I am called Hermes Trismegistus, for I possess the three parts of wisdom of the whole world.
>
> Perfect is what I have said of the work of the sun.[60]

The most important principle among these sayings for the understanding of the order of nature is, of course, the association of the creatures below with those of the world above. There is a reciprocity between the forms of nature here below and the realities of the spiritual or intelligible world, between the Earth and Heaven as understood both cosmologically and alchemically. Furthermore, there are the dual principles, the masculine and the feminine, much like the Chinese *Yang* and *Yin,* which are progenitors of the things of this world. And there is the possibility of the transformation of things in the sense of alchemical transmutation, which also implies inner transformation on the basis of the correspondence between the microcosm and the macrocosm, so foundational to Hermetic philosophy. Finally, it is Hermes Trismegistus, master of knowledge of the realms of Heaven, the Earth, and the intermediate realm, who reveals this knowledge of the order of things, which is not only theoretical but also operative, leading to the production of that inner gold which is the veritable "work of the sun."

Hermeticism repeats in its own way certain of the major theses of the other sapiental schools of philosophy such as Pythagoreanism and Platonism. At the same time it possesses its own unique features including its wedding to the vast enterprise of alchemy with its spiritual, cosmological, psychological, medical, and material dimensions and is of immense religious as well as scientific importance. The esoteric alchemical view of the order of nature derives from Hermeticism as have many of the most important reactions against the mechanization of the concept of the order of nature ever since the Scientific Revolution. Hermeticism must be considered one of the most enduring intellectual currents in Western history despite its marginalization since the seventeenth century.

To summarize the Greek view of the order of nature, it must first of all be remembered that the Greeks did not have one but several views of the order of nature, as we also find in China, India, and the Islamic world. For Plato and Aristotle, natures of things included their goals and the good they actualized, whereas the atomists rejected all teleology and considered the order of nature to be purely mechanical. As for the Skeptics, they held that all attempts to explain nature were futile.[61] As a result of the existence of different schools of the study of nature, three types of cosmology developed:[62]

1. The cosmos is ruled by one supreme Principle who, like a craftsman, has molded the world and created its order, as stated by Plato in *Philebus* and *Timaeus*.
2. The cosmos is balanced between equal and opposite forces, as found in Anaximander, Parmenides, and Empedocles.
3. The cosmos is the scene of universal strife.

Plato and Aristotle accepted the first view, with the difference that Plato considered the "craftsman" of nature to be transcendent and Aristotle considered him to be immanent. As for the Atomists such as Leucippus and Democritus, they strongly opposed the view of any design or order in the universe derived from a Divine Agent, and they were followed in this view by Epicurus and Lucretius, the author of the most detailed source of Epicurean atomism, *De Rerum Natura,* who considered what appears as the order of nature to issue from the mechanical interaction of atoms based upon a law to which all things must conform.[63] Most Greeks, however, opposed this view and considered the Universe to be alive and an organic whole, as asserted by schools as different as the Stoic and the Neoplatonic.

The most important feature of the cosmos accepted by most Greeks was that it is an ordered whole that is intelligible to human beings, although this view was not unanimous and there were certainly some dissenting voices.[64] There was also a hierarchy in the order of nature and, in fact, in the whole of existence, embracing both purely intelligible and natural forms. This hierarchy stretched from the Supreme Good and the Unmoved Mover to the *hylé,* encompassing the world of the intelligences, humans, animals, plants, and numerals in an order that has come to be known as the "great chain of being"[65] and that exercised much influence upon diverse schools of Western thought until its "horizontalization" and temporalization by nineteenth-century evolutionism, which also marked the death of this central metaphysical doctrine in the mainstream of Western thought.[66]

Also, the cosmos was seen as a living organism with an order resembling that of a living being and dominated by the *logos,* which provided both the order and the intelligibility of the cosmos. The Greeks consequently believed in a law (in the cosmic and not necessarily the juridical sense) to which nature conformed, although the interpretation of what this law was differed from one school to another. While Democritus emphasized that things always work in a particular way, much like the mechanistic and mathematical ideas of modern science, and spoke of causal law without speaking of the nature of this law, Aristotle also asserted the necessity of causality while being very much concerned with its nature and purpose. As for the Stoics, they were also keenly interested in the law dominating over the cosmos, law they identified with Fate and at the same time the *logos* of the cosmos.[67] The belief in laws according to which there exists order in nature was, however, shared by most schools of Greek and Roman thought despite differences as to even the meaning of the term law, the Romans being much more juridically oriented than the Greeks.

Furthermore, the great metaphysical and philosophical systems such as Pythagoreanism, Platonism, Aristotelianism, Neoplatonism, Hermeticism, and to some extent Stoicism, although differing on many points, were unanimous in seeing these characteristics in the order of nature and also relating the order of nature to the moral order governing human beings and their society.

But by the end of the Hellenistic period the rebellion of reason against the intellect and the rise of a naturalism that divorced the order of nature from higher orders of reality and that lost sight of the symbolic significance of the cosmos resulted on the one hand in skepticism and on the other in a naturalism and cosmolatry that the early Church Fathers combatted assiduously and that were instrumental in the death of the Greco-Roman civilizations. The great metaphysical and philosophical systems enumerated above did, nevertheless, echo to a large extent but in a speculative and philosophical language many of the principles of the religious vision of the order of nature outlined in the preceding chapter. That is why, once severed from their mythological and naturalistic associations, they came to serve in turn as philosophical categories for the formulation of the religious philosophies of Islam, Judaism, and Christianity in the medieval period and even thereafter. But the development of certain strands of Greek philosophy was also to sow the seeds of the secularization of the cosmos and the destruction of the religious meaning of the order of nature in the West, seeds that were to grow in the Renaissance with the weakening of the Christian civilization of the Middle Ages and the eclipse of the synthesis created between Christianity and Greek philosophy by the Christian philosophers of that period.

MEDIEVAL PHILOSOPHY

During over a millennium that separates Greco-Roman antiquity from the Renaissance, Christian philosophers developed numerous schemes of the order of nature based upon Christian teachings as well as elements drawn from the philosophical heritage of antiquity on the basis of their conformity to various dimensions of the Christian tradition. Among the early figures such men as Origen dealt extensively with this theme, whereas later on such diverse groups as the Dominicans and Franciscans, the Victorines and the Oxford School associated with Robert Grosseteste and Roger Bacon wrote works of great pertinence dealing with this subject. Considering the limitation of space that can be devoted to the medieval view of the subject in our present discussion, we shall limit ourselves to a single example from the Platonic/Neoplatonic and Aristotelian schools of Christian philosophy while remaining mindful of the rich literature that exists on this subject from the point of view of both depth and diversity.

Our representative of the Christian Platonic/Neoplatonic tradition is the ninth-century Irish-Scottish philosopher Johannes Scotus Eriugena (or Erigena) whose best-known writing expounding his metaphysics is entitled *Periphyseon* or *De divisione naturae*. In this major work of Christian philosophy, the author considers Creation not *ab extra* but within the Divine Itself and expands the term "nature" to include all that the mind can conceive of reality.[68] Erigena reshapes and elevates the Boethian concept of nature known to the early Middle Ages to the status of an all-embracing representation of the Universe.[69] In his own words he states:

> As I frequently ponder and so far as my talents allow, ever more carefully investigate the fact that the first and fundamental division of all things which can either be grasped by the mind or lie beyond its grasp is into those that are and those that are not, there comes to mind as a general term for them all what in Greek is called *physis* and in Latin *natura*.[70]

Through His Essence, which is Beyond-Being (*supra-esse*), God creates all creatures in the world of nature and is the efficient cause of all that exists. Man can know the way in which a thing exists (*quia est*) but is unable to unveil the real nature of existents (*quid est*). He can understand Creation and the order of nature but not the true ground of being from which this order issues.

Considering nature as a genus, Erigena divides it into four species as follows:[71]

1. that which creates and is not created—corresponding to God as the Creator.
2. that which is created and creates—corresponding to the intelligible causes and the essences of things.
3. that which is created and does not create—corresponding to the temporal world.
4. that which neither creates nor is created—identified implicitly also with God.

He introduces a nuance between *creare* (to create) and *creari* (to be created), removing the rigid distinction between the Creator and the created, pointing to the esoteric doctrine of Creation in God alluded to in the preceding chapter. Moreover, there is the supernal reality of the Godhead above all categories of conceptual understanding including the universal concept of Being. By virtue of the excellence of His Supra-Being, God creates the intelligible principles or essences of things first *ab intra* before they are existentiated outwardly so that He is the efficient cause of the Universe and the order of nature issues directly from the Divine Order Itself. Also, the very process of nature leads back to God so that He is both the alpha and omega of the order of nature.[72] There is a final "union" between God and the order of nature or Creator and Creation, without this implying pantheism since the *supra-esse* is always transcendent vis-à-vis all that It creates. "Thus the universe which consists of God and creation, previously divided as it were into four forms, is now reduced again to an undivided one, being at the same time principle, cause and end."[73] One might say that the fourfold division of nature is "wrapped up in God"[74] and the order of nature is but the externalization of the Divine Order, God's self-manifestations or theophanies (*dei apparitiones*) being the intermediary stage between God's inaccessible natures and the highest intelligible creatures or angels that mark the descent of the Divine Reality toward Creation and are the immediate principles of the order of nature.

Erigena adds that because man represents all of nature, the damaging of his original state through Original Sin affects all of nature, which has been tainted by the consequences of sin. Consequently, man's vision of the harmony and order of nature is disturbed and he can no longer perceive clearly the beginning and end of this order in God.[75] It is interesting to note in this connection that Erigena considers true philosophy as the means of recovering the original vision of the nature of things. While St. Augustine equated authentic philosophy with religion and identified philosophy as *studium sapientiae,* Erigena went a step further, stating that philosophy stands supreme in that it is concerned with the direct attainment of God. In his *Annotationes in Martianum Capellam* he made his famous assertion *Nemo intrat in caelum nisi per philosophiam* (No one can enter Heaven except through philosophy). He thereby identified philosophy, which as *sophia* exists at the heart of religion, in a manner very similar to numerous Islamic philosophers who identified true philosophy with the *al-Ḥaqīqah* or the Truth lying at the heart of the Divine Law or *al-Sharī'ah*. Little did Erigena know that a few centuries later philosophy in Europe would change in such a way that not only would much of it no longer be the condition for entering Heaven but that the acceptance of the tenets of many of its schools was the best means for being disqualified from entering paradise altogether. Moreover, modern philosophy would become the source of most of the arguments for the denial of the very existence of Heaven.

As for Christian Aristotelian philosophy, no one is more worthy of consideration than the angelic doctor Thomas Aquinas, the thirteenth-century master of Christian philosophy whose influence continues to this day in certain Catholic circles despite the theological transformations of the past three decades.[76] St. Thomas Aquinas is not, of course, a pure Aristotelian as several scholars have demonstrated.[77] Nevertheless, having absorbed the thought of the Islamic Peripatetic philosophers, especially Ibn Sīnā, which itself includes both Aristotelian and Neoplatonic elements, and seeking to respond to the more pure Aristotelianism of the Latin Averroists, Aquinas did create a major synthesis in which basic elements of Aristotelian philosophy, especially in the domain of the philosophy of nature, were incorporated within the matrix of Christian philosophy, leading to the establishment of a new philosophical perspective of vast significance whose views of the order of nature are of great consequence for the understanding of the development of this idea in much of later Western philosophy and also science.[78]

The most important point to emphasize in Aquinas's view of the order of nature is that God rules over His Creation through providence (*providentia*), which for Aquinas means protective care, and it is in this providence that we must seek the root of the order of nature. Creatures are created by God *ex nihilo*, depend completely upon Him, and are moved by God, who is both the efficient cause and the final cause of all things. Furthermore, the ideas of things are contained in the Divine Mind, which "contains the whole pattern of things moving to their end."[79] Providence is the exemplar of things "ordained to their purpose." In fact, God has ordained all things to an end and directs them toward that end.

> Things are said to be ruled or governed by virtue of their being ordained to their end. Now, things are ordered to the ultimate end which God intends, that is, divine goodness, not only by the fact that they perform their operations, but also by the fact that they exist, since to the extent that they exist, they bear the likeness of divine goodness which is the end for things. . . . God, through his understanding and will, is the cause of being for all things. Therefore, he preserves all things in being through his intellect and will.[80]

Although this view seems to imply predestination, it does not preclude the possibility of miracles since God is omnipotent and He does not do violence to the created order in bringing about miracles. In any case, all order and all miracles are effects of God's Will and He is as much present in order as in miracles, which seem to break the order of nature.

For Aquinas, Creation is participation in the Platonic sense in Being,[81] and in contrast to Dionysius who considers God to be above *esse*, he identifies God with *esse* or Pure Being. Creatures participate in being, but the "nature of being" (*natura essendi*) in its infinity and without any limitation belongs to God alone.[82] Creatures come into being from the *rationes ideales* and in their likeness. Aquinas compares this process to art (*natura imitatutur artem divinam*).

> Because all things are related to the divine intellect as artifacts are to art, everything is consequently called true insofar as it possesses the proper form according to which it imitates the divine art. And in this way "being" and "true" are convertible, because every natural thing, through its form, is conformed to the divine art.[83]

In imitating art in its taditional sense,[84] nature fulfills the intention of the Divine Logos. In the same way that the patterns or Forms of artifacts are in the mind of the artificer, the Forms of natural objects are contained in the Divine Intellect. God's knowledge is prior to things and constitutes their "measure," intelligibility, and order.[85]

In the cosmos created by God and "measured" by His knowledge there is both structure and hierarchy based, first of all, upon the distinction between form and matter or actuality and potentiality, form being actuality that determines the nature of *esse* for matter, whereas matter is potentiality, and second between essence and existence. The Universe is arranged in a hierarchical manner on the basis of the degree of actuality, God being pure actuality and below Him standing the levels of angels, souls, sensible forms, and finally matter or potentiality. The universal hierarchy, or great chain of being, is determined by the degree of actuality of the form involved in each level of the hierarchy, but it can also be said that the heirarchy is based upon the degree of likeness to God.[86] The hierarchy is also one of *simplicitas*. The higher the form, the simpler it is as it approaches God, who as Pure Being and also Pure Act is also Pure Simplicity.

The Universe, according to St. Thomas is an *ordo* among whose members there exists proper proportions. The whole order is created by God and bestowed with hierarchy. God has determined the grade of each thing according to His Providence and Justice, the prerequisite of order in the cosmos being the relation of all things to God and not only to each other. The purpose of this order is to fulfill the object of Creation, which is God Himself as the Supreme God. This *ordo ad Deum* is in the nature of things and fulfills their purpose, for the very existence of the order of nature implies the drawing of all Creation by God back to Himself.[87] The universe is an ordered whole, and although each being is good in itself, the total order is of even greater good.[88]

It is important to insist that St. Thomas, like Aristotle, saw intelligibility and therefore order within the world of becoming and not only in the domain of the immutable archetypes.[89] The Thomistic Universe possesses a structure that is ultimately intelligible, a Universe in which all things imitate God through their very existence so that Gilson could refer to the whole cosmology of St. Thomas as *De imitatione Dei*.[90] The attacks against this vast synthesis and masterly exposition of Christian philosophy during the Renaissance and the feeble response of the defenders of the Angelic Doctor, at least in most of Western Europe, caused the eclipse of this grand vision of the order of nature in which the religious element was preserved despite the lack of emphasis upon the symbolic nature of all cosmic reality in the manner of other forms of traditional cosmology and metaphysics.[91] And yet the Thomistic view of the order of nature, far from disappearing from the scene, continued to be cultivated in certain circles and was revived especially in France and Germany through the neo-Thomistic movement at the beginning of the twentieth century.

MODERN PHILOSOPHY SINCE THE RENAISSANCE

The Renaissance marks a rupture with the Middle Ages that is at once abrupt and transitional. On the one hand one observes the rise of humanism, to which we shall turn in Chapter 5, and a new conception of mankind markedly different from his medieval ancestors. On the other hand some of the intellectual trends of the

Middle Ages still continue although they become ever more weakened and marginalized. The Renaissance is witness on the philosophical scene to the continuation of Christian Aristotelianism along with attacks against it, the rediscovery of Platonism and Hermeticism, and intense interest in the esoteric dimensions of Greco-Alexandrian thought in general and yet movements against the esoteric perspective, interest in the philosophy and practice of magic, and at the same time strong opposition to it. The Renaissance intellectual life seems like a chariot driven by several horses moving for a short period together until the chariot is overturned and each horse gallops off in a different direction.[92] Whatever the case, although elements of the medieval and ancient ideas of the order of nature survive, what is most important during this period is that the seeds are sown for what we call modern philosophy and modern science, which were to appear upon the scene during the latter part of the Renaissance and later in the seventeenth century.

As far as the view concerning the order of nature is concerned, much of Renaissance thought displays a general anti-Aristotelian tendency in negating teleology even in its more diluted Aristotelian sense and in seeking to explain things through their efficient causes that exist within them. This opposition to finality and teleology is clearly observable in the thought of Francis Bacon, whose role in the rise of a science based upon power and domination over nature is well known. There was also a tendency to deny the time-honored view that nature imitates eternal Forms, as can be seen in the sixteenth-century philosopher Bernardino Telesio, who emphasized that nature possessed its own innate forms and intrinsic activity, which generated motion, order, and all the structure observable in nature.[93]

Altogether the dominant thought of the Renaissance tended to view nature as something divine and self-creative, and many writers of that period distinguished between complex natural processes and transformations they identified with *natura naturata* and a force immanent within nature that directed these processes, which they called *natura naturans*. This view did not, however, lead to a rediscovery of the sacramental character of nature because the conception of nature as "divine" took place for the most part outside the sacred world of Christianity and was independent of a revealed universe of meaning. "Divine" in this context therefore could not possess the same meaning and efficacy as we find in the primal traditions or for that matter in other religions mentioned earlier in this text. On the contrary, this "divine" view of nature so closely identified with Renaissance *magia*—which also saw nature as a living being—was cut off from the protection of a living tradition, and this gave way very rapidly during the latter years of the Renaissance to a mechanistic view of the world dominated by mathematics. Early Renaissance concerns with magic and astrology and correspondences between various domains of nature were replaced rather quickly with interest in mathematical astronomy and physics, and this profound change of interest was based upon the change in the understanding of the order of nature that can be observed in that short transitional period of European history separating the medieval from the modern period, the period that later revisionist history was to call the Renaissance.

This transitional character of Renaissance cosmology and philosophy of nature can be seen in the transition from Giordano Bruno to Cartesian dualism. For Bruno,[94] who in a sense provided a philosophical interpretation of Copernicanism while drawing from the Hermetic tradition, the cosmos was a living unified whole with the same laws and order dominating over all of it. There was no Prime Mover beyond the cosmos, but all order and movement in nature originated from within itself. The Universe, infinite in spatial extension, was comprised of a plastic matter that was the matrix of all change, and Form or God was the source of this movement but was immanent to nature. Hence the pantheism of which Bruno was accused and for which he was condemned. But philosophically speaking, Bruno was left with a dualism between mind and body, or God and nature, which has characterized much of modern thought to this day, although his dualism functioned within a living unified cosmos. It was in following this background of thought that Spinoza posited both matter and mind as attributes of a single substance he called God but also Nature, which, when extended, became matter and, when thinking, became mind. Monism was, however, not always of the Spinozan kind leading to pantheism, but in certain circles it also became combined with Galilean materialism as seen in Pierre Gassendi and led to that extreme form of materialism that saw all order as issuing from matter and, in fact, identified all of reality with matter, some of its champions even developing a sense of "religious piety" toward matter itself, as one sees in Paul Henri Holbach's *Du Système de la nature*.[95]

A much more significant development of the dualism displayed in Bruno's thought was to be found in the dualism characterizing the ideas of the father of modern Western philosophy, René Descartes. With Descartes one encounters that radical departure from the traditional perspective in the understanding of the order of nature that has characterized and influenced nearly all of later modern thought. For Descartes, extension is an essential attribute of matter, and all genuine properties of matter must derive from extension, which also includes duration. In his *Meditations,* Descartes even considers this conception to be innate to human intelligence like the concepts of God and mind. The basic qualities of things are related to extension and are mathematical, whereas all other qualities are secondary and unimportant.[96] Thus, in the manner of Galileo, Descartes discards all the qualitative aspects of nature, equating all of nature with a kinematic reality that can be explained through geometry. He reduces physics to mathematics and matter practically to space, failing to distinguish between an object and its environment. The order of nature thus becomes nothing but mathematical order and the physical world an entirely mechanical one from which finality is excluded. In his *Principles,* Descartes sought to derive the principles of his physics from metaphysics but not in the traditional sense, for his metaphysics itself was no more than philosophization about a nature completely quantified and mathematicized.

Descartes's physics lost the day to Newton's, but his thoroughly mechanistic conception of the order of nature based on the radical dualism between mind and matter and also between the knowing subject and the known object won the day and wielded an influence that is to be seen everywhere today in the modern view of nature. Descartes removed from nature all its ontological reality save its aspect of quantity, and he helped to create the mechanical notion of the order of nature and the vision of nature as a pure "it" shorn from all spiritual realities, a view that dominates the horizon of modern civilization despite all the later transformations of Western philosophy and science. Like most modern philosophers, Descartes mistook a mathematics of nature for the philosophy of nature and created a philosophy that would serve the purposes of the science of his day, to which we shall turn in the next chapter.[97]

He thus embarked upon the path that led to positivism, which replaced the philosophy of nature with the ideas of Auguste Comte and Ernst Mach in the last century and which severed the links between the order of nature and all questions of ontology and causality. Henceforth, most of the so-called metaphysical systems in European thought, certainly the well-known ones, were based on a philosophy of nature "which was the mechanistic hypothesis of the physico-mathematical method."[98] This was not metaphysics in the traditional sense as one finds in the works of a Śankara or Ibn 'Arabī or within the Western tradition in a Plato or Plotinus or in more recent times in a Böhme or von Baader. Rather, it was a generalization based upon the mathematization and quantification of nature that separated the order of nature from the intelligible world in the Platonic sense, from the moral principles dominating over human life, and from any spiritual reality that human beings and nature could share save through the physical reality of matter and motion. The consequences of such a perspective for the human condition and its catastrophic results for the very survival of life on earth were immense, but they are only now becoming evident for all to see.

Naturally, Descartes had his detractors. His countryman Blaise Pascal expressed his opposition openly when he wrote, "I cannot forgive Descartes. In all his philosophy he would have been quite willing to dispense with God. But he had to make Him give a fillip to set the world in motion; beyond this, he has no further need to God."[99] Pascal himself sought to revive some of the earlier doctrines concerning the order of nature—for example, when he considered nature to be the image of God, displaying perfections that result from being the image of *God* and imperfections due to its being precisely *image* and not the Divine Reality Itself.[100] Pascal was even to meditate upon the order of nature as reflecting the Divine Infinity in a manner reminiscent of the metaphysical doctrines of a Nicolas of Cusa and other masters of Christian gnosis and esotericism. In one of his most famous meditations Pascal observed:

> Let man then contemplate the whole of nature in her full and grand majesty, and turn his vision from the low objects which surround him. Let him gaze on the brilliant light, set like an eternal lamp to illumine the universe; let the earth appear to him a point in comparison with the vast circle described by the sun; and let him wonder at the fact that this vast circle is itself but a very fine point in comparison with that described by the stars in their revolution round the firmament. But if our view be arrested there, let our

imagination pass beyond; it will sooner exhaust the power of conception than nature [will supply] material for conception. The whole visible world is only an imperceptible atom in the whole bosom of nature. No idea approaches it. We may enlarge our conceptions beyond all imaginable space; we only produce atoms in comparison with the reality of things. It is an infinite sphere, the center of which is everywhere, the circumference nowhere. In short, it is the greatest sensible mark of the almighty power of God that imagination loses itself in that thought. [101]

In this passage Pascal seems to grasp intuitively that nexus between the order of nature as ordinarily understood and the Divine Nature, Infinite and Eternal, that encompasses the order of nature and is yet ubiquitous at every point of cosmic manifestation.

Later in the seventeenth century Leibniz, also a mathematician like Descartes, was to oppose certain basic tenets of the Cartesian view of the order of nature. His monadology is in fact a late attempt in the history of European philosophy to preserve some of the characteristics of traditional metaphysics and is significant for this very reason as well as for its role in seventeenth-century European philosophy. [102] The Leibnizian monad is at once a point spatially related to other points and a mind that perceives its environment. The monads have unity and spontaneous activity. They are in the world and a mirror upon the world outside themselves, each monad receiving effects at every moment in such a manner as to mirror what is happening elsewhere. In his *Système nouveau de la nature et de la communication des substances,* Leibniz asserts further that everything that happens to each substance or monad comes from within itself and derives spontaneously from its own nature, the only influence upon each monad being God. Yet there is "a pre-established harmony" created by God by virtue of which all things act in harmony and order rules over the Universe.

Leibniz placed a great deal of emphasis upon the significance of order, and his general principles, which are the foundations of order in nature, include the principle of continuity, the idea that every action involves a reaction, and the motion of cause and effect. There is also the principle that nature is everywhere the same and yet everywhere varied, or in his own famous words *tout comme ici* and *che per variar la natura e bella.* Nature is a vast organism whose lesser parts are also organisms permeated by life, growth, purpose, and effort forming a continuous chain of being from what appears as almost mechanical to the highest consciousness, with a nisus toward higher grades of being that dominate over members of the chain. God, whom Leibniz calls the Monad of monads, has created harmony between monads as well as between the material and mental aspects of monads, each of which possesses its own laws. God has chosen what is best for things by willing them to exist in this "best of possible worlds" dominated by a divinely established order and harmony. [103]

Altogether, Leibniz's view of the order of nature echoes within the context of seventeenth-century European philosophy—already subjugated by the mathematics of nature growing out of the physics of the day—some of the themes of traditional philosophy such as the divinely established harmony of nature and the great chain of being. This is not surprising coming from the pen of one who considered himself to be a follower of the *philosophia perennis*[104] and who played a major role in making this term famous, although he did not have full access to the totality of traditional metaphysics and what traditional authorities understand by perennial philosophy.

Although seventeenth-century philosophers took physics very seriously as definitive knowledge and the mechanical view of the order of nature expounded by Descartes and others won the day, despite the criticisms of a Pascal or a Leibniz, the dualism implied in the view issuing from such a vision of nature encountered many difficulties that became fully manifest in the eighteenth century. This dualism was in fact challenged seriously by a number of philosophers, among whom George Berkeley is particularly interesting, from the point of view of the order of nature. Berkeley pointed out that the idea of nature as pure quantity devoid of quality and movement, moved by a *vis impressa* and the operation of external efficient causes, is itself an abstract idea.[105] The world of pure quantity without quality as depicted by Galileo and Descartes, far from being the fruit of experience, is itself an abstraction, an *ens rationis,* and only an aspect of the reality of nature. Furthermore, if the qualitative aspects of nature exist only in the mind, as claimed by Descartes and also John Locke, and therefore an integral aspect exists only in the mind, then nature itself is the work of the mind.

Berkeley claimed, consequently, that if there is one substance which is real, it is the mind that first creates nature in its fullness and then abstracts from it the physical world of classical physics limited to pure quantity. This mind, however, is not the human mind but the Divine Mind that generates the world through His Thought. In opposing the dualism and materialism of his day, Berkeley therefore reverts to an idealism that views the origin of the order of nature in the mind, not the mind of the individual observer, but the Divine Mind in whom—similar to what one finds in Plotinian doctrine and also in such Islamic philosophers as Ibn Sīnā—contemplation or "thought" coincides with cosmogenesis.

It is in light of Berkeley's thesis, along with the doubts of David Hume about one's ability to know the cause of things and even causality itself, and his opposition to taking physics as the point of departure for philosophizing that one must seek to understand the significance of Kant's critique of knowledge.[106] Kant realized the limitations inherent in the scientific manner of knowing things, a way of understanding that precluded the possibility of knowing the essence of things in themselves. His "physicalism" led him, however, to generalize this agnosticism to all forms of knowing, thereby refusing to intelligence any possibility of knowing the essence of things, a thesis totally opposed to that of traditional metaphysics, and an intellectual suicide to which reference has been made as the most intelligent way of being unintelligent.[107]

In any case, Kant in his "Transcendent Analytics" in the *Critique of Pure Reason* opposes the thesis of Berkeley and claims that it is the purely human mind (*bloss menschliches*) that makes (and not creates) nature as understood by the physicists. Yet this function is not performed by the individual human mind, but neither is it performed by the Mind of God. Rather, it is the "transcendent ego," the pure understanding that is immanent in all human thought which fulfills this function. For Kant, the order of nature envisaged by the physicist is an essentially rational and also necessary product of the human way of understanding things. But the mind has no way of knowing things in themselves.[108] This at least is Kant's view in his first *Critique* concerning the foundations of natural science. In his *Critique of Practical Reason,* however, he states that at least in moral experience we can know our minds as realities in themselves, whereas in his *Critique of Judgement* he implies that the reality underlying the phenomena of nature is of the same character as mind, "so that what we know in our practical or moral experience is of the same kind as what we think, but cannot know, in our theoretical experience as students of natural science."[109]

There is thus a contradiction in Kant's "subjective idealism," which was to be discussed by many a later philosopher. But his view of the imposition of the categories one observes in nature by the mind upon nature, the rejection of those categories that relate the phenomenal world to its Divine Principle, and the rejection of the possibility of essential and principial knowledge all played an important role in further alienating Western thought from its own metaphysical and religious traditions as far as the order of nature was concerned. Kant's theory about nature was not in reality a theory of knowledge, but a theory of scientific knowledge that claimed for itself the status of a theory of knowledge, thereby rejecting other ways of knowing the order of nature.

Moreover, Kant was never clear about *how* we think nor about the question of things in themselves, a question Johann Fichte tried to remove as a problem by claiming that mind produced nature out of nothing and that Hegel was to develop much further. It is also important to note that in arguing for an *a priori* basis for physics while accepting observation in his *Metaphysical Foundations of Natural Science,* Kant was setting the stage for the development of the *Naturphilosophie* associated with Friedrich Schelling and to some extent Hegel, which stood opposed to the mechanical view of the natural world inherited from the seventeenth-century physicists and that served as the point of departure for Kant. Thus, the "subjectivization" of the order of nature and the denial to human intelligence the possibility of knowledge of the essential nature of things in Kant mark an important stage in the separation between the religious and metaphysical views of the order of nature on the one hand, and the prevalent scientific and philosophical views of that order in the West on the other, and they denote the end process of a cycle which begins with the mechanization of the order of nature in the hands of Galileo, Descartes, and other philosophers and physicists of their day.

Schelling, the nineteenth-century near-contemporary of Hegel, is best known for the development of *Naturphilosophie,* which was to have a deep impact in Germany throughout the nineteenth century in not only philosophy but also natural science itself, to which we shall turn in the next chapter.[110] According to Schelling, matter and consciousness or spirit (which gains knowledge of nature) and nature (which is known) are the same. It is this identity that makes it possible to know nature in itself and without imposition of external human factors. Schell-

ing sought to renounce transcendent explanations and to emphasize the immanence of order within nature. He accentuated the autonomy of nature and that "all
its laws are immanent, or, *nature is its own lawgiver*" and "what takes place in
nature must be explained from the active and mobile principles which lie within
it, or: *nature is self-sufficient* (the autarky of nature)."[111]

There exists within nature at once limitation and ever renewed transcending
of these limitations, the tandency toward development and its restraint, which are
identified with *natura naturans* and *natura naturata*. Each product of nature is the
result of a restraint placed upon the infinite productivity of nature by nature
herself. The order of nature must therefore be understood as a process that is
teleological. There are three levels of potency in nature; the first involves the
derivation of matter and the order and structure of the world from the three
principles of repulsion, attraction, and gravitation. The second potency causes the
qualitative nature of the inorganic to be deduced from the three principles of
magnetism, electricity, and chemistry. The third potency involves the organic
world, including plants, animals, and human beings, and it involves the three
principles of reproduction, irritability, and sensitivity. Moreover, the organic and
the inorganic are interdependent and a preestablished harmony embraces both of
them. Schelling strongly opposed the mechanistic view of nature, and he sought
to explain the order of nature as emanating from within it, thereby bestowing a
kind of divine status to nature reminiscent in some ways of the theories of the
Stoics. His views held great interest for a few decades and were taken up even by
some scientists, but they could not overcome the mechanistic conception of order
that continued to dominate the mainstream of European science and which,
despite the philosophy of nature of Hegel, was to give rise to the positivism of
such figures as Comte and Mach at the end of the nineteenth century.

Hegel's views concerning the order of nature appeared upon the scene when
interest in *Naturphilosophie* had already begun to wane to some extent. But his
views were nevertheless very influential, covering the whole spectrum of thought
from conservative Protestant theology to the militant atheism of Marx and his
followers. Hegel's view of the order of nature starts with the question of how we
think of a thing in itself. In contrast to Kant, Hegel rejected scientific claim to
exclusive knowledge of nature and believed that it is possible to know a thing in
itself. What can be known as the thing in itself is the pure being of a thing
without any determinations, but pure being having no particularities cannot be
described. Hence, there is a nothingness that confronts being and there is a
dialectical process of going from being to nothingness, and this precisely is
becoming. Hegel developed what he called the "science of logic" on the basis of
this dialectic. For him a concept is like an organism that moves from potentiality
to actuality, concepts being like Platonic Ideas except in a dynamic state. There
exists a logical process that precedes the process of nature, and God's process of
"self-creator" is at the same time the process of the Creation of the world.[112]

There exists a dynamic world of forms associated with the dialectic reflected
in Hegelian logic that Hegel calls Idea and which is the source of nature and its
order. For Hegel, and in opposition to Berkeley and Kant, Idea is an objective

reality at once the source of nature and mind. [113] According to Hegel's *Encyclopedia of Philosophical Sciences,* philosophy has three parts: logic or the theory of the Idea; the theory of nature; and the theory of mind. The science of logic is the key to the other two, for it deals with the Idea and its dialectical process, which is the principle of the dialectical processes of both nature and mind.

For Hegel, nature is real and not just an illusion, nor is it the product of any mind. Like Plato and Aristotle, Hegel believed that nature is always trying to reach the full embodiment of the forms but does not succeed completely. But there is a nisus in nature seeking to become something definite and approaching this goal asymptomatically without ever reaching it. The laws of nature describe, therefore, general tendencies and are statistical but do not concern all individual cases. Furthermore, the scientific study of nature is always approximate, precisely because of the indeterminacy present in nature where forms are not fully realized.

The forms of nature differ from both the Idea discussed in logic and the forms in the mind because the latter are never fully realized. The reason for the lack of full embodiment of forms in nature is that nature is essentially externality and within it everything is external to everything else—that is, everything is outside everything else (hence space) and everything is outside itself (hence time). The forms in nature are therefore doubly broken up and never fully realized. Nature is also constant activity and process, being a living organism. This view naturally contradicted the Newtonian concept of matter being in a particular place and moment of time and was in conflict with the physics of Hegel's day. The dynamic process of nature, reflecting the dialectic of Hegelian logic, leads, according to Hegel, to the mind in a natural way as an egg leads to a chick, but this transformation does not take place in time. Rather, it is ideal or logical, and he opposed clearly the evolutionary theory of transformation in time, which was to revolutionize the biology of the nineteenth century. For Hegel, each stage in the chain of being involves a new principle and a lower link in the chain; dead matter, for instance, could not evolve into a higher link—for example, life—simply through the passage of time. Hegel sought to understand the order of nature in terms of the dialectical process of what he called logic and in a manner that was opposed to the physics of his day and also the idea of evolution in time, which was to have such a major impact upon later European philosophy and science.

The first major Western philosopher to develop a philosophy of nature to embrace Darwinism at the end of the nineteenth century and beginning of the twentieth century was Henri Bergson, especially in his earlier writings where he espoused the idea of the "life force" or *élan vital.* [114] For Bergson in his *Creative Evolution* the only reality of nature is life, which has created the mind and is open to the process of change leading to genuine novelties. Matter is only what the mind understands of reality in order to manipulate and master it and is only a figment of human reason useful for action but not real. The whole cosmos is brought about by a vital process that Bergson termed "creative evolution." In such a cosmos there is no efficient cause but only the *élan vital.* Nor is there a final cause. The *élan vital* has no goal or *teleos*; it is sheer force not responsible to any law, order, or pattern outside itself. The order of nature and its laws are in fact nothing more than structures that the flow of nature adopts for a while. There is no distinction between substances and the intelligible laws these substances obey. Both are parts of a process of change producing things as well as the ever-changing laws according to which things change.

Bergson's views—which are another form of subjectivism opposed to the objectivity of an intelligible order in the name of an emergent evolution, that denies the very categories of intelligence—mark the final destruction of the understanding of the order of nature as deriving from a principle transcending the world of change, as asserted by Plato, or permanent but immanent within becoming, as one sees in Aristotle. It is the final surrender of all categories of immutability to the world of change and becoming. In his later life Bergson was to turn closer to the tenets of Catholic theology, but his idea of creative evolution continued to draw attention and was to find its followers among such figures as C. Lloyd Morgan, J. C. Smuts, Samuel Alexander, and other champions of emergent evolution, and it marked the beginning of a current of philosophical thought that has played a dominant role in more recently held views of the order of nature in the West.

The twentieth century has witnessed philosophical currents as diverse as positivism, for which the order of nature is meaningless outside operational and scientifically determined definitions, and which marks the final and complete surrender of philosophy to the natural sciences, to the phenomenology of a Max Scheler, which opposed strongly the very tenets of positivism. It is impossible to describe even briefly the many views concerning the order of nature by philosophers of so many diverse views, yet mostly still influenced by the "mathematics of nature" issuing from the physical sciences. We shall therefore limit ourselves to a single figure, but one who is among the most important in the domain of philosophical cosmology and what pertains to the order of nature. That individual is Alfred North Whitehead, whose intellectual activities cover the first half of the twentieth century.[115]

At once a great mathematician and an accomplished philosopher, Whitehead returned to the philosophical understanding of the order of nature something of the Platonic doctrine of intelligibility, although in contrast to Plato he emphasized the significance and reality of nature and its constant becoming, which he saw, however, in terms of moving patterns. For him everything that exists belongs to the "order of nature," which is comprised of actual entities organized into "societies."[116] These "societies" constitute a whole that is always greater than its parts and are "more than a set of entities to which a class name applies; that is to say, it [societies] involves more than a mere mathematical conception of order."[117] Whitehead therefore repudiates categorically the equating of the order of nature with the mere quantitative order of mathematics.

Nature is in fact an organism not merely reducible to its components but dependent upon the pattern or structure in which the parts are composed together as a whole. Nature is also a process and not a substance in the Aristotelian sense of the term; in fact, substance and activity are the same, as also asserted by modern physics. Cosmic process has a direction and possesses two basic characteristics:

extensiveness or development upon the stage of time, and space and teleology. Whitehead also posits other worlds he calls "cosmic epochs," each cosmic epoch possessing laws that are arbitrary and not perfectly obeyed. In fact, the laws of any cosmic epoch are short-lived and are followed by instances of disorder that subvert the existing order, leading to another kind of order. [118] In contrast to other evolutionists such as Samuel Alexander, however, Whitehead considers new patterns that appear in the world to be both immanent and transcendent, being "eternal objects" in the Platonic sense. God is Infinite and as such is the infinite lure toward which all processes direct themselves, in a sense like Aristotle's God in His cosmological role. Also, in contrast to other evolutionists, Whitehead does not consider life to be evolved from matter in time but considers matter as an abstraction. He thereby outlines a theory of the order of nature that, while being another version of modern cosmology, reasserts in its own fashion some of the basic tenets of the traditional philosophies of the West.

We could not conclude this discourse about the philosophical understanding of the order of nature in the West without saying something about the revival of perennial philosophy in the contemporary period and its reassertion of traditional metaphysics. This reconstitutes the deepest meaning of the order of nature and its ontological roots following several centuries of more or less decline of traditional doctrines resulting from the advent of schools of modern philosophy based on the surrender of philosophical thought to a quantitative view of the order of nature emerging from the physical sciences. In recent decades some of the traditional schools of philosophy such as Thomism have been revised along with their philosophy of nature, [119] but the purest expression of the perennial philosophy is to be found in the metaphysical expositions of the traditionalists, and therefore it is to the foremost living figure of this school, Frithjof Schuon, that we turn to conclude our discussion of the philosophical understanding of the order of nature in the West, although "philosophical" in this context must be understood strictly in its traditional and not profane sense. Moreover, these doctrines are far from being limited to the West.

Schuon emphasizes first of all that the world as object cannot but derive its reality, order, and meaning from the Supreme Reality or the Divine Order or, to quote his words, "There is also the metaphysical Object which confers on the world, and thus on what the world contains, all of its reality and all of its meaning." [120] The world or the order of nature derives ontologically from the Divine Principle, which, however, is not only above or beyond the cosmos but also immanent within it.

> The cosmic object—the world—is as if suspended between two complementary dimensions, namely transcendence and immanence: on the one hand, God is the "Other" who is infinitely "above" the world, and on the other hand, the world is His manifestation in which He is present; this implies that without this immanence the world would be reduced to nothing, and that the world—and all that it contains—is necessarily symbolical. [121]

The conditions of existence on the sensible or the relative level cannot but be rooted in the Divine Order, for the order of nature is ultimately nothing but the irradiation of the Divine Principle.

> The Infinite by its radiation brought about so to speak by the pressure—or the overflowing—of the innumerable possibilities, transposes the substance of the Absolute, namely the Sovereign Good, into relativity; this transposition give rise a priori to the reflected image of the Good, namely created Being. The Good, which coincides with the Absolute, is thus prolonged in the direction of relativity and first gives rise to Being, which contains the archetypes, and then to Existence, which manifests them in indefinitely varied modes and according to the rhythms of the diverse cosmic cycles.[122]

The Divine Order, possessing the attributes of Wisdom, Power, and Goodness, comprises three degrees of Reality: the Beyond-Being, Being, and Existence. The latter finds its most perfect expression in the Logos, revelation or Divine manifestation, which is "the direct and central reflection of Being in the cosmic order; it is thus that the Divine Order enters into the cosmos without ceasing to be what it is, and without the cosmos ceasing to be what it is."[123] Macrocosmically this Divine manifestation corresponds in the Abrahamic universe to the archangelic order and in Hinduism to the *Buddhi*. Furthermore, the lower realms of manifestation are of necessity related to this nexus between the Divine and cosmic orders and have their roots ultimately in the Divine Order itself.

The fundamental conditions of sensible existence that determine what we consider to be the order of nature are matter/energy, form, and number situated in space and time. The principle of matter/energy is ether, which is the principle of the elements, and matter may be said to be the sensible manifestation of existence itself. Form is the manifestation of an idea or archetype in the Platonic sense and is contained ultimately as a possibility in Divine Knowledge. As for number, it manifests the unlimitedness of cosmic possibility, which itself reflects the infinitude of the Divine Possibility. It can also be said that ether, the principle of matter/energy, is the direct manifestation of pure existence; the sphere as the perfect form, the image of the primordial archetype and the number one, the principle of all numbers, the direct reflection of the Unique Divine Principle containing innumerable possibilities as the number one already contains all numbers within itself.[124] As for time and space, their possibility is wed to that of things, but even they are not bound to the physical realm but "include psychic as well as physical phenomena, but do not reach the domain of the spirit."[125] Symbolically, however, even time and space have a metaphysical significance and have their root in the Principle itself.

Schuon deals extensively with the poles of subject and object, concrete and abstract time, manner of the delineation of space and the rhythms of time, and many other questions of a cosmological order that reveal the significance of the parameters and conditions of the cosmic order beyond that order and unveil the manner in which the roots of the order of nature are sunk in the Divine Order from which the natural order issues. In expounding this metaphysical doctrine of the meaning of the order of nature, Schuon at once reaffirms the teachings of the traditional schools of thought both in the West and in Oriental metaphysical teachings, and he responds to and repudiates the several centuries of development of Western philosophy based upon the negation of perennial wisdom and the systematization by thinkers of their own limitations and absolutization of their own relative understanding of things. The final result of such a process, which is now so evident, is the denial of the Absolute and even the category of the truth itself from so much of contemporary philosophy, many of whose well-known voices are now declaring its immanent demise.

During the past few centuries, as the mainstream of Western philosophy surrendered itself to the findings of modern science and sought to create a "metaphysics" on the basis of a mathematical understanding of nature taken as a legitimate philosophy of nature, those in the West who sought to preserve the older understanding of the deeper significance of the order of nature became marginalized in the arena of Western intellectual life or were relegated to the realm of the "occult" and the exotic. Modern philosophical schools came to occupy the center of the stage, each containing partial truths integrated into a whole that, taken in its totality, was false and soon was attacked, criticized, and replaced by another "philosophy." Furthermore, parallel with this ongoing process, the traditional understanding of the Divine Origin of the order of nature, the rapport between cosmic and moral law, the hierarchic nature of cosmic order, and many other teachings that various traditional schools of Western philosophy shared with each other, and with the metaphysical teachings of other traditions, continued to be criticized and opposed. The prevalent view in modern Western society of the independence of the order of nature from any other order of reality, the destruction of the spiritual significance of nature, the reductions of the laws of the cosmos to purely mathematical ones, and many other basic concepts foundational to the present-day crisis between man and nature are not only the products of modern science but most of all of modern philosophy, which has sought to create an entire worldview on the basis of a purely quantitative understanding of nature, which itself is a philosophical supposition underlying modern science.

The resuscitation of traditional metaphysics by the expositors of the *philosophia perennis* such as Guénon and Schuon is significant not only in providing a veritable *Sophia* at a time when the well-trodden paths of modern philosophy have reached the impasse announced by so many of their practitioners, but also in opening the door to those other intellectual and metaphysical worlds that have dominated the horizons of the followers of other religions over the millennia. If those followers are participating fully with their Western brothers and sisters in the destruction of the world of nature, they nevertheless do so from a very different intellectual background, a point that we shall discuss further in Chapter 6. For them at least the voices of a Chu Hsi, the masters of the *Sāṃkhya,* or the expositors of *ishrāqī* theosophy have not been completely drowned by such a loud cacophany, and separated by such a wide chasm, as the noise drowning the voice of the Western sages of old and the barrier separating modern Westerners from the teachings of, say, a St. Maximus the Confessor or an Erigena. The exposition of traditional teachings is also of the greatest significance in the light of the existing difference between the Western inheritors of modern philosophy and non-Westerners in that it can make and has in fact already made the living teachings of the East available in a manner that can resonate in the mind and soul of Westerners in quest of the truth. It also makes it easier to penetrate through the philosophical veils of the past few centuries, to which we have alluded in the pages above, so as to reach and appreciate fully the import of the traditional Western schools of philosophy and their very pertinent teachings concerning the order of nature.

Finally, the metaphysical doctrines in general and the meaning of the order of nature in particular contained in the *philosophia perennis* allow us to understand better and more critically both the traditional philosophies of the West, long relegated to the realm of mere historical and archaeological interest, and the misdeeds of modern philosophy and to distinguish more clearly between them. Such knowledge is also essential for the recovery of the deeper meaning of the order of nature as it has been envisaged in various religions and as it has been experienced and lived by countless generations of human beings. Furthermore, traditional metaphysics and cosmology enable us to understand better what distinguishes the traditional sciences from those that were the product of the seventeenth-century Scientific Revolution and the consequence of the mechanization of the world picture. In this way we can gain a greater awareness of the religious, philosophical, scientific, and historical roots of currently held conceptions about the order of nature, conceptions that now threaten not only the harmony of nature but also human life itself. Only perennial wisdom can reveal to us objectively our plight that is the direct consequence of the loss of that wisdom and that is now endangering earthly existence itself for the sake of which the celestial realities and enternal truths were so easily sacrificed and relegated to oblivion.

NOTES

1. We have dealt with this question in *Knowledge and the Sacred*, (Albany: State University of New York Press, 1989) pp. 1–48.

2. Precisely because of limited understanding imposed upon the meaning of philosophy in contemporary European languages, both Henry Corbin and I have often translated *ḥikmat al-ishrāq* as the "Theosophy of the Orient of Light," rather than "philosophy." See Henry Corbin, *En Islam iranien*, Vol. 2 (Paris: Gallimard, 1971), pp. 19ff. and S. H. Nasr, *Three Muslim Sages* (Delmar, N.Y.: Caravan Books, 1975), Chapter 2.

3. This type of difference is, however, of a very different order from the difference between Pythagoreanism and Platonism on the one hand and, say, logical positivism on the other.

4. One should remember that the discussion of philosophy is unavoidable whenever one wishes to deal seriously with the relation between religion and science.

5. See F. Cornford, *From Religion to Philosophy* (Atlantic Highlands, N.J.: Humanities Press, 1980) which describes this process in a profound fashion.

6. "Greek thinkers regarded the presence of mind in nature as the source of that regularity or orderliness of the natural world whose presence made a science of nature possible. . . . They conceived mind, in all its manifestations, whether in human affairs or elsewhere, as a ruler, a dominating or regulating element, imposing order first upon itself and then upon everything belonging to it, primarily its own body and secondarily that body's environment." Robin G. Collingwood, *The Idea of Nature* (Oxford: Clarendon Press, 1949), p. 3.

7. Ibid., p. 44.

8. On the Ionians, see William K. C. Guthrie, *A History of Greek Philosophy*, Vol. 1 (Cambridge: Cambridge University Press, 1962), Part 3, pp. 39ff.; Charles H. Kahn, *Anaximander and the Origins of Greek Cosmogony* (New York: Columbia University Press, 1960); Joseph Owens, *A History of Ancient Western Philosophy* (New York: Appleton-Century-Crofts, 1959), Chapter 1, p. 3; Kathleen Freeman, *The Pre-Socratic Philosophers: A Companion to Diels, Fragmente der Vorsokratiker* (Oxford: Basil Blackwell, 1966), B; pp. 49ff.; and James B. Wilbur and Harold J. Allen (eds.), *The Worlds of the Early Greek Philosophers* (Buffalo, N.Y.: Prometheus Books, 1979), Part 1, "The Ionians," pp. 27ff.

9. See Collingwood, *The Idea of Nature,* pp. 29–30.

10. Annemarie Schimmel, *The Mystery of Numbers* (Oxford: Oxford University Press, 1993), p. 11.

11. See Frithjof Schuon, *Esoterism as Principle and as Way,* trans. W. Stoddart (Pates Manor, U.K.: Perennial Books, 1990), "Hypostatic and Cosmic Numbers," pp. 65ff.

12. Walter Wili, "The History of the Spirit in Antiquity," in Joseph Campbell (ed.), *Spirit and Nature,* trans. R. Manheim and R.F.C. Hull (Princeton, N.J.: Princeton University Press, 1982), Bollingen Series XXXI, p. 86. On Pythagoras as seen by academic scholarship, see Cornelia J. Vogel, *Greek Philosophy: A Collection of Texts: Vol. 1. Thales to Plato* (Leiden: E. J. Brill, 1950); W. K. C. Guthrie, *A History of Greek Philosophy;* Walter Burkert, *Love and Science in Ancient Pythagoreanism* (Cambridge, Mass.: Harvard University Press, 1972). As for works written or compiled by those who identify with the tenets of Pythagoreanism, see Kenneth S. Guthrie (trans.), *The Pythagorean Sourcebook and Library* (Grand Rapids, Mich.: Phanes Press, 1987); Hans Keyser, *Lehrbuch der Harmonik* (Zurich: Occident, 1950); Matila Ghyka, *Le Nombre d'or,* 2 vols. (Paris: Gallimard, 1931); and Antoine Fabre d'Olivet, *The Golden Verses of Pythagoras,* trans. N. L. Redfield (New York: Samuel Weiser, 1975).

13. See Von Thimus, *Die harmonikale Symbolik des Alterthums,* 2 vols. (Hildesheim, Germany: Olms, 1972).

14. A great deal of attention has been paid during the past few decades to Pythagorean harmonics and their application to the sciences and the arts including, of course, music itself. See, for example, Hans Keyser, *Akróasis: The Theory of World Harmonies,* trans. R. Lilienfeld (Boston: Plowshare, 1970); Ernest Levy, "The Pythagorean Concept of Measure," *Main Currents in Modern Thought* (Vol. 21, no. 3, Jan.–Feb. 1965), pp. 51–57; and with Siegmund Levarie, *Tone: A Study in Musical Acoustics* (Kent, Ohio: Kent State University Press, 1968); Ernest G. McClain, *The Myth of Invariance* (York Beach, Maine: Nicolas Hays, 1984); McClain, *The Pythagorean Plato: Prelude to the Song Itself* (Stony

Brook, N.Y.: Nicolas Hays, 1978); and Jocelyn Godwin, *Harmonies of Heaven and Earth* (Rochester, Vt.: Inner Traditions International, 1987).

15. On the Islamic view of Pythagoras and Pythagoreanism see S. H. Nasr, *An Introduction to Islamic Cosmological Doctrines* (Albany: State University of New York Press, 1993), pp. 47ff.

16. See Christopher Bamford (ed.), *Homage to Pythagoras: Rediscovering Sacred Science* (Hudson, N.Y.: Lindisfarne Press, 1994); and K. S. Guthrie, *The Pythagorean Sourcebook and Library*, pp. 60–61.

17. This includes both serious students of the Western esoteric tradition and occultists with all kinds of background and claims.

18. "Not only are all of Plato's mathematical allegories capable of a musical analysis—one which makes sense out of every step in his arithmetic—but all of his allegories taken together prove to be a united treatise on the musical scale so that each one throws light on the others. However, it is perhaps even more remarkable that, when the *Republic, Timaeus, Critias,* and *Laws* are studied as a group—as a unity—it then proves possible to explain virtually every Platonic mathematical riddle with help from related passages, that is, in Plato's own words." McClain, *The Pythagorean Plato,* p. 3. On Plato's views concerning nature interpreted from different philosophical perspectives, see Hans-Georg Gadamer, *Idee und Wirklichkeit in Plato Timaios* (Heidelberg: Winter, 1974); Karen Gloy, *Studien zur Platonischen Naturphilosophie in Platons Timaios* (Wurzburg: Koningshausen and Neumann, 1986); Alfred E. Taylor, *A Commentary on Plato's Timaeus* (Oxford: Oxford University Press, 1921); Francis M. Cornford, *Plato's Cosmology: The Timaeus of Plato* (London: Routledge and Kegan Paul, 1948); and Carl F. von Weizsäcker, *The Unity of Nature,* trans. F. J. Zucker (New York: Farrar, Straus & Giroux, 1980), pp. 368ff. On Plato's mathematics see also Robert Brumbough, *Plato's Mathematical Imagination* (New York: Kraus Reprint, 1968).

19. *Epinomis,* 991a, 992a. Quoted in McClain, *The Pythagorean Plato,* p. 7.

20. Cornford, *Plato's Cosmology,* p. 25.

21. *Timaeus,* 29–30d and e; ibid., p. 33.

22. See Ernan McMullin, "Cosmic Order in Plato and Aristotle," in Paul Kuntz (ed.), *The Concept of Order* (Seattle and London: University of Washington Press, 1968), pp. 63ff., especially pp. 65–67.

23. *Timaeus,* 30c; Cornford, *Plato's Cosmology,* pp. 39–40.

24. McClain, *The Pythagorean Plato,* p. 60. For a thorough musical analysis of this series see pp. 61ff of McClain's book.

25. Ibid., p. 58. Cornford, who differs from McClain in his interpretation of the numbers associated with the harmony of the World Soul, writes, "The soul must be composed according to a harmonia and advance *as far as solid numbers* and be harmonised by two means, *in order that, extending throughout the whole solid body of the world,* it may grasp all the things that exist." *Plato's Cosmology,* p. 68.

26. According to the *Timaeus,* "When the ordering of the universe was set about, God first began by laying out by figure and number the patterns of fire and water and earth and air, which theretofore, though showing some vestiges of their structure, were altogether in such a state as might be expected when God is absent. *That He shaped them to be, as they had not been before, wholly beauteous and good, as far as might be, one must assume throughout as our standing principle.*" Benjamin Farrington, *Greek Science: Its Meaning for Us* (Baltimore: Penguin Books, 1961), p. 119.

27. Scholars have debated about imitation versus participation in Platonic doctrine.

The two, however, are not contradictory but can be understood in a complementary fashion and imply one another. See Collingwood, *The Idea of Nature,* pp. 61–63.

28. Ernan McMullin, "Cosmic Order in Plato and Aristotle," p. 23. See also the all-important late dialogue of Plato's *Laws* where his conception of human and cosmic law is fully developed.

29. This is stated in *Metaphysics,* Book Δ, as well as in the *Physics.*

30. W. D. Ross, *Aristotle* (London: Methuen, 1930), p. 68.

31. Collingwood, *The Idea of Nature,* p. 92. On Aristotle's view of form and matter and natural philosophy based upon it, see Frederick J. E. Woodbridge, *Aristotle's Vision of Nature* (New York: Columbia University Press, 1966); and Ross, "Philosophy of Nature," in *Aristotle,* pp. 62ff; David Lindberg, *The Beginning of Western Science* (Chicago: University of Chicago Press, 1992), pp. 48ff.; and Ingrid Craemer-Ruegenberg, *Die Naturphilosophie des Aristoteles* (Freiburg: Alber, 1980). For an extensive bibliography of works pertaining to Aristotle's philosophy of nature see Gustav A. Seeck, "Bibliographie zur Naturphilosphie des Aristoteles," in A. Seeck (ed.), *Wege der Forschung,* Vol. 225 (Darmstadt: Wissenschaftliche Buchgesellschaft, 1975), pp. 404–410.

32. Collingwood, *The Idea of Nature,* p. 85.

33. Ibid, p. 90.

34. Samuel Sambursky, *The Physical World of the Greeks,* trans. Merton Dagut (London: Routledge and Kegan Paul, 1963), pp. 84–85. The teleological nature of movement in nature is discussed by Aristotle in the second book of his *Physics,* e.g., 198b. For design in nature according to Aristotle see also John Hermann Randall, *Aristotle* (New York: Columbia University Press, 1960), p. 186.

35. "The cosmic order of Aristotle, the empirist, can thus be viewed as somewhere halfway between the teleological order of Plato, consciously directed to the good, and the mechanistic cosmic order of the Newtonians, where considerations of the good are no longer scientifically relevant." McMullin, "Cosmic Order in Plato and Aristotle," p. 76.

36. "The universal *physis* was defined by the Stoics both as the generative force in the universe, causing life ad growth, and as the force that held the universe together and in order; in its role as ordering force, *physis* is equivalent to the 'true order' (*orthos lógos*) of the universe and is responsible for its 'orderly arrangement' (*dioikēsis*)." Michael Lapidge, "Stoic Cosmology," in John M. Rist (ed.), *The Stoics* (Berkeley: University of California Press, 1978), p. 161. On Stoicism and its history in general, see Marcia L. Colish, *The Stoic Tradition from Antiquity to the Early Middle Ages,* 2 vols. (Leiden and New York: E. J. Brill, 1990), especially Chapter 1 dealing with physics and cosmology; Emile Bréhier, *The Hellenistic and Roman Age (The History of Philosophy,* trans. Wade Baskin (Chicago: University of Chicago Press, 1965); André Bridoux, *Le Stoicisme et son influence* (Paris: J. Vrin, 1966); Johnny Christensen, *An Essay on the Unity of Stoic Philosophy* (Copenhagen: Munksgaard, 1962); Ludwig Edelstein, *The Meaning of Stoicism* (Cambridge, Mass.: Harvard University Press, 1966); Maximillian Forschner, *Dei stoische Ethik: Über den Zusammenhang von Natur-, Sprach-und Moralphilosophie in altstoischen System* (Stuttgart: Klett-Cotta, 1981); Max Pohlenz, *Die Stoa: Geschichte einer geistigen Bewegung,* 2 vols. (Göttingen: Vandenhoeck & Ruprecht, 1955–59); Gerard Verbeke, *L'Évolution de la doctrine du pneuma du Stoicisme à S. Augustin* (Paris: Desclée de Brouwer, 1945); Whitney J. Oates (ed.), *The Stoic and Epicurean Philosophers* (New York: Random House, 1940); and Fritz Jurss (ed.), *Geschichte des wissenschaftlichen Denkens in Altertum* (Berlin: Akademie Verlag, 1982).

37. "The Stoic God, it has often been noted, is like a Platonic demiurge who does not, however, copy a pattern but brings himself as a pattern to the creation and structuring

of a universe that directly embodies his identity." Robert B. Todd, "Monism and Immanence: The Foundations of Stoic Physics," in Rist (ed.), *The Stoics,* p. 159.

38. Ibid., p. 166.

39. It is interesting to note that the Stoics even derived the word *Dia* (God) from the verb *diēkō,* meaning to pervade, because *pneuma* pervaded the entire cosmos.

40. Rist (ed.), *The Stoics,* p. 171.

41. "One comes to realize that pneuma derived its central position in Stoic physics from its dual significance. It was power (viz. Force) impressing a definite state upon matter on the one hand, and causal nexus linking the successive states of matter on the other, and in both of these aspects it revealed itself as a spatially and temporally continuous agent." Samuel Sambursky, *Physics of the Stoics* (New York: Macmillan, 1959), p. 37

42. "Nothing exists or has come into being in the cosmos without a cause." Sambursky, *Physical World of the Greeks,* p. 170.

43. Sambursky, *Physics of the Stoics,* p. 41.

44. Ibid., pp. 42ff.

45. *Astronomica* 2.60–66; quoted by Lapidge in Rist (ed.), *The Stoics,* p. 185.

46. On Plotinus and Neoplatonism in relation to the question of the order of nature, see Plotinus, *Enneads,* trans. S. MacKenna (New York: Larson Publications, 1992); William Ralph Inge, *The Philosophy of Plotinus,* 2 vols. (London: Longmans, Green & Co., 1948); Maurice de Gandillac, *La Sagesse de Plotin* (Paris: J. Vrin, 1966); Ludger Koreng, *Die Grundlagen des Wissenschaftsbegriffes bei Plotins* (Zurich and New York: Georg Olms Verlag, 1990); Joseph Katz, *The Philosophy of Plotinus* (New York: Appleton-Century-Crofts, 1950); A. Hillary Armstrong, *The Architecture of the Intelligible Universe in the Philosophy of Plotinus* (Cambridge: Cambridge University Press, 1940); and A. Hillary Armstrong (ed.), *Classical Mediterranean Spirituality,* Vol. 15 of "World Spirituality: An Encyclopedic History of the Religious Quest" (New York: Crossroad Publications, 1986), Chapter 10, "I. Plotinus and Porphyry" by Pierre Hadot, pp. 230–249, and "II. From Iamblichus to Proclus and Damascius," pp. 250–265.

47. See *Enneads,* 6.3 and 6.8. This quotation is from Inge, *Philosophy of Plotinus,* Vol. 1, p. 152. On the Plotinian doctrine of matter see Hubert Benz, *'Materie' und Wahrnemung in der Philosophie Plotins* (Würzburg: Königshausen u. Neumann, 1990), especially pp. 85ff. As to how nature functions, see Katz, *Philosophy of Plotinus,* the citations from the *Enneads* on the subject are assembled.

48. "It [*lógos-lógoi*] is that which, proceeding from Spirit, either directly or indirectly through the medium of the World-Soul, and identical in its nature with Soul conveys the energy of Spirit and Soul into matter. And that which proceeds from Soul to irradiate Matter is Nature." Inge, *Philosophy of Plotinus* p. 156.

49. "The 'unfolding of the Logoi' in the *Enneads* is not a real process of evolution. It is the necessary and undeliberate actualization of the potentialities which the higher contains for producing the lower, and results from the capacity in the higher for contemplating that above itself again." Armstrong, *Architecture of the Intelligible Universe,* p. 100.

50. *Enneads,* p. 275.

51. *Enneads,* IV, 4, 35, vv. 8–17, quoted in Gary M. Gurtler, S. J., *Plotinus: The Experience of Unity* (New York: Peter Lang, 1988), pp. 113–114. A somewhat different translation is given by MacKenna in *Enneads,* p. 364.

52. On this and the more general question of the relation of God to the cosmos and the soul in Plotinus see A. Hillary Armstrong, *Plotinian and Christian Studies* (London: Variorum Reprints, 1979), "The Apprehension of Divinity in the Self and the Cosmos in Plotinus," XVIII.

53. See Armstrong, *Architecture of the Intelligible Universe,* p. 98.

54. "The treatises *On Providence* from a theodicy, a justification of the moral order in our world. The Logos, as cause of this order, is representative of *Noūs,* of the transcendent divine order because of which the world is an ordered whole." Ibid, p. 103.

55. Assembled together as the *Corpus Hermeticum,* these works reached the West mostly through Arabic renditions from the tenth and eleventh centuries onward and were not translated directly from Greek until the fifteenth century when Marsilio Ficino rendered them into Latin in Florence. See *Présence d'Hermès Trismegiste* (Paris: Albin Michel, 1988), especially Antoine Faivre, "D'Hermès—Mercure à Hermès Trismégiste: au confluent du mythe et du mythique," pp. 24–48.

56. On Islamic Hermeticism, which was the source for Western Hermeticism in the Middle Ages, see Louis Massignion, "Inventaire de la littérature hermétique arabe," Appendix III of André J. Festugière and Arthur D. Nock, *La Révélation d'Hermès Trismégiste,* Vol. 1 (Paris: J. Vrin, 1949); Fu'ad Sezgin, *Geschichte des arabischen Schrifttums,* Vol. 4 (Leiden: E. J. Brill, 1971), pp. 38ff.; S. H. Nasr, "Hermes and Hermetic Writings in the Islamic World," in Nasr, *Islamic Life and Thought* (Albany: State University of New York Press, 1981), pp. 96–119; and Pierre Lory, "Hermès/Idris, prophète et sage dans la tradition islamique," in *Présence d'Hermès Trismégiste,* pp. 100–109. Concerning the text of *Tabula Smaragdina* see Julius Ruska, *Tabula Smaragdina: Ein Beitrag zur Geschichte der hermetischen Literatur* (Heidelberg: Winter, 1926).

57. See Mirko Sladek, *Fragmente der Hermetischen Philosophie in der Naturphilosophie der Neuzeit* (Frankfort-am-Main: Peter Lang GmbH, 1984), where the history of the influence of Hermeticism is traced along with an analysis of the Hermetic philosophy of nature.

58. This is particularly true of Germany and France where the last few years have been witness to the appearance of a number of important studies concerned with Hermeticism not only historically but also philosophically. In this context it is of interest to point out the publication of *Bibliothèque de l'Hermétisme* directed by Antoine Faivre in France and the works of the French philosopher Gilbert Durand, especially his *Science de l'homme et tradition: Le "nouvel esprit anthropologique"* (Paris: Tête de Feuilles; Sirac, 1975), where he speaks of the Hermetic science of man as a new anthropology that would go beyond the limited conception of the *anthropos,* which has been entertained by "scientific" anthropology since the last century. As for the English-speaking world, despite important research by Frances Yates and others, which has brought out the historical significance of Hermeticism during the period of genesis of modern science, less philosophical interest has been shown in Hermeticism than in continental Europe, certain British occultist circles being an exception. But the interests of the latter have not entered into formal scholarly circles and the mainstream of philosophy.

59. Alchemy is, of course, based upon the Hermetic philosophy and may be considered to be an application of Hermetic philosophy to the domain of material substances in their relation to the soul and the cosmos. See Titus Buckhardt, *Alchemy: Science of the Cosmos—Science of the Soul,* trans. William Stoddart (Longmead, U.K.: Element Books, 1986).

60. R. A. Schwaller de Lubicz, *Nature Word—Verbe Nature,* trans. D. Lawlor (West Stockbridge, Mass.: Lindisfarne Press, 1982, pp. 35–36) in the Foreword by Christopher Bamford. As Bamford mentions, Schwaller de Lubicz's book is itself a contemporary commentary upon the principles of Hermetic philosophy. This fact is an indication of the still living nature in the West of Hermeticism, which forms the foundation of the

worldview of perhaps the most perceptive contemporary student of ancient Egypt and an important intellectual figure in his own right.

61. See G. E. R. Lloyd, *Methods and Problems in Greek Science* (Cambridge: Cambridge University Press, 1991), pp. 418ff.

62. Ibid, p. 150.

63. Samuel Sambursky calls this "the law of conservation of matter" according to which nothing can be created out of nothing nor destroyed and returned to nothing and nothing happens at random." See Samuel Sambursky, *Physical World of the Greeks* (London: Routledge and Kegan Paul, 1963), p. 107.

64. See Myles F. Burnyeat (ed.), *The Skeptical Traditon* (Berkeley: University of California Press, 1983).

65. Following the classical work of Arthur Lovejoy, *The Great Chain of Being* (Cambridge, Mass.: Harvard University Press, 1933), where the development of this central idea has been traced from Plato and Aristotle to modern times.

66. Huston Smith in his *Forgotten Truth* (New York: HarperCollins, 1992), discusses both the centrality of this doctrine for traditional metaphysics and the consequences of its loss for modern philosophy and science.

67. In his book *On Providence* Chrysippus says, "Fate is a certain physical order wherein one thing is always caused by and results from another, in such a way that this interrelation cannot be changed." Quoted in Sambursky, *Physical World of the Greeks,* p. 171. It is easy to see how the concept of fate expressed here differs from the early Greek religious conception of the term. Yet, the idea of fate as law, which all things must follow, continues through most periods of Greek philosophical speculation, having its roots in the Greek religious conception of fate discussed in the preceding chapter.

68. For Erigena, "Nothing at all can occur in our thoughts that would fall outside this name [nature]." *Periphyseon,* Vol. 1, ed. I. P. Sheldon-Williams (Dublin: The Dublin Institute of Advanced Studies, 1978), p. 37. On works about Erigena's masterpiece and philosophy of nature especially as they concern the subject under discussion, see Henry Bett, *Johannes Scotus Eriugena, A Study in Medieval Philosophy* (Cambridge: Cambridge University Press, 1925); John J. O'Meara and Ludwig Bielu (eds.), *The Mind of Eriugena* (Dublin: Irish University Press, 1973); John J. O'Meara, *Eriugena* (New York: Oxford University Press, 1988; René Roques, *Libres sentiers vers l'erigénisme* (Rome: Edizione dell'Ateneo, 1975); Gisela Kaldenbach, *Die Kosmologie des Johannes Scottus Erigena* (Munich: Inaug. Diss., 1963); Gregory Tullio, *Giovànni Scoto Eriugena, Tre Studi* (Florence: F. Le Monnier, 1963); Gangolf Schrimpf, *Das Werk des Johannes Scottus Eriugena in Rahmen des Wissenscheftsverständnisses seiner Zeit. Ein Hinführung zu Periphyseon* (Münster: Beitrage zur Geschichte der Philosophie und Theologie des Mittlealters. Neue Folge Band 23, 1982); Willemien Otten, *The Anthropology of Johannes Scottus Eriugena* (Leiden: E. J. Brill, 1991); and S. H. Nasr, *Knowledge and the Sacred,* pp. 20ff. See also John Scotus Erigena, *The Voice of the Eagle: The Heart of Celtic Christianity,* trans. Christopher Bamford (Hudson, N.Y.: Lindisfarne Press, 1990).

69. See D. J. O'Meara, "The Concept of Nature in John Scottus Eriugena" (De divisione naturae Book I), *Vivarium* (Vol. 19, 1981), pp. 126–145.

70. *Periphyseon,* Vol. 1 p. 37.

71. Ibid.

72. "God seems to epitomize both the beginning and the end of the unfolding of *natura* as a process which advances through the logical stages of divisions and analysis." Otten, *Anthropology of Eriugena,* p. 24.

G. Scrimpf writes, "Die *divisio naturae* zerlegt als den Begriff für den Prozess, den die Wirklichkeit in Ganzen notwendig durchläuft, Hilfe des formalen Verfahrens der logischen Einteilung vollständig in die Begriffe jener Aspekte, unter denen allein Prozess als ein jeweils anderer Ausdruck der Wirklichkeit in Ganzen zum Gegenstand einer wissenschaftlichen Aussage gemacht werden kann." Schrimpf, *Das Werk des Johannes Eriugena*, p. 157.

73. *Periphyseon*, Vol. 2, 1972, p. 13.

74. Otten, *Anthropology of Eriugena*, p. 32.

75. Ibid., p. 165.

76. See, for example, Jacques Maritain, *Philosophy of Nature* (New York: Philosophical Library, 1951), where the author defends the Thomistic philosophy of nature as a living alternative to modern positivism. Naturally, this work belongs to the period preceding Vatican II, the spread of Teilhardism and Liberation Theology and other non-Thomistic schools of thought within Catholic circles. But the influence of St. Thomas Aquinas and such Thomists as Maritain himself has certainly not disappeared.

77. On Platonic elements in St. Thomas Aquinas see Louis-Bertrand Geiger, *La Participation dans la philosophie de S. Thomas d'Aquin* (Paris: J. Vrin, 1942); Joseph Santeler, *Der Platonismus in der Erkenntnislehre des Heiligen Thomas von Aquin* (Innsbruck: F. Rauch, 1939); and Robert J. Henle, S. J., *Saint Thomas and Platonism: A Study of the Plato and Platonici Texts in the Writings of St. Thomas* (The Hague: Martinus Nijhoff, 1956).

78. There is such a vast literature on Aquinas, even concerning the more limited subject of his views concerning the order of nature, that is not possible to mention even most of the pertinent writings here. Some of the more important works concerning his philosophy of nature and understanding of the order of nature include Etienne Gilson, *The Christian Philosophy of St. Thomas Aquinas*, trans. L. K. Shook (New York: Random House, 1966), particularly Part 2; Joseph Legrand, S. J., *L'Univers et l'homme dans la philosophie de Saint Thomas* (Paris: Desclée de Brouwer, 1946), especially Part 1; E. Gilson, *The Spirit of Thomism* (New York: P. J. Kennedy & Sons, 1964), Part 2; Gallus Manser, *Das Wesen des Thomismus* (Freiburg: Paulusverlag, 1949), pp. 561ff.; Paul Grenet, *Thomism: An Introduction*, trans. J. F. Ross (London and New York: Harper & Row, 1967), Part 1; Brian Davies, *The Thought of Thomas Aquinas* (Oxford: Clarendon Press, 1992); Jan Aertsen, *Nature and Creature: Thomas Aquinas's Way of Thought* (Leiden: E. J. Brill, 1988); Karl Rahner, *Geist in Welt: Zur Metaphysik der endlichen Erkenntnis bei Thomas von Aquin* (Munich: Kosel-Verlag, 1957), especially pp. 69ff.; Hampus Lyttkens, *The Analogy between God and the World: An Investigation of Its Background and Interpretation of Its Use by Thomas of Aquinas* (Uppsala: Almquist & Wiksells Boktryckeri AB, 1952); and B. Coffey, "The Notion of Order According to St. Thomas Aquinas," *Modern Schoolman* (Vol. 27, 1949), pp. 1–18.

79. *Summa Theologica*, part I, question 22, article 1. See also Brian Davies, *The Thought of Thomas Aquinas*, p. 158.

80. *Summa Contra Gentiles*, 3.65.2f; also Davies, *op. cit.* p. 159.

81. "The divine Being is the *ratio creandi*, for through creation all things participate in being." Aertsen, *Nature and Creature*, p. 123.

82. *Summa Theologica*, I, 45, 5 and 1.

83. From St. Thomas Aquinas, *In libros Peri Hermeneias Aristotelis exposito, lect.* 3, 30, quoted in Aertsen, *Nature and Creature*, p. 165.

84. On St. Thomas's view of art, see Ananda K. Coomaraswamy, *Christian and Oriental Philosophy of Art* (New York: Dover, 1956), especially Chapter 2, p. 23ff.

85. For an exposition of St. Thomas's cosmology, see Rahner, *Geist in Welt*, pp. 69ff.

86. Lyttkens, *Analogy between God and the World*, pp. 171ff.

87. "To order the things with God as their purpose is equivalent to God's drawing all created things back to Himself." Lyttkens, *Analogy between God and the World*, p. 173.

88. "The universe is an ordered whole, a hierarchy of beings, and although each particular being is good in itself, their general order is better still, since it includes, over and above the perfection of each individual thing, that of the whole." Gilson, *The Spirit of Thomism*, pp. 40–41.

89. See Maritain, *Philosophy of Nature*, pp. 93ff. See also Mary Cosmos Hughes, *The Intelligibility of the Universe* (Washington, D.C.: Catholic University of America Press, 1946).

90. "The whole cosmology of Aquinas could have for its title, *De imitatione Dei*. Indeed, a certain inborn desire to imitate God and to emulate His perfection is the secret that even the physical universe is revealing in its existence as well as in its operations." Gilson, *The Spirit of Thomism*, p. 44.

Aquinas's view of the order of nature and Creation is summarized in a masterly fashion by Gilson in his *The Philosophy of St. Thomas Aquinas*, trans. Edward Bullough (Cambridge: W. Heffer & Sons, 1929), pp. 107ff.; and his *The Christian Philosophy of St. Thomas Aquinas*, pp. 145ff.

91. In *Man and Nature* we have pointed to the rationalistic tendencies and empirical epistemology of Thomism as being instrumental to some extent in paving the way for the rise of that combination of rationalism and empiricism in the seventeenth century that was to destroy the sacred significance of the cosmos in the West. But we do not agree with those who accuse Aquinas as being directly responsible for the destruction of the Christian view of nature as a result of adopting the Aristotelian theory of hylomorphism—for example, Philip Sherrard in his book *The Rape of Man and Nature* (London: Golgonooza Press, 1987).

92. See Georgio Di Santillana, *The Age of Adventure: The Renaissance Philosophers* (New York: George Braziller, 1957), especially the Introduction.

93. On Telesio see Giovanni Gentile, *Il pensiero italiano del rinascimento* (Florence: G. C. Sansoni, 1955). On Telesio and the Renaissance philosophy of nature in general, see also Alfonso Ingegno, "The New Philosophy of Nature," in Charles B. Schmitt et al. (eds.), *The Cambridge History of Renaissance Philosophy* (New York: Cambridge University Press, 1988), pp. 236ff.

94. On Bruno and his view of the cosmos see Alexander Koyré, *From the Closed World to the Infinite Universe*, (New York: Harper Torchbook, 1958); Frances Yates, *Giordano Bruno and the Hermetic Tradition* (Chicago: University of Chicago Press, 1991); Irving L. Horowitz, *The Renaissance Philosophy of Giordano Bruno* (New York: Coleman-Ross, 1952); Dorothea W. Singer, *Giordano Bruno, His Life and Thought* (New York: Henry Schuman, 1950, which contains the text of Bruno's work, *On the Infinite Universe and Worlds*); Paul-Henri Michel, *The Cosmology of Giordano Bruno*, trans. R. E. W. Maddison (London: Methuen, 1962, and Ithaca, N.Y.: Cornell University Press, 1973); and Jochen Kirchhoff, *Giordano Bruno* (Reinbeck bei Hamburg: Rowolt, 1980).

95. See Collingwood, *The Idea of Nature*, pp. 104–105.

96. Descartes practically identified mathematics and natural science as seen in his *Regulae ad Directionem Ingenii*. See John Beck Leslie, *The Method of Descartes: A Study of the Regulae* (Oxford: Clarendon Press, 1952); and Jean-Luc Marion, *Sur l'ontologie grise de*

Descartes (Paris: J. Vrin, 1975). On Descartes' philosophy as it concerns nature see Daniel Garber, *Descartes' Metaphysical Physics* (Chicago: University of Chicago Press, 1992); and William Shea, *The Magic of Numbers and Motion: The Scientific Career of Rene Descartes* (Canton, Mass.: Science History Publications, 1991).

97. "You can see how Descartes' rigorously mechanistic philosophy of nature was— and this indeed is what condemns it as a philosophy—a marvelously servile adaption of philosophy to the dynamic state of the sciences and of scientific research during his time." Maritain, *Philosophy of Nature,* p. 43.

98. Ibid, p. 44.

99. Blaise Pascal, *Pensées: The Provincial Letters,* trans. W. F. Trotter (New York: Random House, 1941), letter 77, p. 29.

100. "La nature a des perfections pour montrer qu'elle est l'image de Dieu, et des defauts pour montrer qu'elle n'en est que l'image." *Les Pensées de Pascal,* ed. Francis Kaplan (Paris: Les Editions du Cerf, 1982), No. 1310, p. 546.

101. Blaise Pascal, *Pensées: Thoughts on Religion and Other Subjects,* trans. W. F. Trotter (New York: Washington Square Press, 1965), pp. 19–20 (slightly modified).

102. On this question see Fernand Branner, *Etudes sur la signification historique de la philosophie de Leibnitz* (Paris: J. Vrin, 1950). On Leibniz's view of the order of nature see Ernst Cassirer, *Leibnitz' System in seinem wissenschaftlichen Grundlagen* (Marburg: N. G. Elwert, 1902); Martial Guéroult, *Dynamique et métaphysique leibniziennes* (Paris: Les Belles Lettres, 1934); Bertrand Russell, *A Critical Exposition of the Philosophy of Leibnitz* (Cambridge: Cambridge University Press, 1937); Kathleen Okruhlik and James R. Brown (eds.), *The Natural Philosophy of Leibnitz* (Dordrecht and Boston: D. Reidel, 1985); and Albert Heinekamp (ed.), *Leibnitz' Dynamica* (Stuttgart: F. Steiner Verlag, 1984). On the philosophy of nature based especially on the German school from Leibniz to the present but also including Greek and medieval sources, see Gernot Böhme (ed.), *Klassiker der Naturphilosophie* (Munich: C. H. Beck, 1989).

103. See Yvon Belaval, *Leibnitz: Initiation à sa philosophie* (Paris: J. Vrin, 1962).

104. On the history of the usage of this term and the role of Leibniz therein, see C. Schmitt, "Perennial Philosophy: Steuco to Leibnitz," in his *Studies in Renaissance Philosophy and Science* (London: Variorum Reprints, 1981), pp. 505–532.

105. See Collingwood, *The Idea of Nature,* pp. 113ff. On Berkeley's view of the order of nature see Gabriel Moked, *Particles and Ideas: Bishop Berkeley's Corpuscularian Philosophy* (Oxford and New York: Clarendon Press, 1988); Gavin Ardley, *Berkeley's Philosophy of Nature* (Auckland: University of Auckland, Bulletin 63, 1962); and Richard J. Brook, *Berkeley's Philosophy of Science* (The Hague: Martinus Nijhoff, 1973).

106. We cannot at all deal with Kant's critical philosophy here but must limit ourselves to his views concerning the order of nature. There is a vast literature on this subject, only a few of whose titles we mention by way of example: Erich Adickes, *Kant als Naturforscher,* 2 vols. (Berlin: W. de Gruyter, 1924/25); Martin Heidegger, *Kant and the Problem of Metaphysics,* trans. James Churchill (Bloomington: Indiana University Press, 1962); Gottfried Martin, *Kant's Metaphysics and Theory of Science,* trans. P. G. Lucas (Manchester: Manchester University Press, 1955); James Ellington, *Kant's Philosophy of Material Nature* (Indianapolis, Ind.: Hackett, 1985); Christopher B. Garnett, *The Kantian Philosophy of Space* (Port Washington, N.Y.: Kennikat Press, 1965); Gernot Böhme, *Philosophieren mit Kant: Zur Rekonstruktion der Kantischen Erkenntnis-und Wissenschaftstheorie* (Frankfurt: Suhrkamp, 1986); Gordon G. Brittan, *Kant's Theory of Science* (Princeton, N.J.: Princeton University Press, 1978); Gerd Buchdahl, *Metaphysics and the Philosophy of Science: The Classical Origins: Descartes to Kant* (Lanham, Md.: University

Press of America, 1988); Robert E. Butts (ed.), *Kant's Philosophy of Physical Science* (Dordrecht and Boston: D. Reidel, 1986); H. Hoppe, *Kant's Theorie der Physik* (Frankfurt: V. Klostermann, 1969); Lothar Schäfer, *Kants Metaphysik der Natur* (Berlin: W. de Gruyter, 1966); Jules Vuillemin, *Physique et métaphysique kantienne* (Paris: Presses Universitaires de France, 1955); and von Weizsäcker, *The Unity of Nature* (New York: Farrar Straus Giroux, 1980), pp. 308ff.

107. "Reason, then, to the extent that it is artificially divorced from the Intellect, engenders individualism and arbitrariness. This is exactly what happens in the case of someone like Kant, who is a rationalist even while rejecting 'dogmatic realism'; while the latter is doubtless rationalism, the Kantian critical philosophy is even more deserving of the name; indeed, it is the very acme of rationalism. As is well known, this critical philosophy looks upon metaphysics, not as the science of the Absolute and of the true nature of things, but as the 'science of the limits of human reason,' this reason (*Vernunft*) being identified with intelligence pure and simple, an utterly contradictory axiom, for in terms of what can the intelligence limit itself, seeing that by its very nature it is in principle unlimited or it is nothing? And if the intelligence as such is limited, what guarantee do we have that its operations, including those of critical philosophy, are valid?" Frithjof Schuon, *Logic and Transcendence*, trans. Peter Townsend, (London: Perennial Books, 1984), pp. 34–35.

108. "Nature of the material world is known to us only as a collection of phenomena, owing their existence to our own thinking activities and essentially relative to those activities." Collingwood, *The Idea of Nature*, p. 117.

109. Ibid., p. 118.

110. Schelling's most important works in the domain of *Naturphilosophie* are *Ideen zu einer Philosophie der Natur, Erster Entwurf eines Systems der Naturphilosophie*, and *Einleitung zu dem Entwurf eines Systems der Naturphilosophie order über den Begriff der spekulativen Physik*. On Schelling, see Ernst Block, *Das Materialproblem, seine Geschichte und Substanz, Bloch Gesamtausgabe*, Vol. 7 (Frankfurt: Suhrkamp, 1972); Marie-Luise Heuser-Kessler, *Die Produktivität der Natur: Schellings Naturphilosophie und das neue Paradigma der Selbstorganisation in den Naturwissenschaften* (Berlin: Duncker & Humbolt, 1986); and Wolfdietrich Schmied-Kowarizk, *Das dialektische Verhältnis des Menschen zur Natur* (Freiburg-Munich: Alber-Broschur, 1984).

111. Schelling, *Erster Entwurf*, 1799. In *Werke* 2 (Munich: Beck, 1927), p. 17. Quoted by Dietrich von Engelhardt in "Natural Science in the age of Romanticism," in Antoine Faivre and Jacob Needleman (eds.), *Modern Esoteric Spirituality*, Vol. 21 of *World Spirituality: An Encyclopedic History of the Religious Quest* (New York: Crossroad Publications, 1992), p. 103. This analysis of the thought of Schelling is based primarily but not exclusively on this study.

112. "God is the self-creating and self-subsisting world or organism of pure concepts, and mind is only one, though the highest and most perfect, of the determination which God acquires in that process of self-creation which is also the process of creating the world." Collingwood, *The Idea of Nature*, p. 122.

113. On Hegel's philosophy of nature and cosmology, concerning which there is an extensive bibliography, see by way of example Walter C. Stace, *The Philosophy of Hegel* (New York: Dover, 1955); John M. E. McTaggart, *Studies in Hegelian Cosmology* (Cambridge: Cambridge University Press, 1901); Theodor L. Haering, *Hegel: Sein Wollen und Sein Werk*, 2 vols. (Leipzig and Berlin: B. G. Teubner, 1929); Olaf Breidbach, *Das Organische in Hegels Denken: Studie zur Naturphilosophie und Biologie um 1800* (Würzburg: Königshausen und Neumann, 1982); Rolf-Peter Horstmann and Michael J. Petry (eds.),

Hegels Philosophie der Natur: Beziehungen zwischen empirischer und spekulativer Naturerkenntnis (Stuttgart: Klett-Cotta, 1986); Henry S. Harris, *Hegel's Development: Night Thoughts (Jena 1801–1806)* (Oxford: Oxford University Press, 1983); and Michael J. Petry (ed.), *Hegel und die Naturwissenschaften* (Stuttgart-Bad Cannstatt: Fromann-Holzboog, 1986).

114. On Bergson's philosophy of nature and science see Milic Čapek, *Bergson and Modern Physics: A Re-Interpretation and Re-Evaluation* (Dordrecht: D. Reidel; and New York: Humanities Press, 1971); Peter A. Gunter (ed.), *Bergson and the Evolution of Physics* (Knoxville: University of Tennessee Press, 1969); Newton Stallknecht, *Studies in the Philosophy of Creation with Special Reference to Bergson and Whitehead* (Princeton, N.J.: Princeton University Press, 1934); Pierre Trotignon, *L'Idee de vie chez Bergson et la critique de la métaphysique* (Paris: Presses Universitaires de France, 1968).

115. Whitehead's own most important works dealing with the order of nature are *Process and Reality: An Essay in Cosmology* (New York: Social Science Bookstore, 1941); and *The Concept of Nature* (Cambridge: Cambridge University Press, 1971).

Concerning Whitehead's views about nature see Murray Code, *Order and Organism: Steps to a Whiteheadian Philosophy of Mathematics and Natural Sciences* (Albany: State University of New York Press, 1985); Ivor Leclerc, *The Nature of Physical Existence* (London: Allen & Unwin, 1972); Victor Lorne, *Understanding Whitehead* (Baltimore: John Hopkins University Press, 1962); Robert M. Palter, *Whitehead's Philosophy of Science* (Chicago: University of Chicago Press, 1960); Ernst Wolf-Gazo (ed.), *Whitehead-Einführung in seine Kosmologie* (Freiburg-Munich: Alber Hans-Joachim Sander, 1980), with Harold Hotz (eds.), *Whitehead und der Prozeßbegriff* (Freiburg-Munich: Alber, 1984), especially parts III and IV; Hans-Joachim Sander, *Natur und Schopfung: die Realität in Prozess* (Frankfurt am Main: Peter Lang, 1991); George R. Lucas, *The Rehabilitation of Whitehead: An Analytic and Historical Assessment of Process Philosophy* (Albany: State University of New York Press, 1989), especially Chapter 6, "Whitehead, Hegel, and the Philosophy of Nature," pp. 93ff., and Chapter 10, "Philosophy of Science and Philosophy of Nature," pp. 180ff., where Whitehead's views are appraised in the light of current developments in physics such as Bell's theorem and David Bohm's "Implicate Order"; also John B. Cobb and David A. Griffin, *Mind in Nature: Essays on the Interface of Science and Philosophy* (Washington, D.C.: University Press of America, 1977).

On Whitehead's views of nature in comparison to Kant's, see Gordon Treash, "The Nature of Nature: Kant and Whitehead," in Paul A. Bogaard and Gordon Treash (eds.), *Metaphysics as Foundation: Essays in Honor of Ivor Leclerc* (Albany: State University of New York Press, 1993), pp. 42–58.

116. See Whitehead, *Process and Reality*, ii., iii.

117. Ibid., p. 124.

118. Ibid., p. 127. See also Collingwood, *The Idea of Nature*, p. 165, where he provides a clear summary of Whitehead's cosmology.

119. See Maritain, *The Philosophy of Nature*.

120. Schuon, *To Have a Center* (Bloomington, Ind.: World Wisdom Books, 1990), "Universal Categories," p. 80. This essay is among Schuon's most important in relating the cosmic categories to their Divine Principle. On his view about the relation between the order of nature and the Divine Order see also his *Survey of Metaphysics and Esoterism*, trans. G. Polit (Bloomington, Ind.: World Wisdom Books, 1986), pp. 25–35; and *From the Divine to the Human*, trans. G. Polit and D. Lambert, (Bloomington, Ind.: World Wisdom Books, 1982), pp. 57–71. For an analysis of the teachings of Schuon in general,

see our Introduction to Nasr (ed.), *The Essential Writings of Frithjof Schuon* (Rockport, Mass.: Element Books, 1986), pp. 1–64.

121. Schuon, *To Have a Center*, p. 81.

122. Schuon, *Survey of Metaphysics and Esoterism*, p. 29.

123. Ibid., pp. 32–33.

124. Schuon, *From the Divine to the Human*, p. 57.

125. Schuon, *To Have a Center*, p. 83.

4

The Traditional Sciences, the Scientific Revolution, and Its Aftermath

چرخ گیتی دائماً در گردش است   همچو چرخ ساعت دوّار ما

لیك این تشبیه بی سامان بود   حاصل اندیشهٔ گمراه ما

جنبش عالم زافعال خداست   گرچه خارج باشد آن از درك ما

پرده بردار از نمای این جهان   تا زجهل آسوده گردد جان ما

A living being, locus of Divine Energy
Outward image of our inner reality,
Thus did men conceive the cosmos in ages gone,
And even now do behold her thus here and there.
But then there appeared models of wheels within wheels.
And a vision bound by matter in constant motion,
Nature reduced to a machine, purposeless, lifeless,
Grinding under laws in numbers written,
Shorn from the world of the Spirit and Life Divine,
Even if now no longer bound to the clock-like view of things.
What poverty to behold creation in such sight!
And how tragic its results for us who live on Earth,
In a paradise which we destroy so readily,
Armed with that truncated vision of what the world is,
And who we are who behold it as we do.

THE TRADITIONAL SCIENCES

To understand the radical transformations brought about by modern science concerning the order of nature, it is necessary first to mention, albeit briefly, the significance of the traditional sciences of the cosmos and the fact that they shared, in contrast to modern science, the same universe of discourse with the religion or religions of the civilization in whose bosom they were cultivated. In fact, modern science not only eclipsed the religious and traditional philosophical understanding of the order of nature in the West, but it also all but destroyed the traditional sciences, relegating them in the Occident at best to the margin of intellectual activity and most often to the category of superstition or the domain of occultism and pseudo-esoterism as one finds on the Continent as well as in England from the seventeenth century onward.[1] The traditional sciences, however, are not simply occult sciences as usually understood; rather, they are sciences of nature based upon metaphysical principles that differ markedly from the philosophical presumptions of modern science. But in any case they *are* sciences of nature with their own view concerning nature, and they are much more than rudimentary preludes to modern science as envisaged by positivistic historians of science. They are also the foundations upon which modern science was constructed after that science rejected the worldview of Islamic and later medieval Latin science. Modern science is, therefore, not simply the continuation of Islamic or Latin science. A major change of worldview or paradigm separates modern science from its medieval past. Yet as far as many theories and facts are concerned, modern science is based upon these traditional sciences.

Until recently the traditional sciences have been by and large neglected in the West, being viewed as superstition or as elementary steps in the direction of modern science. Even those scientists attracted to Oriental doctrines and who want to create a rapprochement between modern science and Oriental wisdom usually turn only to Oriental metaphysics and psychology, ignoring almost completely the Oriental traditional sciences of nature cultivated over the millennia in the bosom of that very wisdom that such figures are now trying to correlate with the latest discoveries of modern science.[2] And yet there is such a thing as traditional science distinct from both religion and philosophy but closely related to them.[3] Such sciences contain a profound view of the order of nature seen from a perspective different from that of modern science. Through them one is able to behold other faces of nature than the one studied so thoroughly, successfully, and also triumphantly by modern science, with the assumption that the face thus studied is the only face or aspect of nature and that modern science is the only legitimate science of the natural order, a claim based on a totalitarian perspective rarely perceived for what it is and which has been hardly ever challenged seriously in the West until fairly recently.

There are many traditional sciences—Egyptian, Chinese, Indian, Greek, Islamic, and others—and even many traditional sciences within a single tradition. These sciences are based upon certain metaphysical principles that also constitute the principles of the religion and tradition within whose context these sciences have been cultivated. Some in fact have quite legitimately called them "sacred science" to distinguish them from "profane science," which has cut off its links with the sacred.[4]

Each of the great traditional civilizations developed many such sciences, ranging from medicine to astronomy, and all were based on an understanding of the order of nature that they shared with the religion of the civilization to which these sciences belonged. Our goal here is not to discuss these sciences in themselves, which would require a vast separate undertaking, but to display how such sciences shared the same universe of meaning with religion as far as the order of nature was concerned.[5] Such a discussion will make clearer the radical change brought about in the West when a science was created that did not participate in the same discourse concerning the order of nature with religion. This had consequences of the greatest import for human existence as a result of both inner conflicts thus created and the unbridled development of a technology based upon that science, and for that very reason was totally divorced from any principles of a religious nature unless it be in rare individual cases whose very exception proves the rule.

As an example of the traditional sciences, we have chosen Islamic science, with which we are more familiar than with other traditional sciences, while remaining aware that the common universe of discourse found between science and religion in the Islamic context can also be found elsewhere—for example, in China where such key concepts as *Tao, Yin,* and *Yang* are shared by religion, physics, and medicine, just to name a few fields, or in India where the doctrine of the *guṇas* is found in religious rites and doctrines, yoga, medicine, and even dietary regulations.

As for Islamic science, its sharing the same universe of meaning with religion as far as the order of nature is concerned can be demonstrated through our analysis of a single concept, that of the balance (*al-mīzān*), a term that appears in the Quran. In Chapter 50 of the Quran, "The Beneficient" (*al-Raḥmān*) God states, "And the sky He hath uplifted; and He hath set the balance [*al-mīzān*]. That ye exceed not the balance [*al-mīzān*]. But observe the measure [*al-wazn*] strictly, nor fall short of the balance [*al-mīzān*] (vv.7–9, Pickthall translation somewhat modified). Numerous Quranic commentators of this verse have sought to explain the meaning of the key term *al-mīzān,* which is related etymologically to "measure" or *al-wazn.* Some have interpreted *al-mīzān* as the balance by which the consequences of human action are weighed in the next world as well as the necessity of leading a morally balanced life in this world. In fact, many Islamic works on ethics have appeared over the ages with the title of *mīzān al-'amal* or "balance of human actions." Others have interpreted the term to mean the discernment that allows us to establish balance in all aspects of life and have identified it with the Quran itself, one of whose names is *al-Furqān,* or discernment. In fact, one of the most important Quranic commentaries of this century, by 'Allāmah Sayyid Muḥammad Ḥusayn Ṭabāṭab'ī, is entitled *al-Mīzān.*[6]

In certain schools of Islamic philosophy the *mīzān* is associated with the balance of the Universe itself through that Divine Wisdom which preserves everything in its place and has created everything according to a just measure so that the term becomes closely associated with the order prevalent in nature.

Jābir ibn Ḥayyān, the founder of Islamic alchemy, formulated a whole cosmology and physics based upon the concept of the *mīzān,* which measures not quantity but the tendency of the World Soul and the balance between the inner and outer aspects of physical substances. In fact, the *mīzān* is central to Jābir's entire alchemy,[7] and through him it deeply influenced many later alchemists.

Then there is use of the same terms of *al-mīzān* and *al-wazn,* or balance and measure, but understood in their physical sense by physicists like al-Bīrūnī and al-Khāzinī who wrote treatises on the use of the physical balance for the measurement of weights following the Greek tradition associated especially with Archimedes. Abu'l-Fatḥ al-Khāzinī's twelfth-century work, *Kitāb mīzān al-ḥikmah* (The Book of the Balance of Wisdom)—dealing with mechanics and hydrostatics and containing the views of earlier Muslim scientists such as al-Rāzī and al-Bīrūnī as well as such Greeks as Heron and Archimedes—is a major book in the history of science even if viewed from the point of development of modern science.[8] If one ponders over works ranging from those of al-Khāzinī to those of Jābir and then the writings on ethics, psychology, eschatology, and metaphysics—all using the terms *mīzān* and *wazn* drawn originally from the Quran—one realizes in a concrete fashion the unity of the universe of discourse that was shared by physicists, alchemists, and philosophers as well as Quranic commentators for whom the resonances of the meanings of this term on various levels were very real, while each relied on a particular level of meaning of this polysemic term. The order of nature studied and explained by the traditional sciences not only corresponded to an aspect of reality, as seen concretely in the practical efficacy of certain forms of traditional medicine now avidly sought by many Westerners, but was also wed to the religious universe. These sciences were not subservient to religious disciplines such as exoteric hermeneutics, theology, or jurisprudence; they never rebelled against those principles of a metaphysical order that they shared with the religion of the society in which they were cultivated.

It was this common universe of discourse that was rent asunder by the rise of modern science as a result of which the religious view of the order of nature, which is always based on symbolism, was reduced either to irrelevance or to a matter of mere subjective concern, which made the cosmic teachings of religion to appear as unreal and irrelevant. Also, it was through the destruction of the unitary vision of the cosmos that the "laws of nature" became divorced from moral laws and the sciences of nature became divorced at their roots from the foundations of religious ethics. The consequence of this segmentation and separation was the alienation of man from an image of the Universe created by himself but given a purely objective and nonanthropomorphic status and the surrender of nature as a mass without spiritual significance to be analyzed and dissected with impunity on the one hand and plundered and raped with uncontrolled avidity on the other. Thus, it is of the utmost importance to try to understand in depth how the modern scientific view of the order of nature was founded and how it has evolved during the past four centuries to the present day. This subject is vast, and countless studies have been devoted to it; in turning to this subject here, therefore, we can do no more than summarize some of the most important features of this development without in any way being able to exhaust the subject or even do justice to its multifarious aspects and the numerous interpretations it has received from scholars over the years.[9]

THE MECHANIZATION OF THE WORLD PICTURE
IN THE RENAISSANCE AND THE SCIENTIFIC REVOLUTION

Why is it that the Scientific Revolution took place in Europe and not elsewhere, and why was it the Christian view of the order of nature that was eclipsed rather than the view of other religions? The answer to such a complex question requires examining many parameters and factors lying outside the scope and aim of this study. [10] As far as we are concerned, at the heart of the cluster of reasons as to why religion lost the cosmos in the West lies the following: The weakening of the sapiental dimension, with its emphasis upon the symbolic significance of the cosmos within Christianity; the rise of a rationalism already embedded to some extent in the Thomistic synthesis; the dominance of nominalism in the late Middle Ages; the eclipse and marginalization of Christian philosophy during the period, which marks the incubation and formation of modern science; and the all-important rise of humanism in the Renaissance, with which we shall concern ourselves in the next chapter. [11]

In any case, the traditional Christian understanding of nature was overturned with the Scientific Revolution; consequently, Christian thinkers either turned away from serious concern with a metaphysics and theology of nature or simply adopted whatever happened to be the prevalent scientific view and then tried to theologize about it and interpret it in a Christian manner. After the trial of Galileo little serious protest or effective criticism was made by Catholic theologians about the claims of modern science concerning the order of nature, and most Protestant theologians either pursued their acosmic theology or fought a rearguard action in retreat before the onslaught of scientific claims concerning the natural order, including the human body. It is only during the past generation, and thanks to the environmental crisis, as we shall see in Chapter 6, that the situation as far as renewed interest in nature is concerned has changed within the mainstream of Christian thought in the West. Whatever the causes and the nature of the consequences of the Scientific Revolution, it is important to remember that it marked the first occasion in human history when a human collectivity completely replaced the religious understanding of the order of nature for one that was not only nonreligious but that also challenged some of the most basic tenets of the religious perspective.

Although the Renaissance marks a rapid break with medieval Christian civilization and is characterized by the rise of skepticism and humanism, it was not during this period that the Scientific Revolution took place. The science of the Renaissance was still for the most part the continuation of Islamic and medieval Latin science, and even if a Paracelsus burned the medical works of al-Rāzī and Ibn Sīnā, he was still operating within the same universe, shared to a large extent by Islamic and late Latin science. [12] And yet the seeds of the Scientific Revolution were sown in the Renaissance, many of whose thinkers displayed great interest in cosmology and the philosophical significance of the order of nature.

Before the Scientific Revolution could take place, the Aristotelian worldview had to be destroyed, and this destruction came not only from the rise of the new astronomy but also from several other sources. There was first of all the spread of Hermeticism, alluded to in the previous chapter, following the translation of the Hermetic Corpus by Marsilio Ficino. Interest arose in sympathetic magic and in many of the traditional sciences based upon correspondences between various levels of cosmic reality, of which Renaissance astrology is a well-known example. All of these schools and tendencies were based upon a view of the order of nature very different from both the Aristotelian and the mechanical, which would soon become dominant. They were in fact extensions of traditional and esoteric cosmological sciences but now divorced for the most part from their metaphysical principles and cultivated to an ever greater degree, although not completely, outside the universe of traditional Christianity. They helped to destroy the Aristotelian understanding of nature before being replaced themselves by the new "mechanical philosophy."

Moreover, the Renaissance was witness to the rise of the artist-engineer, especially in Italy. Such men as Filippo Brunelleschi presented a view of nature that challenged the prevalent Aristotelianism and helped to weaken and destroy it.[13] They also helped to create the image of an order imposed upon nature in accordance with both the prevalent humanism and the Baconian view of science that appeared during the last part of the Renaissance in the sixteenth century, which was to witness the beginnings of the Scientific Revolution. And it was precisely during this later phase of the Renaissance that the idea of nature as a mechanism came to the fore, replacing the concept of nature as possessing both intelligence and life as asserted by not only Greek and medieval Christian philosophers and scientists but also most earlier Renaissance thinkers still imbued with elements drawn from various traditional cosmologies.

The rising view of nature as a machine and the order of nature as a mechanical order was based on the thesis that, because nature itself was devoid of intelligence and life, its order was due to laws imposed upon it by an intelligent being outside of nature—that is, God as the author of nature—but in a sense divorced from it. The human mind was able to study these laws, which in themselves were immutable and not subject to any change. Thus there arose that dualism which is so evident in Descartes and even Spinoza, who, despite his insistence upon the one Substance, was forced to admit that thought and extension were distinct attributes of that one Substance. This dualism also remained the prime occupation of later Western philosophers such as Hume, Kant, Berkeley, and Hegel, all of whom, despite their many differences, came to the same conslusion. "In every case their answer was at bottom the same: namely, that mind makes nature; nature is, so to speak, a by-product of the autonomous and self-existing activity of the mind."[14] Reduced to a machine by the new mental conception of what constituted physical reality, nature was to be studied by the human mind through laws that it was in the nature of the mind to understand, and God was reduced to the role of a millwright or a clockmaker, a role that also came to be considered as redundant by many of the later Newtonians. The radical transformation in the understanding of the order of nature that was to serve as the background for modern science was thereby established in the late Renaissance despite the survival of nonmechanical views that continued to be of some significance well into the seventeenth century.

The Rise of the Idea of "Laws of Nature"

The divorce of the meaning of order in nature from its traditional sense and the substitution for it of laws governing the running of a machine—an idea so central to the rise of the Scientific Revolution and the eclipse of the traditional religious understanding of nature—is closely related to the modern idea of "laws of nature" that appeared at this time and became widely held in the seventeenth century. To understand how such a concept came to be accepted in the West in contrast to other civilizations, it is necessary to delve briefly into its history. As mentioned already, in nearly every religion, moral law and the laws dominating over nature were considered as being interrelated.[15] Among Semites already in 2000 B.C., Marduk, the Sun-God, was considered as the celestial lawgiver, whereas in the Abrahamic religions one of the main functions of God is to legislate laws for both human society and nature, one of the Names of God in Islam being *al-Shāri'* or the Lawgiver. In the Psalms (148:6) it is said concerning God's laws, "He hath also established them for ever and ever; he hath made a decree which they shall not pass." The divine origin of law is also emphasized in both the Indian and Far Eastern traditions, as the central role of such terms as *dharma* and *li* demonstrate.[16]

In ancient Greece and Rome the idea of the cosmos being ruled by law is already mentioned by Demosthenes in the fourth century B.C.[17] but is especially emphasized by the Stoics, who identified Zeus with Universal Law and who influenced the Roman idea of natural law, as the law common to all men whatever might be their cultures and local traditions. The Jews had also developed the idea of natural law corresponding to the *jus gentium* of Roman law when they spoke of "The Seven Commandments for the Descendents of Noah." Christians continued to accept this view, and in the sixth century Justinian in his *Corpus of Civil Law* (*Corpus Juris Civilis*) even spoke of natural law extended to the animal realm.

It was Thomas Aquinas who synthesized all the different strands of thought concerning natural law in a Christian context. According to him there are three systems of law:[18]

1. *lex aeterna*—the eternal laws governing all things at all times
2. *lex naturalis*—natural laws governing humans
3. *lex positiva*—positive laws laid down by humans and consisting of *lex divina*, or ecclesiastical laws inspired by the Holy Spirit, and *lex humana*, or human laws enacted by rulers and legislatures.

Because the laws governing nature were of divine origin, St. Thomas asserts, "Every law framed by man bears the nature of a law only to the extent to which it is derived from the laws of nature."[19] He confirmed a view found in worlds as far apart as China and Islam. In China manmade laws (*fa*) were always subservient to the cosmic principles or laws (*li*), and if *fa* went against *li*, it had to be abandoned.

In the same way in Islam *al-qānūn,* or manmade law, is always subservient to *al-Sharī'ah* or Divine Law, which governs not only men but also the cosmos.[20]

In the West in contrast to other civilizations, this idea of law pertaining to both men and nature and legislated by God became rapidly secularized, and with the Reformation and its aftermath human reason came to replace Divine Will. It is this transformation that created the idea of "laws of nature" in the modern sense, laws that even if accepted as having been made originally by God were completely rational and discernible to human reason and no longer depended upon the Divine Will. By the seventeenth century the new meaning had become firmly established. Giordano Bruno had already tried to draw laws of nature from the *lex aeterna* of St. Thomas. Kepler used the concept of law of nature in contrast to Galileo, who avoided it. In his *Discourse of Method,* Descartes developed the idea fully and spoke of laws that God had put into nature, and Boyle and Newton used the idea freely.

From the idea of cosmic order and laws created by God through His Will and applicable to both and men and nature to the idea of "laws of nature" discoverable completely by human reason and usually identified with mathematical laws, divorced from ethical and spiritual laws, there is a major transformation that played a central role in the rise of modern science. This new idea of laws of nature also eclipsed the earlier Christian understanding of the subject, although later theologians tried to "Christianize" the seventeenth-century scientific concept of laws of nature. Interestingly enough, such an event did not take place in other civilizations with a long scientific tradition such as the Chinese, Indian, and Islamic, and this is of great significance in the parting of ways between the modern West and other civilizations as far as the understanding of the order of nature and its religious significance are concerned.

Copernicus, Copernicanism, and the "Infinite Universe"

The advent of Copernicus marks the beginning of the destruction of the traditional idea of cosmic order, which was to culminate in the Newtonian vision of the world as a machine. Before Copernicus others in both Greece and the Islamic world had spoken of the possibility of a heliocentric system that could be explained metaphysically as part of an esoteric cosmology in which the Sun, the symbol of the Divine Intellect, was central. But in those earlier instances the appearance of nature was never destroyed, nor was the hierarchy of existence, which the Ptolemaic cosmology symbolizes, so clearly eclipsed. With Copernicanism the destruction of the symbol and the symbolized went hand in hand, bringing about an intellectual and spiritual dislocation that was to have the deepest effect upon Western man's image of himself and his relation to the cosmos.[21] With the destruction of the Ptolemaic model the aspect of order as hierarchy was destroyed, leading to the loss of man's "home" and sense of "place" in the vast Universe that surrounded him.

The Copernican Revolution implied not only changing the center of the cosmos from Earth to the Sun or destroying the significance of the role of man at the center of the world, but it denied finally that the cosmos had any center at all.[22] Later Copernicanism also transformed the metaphysical idea of an infinite Universe as developed by Nicholas of Cusa into an astronomical one, as we see in the work of the English Copernican Thomas Digges. In the hands of Bruno this infinite Universe was shown to need no center at all since the Sun was one among countless stars scattered through infinite space populated by many planets such as Earth. Therefore, even the Sun was reduced along with Earth to an insignificant speck.[23]

It was Giordano Bruno in particular who was the first to supply an outline and was the primary representative of the "doctrine of the decentralized, infinite and infinitely populous universe,"[24] although Thomas Digges had been the first to expand the Copernican world to an open one. Bruno is the father of the idea of an infinitely expanded Universe that has been popular in modern science over the past two centuries, although he was far from being a modern mind as shown by his attachment to Hermeticism, mentioned earlier.[25] The view of the infinity of the Universe obviously destroyed the traditional vision of harmony and even mathematical order that had dominated the worldview of most Western scientists and philosophers until that time. For those very reasons, in fact, it was not accepted by many scientists, and no less a figure than Johannes Kepler considered this view to be scientifically meaningless. Bruno also combined Copernicanism with atomism, thereby preparing the birth of the atomistic cosmology that was to replace the hylomorphism of Scholastic cosmology in the seventeenth century, as we see in the works of Descartes and of course Newton, who, while rejecting Cartesian physics, accepted the idea of the world of nature as a "corpuscular machine."

All of these developments beginning with Copernicus's own thesis of heliocentrism helped to destroy the idea of nature as a living reality and reduced the cosmos to simply structured matter. The spiritual nature of the substance of the heavens and the angelic nature of the forces moving the planets and the stars came to an end in the eyes of modern man, resulting in the enhancing of his power. Man could now extend his knowledge to the heavens and, in fact, the whole cosmos by simply studying Earth.[26] The apple that fell on Newton's head reminded him of the force that moved the planets owing to the homogenization of the cosmos introduced by Copernicanism. Henceforth all qualitative differences were irrelevant. There was but one substance comprising the entire Universe, and that substance was characterized by quantity, the only differences between things being those of quantity and mathematical structures. The era of the mechanization of the cosmos and the reduction of the order of nature to a mechanical one had arrived. No wonder then that the great Elizabethan poet John Donne was to lament,

> . . . new Philosophy calls all in doubt,
> The Element of fire is quite put out;
> The Sun is lost, and th' earth, and no mans wit
> Can well direct him where to looke for it.
> And freely men confesse that this world's spent,

When in the Planets, and the Firmament
They seeke so many new; then see that this
Is crumbled out again to his Atomies.
'Tis all in peeces, all cohaerence gone;
All just supply, and all Relation.[27]

Bacon and Gilbert

The English philosopher Francis Bacon and the scientist William Gilbert demonstrate each in his own way the rise of the new mechanical philosophy in the ambience of the English world given much more to empiricism than to rationalism. The role of Bacon in the rise of modern science has been exaggerated as far as the so-called scientific method of induction introduced by him is concerned, because one knows only too well that there is in fact strictly speaking no such thing as *the* scientific method if one only ponders how Einstein came up with the theory of relativity or Niels Bohr with his model of the atom. But Bacon was important in popularizing the new science and defining its role as a search for power to dominate over nature and not only to understand it. In him can be found the genesis of that aspect of modern science which is concerned not so much with understanding the order of nature as with dominating over it, with the result of imposing upon nature a purely human order aimed at the attainment of material goals.

Bacon was on the one hand a rabid enemy of Aristotelianism and especially Aristotelian logic against which he wrote his *Novum Organum*.[28] On the other hand he was not simply a rationalistic empiricist but showed interest in the "chemical philosophy" of his day along with Renaissance magic. And yet, in his works, he rejected the ultimate significance of qualities in nature, reducing qualitative distinctions to functions of structures to be treated mathematically. Bacon did not, however, have a full grasp of the meaning of the quantitative unity of the substance of the cosmos and the significance of the role of mathematics in science. His own contribution to the new mechanical science was far from being as significant as that of a Descartes or a Galileo and must be understood most of all in the public support he was able to gather, as a powerful political figure, for the new science in England.

Gilbert was a more important figure as far as the new science itself was concerned. In 1600 he published his well-known *De Magnete* on magnetism, claiming that attractive forces, as one finds in the case of the magnet, pervade the whole of nature.[29] The significance of this work was of course its experimental basis, which makes it significant for the rise of the new science, although Gilbert still envisaged magnetism in terms of an animistic force.[30] Making use of centuries of observation and study of magnetism going back to Peregrinus Proteus, Gilbert proceeded step by step through experimentation. He belongs to that group of men in the Renaissance and the seventeenth century who mediated between science and technology.

According to Gilbert there was a soul in the magnet that would awaken a kindred psychic potency dormant in the iron, thus causing attraction. In contrast to Galileo and other contemporaries, he was asking the question: What is the nature of magnetism? His answer was the animistic force that was part of the vitalistic theory of Earth. For Gilbert, Earth was still the *mater communis* whose interior was like a womb in which metals grew; he opposed the mechanistic view of nature although he accepted the view of the infinity of the Universe with an infinite number of stars with varying distances from the center of the Universe and extending to infinity.[31] Gilbert was therefore a transitional figure belonging on the one hand to the vitalistic world of the earlier physics and the experimental science that was soon to deplete nature completely of any spiritual and even vital elements. His view of Earth as a great magnet and his emphasis upon experimentation mark him as an opponent of the older view of the order of nature. There is no doubt that it was Gilbert's insistence that attractive forces pervade nature that led Kepler to assert that one body attracts another because of the "natural affection" of bodies for each other and hence the necessity to substitute in physics the word *vis*, which implies a mechanical rather than vital force, for the word *anima*.

Galileo

Despite the significance of Descartes and Cartesian mathematics, it is Galileo whom one must accept as the founder of the idea of mathematical physics.[32] In a famous passage in *Il Saggiatore* he noted:

> Philosophy is written in this grand book, the universe, which stands continually open to our gaze. But the book cannot be understood unless one first learns to comprehend the language and read the letters in which it is composed. It is written in the language of mathematics, and its characters are triangles, circles and other geometric figures, without which it is humanly impossible to understand a single word of it; without these, one wanders about in a dark labyrinth.[33]

In this, one of the most significant statements of the Scientific Revolution, Galileo transformed the book of nature, which had been considered by Muslim, Jews, and Christians for centuries to have contained the "signs of God" (*āyāt Allāh* or *vestigia Dei*), into a book of mathematics to be understood by the mathematical knowledge innate to the human mind. In a most abrupt manner he destroyed the very understanding of *natura* as held by ancient and medieval philosophers and scientists and deprived nature of her substance, colors, forms, qualities, and all other aspects of physical reality that traditional religions everywhere had identified with the imprint of the Divine upon the cosmic order.[34] By destroying the significance of what he called "secondary qualities" or qualities as such and emphasizing only the "primary qualities," which for him were none other than pure quantity, Galileo also rejected the religious understanding of the order of nature.

Of course, Galileo claimed such a view as being Platonic and attacked the existing Aristotelianism in the name of the venerable Platonic tradition. More-over, many of his well-known modern students have confirmed his Platonism.[35] Although not doubting that there are certain Platonic elements in Galileo, it is difficult to see how a scientist who reduces nature to a vast machine whose movement studied mathematically he consideres as the goal of the new physics he is establishing could be identified with the author of the metaphysics of Platonic Ideas, which are both ontological principles of the physical world and the source of its order. Is one simply to equate mathematical entities with the Platonic Ideas while considering mathematics only in its quantitative and not symbolic aspect? Are the triangle and circle mentioned by Galileo in the *Il Saggiatore* to be identified with the symbolic figures of Pythagorean geometry? It seems that nothing was further from Galileo's mind as one can see from the results of the physics he helped to create in which there would surely be no possibility of the incarnation in the substance of this world of the Logos nor of the *lógoi* as stated by Christian Platonists such as St. Maximus mentioned earlier. Insistence upon the mathematical nature of physical reality, far from being a return to Platonism, which comprises one of the most important schools of Western metaphysics and theology, marked in fact the death knell of the religious understanding of nature in the Occident and the creation of a science based upon a view of the order of nature totally different from what had existed in Christian religious and philo-sophical thought until then.[36]

The reason why Galileo was more successful than Descartes in the creation of a physics based completely on mathematics was not the insistence of both men upon the primacy of mathematics, but that Descartes failed to distinguish be-tween physics and mathematics and pushed the mathematization of nature to an extreme while Galileo succeeded in applying mathematics to physical reality, thereby creating a new physics albeit not completely. The early Galileo was still immersed in the medieval physics of a Jean Buridan or Ibn Bājjah (Avempace), but two factors turned him to the new science: The first was the mathematical direction of his thought influenced by Archimedes, and the second the Copernican world-picture, which dominated his whole intellectual outlook as he set out to demonstrate that the heliocentric system embodied a physical truth and was not simply mathematically convenient.[37] Thereby he set out on a quest that was to reduce the heavens to an earthly reality and the earthly reality to the subject of a mathematical science contained primarily in the mechanics he developed.

It is true that Galileo never completed his project; for example, although he made important contributions to the theory of inertia, he could not conceive of a body moving perpetually in a straight line since he still held on to the view of a spherical Universe with a finite radius.[38] But he remains nevertheless the founder of that classical mathematical science which reached its culmination with Newton and symbolizes to this day in the popular mind in the West, thanks to his famous trial, the triumph of reason over fanaticism, whereas what he really signifies is the triumph of a purely quantitative understanding of the order of nature over the religious and qualitative one, a triumph that marked not only an ordinary victory but the nearly total obliteration in the West of the order it came to replace.[39] No event in modern European history is more significant than the trial of Galileo in the replacing of the religious understanding of nature with the new "mechanical philosophy," which not only claimed to be a science of nature but also to be the *only* legitimate science of the natural world. The consequences of that event are to be seen in the disappearance of so many species and the destruction of Earth's natural resources today.

Kepler

In contrast to Galileo, Johannes Kepler was concerned with the actual forces and physical causes of celestial motion and not only its geometry, and he may therefore be said to be the first person to have replaced the celestial theology of Scholasticism with celestial physics, taking a step beyond Galileo.[40] Kepler considered the celestial bodies to be lifeless and inert, possessing a property he called "inertia." Such bodies cannot keep moving or put themselves in motion precisely because they possess the property of inertia. Moreover, there was no longer a hierarchy of space, as already indicated by Galileo, space being conceived henceforth as isotropic, and Earth as sharing the same physics with the heavens. Thus Kepler further prepared the ground for the synthesis of Newton.[41]

As to what force actually moved the heavens, Kepler believed it to be magnetic following Gilbert's view of Earth as a giant magnet. But Kepler still combined animistic and mechanistic ideas. In the *Mysterium Cosmographicum* written in 1597, while supporting the heliocentric theory with Pythagorean arguments, he spoke of the World Soul or *anima mundi* being situated in the Sun. In the second edition of the work, however, he had replaced the *anima mundi* with force or *facultas corporea*. Moreover, he emphasized observation and accepted the Platonic solids as models for the planets because they were in accordance with astronomical observation.[42] There is, however, a truly Pythagorean aspect to Kepler. After composing the *Mysterium Cosmographicum,* which dealt only with the geometry of the cosmos, he realized that the cosmos was dynamic and that he must seek harmonic relations, "for God whilst being a geometer, was not solely an architect—a fact which the ancient Pythagoreans had certainly apprehended. He was also, even primarily, a 'musician'."[43]

Being himself a musician and deeply interested in harmonic theory, Kepler set out in 1599 to study harmonic relations especially as they applied to the structure of the Universe. The result of this quest was the *Harmonice Mundi* (1619), which contains the account of his astronomical system and his study of the planets. For Kepler this was the occasion of extreme joy, for he was thereby able to contemplate the harmony of the Universe and discover what he believed to be the secret of the cosmic order that God had revealed to him as a special favor.[44]

The planetary studies of Kepler mark one of the most important instances of the penetration of Pythagorean harmonics into the main body of modern scientific activity. And Kepler, while being perhaps the first person to speak of "the laws of nature" in the modern sense, still conceived of the order and harmony he had discovered in the movement of the planets in a Pythagorean sense. In him elements of Pythagorean mysticism and the new science based upon mathematicization of nature in the modern sense were combined, but his interest in traditional harmonics did little to alter the march of the new science toward a purely quantitative definition of the order of nature as matter in motion. It was his "laws of planetary motion" that were to influence later science,[45] while his joy in the contemplation of cosmic harmony came to be considered as the private musings of an eccentric genius, irrelevant to that quantitative order to whose discovery he had made such a great contribution.

Descartes

In the previous chapter we dealt with the crucial role of René Descartes at the dawn of modern Western philosophy. But now we have to turn to him again as a scientist, who, although criticized by later physicists, left the deepest effect upon the very structure of modern science by his mathematization of space, time, and matter. Descartes sought to develop a physics derived in the manner of mathematics by deduction from axioms, and he considered physics as the trunk of a tree whose root was metaphysics according to his understanding of this term.[46]

For Kepler, Galileo, and Newton the structure of the physical world was essentially mathematical; Descartes, however, went to the extreme of completely identifying mathematics and natural science. According to him, "Natural science is mathematical in character not only in the wider sense that mathematics ministers to it, in whatever function this may be, but also in the much stricter sense that the human mind produces the knowledge of nature by its own effort in the same way as it does mathematics."[47]

Descartes' method in the study of nature is contained in his *Regulae ad Directionem Ingenii* in which he asserts clearly that all scientific knowledge takes place as deduction from axioms as in the case of mathematics, and of course his own contribution to science was primarily in mathematics and more specifically in descriptive geometry. But even in physics, where his theories were to be rejected by Newton, his emphasis upon the identification of matter with its purely quantitative and mathematical features was to have a lasting influence upon modern science. The very idea of matter as pure quantity in fact owes much to Cartesianism, including its epistemological dualism,[48] and Descartes is one of the most important voices during the Scientific Revolution in relegating quality to a purely subjective category.[49] He clearly identified matter with extension when he observed, "It is not heaviness, or hardness, or color which constitutes the nature of body but only extension."[50] Furthermore, "the nature of body, taken generally, does not consist in the fact that it is a hard, or a heavy, or a colored thing, or a thing that touches our senses in any other manner, but only in that it is a *substance* extended in length, breadth and depth." No clearer statement is needed of the transformation of nature from a living "thou" to an "it," which is, moreover, pure quantity. Descartes' physics was to be rejected while that of Galileo was to lay the foundation for classical physics, but the French philosopher-mathematician's concept of corpuscular matter identified with its mathematical properties was to survive as a key element in that new view of nature which saw the order of nature in a purely mathematically cum mechanical order.[51]

Newton

The Scientific Revolution culminated, as confirmed by nearly all historians of science, with Isaac Newton, whose synthesis in the *Principia* was to determine the understanding of the order in nature not only in science but also in most of Western culture to this century. In a sense, there are two Newtons or two sides of this colossal figure of modern science—the well-known Newton of the *Principia* and the *Opticks* and the much less studied and nearly completely neglected Newton who was the author of biblical commentaries and alchemical treatises. The latter aspect of Newton, so much in discord with the rationalistic empirical perspective of modern science, was relegated to oblivion until recent times and even now is only of interest in understanding better the total thought and personality of the most famous of all physicists. However, it does not contribute greatly to our comprehension of the meaning of the order of nature in modern science.[52] It is, therefore, with the former aspect that we are concerned in this study.

The synthesis of Newton as presented in the *Principia* reveals several strands such as Descartes' "Universal Science," the rules and methods outlined by Francis Bacon, the cosmology and physics of Galileo, William Gilbert's theory of attraction between bodies, Kepler's idea of force and inertia and atomism with its roots in neo-Epicurian philosophy.[53] Newton drew from all these sources to complete the creation of a new science that marks the definite termination of the older attitude toward nature and the beginning of a new one. Moreover, with him the new science gained both independence and a prestige that allowed it to exercise vast influence upon Western society and, through the spread of modernism, elsewhere is the world.[54]

As far as order is considered, in both the theoretical *Principia* and the experimental *Opticks,* Newton displayed the same outlook, which involves necessary relations capable of mathematical description of observed phenomena.[55] Like Galileo and Descartes before him, Newton saw the order of nature in quantitative terms. Nature consisted of mass, size, shape, and motion of bodies, other observable qualities being the response of sentient beings to those quantitative "realities" or ultimately the motion of particles. What Newton added to his predecessors and especially Galileo was that, whereas Galilean laws of motion were valid in a vacuum and an ideal mathematicized world, the degree to which the actual physical world deviates from that mathematical world could itself be treated mathematically. Galilean physics was the first-term approximation that could be corrected to the extent needed by corrective terms in an infinite series. Philosophically this implied that the difference between the idealized mathematical world and the actual physical world was itself nothing but quantity to be dealt with mathematically.

The Newtonian concept of the order of nature also implied the uniformity of nature and her laws already indicated by Newton's predecessors in the Scientific Revolution but made more explicit by him. The laws of heavenly motion applied to the Earth and vice versa; terrestrial and celestial physics were but a single science. Moreover, the motion of the heavens could also be calculated on the basis of first-term approximations with multiple inequalities as could motion on Earth.[56]

In contrast to Aristotle, who sought to study causes in nature, and Descartes, whose science was *a priori*, Newton was primarily interested in the order of nature itself, which he saw as mathematical order based upon observation of nature. This order was the result of a demonstrated conclusion rather than a necessary cause. But Newton was not opposed to seeking the cause for the order of nature, which he believed to be God, although he considered order to be observable in nature irrespective of whether one discovers its cause or not. Even force, which Descartes opposed because he considered it to be an occult property, Newton accepted as mathematical relation rooted in the mathematical order of nature. Newton in fact destroyed Cartesian physics by appealing to the very weapon of Descartes, namely mathematical order.

Newton was an observer of nature and claimed that he did not frame any hypotheses (the famous *hypotheses non fingo*). By this assertion Newton did not mean that he did not actually proffer any hypotheses, which in fact he did, but that he did not need to do so as far as his science was concerned. He considered the goal of science to be the discovery of order or, more specifically, the description of the mathematical order of nature from which hypotheses had to be excluded. And yet, Newton's very certitude about the Universe being ordered had a theological basis and rested upon Christian natural theology.[57] That a certain strand of Christian theology should have allowed itself to descend from the exalted level of seeing the cosmos as the theater for the manifestation of the Divine Logos to the plane of accepting the identification of the Divine Order with purely quantitative mathematics is itself a most surprising development.

As an outside observer, one could ask how there could grow within a religion, in which the Logos was considered as the Son of God incarnated in human flesh, a theology where mathematical patterns in a sense took the place of the Logos, as if God had begotten mathematical patterns rather than the Son, and material corpuscles had replaced the flesh in which the Word was incarnated. Such a thesis could have been understood if mathematical patterns had been seen in their Pythagorean and Platonic sense in which Logos itself was understood as harmony, as already mentioned. But for mathematics understood in the Cartesian and Galilean sense to take the place of the Logos, such a theology would have to accept the reduction of primal Divine creativity and activity to purely quantitative relations rather than the Logos "by which all things were made." Such a reduction and impoverishment can only be called a monstrosity that could not but have the direst consequences for later Western civilization. We cannot deal with various aspects of this issue here, but it is necessary to mention in this context that without doubt for Newton himself, but not necessarily his followers, the mathematical order of nature was related to a particular theological vision and the Divine Cause was envisaged as the cause of this order.

In the *Scholium* added to his definitions in the *Principia*, Newton distinguished absolute time from relative time and likewise absolute space from relative space. In contrast to Descartes, who had reduced space to pure quantity, Newton followed Henry Moore, who considered space as an attribute of God. For Newton space was God's *sensorium,* and he called the purely relative conception of time and space vulgar.[58] Newton did not believe that the order observable in the planetary system could be only the result of matter subject to the law of gravity. As he wrote in a letter to Richard Burtley, "to make this System therefore, with all its Motions, requires a Cause . . . and the Velocities with which these Planets could revolve about those Quantities of matter . . . argues that Cause to be not blind and fortuitous, but very skilled in Mechanicks and Geometry."[59] For Newton the supremely elegant structure of the Solar System "was itself proof of an intelligent being who was its cause. It is this being whom he called the Pantacrator, or ruler of the universe, whose Will is the source of the mathematical order observable in nature."[60] Through the actions of God, both order and structure are created in the world.[61]

Newton's cosmology and understanding of order combined the Cartesian conception with Christian natural theology in an unstable wedding that proved to be incompatible.[62] His followers, who for the most part did not share his religious vision, simply discarded the natural theology, which was not at all integral to his physics. What might appear as a new common discourse between religion and the new science was in fact no more than a passing romance that soon turned to a mirage. For most eighteenth-century Newtonians, what was significant was nature seen as a vast machine whose mathematical laws had been discovered by Newton rather than the view of space as a Divine Attribute or the laws of nature as results of Divine Will, which Newton had accepted but which appeared to most of his followers to be irrelevant to science. The very success of Newtonian science blinded men to the reality of the religious understanding of nature, leaving the mechanized view of the world and the purely mathematical character of its order as the only accepted view within the paradigm that came to dominate the mainstream of European thought.

THE QUANTIFICATION OF NATURE IN THE EIGHTEENTH CENTURY

While Newtonian theories became totally dominant in physics and Newtonians sought to apply the mechanical model of the Universe based on purely quantitative and mathematical laws to other fields of the physical sciences, the mathematical method became popularized even beyond the realm of physics and in those sciences that were able to develop along the line of Newtonian physics. A major figure in the popularization of this method was Christian Wolff, a student of Leibniz. Through his efforts and those of others like him, this mathematical or quantifying method became part and parcel of the European philosophical and scientific scene. What the French call *l'esprit géométrique* was highly extolled by the Encyclopedists and came to dominate the more general movement in eighteenth-century Europe to prepare encyclopedias of knowledge of the natural world.[63] There existed a strong impulse drawn from the mathematization of the

My comments on

AUTHOR/EDITOR

TITLE

_____

_____

_____

_____

_____

MAY WE QUOTE YOU? ☐ YES ☐ NO

COURSE NAME _____ DATE _____

WILL YOU ADOPT? ☐ DEFINITELY ☐ POSSIBLE ☐ NO   LEVEL? ☐ FRESH. ☐ SOPH. ☐ JUN. ☐ SEN. ☐ GRAD.

DECISION DATE _____ FOR USE AS: ☐ REQUIRED MAIN TEXT ☐ RECOMMENDED READING

CURRENT TEXT _____ APPROXIMATE ENROLLMENT _____

NAME (PLEASE PRINT) _____

DEPARTMENT _____ POSITION _____

INSTITUTION _____

CITY _____ STATE _____ ZIP CODE _____

VERY IMPORTANT!

E-MAIL ADDRESS _____

TELEPHONE NUMBER _____

BUSINESS REPLY MAIL
FIRST CLASS   PERMIT NO. 4437   NEW YORK, N.Y.

POSTAGE WILL BE PAID BY ADDRESSEE

OXFORD UNIVERSITY PRESS
College Marketing Department
198 Madison Avenue
New York NY 10157-2091

world picture and the success of the "mathematical method" to impose order upon all realms of nature through quantification. Such an impulse is to be seen not only in the *Encyclopédie* but also in Georges Buffon's *Histoire naturelle* and the Linnean encyclopedia, *Systema naturae*, which, although not mathematical in character and still based on morphological descriptions and classifications, are highly quantitative, whereas, the *Encyclopédie* itself is marked by its strongly antimetaphysical stance.[64]

During the eighteenth century, European scientists, active in many different fields, took up enthusiastically what has been called the "systematic" model of order.[65] By "systematics" is meant the classification of objects forming the subject of a particular science, especially the branches of natural history, into groups based on degrees of both identity and difference. Although such a task seems different from the mathematical astronomy and physics of a Galileo or Newton, nevertheless it was an important expression of the quantitative method and *l'esprit géometrique* of the Enlightenment and was definitely connected to the interest in analysis so important to the thought of that period.[66]

Systematics, of course, differed from the mathematical sciences in that it was still concerned with natural forms, but it shared with mathematics a generalized method of analysis that emphasized abstraction and numeration. One could therefore say that in the seventeenth century the dissemination of the idea of mathematical order in nature spread to even those sciences such as natural history in which a Newtonian type of science could not be developed. Through the spread of the quantitative sense of order, the sense of the religious significance of wonder in Creation as manifested in the flora and fauna was also destroyed to a large extent, as was the wonder of the vast darkness of the sky on a starry night. It now only remained for the very reality of the forms of nature to be dissolved into the flow of evolutionary process to destroy whatever sense there might have remained of the sacred origin of life and its forms.

The Scientific Revolution discovered much about the quantitative face of nature but at the expense of that other face which all creatures have turned eternally toward God. Henceforth as long as only the quantitative face of nature was considered as real and the new science was seen as the only science of nature, the religious meaning of the order of nature was irrelevant, at best an emotional and poetic response to "matter in motion." The cosmos could no longer be seen as theophany nor could it be read as so many pages of a revealed book within which were written the signs of God, the *vestigia Dei* or *āyāt Allāh*. Those in the West who still sought such a vision of nature were relegated to the margins of European thought and became associated with occultism and related phenomena.

NATURPHILOSOPHIE AND SCIENCE

Still, there remained a group of philosophers and even scientists who did not submit so rapidly to the mechanistic view of nature. In the decades preceding and following 1800 there existed in Germany a science related to Romanticism and *Naturphilosophie* that rejected the positivistic and mechanistic science of the day in favor of a science that did not reject empiricism but rather sought to integrate the details contained in eighteenth-century encyclopedias of natural history into a whole reflecting the unity of nature. For such scientists the vast amount of detail of the organic and inorganic worlds should reveal rather than veil the unity of nature, and they called for the investigation of this unity. As the Romantic poet and philosopher Novalis wrote, "In physics the phenomena have long been torn from their context and their mutual relations are not pursued. Any phenomenon is a link in an incalculable chain which understands *all phenomena* as links."[67]

For these scientists the idea of hierarchy in nature also continued to be of great significance. It was the gradation of the principles of nature that produced diverse phenomena, and such scientists as Lorenz Oken and Johann Ritter applied their idea of the existence of a hierarchy of orders in nature to chemistry and geology and spoke of potencies that, through metamorphosis, would become parts of a new order. Among them figures such as I. P. V. Troxler envisaged the Infinite Itself as a potency and stated, "The infinite is the *independent substance* of the living from which *accidents* emerge into time only in the dynamism in which the substance limits the potency, and the *attributes* rise up into space only in the organism in which the potency limits the substance."[68]

Practitioners of this kind of science refused to submit to the mechanistic interpretation of the world at that time and sought to preserve the order of nature as related both to the hierarchy and the wholeness characterizing traditional cosmology.

This type of science produced some important figures such as Hans Christian Oersted and made notable discoveries in such fields as galvanism, electromagnetism, anatomy, and medicine. Yet it was fiercely attacked by those practitioners of the sciences who accepted only the empirical and positivistic point of view, and it declined rapidly by the middle of the nineteenth century.[69] Its influence did not, however, die out completely in certain schools of alternative medicine or even among a number of twentieth-century scientists in quest of metaphysical meaning in the physics they were studying. Needless to say, its greatest significance was in constituting a protest against that quantitative view of the order of nature that lay at the heart of the paradigm of science, cultivated and nurtured during a century and a half from Copernicus to Newton, and that became all-powerful and all-embracing in European civilization.

EVOLUTION: DARWINIAN AND NEO-DARWINIAN

Our aim here is not to provide a metaphysical, religious, logical, or even scientific critique of the theory of evolution, which, despite its metaphysical and logical absurdity and a vast amount of paleontological evidence demonstrating the sudden appearance of different species, is accepted by the mainstream scientific and academic establishment in the West, not as a scientific hypothesis but as a dogma.[70] It is not even our purpose to seek to explain how a theory that is metaphysically and logically absurd should become prevalent so rapidly. We will say that such a theory was the only possible choice for those who had denied the creative power of God in the multifarious manifestations of nature to explain the presence of life and various species even if this possibility implied so many improbabilities whose actualization can only be called incredible. Also, we will mention briefly what meaning of order issues from evolutionism, both Darwinian and neo-Darwinian.

Evolution, as scientifically understood, erased the final vestiges of Divine Wisdom from the face of nature and removed whatever ultimate significance natural forms might have by denying all ultimateness and finality and reducing all forms simply to a cross section of the stream of time and flow and process of matter. Whatever remained of the Augustinian *rationes seminales* or the *lógoi* of St. Maximus disappeared, and any nexus that still existed in the minds of people between living things and their archetypal realities in the Mind of God was destroyed. Furthermore, the denial of teleology, which was part and parcel of classical physics as far as it concerned the inanimate world, was extended to the domain of life.

In fact, Darwinism continued the mechanistic conception of the world although it introduced life as a force or principle between the mind and matter of Cartesian dualism in which life was simply included within the domain of matter. Life resembled matter in being devoid of purpose and "blind." Darwin spoke often of natural selection as if there were teleology in nature, but he did not for one moment accept a conscious will operating in nature and denied all teleology in the traditional sense of the term. In any case Darwinism has been closely allied to a purely materialistic genetics and, while philosophically speaking the vital process must be considered as a new element introduced into the scientific understanding of the order of nature, life itself was interpreted by most Darwinians in purely physical and mechanistic terms, which still dominate modern biology.[71]

Darwin himself did not speak to any extent about order in nature save to describe the various species in evolutionary terms, which subverted the vertical hierarchy of the chain of life or the chain of being that was understood traditionally to be "spatial"—that is, always present—to a temporal and horizontal one in which order as hierarchy in the traditional sense lost all its meaning.[72] It was mostly the Darwinians Herbert Spencer and Thomas Huxley who both popularized and expanded upon the Darwinian understanding of the order of nature. They made it clear that Darwinism was based upon the seventeenth-century mechanistic view that saw all nature as matter in motion according to mathematically determined laws. Both Spencer and Huxley stated explicitly that all biological activities are based on matter and motion and nothing else, and they saw Darwinism as the natural outcome of the views of Descartes and Galileo.

They did, however, introduce a major change by refusing to accept mind as an independent substance. Rather, they reduced mind to the result of evolutionary development—that is, purely material processes—that moved toward ever greater organization, resulting finally in human life and consciousness. The reductionism of modern science thereby took a giant step by reducing the other half of Cartesian dualism to matter and ending with a monistic materialism that characterizes so much of modern biology and the views of those who try to derive general philosophical conclusions from it.[73]

The Darwinians saw an order in nature demonstrated by the effect of natural selection always leading to progress that Spencer considered to be a law which he extended from biology to society. Huxley also spoke of a harmonious order governing the universe.[74] But whereas for Descartes and Newton this order was imposed by God and for Kant it proved His existence, for Darwin, Huxley, and other Darwinians such a conception of order was totally destroyed and nature could not in any way lead to God. The order in nature was in fact of a purely statistical kind and was in no way related to design or preestablished harmony. No wonder that Huxley was the first person to coin the word "agnostic" which spread rapidly in a world in which there were so few veritable gnostics. Darwinism was the final blow to a precarious "static" view of nature as far as seeing the processes of nature and the natural species possessing an immutable character. With Darwinism all traces of the view of the existence of the Wisdom of God in His Creation disappeared, marking the complete and final triumph of a materialistic view of nature over the traditional religious one in the West as far as both the scientific world and the so-called intellectual establishment were concerned.[75]

The nineteenth-century Darwinian theory has met so many obstacles that its contemporary adherents, now called neo-Darwinians, have been forced to propose certain new theories of order that differ greatly from older Darwinian views. Thus, Niles Eldridge and Stephen Gould propose an alternative interpretation of Darwinism according to which there are unstable or chaotic states of "punctuated equilibrium" during which "peripheral isolates" may transform a system into a new form.[76] Chaos thus leads to order, which leads to chaos, and then to order, etc. There are also eminent biologists in Europe who, rather than modifying Darwinism in such a manner, reject it completely and speak not of evolution but "organicistic revolutions," which suddenly bring about new life-forms demonstrating discontinuity vis-à-vis what existed before.[77]

Although far from being a scientific fact but rather a philosophical theory and scientific hypothesis, evolutionary theory has presented the greatest challenge in the West to the traditional understanding of the order of nature, being itself in a sense the "religion" of the modern world. It has caused much of Christian theology to recede before its onslaught and to seek to redefine its understanding of man and his destiny. During the twentieth century it has even moved a step further into the domain of religion itself and has resulted in the kind of "evolutionary religion" demonstrated in Christianity by Teilhardism[78] and many current eco-theologians and outside of Christianity by the teachings of Śrī Aurobindo in India. It is also a main feature of nearly all the "New-Age religions" and contemporary occult movements. As for the understanding of the order of nature, the spread of evolutionism destroyed the very meaning of the sacredness of life and removed from nature any possibility of bearing the imprint of the immutable and the eternal.

MODERN PHYSICS: RELATIVITY AND QUANTUM MECHANICS

Modern physics is at once the reversal of the worldview of classical physics and its continuation. This can be seen particularly in the theory of relativity, which rejects completely the Newtonian concept of space and time and the eighteenth-century conception of matter and yet remains faithful to the mathematical view of the order of nature so central to Newtonian thought. Moveover, Einstein continued to consider the order dominating over the Universe as being related to God, who strictly imposed causality over the Universe in which chance did not exist since God "did not play dice" with the Universe. In the same way that Newtonian laws of motion are special cases of relativistic laws of motion, Einsteinian relativity shares the basic conception of the order of nature with classical physics as far as relating order to mathematical patterns is concerned. The major differences between the two are to be seen, first, in the notion of matter, which becomes convertible to energy in modern physics, while being "neither created nor destroyed" in classical physics and chemistry, and second, in the transfer of absoluteness from space and time in Newtonian physics to the velocity of light in relativity. The vision of the Universe issuing from the two schools of physics is different, yet the idea of mathematical order permeating the two visions of the natural world is the same.

With quantum mechanics the departure of the understanding of order in nature from that of classical physics becomes more radical, and even the mathematical order that quantum mechanics shares with classical physics is different in that the latter accepts this order only in the statistical sense. Indeterminacy and uncertainty lie at the heart of quantum mechanics, going back to the question of the wave or corpuscular nature of light and including the formal principle of uncertainty stated by Werner Heisenberg.

The debate as to whether light is a wave or a stream of corpuscles goes back to Newton and Christian Huygens, each of whom had their defenders in the eighteenth and nineteenth centuries, Newton's view being supported by such figures as Ruggiero Boscovich and Pierre Simon de Laplace and Huygens by Robert Hooke and Thomas Young. These views remained, however, exclusive of each other and did not become accepted at the same time within a single view of physics.

In quantum mechanics, however, the two views become combined in such a way as to be logically and even imaginably difficult to conceive. On the one hand Max Planck discovered the discontinuous emission of energy, and Einstein proposed the theory of photons or particles of lights, called also "quanta of action," which were discovered by Arthur H. Compton and Chandrasekhara V. Raman, all leading to the theory of the granular nature of light. On the other hand the de Broglie-Schrödinger theory led to the view that matter and light had wavelike structure. This led to the "wave-particle" duality, which was seen by the physicists of the day and continues to be viewed by most physicists as being irreducible to a single reality. The result of this discovery of quantum mechanics led to the Copenhagen School, which argues that no picture of reality is possible and that micronature is bipartite in an ultimate way, with the result that the nexus between physics and what philosophical understanding of nature it might possess has thus become severed, at least for those who accept the interpretation of this school.

As we shall see, there are other interpretations of this "ambiguity" as well as other main features of quantum mechanics: These include Paul Dirac's assertion that we can only know a defined state *partially;* Heisenberg's uncertainty principle, which involves the very concept of our understanding of nature; the denial of local causality; all laws of quantum mechanics being probabilistic; and the denial of classical determinism.[79]

Modern physics also presents a radically different view of the subatomic world from the simple atomism of classical physics, which considered nature to be comprised of indivisible particles—that is, atoms (from *atomos,* meaning literally "indivisible" in Greek). At the beginning of the twentieth century physicists looked for "ultimate" building particles of matter, and many continue to do so today. But as more and more particles came to be discovered in addition to protons, electrons, and neutrons there now exists such an array of particles, called by some physicists "a particle zoo," that many have given up on the idea of finding the "ultimate" particles or building blocks of matter and rather envisage a vast ocean of energy from which different particles with various lifetimes issue forth and into which they disappear.[80] One might say that whereas Newtonian physics saw an order underlying what appears outwardly as chaos in the perceptible world, for quantum mechanics there is chaos or at least an unknowable reality underlying the order of macro- and even micronature. Some have concluded from this that the limits of human knowledge in the understanding of nature have been reached beyond which one can only appeal to wisdom and other modes of cognition; others, needless to say, reject any other possible mode of knowing. Whatever the case, it is here that metaphysical and religious modes of knowledge concerning even the natural world are entering into the intellectual world of at least some physicists for the first time since the Scientific Revolution, even if until now most physicists who have turned to those other modes of knowledge (usually drawn from non-Western sources) have not been able to gain a profound grasp of those alternative modes of understanding the nature of reality.

Perhaps the greatest challenge to the modern scientific understanding of order comes from the consequences of the Bell theorem, which implies a fundamental interconnectedness of the parts of the Universe denied by both classical and modern physics until only recently.[81] (John Stuart) Bell's theorem asserts that if quantum mechanics is correct then the principle of local causes and the whole notion of locality as we understand it is false. And because it has been shown that the predictions based upon quantum mechanic calculations correspond to experimental results, the whole idea of local causality must be false. The theorem itself is based on the remarkable behavior of particles in two different points in space in which the change of the state of one is detected *immediately* in the other without an apparent causal nexus between them, leading some physicists to speak of the transfer of information at superluminal speeds, something that Einstein rejected.[82]

One of the most notable interpretations of the consequences of Bell's theorem is that of David Bohm, who speaks of the unbroken wholeness of physical reality and denies one of the basic tenets of classical physics, which is the divisibility and analyzability of the physical world. Rather than the world being composed of separate objects in an "explicate order," it is, according to Bohm, an *implicate order*[83] or an unbroken wholeness, about which one can only say that it is. "There is an order unfolded into the very process of the universe but that unfolded [or implicate] order may not be readily apparent."[84] Particles appear to be discontiguous in the explicate order, but they are in reality continuous in that implicate order which our ordinary consciousness does not perceive. Matter itself is a form of the implicate order, and in contrast to what we perceive through our segmented consciousness it cannot be reduced to particles. If only we were to acquire the right consciousness which could know the whole or that-which-is, one would see the separate elements related to the implicate order as the implicate order.

In this interpretation of quantum mechanics and especially Bell's theorem, not only is there an insistence upon wholeness as coming before all parts and segments, but also an insistence upon the significance of consciousness for the mode in which we preceive nature,[85] and the necessity to have a transformation of consciousness in order to perceive that whole in whose matrix alone the behavior of the "parts" can be understood. What implication such a view has for the religious understanding of the order of nature and the reassertion of the significance and validity of its view we shall deal with later in this book. But it needs to be added here that the views of Bohm have not gained the adherence of every physicist, although many have been attracted to it. The prevalent attitude remains that of the Copenhagen School and the identification of the order of nature with laws determined by statistical probabilities and by mathematical models using statistical methods.

ORDER AND CHAOS: THE PRIGOGINIAN VIEW

Another significant challenge to the understanding of the order of nature in classical science has come in recent years from the study of chaos in relation to order, a subject most closely associated with the name of Ilya Prigogine.[86] Classical physics was based upon a reversible conception of time, and theoretically any physical process could be reversed, as in the case of the movement of a wheel. Already in the nineteenth century the first challenge to Newtonian physics came when Jean-Baptiste Fourier formulated the law of the flow of heat, which for the first time presented in a quantitative fashion a nonreversible process. The study of heat led to the science of thermodynamics, which Prigogine calls the first non-classical science. Ludwig Boltzmann realized that thermodynamics cannot be derived from mechanics and introduced into physics the notion of probability, which is closely related to irreversibility. The reality of the arrow of time implied that the future is not simply determined by the past. Moreover, according to the second law of thermodynamics, in any process *entropy*, which is defined as the amount of disorder, increases in an irreversible fashion and "irreversible thermodynamic change is change toward states of increasing probability."[87] Thus, according to the thermodynamic view, there is an irreversible process in the cosmos, and this process is toward ever greater disorder.

Prigogine begins from this background and through the study of what appears to be chaos in relation to order seeks to synthesize the concept of reversible and irreversible time, claiming that entropy itself can be the source of both order and disorder. Critical of the reductionism and determinism implied by modern science, he asserts, "In this sense the dialogue with nature isolated man from nature instead of bringing him closer to it. A triumph of human reason turned into a sad truth. It seems that science debased everything it touched."[88] Prigogine believes that his study of chaos is able to change the terms of this dialogue and inaugurate a new scientific study of order in nature. His studies of chaos and randomness have led him to deny materialistic determinism in nature and the idea of passive matter, which only obeys ineluctable mathematical laws. Rather, for him matter itself is associated with spontaneous activity. Nonequilibrium conditions, far from being simply a nuisance as envisaged by classical physicists, lead to new types of structures that originate spontaneously. "In far-from-equilibrium conditions we may have transformation from disorder, from thermal chaos, into order."[89] Irreversibility, whose significance was denied by so many physicists including Einstein, may in fact be a source of order and organization and bring order out of chaos, and instability may give rise to self-organization as seen in the case of the Berard instability.[90] Prigogine insists that "at all levels, be it the level of macroscopic physics, the level of fluctuations, or the microscopic level, *nonequilibrium is the source of order; nonequilibrium brings 'order out of chaos.'*"[91] The very movement of things involves the arrow of time, which as also shown by Norbert Wiener is irreversible in any given physical universe and leads not only to the ever greater disorder implied by the increase of entropy but also to the creation of new order.

Prigogine thus conceives of order as issuing from the very process of the flow of time in a creative and spontaneous manner as if he had accepted the idea of the immanent *pneuma* of the Stoics. He claims that the new concept of order bestows upon nature once again its "enchantment" and creative power and even formulates a new link between science and ethics. As he observes: "Today we know that time is a construction and therefore carries an ethical responsibility."[92] Altogether the Prigoginian vision of order in relation to chaos represents one of the most significant challenges of twentieth-century science to the view of classical physics concerning order in nature, although it still operates within the scientific worldview and paradigm established by the seventeenth-century Scientific Revolution.

SCIENTIFIC POSITIVISM AND ITS CRITIQUE

The scientific view of the order of nature led to a positivism that spread far beyond the confines of the physical sciences themselves and influenced not only philosophy, as mentioned in the last chapter, but also the social sciences and the humanities as well as the general outlook of modern man. Even today when many scientists have disavowed positivism, and despite the significantly different interpretations given to the meaning of the order of nature by scientists such as David Bohm and Ilya Prigogine, the general influence of positivism continues in fields as diverse as philosophy and medicine. In fact, the exclusivism of the modern scientific view and the refusal to accept other modes of knowledge of nature, including the religious one, can be traced back to the Newtonian synthesis itself.[93]

The philosophical origin of positivism, however, dates back to Kant, who, while showing that modern science can only be a science of phenomena and not the existence of things, denied the possibility of other ways of knowing the world of nature. This kind of empiriological thought, or a science based solely on phenomena, claimed for itself exclusivity of all knowledge of nature.[94] As a result of Kant and his followers, the quantitative and mathematical science of the eighteenth century was no longer mistaken for the philosophy of nature as it had been a century before, but came to take its place.[95] A century later metaphysics was to be banished completely from science with Auguste Comte, who marks the beginning of formal philosophical positivism already inherent in Newtonian physics. All causes were banished and science came to be regarded solely as being concerned with laws connected to phenomena. It was this thesis that was elaborated later by Ernst Mach and came to influence so much of twentieth-century scientific thought with its dread of causality (in the metaphysical sense of the term), finality, and intelligibility. The influence of this type of thought was so great that even Western philosophers interested in metaphysics accepted empiriological knowledge was the sole knowledge of nature.

A scientism that had existed before in small circles developed on a much wider scale and came to dominate the intellectual scene, affecting not only philosophy but also theology despite the opposition of many scientists who were more aware of the limitation of their field than others who had bestowed the halo of infallibility and omniscience upon them. Reactions did arise against positivism from Pierre Duhem, one of the founders of the history of science, from Emile Meyerson, a leading voice among the philosophers of science,[96] and from the German phenomenologists such as Edmund Husserl and Max Scheler who spoke of penetrating intuitively into the real itself (*vestehen*) rather than simply explaining in mechanical terms (*erklären*). But such criticisms hardly carried the day, deprived as they were of an integral metaphysics, whereas in the case of Duhem his work was passed over in silence as the positivistic approach came to dominate the entire field of the history of science.

During the last few decades, the Thomistic philosophy of nature has been revived by certain Catholic thinkers such as Jacques Maritain, and the criticism of scientific positivism has continued by a number of philosophers of science such as

Stanley Jaki, Paul Feyerabend, and Jerome Ravetz.[97] The symbolic view of nature, which presents another science of nature based upon its symbolic rather than external and factual significance of its external forms and which had existed in certain metaphysical and mystical schools in the West, has received new attention. Also, numerous scholars, philosophers, and even scientists have tried to go beyond the borders of the West to seek freedom from the debilitating confines of positivism and scientism. Some scientists have written openly about the limitations of science[98] and many have gained serious interest in theology as theology has become, at least until quite recently, ever less interested in the theology of nature independent of the scientific view of the world. And yet the positivism and scientism flowing from the modern scientific view still dominate the mental landscape and consciousness of most people in the West to such an extent as to leave no room for other views of the order of nature to manifest themselves and to be taken seriously as knowledge. Even postmodernist deconstructionism has been much more successful in destroying what remained of the traditional understanding of sacred Scripture and classical works of Western literature than deconstructing the assertive categories of modern science.

Here and there one sees attempts to reassert a view of the order of nature based on the wholeness of nature as a living being determining its parts in not only biology but also physics,[99] and one must recall the famous assertion of Lewis Thomas that the entire Earth is a cell.[100] Still, it is not as yet realized widely enough that traditionally the principles and conception of science employed in natural philosophy did not originate from the sciences themselves but from metaphysics as implied by the Greek notion of *epistēmē*,[101] whereas in contrast, ever since the seventeenth century, the theory of the sciences came to be based on the sciences themselves in an *a posteriori* and not an *a priori* manner. A new philosophy of nature was thus developed that was based on the sciences of nature and thereby divorced from metaphysical principles, which in all traditional climates had provided the common principles and ground for discourse between the religious and scientific understanding of nature.[102]

Through all the important transformations in modern science from Newtonian mechanics to Bohm's implicate order, it is the scientific understanding of the order of nature that continues to dominate the contemporary scene so as to make a dialogue with the authentically religious view of nature difficult if not well nigh impossible. Even those interested in such a dialogue tend to equate the dogmatism of purely manmade science with sacred doctrines of a Divine Origin, asking both sides to put aside their "dogmatism" to bring about mutual understanding.[103] And then there are those scientists who think they can reach the sacred and metaphysical truth contained in the heart of religions by analyzing to an even greater degree the complex structures of the material world as if one could ever cast aside the veil of Isis.[104] The truth remains that no matter how much it changes, modern science cannot but deal with phenomena, whereas the religious understanding of the order of nature is based ultimately upon knowledge of the ontological reality and root of things in the Divine and the significance of their form and qualitative characteristics on the phenomenal plane as reflecting noumenal realities belonging to the Divine Order. No serious dialogue is possible unless the empirical or scientific view of the order of nature is forced to abdicate from its absolutistic domination over the contemporary dominion of knowledge and the religious understanding of the order of nature comes to be taken seriously in all its depth and grandeur and not as the pale shadow of its real self as it has become during its period of retreat and dilution in the past few centuries in the West.

To revive the religious understanding of nature and to re-sacralize the vision of the natural world, a theme to which we shall turn in the last chapter of this work, it is essential to revive in the West sacred science, a knowledge that is at once a veritable science of nature and possessed of a sacred quality. Except for the rediscovery of metaphysics or Divine Knowledge concerning the Principle Itself, there is no greater need today than the reconstitution of sacred science, which must of necessity always remain in the bosom of a living and sacred tradition.[105] Only in understanding in depth the scientific understanding of the order of nature and the manner in which it eclipsed the religious understanding of nature can one clear the ground to create "space" for the re-creation of a sacred science. And only through such a re-creation and expansion embracing what the contemporary situation demands can the common universe of discourse between religion and science, which characterized the traditional world and to which we alluded at the beginning of this chapter, be reconstituted.

As for those who doubt the necessity of such an undertaking, let them be reminded of the words of Oscar Milosz: "Unless man's concept of the physical universe does accord with reality, his spiritual life will be crippled at its roots, with devastating consequences for every other aspect of his life."[106] The forging of a link between humanity's concept of the physical Universe and reality in such a manner as not to distort reality implies nothing less than the rediscovery of the science of the Real of which sacred science is an application to the domain of physical reality. Without such a science rooted in the religious understanding of Reality, religion being understood in its sapiential dimension, it is not only our spiritual life that becomes devastated but also life on the very Earth upon which we stand and for which modern man accepted to sacrifice Heaven begins to wither away. The reason is that Earth no less than Heaven is in need of that Spirit whose very presence has been made irrelevant in the worldview issuing from the modern scientific understanding of the order of nature. It must not be forgotten that this understanding, while it has discovered much about nature, has also helped to veil the deepest meaning of the order of nature, which concerns us not only here and now but also in the most ultimate sense, as beings born in the bosom of the Earth but destined for the heavenly Empyrean.

NOTES

1. During the Elizabethan period such figures as the "esoterist-scientist" John Dee were still at the center of the intellectual stage, whereas in the eighteenth and ninteenth centuries they were hardly permitted to participate in any intellectual discourse taken seriously by English society. The same holds true for Germany and France despite their

more extensive interest in such matters. It is only during the present century that such figures as Eckarthausen and Saint Martin are being studied seriously outside occultist circles. See Antoine Faivre, *Accès à l'ésotérisme occidentale* (Paris: Gallimard, 1986); also see his *Eckhartshausen et la théosophie chrétienne* (Paris: Klincksieck, 1969); Pierre Riffard, *L'Ésotérisme* (Paris: Robert Laffont, 1990; valuable for its extensive bibliography); and Faivre and Needleman, *Modern Esoteric Spirituality* (New York: Crossroad Publications, 1992).

One must remember the well-known saying of René Guénon that there are no occult sciences but only occulted ones. Cut from their metaphysical principles in a world where such principles came to be denied to an ever greater degree, the traditional sciences could not but become occult sciences, losing their deepest meaning and significance as far as the prevalent understanding of the order of nature was concerned.

2. We have in mind such popular works as Frithjof Capra's *The Tao of Physics* (Berkeley, Calif.: Shambhala, 1975) and *The Turning Point: Science, Society, and the Rising Culture* (New York: Simon & Schuster, 1982); and Gary Zukav, *The Dancing Wu Li Masters: An Overview of the New Physics* (New York: William Morrow, 1979). There are, however, some contemporary scientists aware of the greater significance of the traditional sciences as ways of knowing the world of nature. See, for example, Charles Moraze, *Les Origines sacrées des sciences modernes* (Paris: Fayard, 1986).

3. See S. H. Nasr, *The Need for a Sacred Science* (Albany: State University of New York Press, 1993), Chapter 7, "The Traditional Sciences," p. 95.

4. See René Guénon, *The Crisis of the Modern World*, trans. M. Pallis and R. Nicholson (London: Luzac, 1975), Chapter 4, "Sacred and Profane Science," p. 37.

Many of those who have discovered mathematics and other traditional sciences of the Egyptians and Greeks speak of sacred science or sacred geometry. See, for example, R. A. Schwaller de Lubicz, *Sacred Science: The King of Pharaonic Theocracy*, trans. Andre and Goldian Vanden Broeck (New York: Inner Traditions International, 1982); Robert Lawlor, *Sacred Geometry* (New York: Crossroad Publications, 1982); Nigel Pennick, *Sacred Geometry: Symbolism and Purpose in Religious Structures* (Wellingborough, U.K.: Turnstone Press, 1980); and the works of Keith Critchlow, especially his *Order in Space* (London: Thames & Hudson, 1970).

5. Sharing the same universe of discourse does not mean being the same as religion is usually understood. Rather, it means that these sciences shared the same metaphysical principles and also the same symbolic and formal language as the religion in question, especially the sapiental dimension of the religion and not simply its exoteric, legal, and social aspects.

6. This vast commentary in some 24 volumes was written in Arabic and later translated into Persian. It is now being translated into English. See a-'Allāmah aṭ-Ṭabāṭabā'ī, *Al-Mīzān: An Exegesis of the Quran* (Tehran: World Organization for Islamic Sciences, 1983).

7. See Henry Corbin, *L'Alchimie comme art hiératique* (Paris: L'Herne, 1986), Part 3, p. 145; Paul Kraus, *Jâbir ibn Ḥayyân: Contribution à l'histoire des idées scientifiques dans l'Islam* (Paris: Les Belles Lettres, 1986), p. 223; Pierre Lory, *Alchimie et mystique en terre d'Islam* (Paris: Verdier, 1989), p. 124; and Syed Nomanul Haq, *Names, Natures and Things* (Dordrecht and London: Kluwer, 1994), which deals with the *Kitāb al-ahjār* that is especially concerned with the Jābirean doctrine of the balance.

8. On al-Bīrūnī and al-Khāzinī and the science of the balance, see S. H. Nasr, *Science and Civilization in Islam* (New York: Barnes & Noble, 1992, and Cambridge: Islamic Text Society, 1987), p. 138; and S. H. Nasr, *Islamic Science: An Illustrated Study*

(London: World of Islam Festival Publishing Co., 1976), p. 143, where the tradition of balance and measurement in Islamic science is discussed in general.

9. Past generations of scholars have been deeply influenced by the writings of such figures as Ernst Cassirer, Edwin A. Burtt, and Alexandre Koyré, whose emphasis upon the significance of mathematics and mathematical astronomy in the rise of modern science was in turn challenged by scholars such as Walter Pagel and Allen Debus, who emphasized the inportance of the nonmathematical disciplines such as alchemy, medicine, and Hermeticism. Also, philosophical differences as one finds between Ernst Mach and Pierre Duhem have colored their understanding of the rise of modern science. We cannot deal with these differences here but must point at least to their existence.

10. As far as why the Scientific Revolution did not occur in China, Joseph Needham has discussed it extensively in his monumental work *Science and Civilization in China* (Cambridge: Cambridge University Press, 1954). We have also dealt with this issue for the case of Islam in *Science and Civilization in Islam,* presenting reasons very different from those of Needham.

11. See Etienne Gilson, *The Unity of Philosophical Experience* (Westminster, Md.: Christian Classics, 1982). We have examined this in *Man and Nature: The Spiritual Crisis of Modern Man* (London: HarperCollins, 1989), Chapter 2, "The Intellectual and Historical Causes," p. 51.

12. For a Paracelsus, who spoke of the light of nature (*lumen naturae*), nature far from being closed upon itself was still open to the world of the Spirit and in fact a reflection of that world. "Pour Paracelse, le monde immanent n'a pas de realité indépendante. La nature n'est point close sur elle-même à la manière d'un Ourouboros mais s'ordonne en une spirale prophétiquement ouverte à l'intervention extérieure du Saint-Esprit. A l'idée d'une nature opaque, réduite à une sorte de mécanisme sans maître, Paracelse oppose la vision d'une nature en tant que reflet." Luc-Olivier d'Algange, "Paracelse: Une poétique de la transparence," *Connaissance des Religions* (Vol. 8, no. 3, Dec. 1992), p. 275.

13. See Giorgio Di Santillana, "The Role of Art in the Scientific Renaissance," in Marshall Clagett (ed.), *Critical Problems in the History of Science* (Madison: University of Wisconsin Press, 1959), p. 34.

14. Collingwood, *The Idea of Nature* (Oxford: The Clarendon Press, 1949), p. 7.

15. "Natural law in the juristic sense, law which it is natural for all men to obey, has always been closely linked in men's minds with the concept of laws enacted by God the creator for nature; both go back to the same common root." Colin A. Ronan, *The Shorter Science and Civilization in China: An Abridgement of Joseph Needham's Original Text,* Vol. 1 (Cambridge: Cambridge University Press, 1978), p. 276. On an extensive discussion of the Chinese concept of law, at once human and cosmic, in comparison with Western ideas of "laws of nature," see Joseph Needham, *Science and Civilization in China,* Vol. 2 (Cambridge: Cambridge University Press, 1956), pp. 518ff.

16. See Chapter 2 where we have dealt extensively with this issue.

17. "Since also the whole world, the things divine, and what we call the seasons, appear, if we may trust what we see, to be regulated by Law and Order." Ronan, *Shorter Science,* p. 286. Also Cicero asserts, "The Universe obeys God, seas and law obey the universe, and human life is subject to the decree of the Supreme Law." Ibid., p. 286.

18. On St. Thomas Aquinas's views of natural law, see Odon Lottin, *Le Droit natural chez saint Thomas d'Aquin et ses predecesseurs* (Bruges: C. Bayaert, 1931); Karl Kreilkamp, *The Metaphysical Foundations of Thomistic Jurisprudence* (Washington, D.C.: Catholic University of America Press, 1939); Gallus Manser, *Das Naturrecht in Thomistischer Beleuchtung* (Freiburg: Verlag des Paulusdruckerei, 1944); Thomas Aquinas, *The Treatise on*

Law, ed. R. J. Henle (Notre Dame, Ind.: University of Notre Dame Press, 1993); Thomas Aquinas, *On Law, Morality and Politics,* eds. William Bavengarth and Richard Regan (Indianapolis, Ind.: Hackett, 1988); and Jacques Maritain, *La Loi naturelle ou loi non écrite,* text established by Georges Brazzola (Fribourg: Editions Universitaires, 1986).

19. Ronan., *Shorter Science,* p. 289.

20. Muslims also use the term *al-nāmūs* for cosmic law and almost equivalent of *al-Sharī'ah,* although it is derived etymologically from the Greek *nomos.* The traditional Islamic understanding of laws governing Creation is precisely as *nāmūs al-khilqah* (or *nāmūs* of Creation).

21. "The heliocentric system itself admits of an obvious symbolism, since it identifies the centre of the world with the source of light. Its rediscovery by Copernicus, however, produced no new spiritual vision of the world; rather, it was comparable to the popularization of an esoteric truth. The heliocentric system has no common measure with the subjective experiences of people; in it man has no organic place. Instead of helping the human mind to go beyond itself and to consider things in terms of the immensity of the cosmos, it only encouraged a materialistic Prometheanism which, far from being superhuman, ended by becoming inhuman." Titus Burckhardt, *Mirror of the Intellect* (Albany: State University of New York Press, 1987), p. 21.

22. See Collingwood, *The Idea of Nature,* p. 27.

23. "Not only the earth but the sun and the entire solar system were transformed into insignificant specks lost in the infinitude of God's creation; the compact and ordered cosmos of the scholastics had become a vast chaos; the Copernican departure from tradition had reached its maximum." Thomas Kuhn, *The Copernican Revolution* (Cambridge, Mass.: Harvard University Press, 1976), p. 235. On Copernicus and Copernicanism see also Allen Debus, *Man and Nature in the Renaissance* (Cambridge: Cambridge University Press, 1986), pp. 79ff.; I. Bernard Cohen, *Revolutions in Science* (Cambridge, Mass.: Harvard University Press, 1985), pp. 105ff.; E. J. Dijksterhuis, *The Mechanization of the World Picture: Pythagoras to Newton,* trans. C. Dikshoorn (Princeton, N.J.: Princeton University Press, 1986), p. 288; Francis R. Johnson, *Astronomical Thought in Renaissance England* (Baltimore: Johns Hopkins University Press, 1937); Hans Blumberg, *The Genesis of the Copernican World,* trans. R. M. Wallace (Cambridge, Mass.:, and London: M.I.T. Press, 1987); and Alexandre Koyré, *From the Closed to the Infinite Universe* (New York: Harper Torchbook, 1958).

24. Koyré, *Infinite Universe,* p. 35. See also Arthur Lovejoy, *The Great Chain of Being* (Cambridge, Mass.: Harvard University Press, 1936), p. 116.

25. "Bruno's world-view is vitalistic, magical; his planets are animated beings that move freely through space of their own accord like those of Plato or of Pattrizzi. Bruno is not a modern mind by any means." Koyré, *Infinite Universe,* p. 216.

26. The effect that was both the consequence of Renaissance humanism and helped strengthen its hold will be discussed in the next chapter. Here it is sufficient to recall the fact that, on the one hand, Copernicanism belittled the role and centrality of man in the cosmos; on the other hand it aggrandized his power and earthly knowledge and contributed significantly to the rise of the Prometheanism so characteristic of the Renaissance.

27. From *Anatomy of the World* quoted in Koyré, *Infinite Universe,* p. 29.

28. On this work and Bacon in general see Francis Bacon, *The New Organon and Related Writings,* ed. Fulton H. Anderson (New York: Bobbs-Merrill, 1960); and Anthony Quinton, *Francis Bacon* (Oxford: Oxford University Press, 1980).

29. On Gilbert, see Cohen, *Revolutions in Science,* pp. 133–135; and Dijksterhuis, *World Picture,* pp. 391–396.

30. Debus, *Man and Nature*, p. 89.

31. Francis R. Johnson, *Astronomical Thought in Renaissance England* (New York: Octagon Books, 1968), p. 216.

32. "It is in his [Galileo's] work and not in that of Descartes that the idea of mathematical physics, or rather the idea of the mathematization of the physical, was realized for the first time in the history of human thought." A. Koyré, *Galileo Studies,* trans. J. Mepham (Atlantic Highlands, N.J.: Humanities Press, 1978), p. 201.

33. Stillman Drake, *Discourses and Opinions of Galileo* (New York: Doubleday Anchor Books, 1957), pp. 237–238.

34. In referring to the statement of Galileo in *Il Saggiatore,* R. Lenoble writes, "This phrase . . . expressed a singularly revolutionary idea. By a stroke of the pen, Galileo had abolished the *natura* of the ancients, with its substances, forms and qualities. Nature had become the sum total of quantitative phenomena." "Machanism and Dynamism," in René Taton (ed.), *History of Science: The Beginnings of Modern Science,* trans. A. J. Pomerans (New York: Basic Books, 1964), p. 186.

35. This view was asserted by E. A. Burtt and especially A. Koyré, who noted: 'From our vantage point we can see that the advent of classical science was a return to Plato." Koyré, *Galileo Studies,* p. 202. See also his "Galileo and Plato," *Journal of the History of Ideas* (Vol. 4, 1943), p. 400; and *Etudes d'histoire de la pensée scientifique* (Paris: Presses Universitaires de France, 1966), pp. 147ff. In his *Newtonian Studies,* pp. 212–220, Koyré states that Galileo took Plato's cosmology seriously in both the *Dialogo* and the *Discorsi.*

36. More recent scholars have in fact begun to challenge the views of Burtt, Koyré, and others concerning Galileo's Platonism. For example, Edward Strong observed: "We cannot conclude from this [*The Two Great Systems of the World*], however, that Galileo is a Platonist, or that he is conducting his science upon a Platonic foundation of a mathematical structure of nature." *Procedures and Metaphysics: A Study in the Philosophy of Mathematics–Physical Science in the Sixteenth and Seventeenth Centuries* (Merrick, N.Y.: Richwood Publishing, 1976), p. 164.

Likewise, Gary Hatfield challenges the views of Cassirer, Burtt, Whitehead, and Koyré. Hatfield "found a common metaphysical core shared by adherents of the new science," this being of course their insistence that material bodies have mathematical properties and that these are related to Platonic and Pythagorean metaphysics. He asserts that their motivation for the use of mathematics was completely different from that of the traditional Platonists and that in the works of the founders of modern science, including Galileo, "No unified, historically efficacious metaphysical doctrine regarding the relationship between mathematics and nature is to be found." Quoted in David C. Lindberg and Robert S. Westman, *Reappraisals of the Scientific Revolution* (Cambridge and New York: Cambridge University Press, 1990), "Metaphysics and the New Science," pp. 93–94.

37. See Dijksterhuis, *World Picture,* p. 337.

38. See ibid., p. 348; and Stillman Drake, *Galileo Studies: Personality, Tradition and Revolution* (Ann Arbor: University of Michigan Press, 1970), pp. 240ff.

39. On the controversial life and trial of Galileo see Stillman Drake, *Galileo at Work: His Scientific Biography* (Chicago: University of Chicago Press, 1978); Jerome J. Langford, *Galileo, Science and the Church* (New York: Desclee, 1966); Giorgio Di Santillana, *The Crime of Galileo* (Chicago: University of Chicago Press, 1976), and the somewhat more popular work of James Reston, Jr., *Galileo: A Life* (New York: HarperCollins, 1994), especially Chapter 13, pp. 223ff.

40. See Cohen, *Revolutions in Science,* pp. 127ff.

41. "Keplerian physical principle of inertia, force, and motion implied the end of the Aristotelian cosmos and readied the scientific stage for Newton." Ibid., p. 129.

42. See Strong, *Procedures and Metaphysics,* p. 165.

43. Alexandre Koyré, *The Astronomical Revolution: Copernicus, Kepler, Borelli,* trans. R. E. W. Maddison (London: Methuen, 1973), p. 327.

44. Ibid., p. 342.

45. It must be added, however, that for Kepler himself the distances and dimensions of the planets are caused by "archetypical laws" whose consequence is the motion of the planets determined by "laws of nature" understood in the ordinary sense. As A. Koyré observed, the dimensions and distances of the Solar System are "determined by the action of structural 'archetypical' laws: as a consequence of which their motions, that is to say, the form of their orbits and their speeds of revolution are determined by purely natural laws." Koyré, *Newtonian Studies* (London: Chapman & Hall, 1965), p. 203.

46. As mentioned already, the term "metaphysics" used by modern philosophers such as Descartes must not be confused with metaphysics as traditionally understood. See Rene Guénon, "Oriental Metaphysics," in Jacob Needleman (ed.), *The Sword of Gnosis* (London and Boston: Arkana, 1986), pp. 40–56; and S. H. Nasr, *Knowledge and the Sacred* (Albany: State University of New York Press, 1989), pp. 130ff. Descartes believed in the "unity of all knowledge, scientific and philosophical, which he symbolized in the metaphor of a tree whose roots are metaphysics, whose trunk is physics, and whose branches are specific topics: medicine, mechanics, morality." Cohen, *Revolutions in Science,* p. 153.

47. Dijksterhuis, *World Picture,* p. 404. See pp. 403ff. of this work for a summary of Descartes' views concerning the order of nature.

48. On the development of the modern idea of matter see Max Jammer, *Der Begriff der Masse in der Physik* (Darmstadt: Wissenshaftliche Buchgesellschaft, 1964).

49. "The material bodies we perceive also have physical qualities such as colour, odour and taste, hardness, softness, brittleness, & c., but all of these words merely designate states of consciousness with which we react to the presence of or the contact with particular parts of space; they are subjective reactions which the latter generate in us, and which cannot therefore be the subject of scientific knowledge." Dijksterhuis, *World Picture,* p. 406.

50. Descartes, *Principia philosophiae,* Part 2, No. 4, in Adam Tannery (ed.), *Oeuvres* (Paris: Les Editions du Cerf, 1905), Vol. 8, p. 42.

51. Considering the role of Descartes, Charles Gillispie notes: "The thought of René Descartes moved across the gap in the scientific revolution between the physics of Galileo and the prophecies of Bacon. In its success it complemented each. In its failure it announced the need for a scientific declaration of independence from philosophy." *The Edge of Objectivity: An Essay in the History of Scientific Ideas* (Princeton, N.J.: Princeton University Press, 1960), p. 83. One might add by way of comment that although modern science did declare its independence from a certain type of philosophy, it itself remains based upon a particular philosophical understanding of both the nature of the world and our knowledge of it, and that even an important element of Cartesianism has survived as part and parcel of the modern scientific worldview as mentioned in the previous chapter.

52. Its systematic neglect in the historiography of science until recently does, however, reveal much about the supposed objective character of such histories and the hidden philosophical presumptions that determine in so many cases what is to be studied and what is to be discarded even if it comes from the pen of no lesser a figure than Isaac Newton.

53. See Collingwood, *The Idea of Nature,* pp. 106ff. On Netwon's physics and background of his thought, see also Koyré, *Newtonian Studies;* I. Bernard Cohen,

The Newtonian Revolution: With Illustrations of the Trasnformation of Scientific Ideas (Cambridge: Cambridge University Press, 1980); Cohen, *Revolutions in Science,* pp. 161ff.; Dijksterhuis, *World Picture,* pp. 463ff.; and Frank Manuel, *A Portrait of Isaac Newton* (Cambridge, Mass.: Harvard University Press, 1968).

54. "With Isaac Newton an old period in the attitude of philosophers towards nature ended and a new one began. In his work classical science . . . attained an independent existence, and from then on it began to exercise its full influence on human society." Dijksterhuis, *World Picture,* p. 463.

55. "Order in nature presents itself to observation as a set of necessary relations capable of exact mathematical description." Richard S. Westfall, "Newton and Order," in Paul Kuntz (ed.), *The Concept of Order* (Seattle and London: University of Washington Press, 1968), p. 78.

56. "All of nature follows a uniform pattern, not of ideal mathematical relations, but of mathematically computable deviations from the ideal relations." Ibid., p. 80.

57. "The fact is that Newton was convinced from the beginning that the universe is an ordered cosmos because he knew as a Christian that God had created it. . . . It seemed appropriate to Newton that God had formed the cosmos on the principle of geometry; therefore the geometric ratios ought to be found throughout nature." Richard S. Westfall, *Science and Religion in Seventeenth-Century England* (New Haven, Conn., and London: Yale University Press, 1958), p. 197.

58. Koyré, *Infinite Universe,* p. 160.

59. Quoted in Koyré, *Newtonian Studies,* p. 204.

60. See Ernest Wolf-Gazo, "Newton's Pantakrator and Hegel's Absolute Mind," in Michael J. Petry (ed.), *Hegel and Newtonianism* (Dordrecht and London: Kluwer, 1993) p. 129.

61. In Query 23 of the enlarged Latin edition of the *Opticks,* Newton writes, "It seems to me further, that these Particles have not only a *vis inertiae,* accompanied with passive Laws of motion as naturally result from that Force, but also that they are moved by certain active Principles. . . ." To which Koyré adds by way of commentary, "And it is the action of these principles or, more exactly, the action of God by means of these principles that gives to the world its structure and order that enables us to recognize that the world is an effect of choice, and not chance or necessity. Natural philosophy—at least the good one, that is, the Newtonian and not the Cartesian—thus transcends itself and leads us to God." Koyré, *Newtonian Studies,* p. 218.

62. Concerning the two elements of Newton's view of nature—that is, the idea of nature as a law-bound system of matter in motion, and as a stage for intelligent beings— John C. Greene observed: "The first component came to him from the seventeenth-century revolution in physics and cosmology that began with Galileo and Descartes and found consummate expression in his own *Principia.* The second was derived from Christian natural theology, from the static vision of the doctrine of creation in the special form this doctrine assumed in the late seventeenth century. In the long run, however, the two views of nature which Newton and his English colleagues attempted to fuse into a single view proved incompatible." Greene, "The Concept of Order in Darwinism," in Kuntz (ed.), *The Concept of Order,* pp. 90–91.

63. See Tor Frangmyr, J. L. Heilborn, and Robin E. Rider (eds.), *The Quantifying Spirit in the 18th Century* (Berkeley and Oxford: University of California Press, 1990).

64. See Gunner Broberg, "The Broken Circle," in Frangmyr et al., *Quantifying Spirit,* p. 45.

65. "During the 18th century, European thinkers embraced a systematic model of

order with an enthusiasm and conviction unprecedented before and unmatched since." John E. Lesch, "Systematics and the Geometrical Spirit," in Frangmayr et al., *Quantifying Spirit*, p. 73.

66. See Ernst Cassirer, *The Philosophy of the Englightenment*, trans. Fritz C. A. Koelln and James P. Pettegrove (Princeton, N.J.: Princeton University Press, 1951). Cassirer insists on the significance of analysis as being the heart of Enlightenment thought.

67. Novalis, *Fragmente und Studien, 1799–1800*, in *Schriften*, Vol. 3, pp. 556–693 (Darmstadt: Wissenschaftliche Buchgesellschaft, 1968), 574, quoted in Dietrich von Engelhardt, "Natural Science in the Age of Romanticism," in A. Faivre and J. Needleman (eds.), *Modern Esoteric Spirituality*, p. 109. On this "Romantic" science related to *Naturphilosophie,* see also B. Gower, "Speculation in Physics: The History and Practice of 'Naturphilosophie,'" in *Studies in the History and Philosophy of Science* (Vol. 3, 1972/73), pp. 301–356.

68. Quoted by von Engelhardt, "Natural Science," p. 112.

69. Ibid., pp. 121ff.

70. As can be seen by the type of reactions that usually take place against those who criticize evolutionary teachings, this theory does not play the role similar to any other theory such as that of quantum mechanics but of a pseudo-religious dogma defended with the same passion and tenacity as one sees in those defending a religion.

We have dealt with this issue in our book *Knowledge and the Sacred,* Chapter 7, where in the footnotes we have provided the name of a number of works dealing with the criticism of evolutionary theory from different points of view. In addition to those works, see Osman Bakar (ed.), *Critiques of the Theory of Evolution* (Kuala Lumpur: The Islamic Academy of Science, 1987); and Wolfgang Smith, *Cosmos & Transcendence* (La Salle, Ill.: Sherwood Sugden, 1984), Chapter 4, "Evolution: Fact and Fantasy," p. 66. On the history of the theory of evolution, see Walter Zimmermann, *Evolution: Die Geschichte ihrer Probleme und Erkenntnisse* (Freiburg-Munich: Verlag Karl Alber, 1953). As for the exposition of the theory of evolution by a proponent, see the well-known work of George G. Simpson, *The Meaning of Evolution: A Study of the History of Life and Its Significance for Man* (New Haven, Conn.: Yale University Press, 1964). For a more recent treatment of the subject, see Ervin Laszlo (ed.), *The New Evolutionary Paradigm* (New York and London: Gordon and Breach Science Publishers, 1991).

71. Collingwood sees the Darwinian conception of life-force to imply a force that is at once transcendent and immanent vis-à-vis each organism, "immanent as existing only as embodied in these organisms, transcendent as seeking to realize itself not merely in the survival of the individual organisms, nor merely in the perpetuation of their specific type, but as always able and always trying to find for itself a more adequate realization in a new type." Collingwood, *The Idea of Nature*, p. 135.

72. For the view of order of Darwin and his followers, see John C. Greene, "The Concept of Order in Darwinism," in Kuntz (ed.), *Concept of Order*, pp. 89–103.

73. It is significant that to this day the most virulent form of atheism supposedly supported by science comes from biologists rather than physicists, as one sees in Great Britain today if one compares a Stephen Hawkins and a Richard Dawkins.

74. Greene, "Concept of Order in Darwinism," p. 95.

75. "By Darwin's time the static view of nature was in a precarious conditon. Darwin delivered the *coup de grace* by propounding a mechanism of organic change that seemed to eliminate the last trace of wise design in the formation of the species." John C. Greene, *Darwin and the Modern World View* (Baton Rouge: Louisiana State University Press, 1961), p. 43.

76. See David Loye, "Chaos and Transformation," in Laszlo (ed.), *Evolutionary Paradigm*, p. 15. "Self-organizing is the capacity of open and living systems, such as we live in and we ourselves are, to generate their own new forms from inner guidelines rather than the imposition of form from without." Loye, "Chaos and Transformation," in ibid., p. 15.

77. See Roberto Fondi, *La Révolution organiciste* (Paris: Le Labyrinthe, 1986).

78. For a profound critique of Teilhardism see Wolfgang Smith, *Teilhardism and the New Religion* (Rockford, Ill.: Tan Books, 1986); and Burckhardt, *Mirror of the Intellect*, pp. 32ff.

79. On the major features of quantum mechanics and its worldview see Paul A. M. Dirac, *The Principles of Quantum Mechanics* (New York and Oxford: Oxford University Press, 1947); Leonard Schiff, *Quantum Mechanics* (New York: McGraw-Hill, 1955); Henry Margenau, *The Nature of Physical Reality* (New York: McGraw-Hill, 1950); Victor Weiskopf, *Physics in the Twentieth Century* (Cambridge, Mass.: M.I.T. Press, 1972); John von Neumann, *The Mathematical Foundations of Quantum Mechanics*, trans. R. Beyer (Princeton, N.J.: Princeton University Press, 1955); Max Jammer, *The Philosophy of Quantum Mechanics* (New York: Wiley, 1974); David Bohm and Basil Hiley, *The Undivided Universe: An Ontological Interpretation of Quantum Theory* (London: Routledge, 1993); and the more popular work of Gary Zukav, *The Dancing Wu Li Master: An Overview of the New Physics* (New York and London: Bantam Books, 1984).

80. "The world of particle physics is a world of sparkling energy forever dancing with itself in the form of its particles as they twinkle in and out of existence, collide, transmute and disappear again." Zukav, *Dancing Wu Li*, p. 194.

81. Henry Stapp calls Bell's theorem "the most profound discovery of science." See Stapp, "Bell's Theorem and World Process," in *Il Nuovo Cimento* (Vol. 29B, 1975), p. 271.

82. Bell's theorem has many metaphysical and philosophical implications, some of which have been examined by a number of philosophers and scientists. See especially Wolfgang Smith, "Bell's Theorem and the Perennial Ontology" (in press).

83. See David Bohm, *Wholeness and the Implicate Order* (Boston: Routledge and Kegan Paul, 1980).

84. Zukav, *Dancing Wu Li*, p. 306, from a lecture given by Bohm.

85. Of course, ever since the pioneering work of Eugene Wigner in quantum mechanics, consciousness has been considered as an important element of physics by many physicists in contrast to the view of classical physics whose description of the mathematical order of the universe is considered to be completely independent of the mode of consciousness of the person who perceived that order or of consciousness itself.

86. See Prigogine's well-known work (with Isabelle Stengers), *Order Out of Chaos: Man's New Dialogue with Nature* (New York and London: Bantam, 1984).

87. Ibid., p. 124.

88. Ibid., p. 6.

89. Ibid., p. 12.

90. Ibid., pp. 142–143.

91. Ibid., pp. 286–287.

92. Ibid., p. 312. See also Prigogine, *From Being to Becoming: Time and Complexity in the Physical Sciences* (San Francisco: W. H. Freeman, 1980).

93. See Wolfgang Smith, *Cosmos & Transcendence*, p. 16.

94. See Maritain, *The Philosophy of Nature* (New York: Philosophical Library, 1951), pp. 45ff.

95. As Maritain states, "At first it was confused with the philosophy of nature, and then it replaced it." Maritain, *Philosophy of Nature*, p. 50.

96. See Emile Meyerson, *De l'Explication dans les sciences* (Paris: Payot, 1921), p. 21, where he asserts that genuine science does not in any way conform to the positivistic scheme. See especially page 21.

97. See among the many works of Stanley Jaki, *The Road of Science and the Ways to God* (Chicago: University of Chicago Press, 1980), especially Chapter 10, "The Price of Positivism," p. 145; Paul K. Feyerabend, *Against Method* (New York and London: Verso, 1988); and Jerome Ravetz, *Scientific Knowledge and Its Social Problems* (Oxford: Clarendon Press, 1971).

98. The Swiss scientist and philosopher of science Andre Mercier writes, "Science is one royal way to grasp Nature, but it is not identical with our knowledge about Nature." In George F. McClean (ed.), *Man and Nature* (Calcutta: Oxford University Press, 1978), p. 24.

99. E. E. Harris writes that the whole cosmos is a "single, individual totality, organistic throughout." Ibid., p. 30, adding that according to this view *Totum in toto et totum in qualibet parte.*

100. See *The Lives of a Cell* (New York: Viking Press, 1974), p. 5.

101. The concept of science outlined by Aristotle in his *Posterior Analytics* was certainly not based on his biology or physics. See Ernan McMullin, "Concepts of Science in the Scientific Revolution," in David Lindberg and Robert Westman (eds.), *Reappraisals of the Scientific Revolution* (Cambridge and New York: Cambridge University Press, 1990), p. 28.

102. For the necessity of any veritable science to be rooted in metaphysical principles in the authentic and traditional sense of metaphysics, see Fernand Brunner, *Science et realité* (Paris: Aubier, 1954).

103. An example of such an approach is to be found in the recent work of Brian Swimme and Thomas Berry, *The Universe Story* (San Francisco: Harper, 1992), which despite its good intentions does not distinguish between doctrines of a sacred character and mental crystallizations that have paraded as scientific dogmas as if the Holy Ghost and the mathematical or physical inspiration of a scientist are on the same level.

104. See Frithjof Schuon, *Roots of the Human Condition* (Bloomington, Ind.: World Wisdom Books, 1991), "The Veil of Isis," pp. 15ff.

105. We have dealt with this theme in *The Need for a Sacred Science.*

106. Quoted by Philip Sherrard, *Human Image: World Image—The Death and Resurrection of Sacred Cosmology* (Ipswich, U.K.: Golgonooza Press, 1992), p. 135.

5

The Tragic Consequences of Humanism in the West

در ازل انسان انیس حق بدی

در زمان نسیان بر او غالب شدی

ارج تو زانسان کامل چون بود

جستجو کن در درون راز خودی

The signature of God on Earth,
Half angel half beast, cast into this world,
Abode of dispersion and forgetfulness,
Yet bearing the seal of Divine Proximity
Within the very substance of his soul.
Thus was man envisaged before being severed
From his heavenly mold to be conceived
As a creature solely of this lowly clime,
Subject of a humanism, earthly bound,
Which searching for human meaning in man alone
Has ended by casting man to the realms below,
To what, being not normal, has infra-human become,
And destructive of that very natural order
For whose sake the bond with Heaven was rent asunder,
Giving birth to that Promethean creature
Who now devours the Earth with such avidity.

If one were to travel in the beautiful hills of Tuscany during the spring and behold the luxuriant colors of the rolling hills and the gentle breeze caressing the treetops shimmering in the Italian sun, one would wonder how an Italian by the name of Galileo, who also beheld the beauty of these sites, could reduce nature to matter in motion and the beauty of nature to an irrelevant category and yet become not only a national hero, but the hero of a whole civilization. Nor is it easy to understand how fewer than two hundred men from western Spain could defeat the entire Incan Empire in Peru and bring about the death of 4 million of the 8 million inhabitants of that land in a decade, while debating whether the people the invaders were slaughtering had souls and whether or not they were human.

To account for both of these very different historical facts, it is essential to comprehend the new understanding of man that arose during the European Renaissance in conjunction with that humanism which marks that period and, in a modified fashion, all subsequent periods of Western history to this day. The transformation of the meaning of the order of nature in both philosophy and science cannot be fully understood without delving fully into Renaissance humanism and the new conception of man that appears in stages at that time and leads within a short period to an image of man and his relation to God, of other peoples, and of the order of nature radically different from what had existed in the medieval period in the Christian West and also from what exists today in all non-Western civilizations to the extent that they remain faithful to their own traditions.

To understand this process of the formation of humanism in its secularist sense—a process whose end results can only be called tragic in the light of the consequences of the actions of this "newly" independent or Promethean man reflected in the destruction of the natural environment as well as of other civilizations—it is first necessary to deal with humanism as it came to be understood in the Renaissance along with its prolongation into later centuries of Western history. Scholars of the Renaissance have quite justifiably distinguished between two understandings of humanism: the first, the educational and intellectual program that came to be known as *studia humanitatis,* and the second, the general values associated with making man the measure of all things and the center of the Universe.[1] The two were of course closely related during the Renaissance but were not identical. Humanism as a distinct intellectual program was one among three major philosophical currents during the Renaissance, the other two being Platonism and Aristotelianism, which also expressed views concerning man in relation to God and the cosmos. Also, the worldview of humanism is to be found not only in texts and intellectual activities but also in the arts, crafts, and other aspects of Renaissance culture. But in any case it is especially with humanism as the general understanding of the meaning of man and not only the specifically "humanistic studies" with which we are concerned here while we are fully aware of the survival of various types of traditional philosophy at this time, which were, however, soon eclipsed, as we have had occasion to mention in Chapter 3.

THE MEANING OF RENAISSANCE HUMANISM

There is much debate among scholars as to the real meaning of Renaissance humanism despite some of its clear and salient features. The noted Italian scholar Giorgio Di Santillana observed:

> *Humanitas* was born in Rome, out of the circle of the Scipios, around 150 B.C. It was the watchword of the new imperial civilization, the heir of Greece. It stood opposed to *barbaritas* or *feritas,* "the way of the wild ones," and it meant cultivated intelligence.

In the Christian era, the term took on a connotation of transiency and misery in the face of eternity: *"Chetive creature humaine. . . ."* The Renaissance inherits thus an ample meaning: *Humanitas* is again man's "high state," but it implies also fallibility and frailty: hence venture, risk, responsibility, freedom, tolerance.[2]

One wonders how many Renaissance thinkers ever imagined that the new *humanitas* would lead in a few centuries to the worst kind of *barbaritas* seen in human history. Others have associated *humanitas* with the Greek *paideia* and the "rebirth" of the human spirit, which could be "freed" through the study of the Greek and Latin classics. Through this study man could regain the power he possessed in classical times but had lost in the Middle Ages. Hence the significance of such disciplines as poetry, rhetoric, and history, which would provide such a widening of the horizon for man and enable him to interact in a new way with nature and history.[3] And yet other scholars have emphasized the significance of humanism in enlarging the meaning of man's awareness of himself and the very meaning of "I am,"[4] although such a view is hard to grasp in light of the veritable ontological descent that the newly discovered understanding of man implies.

The debate about humanism also involves its relation to its medieval past. Certain scholars of Catholic background distinguish between humanism and the Renaissance, indicating that such main figures of the Renaissance as Rabelais were not humanists.[5] Some do not even accept the classical views of Jules Michlet and Jacob Burckhardt, who believe the Renaissance to be the opposite of the Middle Ages and insist, against the view of such scholars, upon the existence of a sixteenth-century Christian humanism. Others speak of an eternal humanism that includes the Church Fathers, the Scholastics, and the Christian mystics.[6] To this day a number of Catholic philosophers speak of a continuing tradition of Christian humanism,[7] and following their example some works concerning Islamic and other non-Western traditions have also sought to incorporate this term.[8] However, such amorphous uses of humanism tend to destroy its specific meaning associated with the Renaissance and modern Western civilization and the concept of man that issued from it, a concept that is as different from the Islamic, or for that matter Buddhist, concept of man as night is from day. In any case, in this work we are especially interested not in the general usage of the term "humanism" but in humanism as it grew in the European Renaissance and led to a radically new conception of man independent from any sacred hierarchy and dominant over the world of nature.

The origin of this humanism is of considerable interest for the understanding of the deeper issues involved in the Renaissance revolt against not only its European medieval past, but also tradition in general and in particular the Islamic intellectual tradition from which the West had inherited a great deal.[9] Most scholars consider Petrarch as the father of humanistic studies and even of humanism in the wider sense of the term, Petrarch being a figure who hated the study of logic, natural science, and, needless to say, the whole Scholastic tradition. To understand the nature of the change in attitude that his views imply vis-à-vis the opinions of his medieval predecessors, it is important to note that he was particularly opposed to Islamic science and thought. In a letter to his physician friend Giovanni de'Dondi dell'Orologio, Petrarch wrote:

> Before I close this letter, I implore you to keep these Arabs [meaning of course Muslims] from giving me advice about my personal condition. Let them stay in exile. I hate the whole lot. . . . You know what kind of physicians the Arabs are. I know what kind of poets they are. Nobody has such winning ways; nobody, also, is more tender and more lacking in vigor, and, to use the right words, meaner and more perverted. The minds of men are inclined to act differently; but, as you used to say, every man radiates his own peculiar mental disposition. To sum up: I will not be persuaded that any good can come from Arabia. [10]

This attitude of the father of humanism is significant because it indicates not only the hatred of Renaissance humanism of Islam, but Islam, being the only non-Western civilization known to the West at that time, by implication its hatred of non-Western people and traditions in general. The oft-stated character of tolerance of Renaissance humanism certainly did not include non-European people, as the encounter of men imbued with the spirit of this humanism with other sectors of humanity from the West Indies to the East Indies displays so clearly. This hatred of the Islamic tradition on the part of the purported founder of humanism becomes even more intriguing when one turns to recent scholarship that reveals a surprisingly close historical relation between the Islamic literary or *adab* tradition and *studia humanitatis,* a relation that is no less close than the rapport between Latin Scholasticism and Islamic philosophy and theology.

The idea of the uniqueness of Renaissance man and the subsequent Eurocentric view of history based upon it has prevented the Islamic influence upon the *studia humanitatis* to be taken seriously in the West until now, especially since the Islamic conception of man as in perfect surrender to the Will of God[11] stands so diametrically opposed to the Promethean and Titanic view of man cultivated in the Renaissance. After all, what can be more different from the description of the biblical prophet David in such Islamic sources such as the *Fuṣūṣ al-ḥikam,* in which Ibn 'Arabī emphasizes the perfect surrender of David to the Will of God in receiving the Divine Gift bestowed by God upon him, and the David of Michelangelo, which depicts man as a creature certain of himself as an independent, earthly being, and depicted as if he wanted to conquer Heaven through his own might? Until recent years the views of such scholars as Oscar Kristeller that humanism in the sense of *studia humanitatis* originated as a result of influences emanating from France or Byzantium have been widely accepted. [12] Others have considered this development to be simply spontaneous in southern Italy. In any case, most Western scholars have resisted obstinately any suggestions of Islamic influences. It is therefore quite revealing and shocking to many to come across a recent study by George Makdisi that lays out in scholarly detail the historical link between the Islamic *adab* tradition and the *studia humanitatis.* [13]

ISLAMIC *ADAB* AND RENAISSANCE *STUDIA HUMANITATIS*

After dealing in the first and second parts of his book with what he calls "Scholasticism," consisting mostly of law and theology, which also had considerable influence upon the medieval West and its related institutions,[14] Makdisi turns to the organization of knowledge in the *adab* tradition and the role of *adab,* or what he calls humanism in religious knowledge. He then recounts the major fields of *adab,* consisting of grammar, poetry, eloquence, oratory, epistolary arts, history, and moral philosophy. He then turns to methods of instruction and methodology of learning of *adab,* which includes memory, disputation and instructive conversation, dictation, self-teaching, etc. There is also a discussion of the patron, scholar-humanist, amateur-humanists, and other members of the *adab* community, which include not only professional *adībs* (or scholars of *adab*) such as tutor-professors (*mutadassir*), librarians, secretaries, etc., but also boon companions. Throughout Makdisi's detailed and scholarly study, one is struck with the remarkable similarity as far as subjects of study, manner of teaching, and even formal institutions are concerned between the Islamic world and what developed in Italy in the fourteenth century as *studia humanitatis.*

Makdisi turns in fact in the last part of his book to an in-depth comparison discussing the views of such well-known Renaissance scholars as Robert Weiss, Oscar Kristeller, Jakob Burckhardt, and others, none of whom paid attention to the link between the Islamic *adab* tradition and the *studia humanitatis.*[15] Makdisi questions their view and asks why it is that, while Italy lagged behind France and Germany in science, theology, and even vernacular Latin poetry, Renaissance humanism in the sense of *studia humanitatis* began in Italy. He answers by pointing to the presence of a strong tradition of grammar and rhetoric in Italy closely resembling *adab* and in historical contact with it as can be seen in the very subjects included in *adab* on the one hand and the *studia humanitatis* on the other, as well as similarity of conception of a literary education, organization of literary circles, methods of instruction, and many other elements between the two. Makdisi goes into great detail about the influence of *adab* upon *studia humanitatis,* drawing attention to correspondences that can hardly be denied, as when he points to the correspondence between the title of a man of *adab* as *farīd dahrih* and *nasīj waḥdih* and the Italian *uomo singolare* and *uomo unico,* which correspond exactly to the Arabic terms.[16]

We have taken this short detour from the main subject of this chapter for two reasons. The first is to demonstrate how the type of humanism that grew in the Renaissance and that we identify with humanism as such in this work developed in a direction so different from other traditions that it denied all historical links with the Islamic *adab* tradition from which it had drawn so much and even developed a particular hatred for Islam, as demonstrated by the words of Petrarch mentioned above. The second is to show how the Renaissance conception of man made use of Islamic learning, based on a completely different understanding of man, for purposes completely alien to the Islamic worldview, as we also witness in the sciences, theology, and philosophy. The close historical link between *adab* and *studia humanitatis* and yet the total departure of the conception of man contained in the latter from the former is one of the clearest signs of the departure of Western civilization during the Renaissance from not only its own medieval past but also from traditional worlds comprising the rest of humanity. This had dire consequences for which, paradoxically, the whole of humanity is now paying so dearly.

PHILOSOPHICAL CURRENTS IN THE RENAISSANCE

To turn to Renaissance humanism itself, before dealing with its characteristics, it is necessary to mention a few words about the other major strands of Renaissance thought that, along with what is technically called humanism, helped to mold the Renaissance conception of man. [17] The first is Platonism, which was avidly pursued in the Renaissance. [18] The humanists or *humanista* were also interested in Platonism but turned it for the most part into a "this-worldly" philosophy of the imagination while the members of the Florentine Academy, especially Marsilio Ficino and Giovanni Pico, were more deeply rooted in the medieval philosophical tradition and were not even opposed to Islamic thought as we can see especially in the case of Pico. [19] But by and large Platonism became both more eclectic and also divorced from what is known as Christian Platonism, which dominated most of Christian theology and philosophy up to the thirteenth century. Because the Renaissance was a transitory period marked by so many diverse and often contradictory currents of thought, there is even a major exception to this statement in the person of Nicholas of Cusa, who, although living during the Renaissance, cannot be associated with Renaissance humanism in the sense discussed here but rather represents one of the major voices of traditional metaphysics in its Christian context in the West. [20]

Another important philosophical current of the Renaissance was Aristotelianism, which was revived in Italy by such figures as Pietro Pomponazzi and Giacomo Zabarella, but here again this Aristotelianism was not the one associated with a Thomas Aquinas or Duns Scotus—that is, the Scholasticism so hated by the Renaissance—but the scientific Aristotle studied as a background for medicine and natural science. [21] But these figures were also interested in the question of man and his destiny and were hardly opposed to humanism. Italian Aristotelians were also more attached to Averroes than to Aristotle. In fact, Latin Averroism took refuge in the fifteenth and sixteenth centuries in Italy rather than in Paris, and there was even a new wave of translations of Averroes into Latin at that time in Italy. [22] In contrast to the original Ibn Rushd (Averroes), who was at once philosopher and chief judge of the Islamic courts of law in Cordova, the Latin Averroists such as John of Jandun were open rationalists accepting only reason as authority. Their position stood therefore in stark contrast to that of the Muslim Ibn Rushd, who never ceased to believe in the authority of divine revelation. [23]

This current of Renaissance philosophy led eventually to skepticism and an antisupernaturalism that contrasted with the positive naturalism characterizing the humanism of northern Italian cities. In any case both currents influenced humanism, the first being more impersonal and the second more individualistic. Pomponazzi tried especially to introduce humanistic values into Italian Aristotelianism, which soon became a secular humanism leading to seventeenth-century free thought. A figure such as Zabarella—who marks the peak of Italian Aristotelianism, who wrote influential logical and methodological works, and who also incorporated certain aspects of humanism into Aristotelianism—prepared the ground for Galileo, who, while in Padua, had come into direct contact with Aristotelian thought for which that university was a major center. Thus, both Platonism (often in combination with Hermeticism) and Aristotelianism were philosophical currents that intermingled in various ways with what is technically called humanism and contributed heavily to the characteristics we associate with Renaissance humanism understood not simply as *studia humanitatis,* but essentially as a philosophy of man and his relation to God and the order of nature.

CHARACTERISTICS OF RENAISSANCE HUMANISM

The more general Renaissance humanism, as understood in the sense of a new philosophy growing out of not only *studia humanitatis* but also influenced by other philosophic currents of the period, possesses certain basic characteristics that it is of the utmost importance for us to examine. The first characteristic of this humanism is that it conceives of man as an independent earthly being no longer integrated into the total cosmos of faith of medieval Christianity. To be sure, there were still men and women of faith, but the new man envisaged by humanism was no longer defined by his or her faith in God and the hereafter. This new conception of humanity is closely related to the rather rapid loss of the significance of angels and the angelic hierarchy, delineated by Dionysus, which had dominated the medieval worldview. Rather than being a half-angel, half-man cast on Earth, man now became completely terrestrial, at home in a newly discovered Earth and no longer an exile from the paradisal realm, which did not mean that he did not and does not continue to wreak havoc upon this newly discovered "home." Having banished the angels from the cosmos, the new man also became the only intelligent being on Earth, the only one possessing a "mind."

Worldliness became man's "natural" state, and the otherworldliness of medieval Christian conception of man began to be looked upon with a sense of derision. Earthly man, rather than man before his fall from his Edenic perfection, became the normal man. It was to this idea of the fallen man taken as the norm that Montaigne, one of the Renaissance figures most responsible for forging the new image of humanity, referred when he asserted, "Every man bears the whole stamp of human condition (*l'humaine condition*)."[24]

In forgetting the Heaven of the medieval period, man now discovered a new Earth with which he identified as "the world" and not as nature over which he now felt the sense of greater domination than ever before. But to be "at home" in such a world he must have already become another man, no longer defined by his celestial archetype and Edenic perfection but by his individuality, reason, the senses, and corporeality. Man was redefined on the basis of a subjectivism that destroyed the objective archetypal reality of the human state and the symbolic and contemplative spirit that was henceforth replaced by individualistic reason.

> The Renaissance thought that it had discovered man, whose pathetic convulsions it admired; from the point of view of laicism in all its forms, man as such had become to all extents and purposes good, and the earth too had become good and looked immensely rich and unexplored; instead of living only "by values" one could at last live fully, be fully man and fully on earth; one was no longer a kind of half-angel, fallen and exiled; one had become a whole being, but by the downward path.[25]

The chief characteristic of this new man was both individualism and rationalism. The subjectivism and lack of objective metaphysical criteria characteristic of Renaissance humanism could not but lead to an individualism that affected even the mysticism of the period. Man's individuality became extolled at the expense of the universal to the extent that the new Renaissance man felt himself deeply different not only from members of other civilizations but even from men of earlier periods of Western history when the individual order was defined in light of the universal. Even the heritage of antiquity was received on the basis of an individualistic interpretation that caused it to differ profoundly from the medieval understanding of the same heritage. The Plato of Hugo St. Victor is not the same Plato as one finds in the works of even a Pico, who issued from the Florentine Academy, the source for the dissemination of Platonic teachings in the Renaissance, and even more different from the Plato of a Galileo.

Closely allied with individualism is the rationalism that began to manifest itself to an ever greater degree in the Renaissance, leading finally to the complete separation of philosophy and revelation. Rationalism does not mean simply the use of reason, but the exclusive use of reason independent of both intellection and revelation and the consideration of reason as the highest and exclusive authority for the attainment of truth. This tendency was to be seen not only in Renaissance Averroism, as already mentioned, but also in certain aspects of humanistic studies themselves, leading to an even greater abandonment of intellection and the symbolic mode of thought in favor of a rationalism that could not but result in the development of seventeenth-century rationalistic philosophy of Descartes and others with which we have already dealt earlier in this work.

As far as the conception of man is concerned, this rationalism came to identify man with a reason that was no longer wed to the intellect, the distinction between the two—that is, *intellectus* and *ratio*—in fact soon becoming obliterated.[26] Man was now identified as a being possessing an independent individuality and a reason seeking to encompass reality without recourse to a principle beyond itself, leading of necessity to the infra-rational, which characterizes so much of modern and especially so-called postmodern thought. Henceforth European man gained a new conception of himself as a being endowed with reason, independent of Heaven and ready to conquer Earth, both its non-European humanity and the order of nature. The whole Enlightenment conception of reason and rational man is rooted in the profound transformation of the meaning of man during the Renaissance.

Renaissance rationalism was also accompanied by skepticism that, on the one hand, opposed the limited certitude reached through reason and, one the other, complemented the claim of rationalism in the exclusive use of human reason in the quest of knowledge. Skepticism was of course known not only in Greece and Rome but is particularly a Greco-Roman heritage. It can mean either that no knowledge is possible, as held by academic skeptics, or that there is not sufficient and adequate evidence to decide whether knowledge is possible or not. This latter view is associated with Pyrrhonism whose foremost authority was Sextus Empiricus, who lived in the late second and early third centuries A.D. It is of much interest to note that while skepticism was known by St. Augustine and refuted by him, it disappeared from the Western intellectual tradition for a millennium after him, during which reason was wed to the Christian revelation or the immanent Logos and had no need to examine the possibility of doubt presented by skeptical philosophies, and that it was resuscitated during the late Renaissance.[27]

This event is of great significance for the understanding of later European thought and the origin of an important strand of the conception of man emanating from the Renaissance. In fact, the seventeenth-century French skeptic Pierre Bayle considered the introduction of skepticism during the Renaissance as the beginning of modern philosophy, and Descartes sought after a new ground for certitude because of the skepticism that had become prevalent. Thus, the Pyrrhonism associated with Sextus Empiricus became widespread with the publication of his complete Latin works in 1569. But even before that date Pyrrhonism had begun to be taken seriously. Already in 1510 Gian Francesco had sought to discredit all ancient philosophy in his *Examen Vanitatis Doctrinae Gentium* in which he mentions Pyrrhonism extensively and makes use of Sextus Empiricus to oppose other schools of philosophy. Even the famous French writer François Rabelais mentions Pyrrhonism in his novels *Gargantua* and *Pantagruel* where the philosopher Trouillogan is called *"pyrrhonien."* Likewise, Agrippa von Nettesheim wrote long diatribes against human knowledge that were read by Montaigne and helped revive ancient skepticism. Such figures as Petrus Ramus and his friend Omer Talon discussed both academic and Pyrrhonic skepticism, and even Giordano Bruno refers to the *pirroni* in his *La Cena de la Ceneri.*

The most important figure influenced by Sextus Empiricus, however, was Montaigne, who, while being instrumental in creating the Renaissance conception of man, also criticized prevalent theories through skepticism. His espousal of Pyrrhonism helped in fact to create what came to be known in the seventeenth century as *la crise pyrrhonienne,* and this left a profound effect upon the religious debates of his day.[28] Renaissance skepticism not only affected later European thought, but it helped create a conception of man whose streak of doubt was not about his power to dominate the order of nature but to know ultimate principles and all that had defined man throughout human history.

In this second departure of Western man from the human family, the first being the Greece of the Sophists and Skeptics, once again the same distinguishing characteristics of rationalism and skepticism came into play. When a Spaniard stood next to a Native American, or a Portuguese next to a Chinese, or a Dutchman before a Javanese, or an Englishman or Frenchman before any African or Oriental in the Age of Exploration and expansion of European powers, among all the factors distinguishing one type of humanity from all others was the presence of this skeptical vein. It led to many scientific discoveries but also to the loss of sacred knowledge and in some cases the sense of the sacred itself. And it remains to this day a salient feature of that type of human being for whom the desecration of nature is meaningless because there is nothing sacred to start with.

Yet another characteristic of Renaissance humanism, again closely related to rationalism and skepticism despite appearances, is "naturalism," understood in the sense that man is part of nature, not in the neo-Confucian or Zen sense, but in that his own bodily pleasures are of importance.[29] This can be seen in Renaissance paintings that emphasize the discovery of nature; but outside those circles that continued to cultivate esoteric cosmologies, which still related nature to its metaphysical principles, this naturalism involved more the rediscovery of pleasure than of the spiritual significance of the body or nature, especially as far as the followers of the new humanism were concerned. This type of naturalism manifested itself by its opposition to medieval asceticism as seen in Lorenzo Valla's *De Voluptate* for which pleasure even became the goal of virtue and the sole goal of human existence. Valla denied the superiority of monastic life as claimed by medieval Christianity, and some of his arguments were echoed by others such as Coluccio Salutati. There was also a reappraisal of Epicurus, then considered by some as the master of human wisdom. Even Aristotle came to be extolled not because of his metaphysics but as a result of his appreciation of the importance of money.

There thus appeared this other important characteristic of modern man so prevalent to this day, that of being a prisoner of his senses, which he must seek constantly to satiate without limit, and that of the follower of a naturalism that is against the order of nature as a value in itself, a being devoted to the bodily gratification without the least interest in the significance of the body in the religious, metaphysical, and cosmological sense. Such a naturalism has not been necessarily opposed to the dualism that has dominated Western thought from Descartes to this day and has emphasized the importance of the gratification of the bodily senses without showing any concern for the body as an integral aspect of the human microcosm.

The new consciousness of man living amidst the world of nature was complemented by a new awareness of man's position in history. There developed at this time a historicism representing the secularization of the Christian doctrine of the march of time and that played an important role in creating a consciousness within the new man of his position in history considered as the secular flow of time rather than his position in the face of eternity. Traditional man, Christian or otherwise, always situates and orients himself vis-à-vis an Origin and a Center, both of which are Divine. The new humanism changed this matrix drastically by substituting historical time for eternity with profound consequences for the future; for it was this very inception of historicism that was to lead to the idea of indefinite material progress, evolution, social Darwinism, "white man's burden," the negation of transhistorical realities, and many other developments that had and continue to have the most profound consequences for the relation between man and the order of nature.

Another basic element of the Renaissance conception of man and the subsequent humanism that has dominated the West since then is the new notion of freedom, which may in fact be considered as the main element of Renaissance and post-Renaissance humanism. This new understanding of freedom meant essentially independence from the sacred world of medieval Christianity and its cosmic order and not freedom from the limitations of the ego and the bonds of material existence as envisaged by seers and sages in East and West over the ages. Such figures as Giannozzo Manetti, Marsilio Ficino, and Giovanni Pico emphasized the ability of man to act independently of any other agent in the Universe. They exalted man's freedom to form and change the world as he willed irrespective of any cosmic laws or even of the Divine Will, at least according to those who developed this idea later on the basis of the Renaissance humanistic notion of freedom. The glorification of man so emphasized in such treatises as Pico's *On the Dignity of Man* was directly based upon what such authors conceived to be the innate freedom of man from all constraints. Man now becomes the independent protagonist in the cosmic drama and he, rather than "Fortune," is now seen to control and direct the ship of human life.[30] Even the emphasis upon the wonders of the human mind by such a figure as Pico is based on the freedom enjoyed by man.[31]

Humanistic Renaissance authors also tended to associate freedom with reason. A case in point is *De libro arbitrio* of Lorenzo Valla, where freedom is judged from the point of view of reason and not religious dogma. Valla, in fact, insists that reason "is the best author" not to be contradicted by any other authority. He then goes on to criticize the sacred hierarchy of the Church and, despite accepting Christianity as pure truth, begins to submit it to the judgments of pure natural reason. There is thus created a link between the understanding of the notion of human freedom and rationalism, which dominated Western thought until the revolt against reason in nineteenth-century Western philosophy.

Even Renaissance Aristotelians—for example, Pietro Pomponazzi, who has been called the last Scholastic—were attracted to the new understanding of the notion of freedom. Pomponazzi emphasized the contrast between faith and reason and was interested in the freedom of man placed in the "field of tension" between the two. In fact, the whole spectrum of Renaissance philosophy extending from Pomponazzi to the Platonists of the Florentine Academy to Valla were interested in the question of the freedom of man related to his grandeur.

Pico, whose views concerning man became especially influential, went a step further in reversing the traditional rapport between being and acting. According to traditional doctrines our actions depend upon our mode of being or, as the Scholastics stated it, *operari sequitur esse*.[32] Pico reversed this relationship and claimed that "the being of man follows from his doing."[33] He thus stated philosophically the thesis of the primacy of action over contemplation and doing over being, which characterizes modern man and which has been of the greatest consequence for the destruction of the world of nature. The unlimited energy of a civilization turned totally outward to remold the natural world in complete "freedom" and without any inner constraints is at the heart of the relentless activity of modern man in the destruction of the natural environment vis-à-vis, which he cannot simply "be" but toward which he must act aggressively to change and transform it.

In relation to this lack of a distinct *esse* that would be the source of human actions, Pico emphasizes the Protean nature of man. Proteus, a sea god of the Greeks, assumed all kinds of shapes and forms and was amoral. He thus became identified with restlessness and change and was attacked by Plato in the *Republic* (II.318D). Yet he came to be extolled by the Renaissance philosophers such as Pico, Giovanni Gelli, and Juan Luis Vives, who helped create that image of a restless creature with whom modern man identifies so closely. While Pico considers man as a chameleon imitating Heaven and Earth, Gelli in his *Circe* talks of Protean man "jumping up and down the Chain of Being at Will."[34] As for Vives, he speaks in his *Fable about Man* of man miming all of Creation including multiform Proteus.[35]

Perhaps the most famous description of this Protean character of man related to his complete freedom to act according to his will is the following passage of Pico from *On the Dignity of Man:*

> We have given to thee, Adam, no fixed seat, no form of thy very own, no gift peculiarly thine, that thou mayest feel as thine own, have as thine own, possess as thine own the seat, the form, the gifts which thou shalt desire. A limited nature in other creatures is confined within the laws written down by Us. In conformity with thy free judgment, in whose hands I have placed thee, thou art confined by no bounds; and thou wilt fix limits of nature for thyself. I have placed thee at the center of the world, that from these thou mayest more conveniently look around and see whatsoever is in the world. . . . Thou, like a judge appointed for being honorable, art the molder and maker of thyself; thou mayest sculpt thyself into whatever shape thou dost prefer. Thou canst grow downward into the lower natures which are brutes. Thou canst again grow upward from they soul's reason into the high natures which are divine.[36]

This celebrated passage echoes in many ways the traditional doctrine of man, conceived as *al-insān al-kāmil* in Islam, who can occupy all levels of existence, and the last part is reminiscent in a certain sense of the famous Quranic passage, "Surely we created man of the best stature, then we reduced him to the lowest of the low"(XCV: 4–5; Pickthall translation). It also contains elements of the esoteric doctrines of man contained in Hermetic and Cabalistic teachings, but all of this is interpreted in a Protean manner with results very different from what the traditions envisaged over the millennia.

The ideas of Pico found their immediate echo in Charles de Bouvelles (Carolus Bovillus), the French philosopher who was influenced by both the Florentine Platonists and Nicholas of Cusa. He was the author of *De sapiente,* written in 1509, which Ernst Cassirer has called "perhaps the most curious and in some respect the most characteristic creation of Renaissance philosophy."[37] While still influenced by traditional ideas of the relation between the microcosm and macrocosm, Bouvelles developed ideas that were much more in accord with modern philosophy than with the thought of his contemporaries and which have been compared to the idealism of Leibniz and Hegel.[38] Bouvelles continued the theme of the Protean nature of man. Being journeys through *Esse, vivere, sentire,* and *intelligere* to arrive at Itself. Man possesses all these levels within himself, and through his reason the cycle of nature is completed and returns to herself. But upon returning, nature no longer has the form with which she started out.

> Once the first separation in man has been completed, once he has stepped out of the simplicity of his original state, he can never again return to this unbroken simplicity. He must go through the opposite in order to pass beyond it to find the true unity of his being—that unity which does not exclude difference but rather postulates and requires it.[39]

Man's freedom in fact issues from the contradictions in his being, from the fact that he does not possess a ready-made nature but a Protean one. Man must acquire his being through *virtus* and *ars* and must pass through the various levels of *Esse, vivere,* etc. In this process he can fall through the vice of inertia or *acedia* to the level of existence without consciousness or rise to the highest level through self-consciousness, which implies also knowledge of the cosmos. According to Bouvelles,

> The man of nature, simple *homo,* must become the man of art, the *homo-homo;* but this difference is already overcome, inasmuch as it is recognized in its necessity. Above the first two forms arises now the last and highest; the trinity *homo-homo-homo,* in which the opposition of potency and act, of nature and freedom, of being and consciousness, is at once encompassed and resolved. Man no longer appears therein as a part of the universe but as its eye and mirror; and indeed, as a mirror that does not receive the images of things from outside but that rather forms and shapes them in itself.[40]
>
> Man is the central point of the cosmos in whom all degrees of being converge, and he can journey through them since he is a Protean being capable of taking on all forms without a fixed place in the cosmos.[41]

Bouvelles compared the wise man to Prometheus, for wisdom confers power upon its beholder and allows man to change his nature. Renaissance thought had in fact resurrected the ancient myth of Prometheus in seeking a pictorial and mythological expression for its idea of man. The new idea of Prometheus, far from being seen negatively as symbolizing man's rebellion against Heaven, came to be viewed in a positive light.[42] The new man who proudly called himself Promethean saw himself as an independent agent free from both the theological and the natural order, which at that time included the astrological influence of the stars, from both *regnum gratiae* and *regnum naturae*.[43] There was thus born the prototype of modern man whom we can call Promethean in contrast to the traditional or pontifical man who always remains aware of his role as bridge (*ponte*) between Heaven and Earth, in submission to Heaven and ruler of Earth in the name of Heaven and in harmony with cosmic laws.[44] The conception of the order of nature as pure quantity perceptible to man's senses and object of man's reason and the development of a science founded upon the exercise of power over nature would not have been possible without the replacement in the West of pontifical man by the Promethean man so much extolled by Renaissance philosophers from Bouvelles to Bruno and celebrated so forcefully by a sculptor and painter such as Michelangelo, who depicts man in the Sistine Chapel as almost the equivalent of God.

Such a vision of man created an egoism and sense of *hubris* that is especially evident in the art of the period.[45] The Renaissance praise of man was not, however, necessarily anti-Christian, as is seen in many Renaissance works such as Ficino's *De Christiana religione,* and sought even to be tolerant, although this tolerance never went beyond the borders of Christianity, as already mentioned and as seen especially in the attitude during that period toward Judaism and Islam.[46] Still, the aggrandizement of man not only brought about as response the skeptical reactions of a Montaigne but was also strongly opposed by both Calvin and Luther, who emphasized the wretchedness of the human condition. But even the Reformation emphasized individualism, as seen in the proliferation of Protestantism into so many branches. Moreover, after Luther even in Germany greater emphasis came to be placed upon the freedom of human will, and the debates between the so-called Christian humanist Erasmus and Luther over free will and determinism influenced many future generations. Contrary views of man and his freedom dominated the scene and found their echo in Shakespeare and other major Western writers.

As far as the significance of the concept of man for the order of nature is concerned, however, what is most significant is the Prometheanism that came to dominate Western civilization to an ever greater degree despite the survival in certain circles of both the traditional Christian understanding of man and even the esoteric doctrines of the Cabala and Hermeticism, which although marginalized did not disappear completely at that time. The main characteristics of Renaissance humanism can be in fact summarized in the new Promethean conception of man, with a reason made independent of revelation, a Protean being ready to rebel against Heaven and to master and dominate the Earth. Of course, the imprint of Christianity could not be obliterated from the soul of the new European man so quickly, but it was weakened enough for the new Promethean man to announce his declaration of independence from religion and revelation in many domains, of which the most significant for our present study was the order of nature.

CONSEQUENCES OF THE NEW HUMANISM

In the matrix of the tapestry of the Renaissance, woven from so many often contradictory strands, from Hermeticism to Lutheranism, from Aristotelianism to the *studia humanitatis,* and from Platonism to experimental science, there grew the outline and form of that humanism which has characterized the modern world since that time and is only now being seriously challenged from below and to some extent from above. At the center of this humanism stood the Promethean vision of man, who now came to occupy the middle of the stage as an ontologically autonomous being. If certain esotericisms such as that of Islam had accepted the thesis that man is the measure of all things because they saw in man the full theophany (*tajallī*) of God's Names and Qualities, now man came to be the measure of all things as a purely earthly being. The consequence was the rise of an anthropomorphic perspective that has dominated all aspects of Western thought for the past half millennium.

Henceforth, man's reason, divorced from both revelation and intellection in the traditional sense of the term,[47] came to be the sole criterion of verification of knowledge along with man's sensory perceptions. Only man's faculties determined knowledge even if faith in God still persisted to some extent. The presence of this faith, however, could not prevent the step-by-step desacralizing of knowledge that characterized European intellectual history from the Renaissance onward and that, beginning with knowledge of the order of nature, was finally to affect even theology itself. All modern modes of thought are in essence anthropomorphic in that they are based completely on purely human faculties. Even modern science, which paints a picture of the world to which human beings are for the most part alien, is purely anthropomorphic in that it is based completely on the human mind and the human senses even when it speaks of the most distant galaxies.

This new humanism was of course challenged by many forces over the centuries following the Renaissance, from religious opposition to the aggrandizement of man, to philosophies such as those of Hegel and Marx, which reduced man to simply an element in the human collectivity and society; to Darwinism, which reduced him to an accident in the process of the evolution of matter. During this century all types of reductionism, whether it be psychological in the behavioristic sense, or biological or social, have sought to destroy the centrality and independence of man declared by those Renaissance writers who first conceived of the idea of humanism in the sense described above. And yet the prevailing image of man, especially as it concerns the order of nature and the crisis that modern man has created vis-à-vis the environment, remains the Promethean image forged during the Renaissance, enhanced by the civilization and rationalism of the Age of Enlightenment and even strengthened in a certain sense by the antirationalistic forces of Romanticism that, despite its love of nature, sought nevertheless to aggrandize human genius, which is in a sense an invention of that age applied especially to the domain of the arts. One can hardly forget the Promethean image of man, at least its heroic aspect, when one hears Beethoven's *Eroica Symphony* or reads the poems of Shelley.

Irrespective of all the differences between various schools of thought in the West, the central image of man as the earthly god, conqueror of nature, and maker of his own destiny and the future of civilization continued. If a Ming Confucian scholar or a Seljuq Persian theologian were presented with the different images of man from Pico to Michelangelo to Montaigne to Descartes to Diderot and Voltaire and then on to the nineteenth-century philosophers and artists such as Hegel and Wagner, and even including Nietzsche with his idea of the *Über-mensch,* they would be much more impressed with the similarities of these individuals than with their differences. They would see in all these modern versions of the Western concept of man a being very different from *jen* or *insān* in the Confucian and Islamic traditions, respectively. They would see a being who was no longer organically linked to either the cosmos or to God, to Heaven or Earth. They would immediately detect the radical difference between the Islamic theocentrism, which is certainly close to the Christian perspective in many ways, and what has been called Confucian anthropocosmism on the one hand and the anthropocentrism prevalent in the domineering culture of the West. They would even experience a closer sympathy with the Augustinian conception of man tainted by Original Sin, which they would reject, than with the humanistic idea of the innately "good" man so much discussed in the Enlightenment and thereafter, for despite all their differences, traditional views of humanity are all within the matrix of a theocentric universe, whereas humanism is of necessity grounded in anthropocentrism.

Or it might be said that all traditional views of man function in a Universe with a Center, and this includes the Shamanic and Chinese religions, which do not speak of Creation but nevertheless are dominated by a Divine Center so that their anthropocosmism is ultimately none other than a form of theocentrism. In contrast, the humanistic view envisages a man and a world that are ultimately without a center, for to place man at the center of things is to deny the reality of a center, the nature of the *anthropos* being too transient and nebulous to be able to act as a center unless the *anthropos* be envisaged in its theomorphic nature, which would bring us back to the traditional view of man. Consequently, the human collectivity characterized by a world having a Divine Center was now challenged by a new type of man who, conceiving himself as the center of things, reduced his world to a circle without a center with devastating consequences for the rest of humanity and the order of nature, for we know only too well that when the center disappears the circumference crumbles.

This new vision of Promethean man and the humanism characterizing it was to have the greatest effect upon the order of nature from a practical as well as theoretical point of view. In a sense, modern man, who is none other than the Promethean man described here, usurped the rights of both God and nature for himself. In all traditional civilizations a boundary was set upon human possibilities from above. Man had certain duties toward God and also certain duties toward His Creation even in the Abrahamic monotheisms, which have been so wrongly accused of late for the sins of postmedieval Western civilization.

In Islam, man is God's vicegerent on Earth (*khalīfat Allāh fī'l-arḍ*), and he has custodianship and rights over other creatures by virtue of this vicegerency and not simply as a result of being a purely earthly creature more clever and cunning than others. Renaissance humanism gave birth to a man who was no longer bound to a Divine Order or sacred hierarchy and who saw no limit upon his right to destroy nature. By stealing *à la* Prometheus the fire of a knowledge of the world that he came to divorce from all divine principles, this new man set out to conquer both other peoples and the world of nature.

Something of Christianity, of course, survived in modern man, but in most cases it was of little consequence as far as the destruction of nature was concerned. Equipped with a Faustian knowledge, secular in character, and based on power over the natural order, the new man began to create unprecedented havoc over the globe, for there was now no limit set by any spiritual laws upon his rights of dominion and no higher knowledge to set a limit upon his profane knowledge of the world. Other conquerers had come and gone, but none were equipped with such knowledge based upon domination, with a technology that knew no bounds in its destructive powers, nor with a self-image so divorced from that of a being in harmony with the cosmic ambience. Five hundred years of the devastating actions of Promethean man, opposed to both tradition and the world of nature, have borne consequences too evident to deny. It is not, therefore, an overstatement to speak of the tragic consequences of humanism understood not as a general appreciation of man but as placing earthly man at the center of the scheme of things and leading of necessity to an even greater secularization of man and ultimately to the subhuman. For to be truly human is to transcend the human. To be satisfied with the merely human is to fall ultimately below the human state.

IS THERE A NON-WESTERN HUMANISM?

The term "humanism" has been used by a number of authors for some non-Western traditions, especially Confucianism and to some extent Islam, and many might take issue with the analysis we have given above of humanism in the West by pointing to the presence of humanism in non-Western traditions. Naturally, much depends upon the definition given to the term "humanist" or "humanism," but if we understand the term in relation to the new conception of man that developed during the Renaissance and later European history, it is easy to show how it differs radically from what has been called humanism in other contexts. To make clear the singular features of Western humanism and its conception of man so radically different from various traditional points of view, a few words need to be said about what has come to be called Confucian as well as Islamic humanism.

Perhaps no other non-Western tradition has been as closely identified with humanism as Confucianism to the extent that many in the West and even a number of Chinese scholars influenced by modern rationalism and scientism have refused to identify Confucianism as a religion but have called it a philosophy of rationalistic and humanistic bent. The idea of Confucian humanism has become prevalent among historians of religion to such a degree that it is necessary to emphasize here its fundamental differences from humanism as it grew in the West. It is hoped that in this way it will become clearer how the latter form of humanism, which we consider as humanism as such in the context of this work, differs from all kinds of traditional doctrines regarding man, even the Confucian, which seems to be so much concerned with man's life in this world and what is now called the secular domain.[48]

If we delve more deeply into the Confucian and also neo-Confucian concept of man, however, we realize its radically different and distinguishing features. Confucius had the deepest sense of Heaven's mandate and he always glorified Heaven (*ti'en*). It was said of him that at the age of fifty he knew the mandate of Heaven. His conception of the perfect man or *chün-tzu* was of a morally perfect being who always stood in the awe of Heaven. The superior man is *jen*—that is, one who is loyal to his moral nature (*chung*) and treats others as himself (*shu*). *Chung* and *shu* in fact comprise the two sides or aspects of *jen*. Moreover, the "others" in the Confucian context include the order of nature or the cosmos from which the Confucian man is never separated.

Moreover, the ideal of self-cultivation, so central to Confucianism and neo-Confucianism, does not involve only the "self" in the modern, Western sense, cut off at once from Heaven, the world of nature, and society, but considers man in relation to both Heaven and Earth from which he is never severed. In fact, his body is one with Heaven and Earth with which it forms a triad constituting an interconnecting reality.[49] What is called Confucian humanism differs radically from Western humanism not only in the anthropocosmic view of the former and the anthropocentric view of the latter, which affects radically the attitude of man toward nature, but also in the different conceptions of the relation of human nature to Heaven. In the Chinese tradition man's nature is united with Heaven; moreover, in contrast to modern Western humanism there was never a rebellion against such a view until the penetration of modern Western schools of thought into China. As for man's relation to nature in the context of Confucian "humanism":

> Confucian humanism is fundamentally different from anthropocentrism because it professes the unity of man and Heaven rather than the imposition of the human will on nature. In fact, the anthropocentric assumption that man is put on earth to pursue knowledge and, as knowledge expands, so does man's dominion over earth is quite different from the Confucian perception of the pursuit of knowledge as an integral part of one's self-cultivation.
> . . . The human transformation of nature, therefore, means as much an integrative effort to learn and live harmoniously in one's natural environment as a modest attempt to use the environment to sustain basic livelihood. The idea of exploiting nature is rejected because it is incompatible with the

Confucian concern for moral development. Once our attention is focused upon the external, as the argument goes, our internal resources will be dissipated.[50]

There is yet another aspect of Confucianism that sets it completely apart from modern humanism and that is its emphasis upon ritual (*li*) and magic as traditionally understood. This side of the Confucian view of man has been brought out by Herbert Fingerette in a well-known study based upon the most authenticated parts of the *Analects*.[51] In his study, Fingerette aims "at revealing the magic power which Confucius saw, quite correctly, as the very essence of human virtue. It is finally by way of the magical that we can also arrive at the best vantage point for seeing holiness in human existence which Confucius saw as so central."[52] Lest one forget, it must be emphasized that magic, traditionally understood, is based upon correspondence and "sympathies" between various domains of reality and levels of being, and sacred rites in the Chinese context as elsewhere established harmony not only with Heaven but also Earth, or the order of nature. Naturally, the interest in magic or *magia* was widespread during the Renaissance, but what emerged as humanism in the West was as far removed from the world of sacred rituals and magical sympathy with the rest of Creation as one can imagine.

Confucius envisaged man as a Holy Vessel not defined either purely as an individual or simply as a member of a social order. Most scholars have tended to emphasize either the individual ethical component or the social-ethical concern,[53] neglecting the bond with the cosmos, the magical, the ritual, and all that makes man what Confucius calls "a sacrificial vessel of jade," which gains its significance neither from its being a vessel nor its being made of jade but rather from its use in a sacrificial ritual.

"By analogy, Confucius may be taken to imply that the individual human being, too, has ultimate dignity, sacred dignity by virtue of his role in rite, in ceremony, in *li*."[54] That is why man is a Holy Vessel and the ritual aspects of life bestow sacredness upon him, a dignity that is embedded in *li*. In participating in communal rites, man gains "a new and holy beauty just as does the sacrificial vessel."[55] It is the flowering of humanity in ceremonial and ritual acts that bestows holiness and dignity upon man, a holiness that man, moreover, shares with nature for "the raiment of holiness is cast upon Nature as well as man, upon the rivers and the air as well as upon youth and song, when they are seen through the image of the Rain Dance."[56] What could be more different, especially as far as man's relation with order of nature is concerned, than the Promethean man who grew out of Western humanism and set out to conquer the world, the last thought in his mind being "the holiness . . . cast upon Nature"? Or what could contrast more with the Confucian ideal of man performing sacred rituals than a humanist of the Enlightenment and his later progeny who drew ever further away from the sacred rites of Christianity?

This brief treatment of Confucianism should be sufficient to evoke the radical differences between humanism as it developed in the West and so-called Confucian humanism. But before terminating this discussion, it is necessary to draw closer to the Western world and mention briefly the case of Islam. During the past century those who have sought to denigrate the historical development of Islam and to criticize it for not having followed the trajectory of Western history have usually been modernists with a positive appraisal of humanism who therefore sought to prove there was no such a thing as Islamic humanism. As a way of belittling Islamic civilization there have also been those sympathetic to both Christianity and humanism who have spoken of Christian humanism while denying the existence of Islamic humanism. Then there have been those scholars who have used humanism in the sense of the *studia humanitatis* or the *artes liberales* in general, especially in reference to the fourth / tenth and fifth / eleventh centuries to which they have referred as the period of Islamic humanism since it was an era when the arts and sciences were widely cultivated, especially in Baghdad.[57]

Certain figures of Islamic history have also been dubbed as humanists, perhaps the most famous among them being the greatest stylist of the Persian language, Sa'dī, whose *Gulistān* and *Būstān* are among the most outstanding masterpieces of Persian literature. A profound observance of the human condition, Sa'dī portrayed man in all his grandeur and misery. Translated into European languages in the seventeenth century, he attracted the attention of many Enlightenment rationalists who saw him as a "humanist" opposed to the theological views of man derived from the Christian tradition.[58] When we examine Sa'dī's works in Persian, however, we discover that he was as far removed from the rationalist-humanist that he was purported to be in the eighteenth century as Ibn Rushd (Averroes), the chief Muslim religious authority of Cordova, was from the Averroes of the European Averroists, that archrationalist and enemy of the authority of revelation.

Sa'dī was at once a Sufi of the Suhrawardiyyah Order, fully aware of the Sufi doctrine of man as God's vicegerent and theophany of His Names, and a seasoned observer of human affairs. Even a cursory study of his verses reveals how far he stood from the modern humanistic view of man with its strong emphasis upon rationalism that characterized humanism at least until the nineteenth century. It is enough to quote one of his famous poems to underscore this difference:

رسد آدمی به جائی که بجز خدا نبیند   بنگر که تا چه حد است مقام آدمیت

Man attains an abode from which he sees naught but God,
Look what heights the station of man has reached.

Even if one were to forget the immortal poems of Sa'dī concerning God and the Prophet, this poem alone would speak eloquently enough about what distinguishes Western humanism from the supposed humanism of a Sa'dī, himself considered as the most "humanistic" among the famous poets or the Islamic world.

Although it is not possible here to analyze the view of man in all the different traditions of the world,[59] enough has been said here about those non-Western

traditions most often associated with humanism to allow us to assert that humanism, as it developed from the Renaissance onward in the West, projected a view of
man radically different from how he had been and continues to be envisaged in
different non-Western traditional climates. In modern Europe a new man set his
foot upon the stage of history; he had no historical precedence and had achieved,
both in the development of a quantitative science of nature and the destruction of
the order of nature, what history had never observed before. It is only now, when
the fire stolen from Heaven by the new Prometheus is beginning to destroy and
consume the world, which Promethean man has created, along with the world of
nature, that at last some people in the West are beginning to question the very
premises of that humanism which is now threatening both the existence of humanity itself and the order of nature.

THE DISFIGURATION OF THE IMAGE OF MAN AND THE
REDISCOVERY OF THE TRADITIONAL *ANTHROPOS*

The man who emerged from the humanism of the Renaissance in rebellion against
Heaven, banishing the angels from the cosmos and reducing the function of God
to the maker of the cosmic clock, could transform the spring of the Tuscany hills
into matter in motion and become the hero of the civilization created by such a
man, independent as a consequence of his reason and will, and master over the will
of other human collectivities and nature. His feats in conquering nature could still
be called "triumphs of the human spirit," but such a man could not prevent the
gradual destruction of the human face and the appearance of a subhuman world
that now threatens to devour the human and before which the very champions of
humanism have to struggle to preserve something of that heritage, which itself
has led to the present dissolution of the human from below.

The history of the modern world during the past few centuries is characterized by a gradual disfiguration of the image of man.[60] Conceived among Greek
Platonists as the *anthrōpos* bearing within himself the divine *noūs*, man was clearly
depicted in Christianity as the theomorphic being bearing the imprint of God and
being in his spiritual reality the *imago Dei*. Through the rise of humanism the face
of man was declared as independent of the Face of God, culminating in the
nineteenth century in the famous Nietzschean declaration of "the death of God."
But the face of man is a reflection of the Face of God or what the Quran calls *wajh
Allāh*. To eradicate His Face is also to deface man and to announce his death, to
which the present century bears witness. In fact, from the point of view of the
traditional understanding of the meaning of the *anthrōpos*, the last half millennium marks the gradual disfiguration of the image of man, resulting finally in the
death of that humanistic conception of humanity so highly praised by defenders of
modern man and his exploitations.

This gradual disfiguration is to be seen in the European art of painting as well
as in the art of dress or attire. The human image was at first none other than the
Divine Image of the icon, which is the origin of Christian painting. The icon is

the meta-human image of the human, revealing the human in its archetypal reality. In the Renaissance the religious image becomes completely anthropomorphic, leading to an even greater naturalism, which ends finally in the decomposition of the image of the face of man in Picasso and his followers. Henceforth an imageless or so-called abstract art comes to the fore, which far from being surrealistic is subrealistic, rising from the lower layers of the psyche and leading often to the infrahuman.[61] As for the art of the dress, or apparel, with the Renaissance the sacerdotal nature of clothing, especially male attire, is destroyed, replaced by various styles that emphasize pompocity, luxury, animality, and almost anything other than man's sacerdotal and pontifical nature. It ends with that casualness in attire which succeeds to the extent possible to hide the nobility of the human body.

The steady process of the disfiguration of the image of man can also be seen in the way in which modern man comes to identify his nature with his creations based upon the forgetfulness of his original nature. He creates the machine and then philosophers and scientists appear who identify man himself as a machine. Then man invents the computer and before long the human brain is itself seen as a computer, and few bother to ask what it was before the computer was invented. The Faustian genius for invention, which must go on ceaselessly, only widens the road for modern man's rapid existential decline, which before the catastrophe of the past few decades almost everyone in the West and their followers on other continents hailed as obvious progress.

This continuous disfiguration of the image of man, despite all the differences among the Renaissance humanist, the Enlightenment rationalist, or the nineteenth-century evolutionist, has not ceased to have one constant feature—namely the aggressive attitude toward nature. All of these stages of the transformation of the image of man have in fact taken place in the matrix of the anthropomorphic worldview, with its subordination of the Divine and the cosmic to the human. The main thrust of the history of humanity in the West has been to substitute the kingdom of man for the kingdom of God.[62] Only now when much of Earth has been despoiled and the rest threatened as never before, a few have awakened to the reality that, although man once sought the kingdom of God seriously, he lived at peace with the world of nature or at least did not threaten the very fabric of the order of nature; now that he is living and striving only for the kingdom of man, he is about to destroy the very order that makes the fabric of human life on Earth possible.

It is at this crucial moment that a number of voices, in realizing that the humanistic image of man as defined above must be totally replaced, have sought to revive the traditional understanding of the *anthrōpos*. Some have turned to Oriental doctrines where the traditional image of man has remained alive, despite the spread of modernism ever since the last century[63]; others have turned to the Western tradition, especially its esoteric dimension, which has become eclipsed during the past several centuries.[64] The latter have tried to bring to center stage the image of man as at once spirit, soul, and body and to emphasize the axis between Heaven and Earth to which so many works of Christian metaphysics and especially Hermetic and Cabalistic writings refer. In both cases, an awareness exists that the image of man as he has been conceived during the past few centuries in the West must die and the traditional image of man revived if the current crisis within both human society and vis-à-vis nature is to be solved. One can only add that there is no possibility of rediscovering the religious understanding of the order of nature without discovering once again the traditional image of man and the process whereby this image came to be forgotten by that type of man who has wreaked havoc upon Earth and, as the Quran asserts, is a veritable "corrupter of the Earth." The recovery of the traditional wisdom concerning nature can only come about if we recall the words of Hildegard of Bingen, that remarkable medieval Christian mystic and poet, who observed:

O Man,
Regard thyself,
Thou hast within thyself
Heaven and Earth.

NOTES

1. See Nicola Abbagnano, "Humanism," in *The Encyclopedia of Philosophy,* Vol. 4 (New York and London: Macmillan, 1972), pp. 69–72, and his "Italian Renaissance Humanism," *Cahiers d'Histoire Mondiale* (Vol. 7, 1962 / 63), pp. 267–282. See also Ernst Cassirer et al. (eds.), *The Renaissance Philosophy of Man* (Chicago: University of Chicago Press, 1948), particularly the Introduction by Paul O. Kristeller and John H. Randall, pp. 3ff.

2. Giorgio Di Santillana, *The Age of Adventure* (New York: George Brazilier, 1957), p. 11.

3. See Abbagnano, "Humanism," p. 70.

4. "This is a deep regard for what is meant by the verb 'to be' and especially 'I am.' The humanist is interested in everything because he wants to compare himself with it." Stevie Davies, *Renaissance Views of Man* (New York: Barnes & Noble, 1979), p. 9.

5. "Il n'est pas forcé que l'homme de la Renaissance soit un humaniste (Rabelabis ne l'est presque point); il l'est moins encore que l'humaniste soil un homme de la Renaissance." Émile Faquet *Siezième siècle, Études littéraires* (Paris: Bouvin & Cie, 1949), pp. XV–XVI; quoted by Augustin Renaudet, *Humanisme et Renaissance* (Geneva: Librairie E. Droz, 1958), p. 32.

6. The work by Renaudet (*Humanisme et Renaissance*) is a case in point. In contrast to this view, Paul Kristeller refutes the notion that such a figure as St. Thomas Aquinas was a medieval humanist. See Kristeller's *Eight Italian Philosophers of the Italian Renaissance* (Stanford, Calif.: Stanford University Press, 1964), pp. 147ff.

7. See, for example, the well-known work of Jacques Maritain, *L'Humanisme integral; problèmes temporels et spirituels d'une nouvelle chrétienté* (Paris: F. Aubler, 1936).

8. See, for example, Mohammed Arkoun, *L'humanisme arabe au IVe-Xe siècle: Miskawayh philosophe et historien* (Paris: J. Vrin, 1982); and Joel L. Kraemer, *Humanism in the Renaissance of Islam* (Leiden: E. J. Brill), 1986.

9. There is a vast literature on Renaissance humanism including questions of its

origin. For works in English see Benjamin G. Kohl, *Renaissance Humanism, 1300–1500: A Bibliography of Materials in English* (New York and London: Garland Publishing, 1985).

10. Cassirer et al. (eds.), *Renaissance Philosophy of Man*, p. 142. See the Introduction by Hans Nachod (pp. 23–33) for an analysis of the thought of Petrarch. On Petrarch see also Jerrold E. Seigel, *Rhetoric and Philosophy in Renaissance Humanism: The Union of Eloquence and Wisdom, Petrarch to Valla* (Princeton, N.J.: Princeton University Press, 1968).

11. On the Islamic conception of man see G. Eaton, "Man," in Seyyed Hossein Nasr (ed.), *Islamic Spirituality: Foundations* (New York: Crossroad Publications, 1987), pp. 358ff.; S. H. Nasr, "Who Is Man? The Perennial Answer of Islam," in Jacob Needleman (ed.), *The Sword of Gnosis* (London and Boston: Arkana, 1986), pp. 203ff.

12. According to Kristeller, humanism "was a development that may have been encouraged by influence from France and from Byzantinum." Cassirer et al. (eds.), *The Renaissance Philosophy of Man*, p. 3.

13. George Makdisi, *The Rise of Humanism in Classical Islam and the Christian West* (Edinburgh: Edinburgh University Press, 1990). The Arabic word *adab* means at once literature (*belles-lettres*), culture, humanities, courtesy, and correct comportment and is almost untranslatable into a single term in English.

14. Makdisi (p. 296) quotes Kristeller's definition of Renaissance humanism as "the general tendency of the age to attach the *greatest importance to classical studies, and to consider classical antiquity as the common standard and model* by which to guide all cultural activities." From Paul Kristeller, *Studies in Renaissance Thought and Letters* (Rome: Edizioni di Storia et Letteratura, 1956), p. 350. Kristeller also emphasizes the importance of eloquence and the production of an enormous number of treatises on literature, poetry, etc.

15. Space does not allow us here to mention the vast amount of scholarly evidence that the author has brought to bear upon the subject, and we can do no more than refer the reader to Part Seven of Makdisi's work as well as the original Arabic, Latin, and vernacular sources cited by him.

16. See Makdisi, *Rise of Humanism*, p. 351.

17. Concerning the thought of two of the leading philosophical figures of the period it has been said: "The philosophies of man of Marsilio Ficino and [Giovanni] Pico are humanistic on a philosophical level. Ficino was the first Renaissance philosopher to formulate a metaphysical view of the nature and place of man in the universe." See the Introduction by P. Miller in Pico della Mirandola, *On the Dignity of Man, On Being and the One*, and *Heptaplus*, trans. Paul J. W. Miller and Douglas Carmichael (New York: Bobbs-Merrill, 1965), p. XIV.

18. On Renaissance philosophy see Charles B. Schmitt et al. (eds.), *The Cambridge History of Renaissance Philosophy* (Cambridge and New York: Cambridge University Press, 1988) which contains also an extensive bibliography on the subject.

19. Pico begins his book *On the Dignity of Man* as follows: "Most venerable fathers, I have read in the records of the Arabians that Abdul the Saracen, on being asked what thing on, so to speak, the world's stage, he viewed as most greatly worthy of wonder, answered that he viewed nothing more wonderful than man." Ibid., p. 3; also Cassirer et al. (eds.), *The Renaissance Philosophy of Man*, p. 225. For an analysis of Pico's philosophy see the Introduction by Paul Kristeller in the same volume (pp. 215–222). As for Ficino, see pp. 185ff. of the same work.

20. It is for this reason that we have not dealt with him in this chapter although we must emphasize Nicholas of Cusa's great significance in the exposition of traditional

metaphysics at that crucial moment in Western history when the medieval world of faith was crumbling before the new Renaissance "Age of Adventure."

21. These currents of thought were analyzed in depth by Ernst Cassirer and others in *The Renaissance Philosophy of Man*, but Cassirer's neo-Kantianism has been challenged by more recent scholarship. See Pauline M. Watts, "Pseudo-Dionysius the Areopagite and Three Renaissance Neoplatonists: Cusanus, Ficino & Pico," in James Hankins et al. (eds.), *Supplementum Festivum: Studies in Honor of Paul Oskar Kristeller* (Binghamton, N.Y.: Center for Medieval and Early Renaissance Studies, 1987), pp. 279ff. Watts points out that in contrast to the views of Cassirer, these men were not just Platonists. The first included in his thought important Aristotelian elements and the last two were eclectics displaying significant Hermetic and Cabalistic elements.

22. It is in reference to this phenomenon that Harry A. Wolfson speaks of the "twice-revealed Averroes." See his essay, "The Twice-Revealed Averroes," *Speculum* (Vol. 36, 1961), pp. 373–392. On Renaissance Aristotelianism, see Charles B. Schmitt, *The Aristotelian Tradition and Renaissance Universities* (London: Variorum Reprints, 1984).

23. We see here once again in the West the remarkable metamorphosis of an aspect of the Islamic intellectual tradition into something derived from, yet differing radically from, its original reality.

24. Quoted in Di Santillana, *The Age of Adventure*, p. 168. Montaigne does not of course mean the inner man, or what Islamic esotericism calls universal man (*al-insān al-kāmil*) but the "ordinary" nature of ordinary men.

25. Frithjof Schuon, *Light on the Ancient Worlds*, trans. Lord Northbourne (Bloomington, Ind.: World Wisdom Books, 1984), p. 31. It is interest to note in this conjunction how Pico belittled the evil in man.

26. We have dealt with this question in our book *Knowledge and the Sacred* (Albany: State University of New York Press, 1989), pp. 160ff.

27. For the history of skepticism in the West, especially during the Renaissance, see Richard H. Popkin, *The History of Scepticism from Erasmus to Descartes* (Assen, the Netherlands: Van Gorcum & Comp. N.V., 1960).

28. "Not only was he [Montaigne] the best writer and thinker of those who were interested in the ideas of the Academies and Pyrrhonians, but he was also the one who felt most fully the impact of the Pyrrhonian theory of complete doubt, and its relevance to the religious debates of the time." Ibid., p. 44.

29. "If by naturalism one means the conviction that man is a part of nature—that nature is his realm, that the features which tie him to nature (his body, his needs, his sensations) are essential to him to the point that he cannot abstract from them or ignore them—then one can speak of a naturalism in humanism." Nicola Abbagnano, "Humanism," p. 70.

30. "The old image of Fortune with a wheel, seizing men and dragging them along, sometimes raising them, sometimes throwing them down into the abyss, now gives way to the depiction of Fortune with a *sailboat*. And this bark is not controlled by Fortune alone—man himself is steering it." Ernst Cassirer, *The Individual and the Cosmos in Renaissance Philosophy*, trans. Mario Domandi (New York: Harper & Row, 1964), p. 77.

31. Pico writes, "The wonders of the mind are greater than the heavens. . . . On earth, nothing is great but man; and nothing is great in man but his mind and his soul. When you rise up to them, you rise up beyond the heavens." Pico della Mirandola, *In astrologiam*, iii, 27, *Opera*, fol. 519, quoted by Cassirer, *The Individual and the Cosmos*, p. 77. The similarity of aspects of Pico's view to the traditional doctrines of man is obvious. The basic difference is to a large extent the anthropomorphic view of the first and the

theomorphic view of the second. After Ficino and Pico this inherent anthropomorphism became more accentuated and central to nearly the whole of Western thought.

32. On the question of being and action or contemplation and action in different traditional worlds, see Yusuf Ibish and Peter Lawborn Wilson (eds.), *Traditional Modes of Contemplation and Action* (Tehran: Imperial Iranian Academy of Philosophy, 1977).

33. Cassirer, *Individual and the Cosmos*, p. 84. There is of course some truth in this statement in the sense that through our actions we weave our future "body of resurrection" and that our actions affect our mode of being without which spiritual practices would be meaningless. But it is it not this understanding of the statement that Pico had in mind.

34. Davies, *Renaissance Views of Man*, p. 10.

35. See Cassirer et al., *The Renaissance Philosophy of Man*, p. 389.

36. Pico della Mirandola, *On the Dignity of Man*, trans. Charles Wallis (Indianapolis: Bobbs-Merrill, 1965), pp. 4–5. See also Cassirer, *The Individual and the Cosmos*, pp. 85ff.

37. Cassirer, *The Individual and the Cosmos*, p. 88. As an example of Bouvelles's own work in modern editions see Carolus Bovillus, *Sur les langues vulgaires et la variété de la langue française*, trans. Colette Dumont-Demaizière (Paris: C. Klincksieck, 1973).

38. Ibid., p. 89.

39. Ibid., p. 91.

40. Ibid., p. 93. The use of the image of the eye and the mirror is strikingly reminiscent of the *Gulshan-i rāz* of Shaykh Maḥmūd Shabistarī, who refers to man as the eye that sees the reflections of the Divine Names and Qualities in the mirror of nothingness, man himself being at the same time the total reflection of those Names and Qualities. In contrast to Bouvelles, however, he emphasizes the objective and Divine Origin of the archetypal realities reflected in man and the cosmos and does not claim that man forms such images. Shabistarī writes,

> *Nonbeing is a mirror, the world the image of the {Universal Man} and man,*
> *Is the eye of the image, in which the person is hidden.*
> *Thou art the eye of the image, and He is the light of the eye.*
> *Who has ever seen with the eye, the eye through which all things are seen?*

See S. H. Nasr, *Science and Civilization in Islam* (Cambridge: Islamic Text Society, 1987), p. 345.

41. "Man is a mirror who stands outside and opposite the rest of creation in order to observe and reflect the world. He is thus the focal point of the universe in which all degrees of reality converge." Jill Kraye, in reference to Bouvelles in "Moral Philosophy," Schmitt et al., *The Cambridge History of the Renaissance*, p. 314.

42. On the changes in the concept of Prometheus during the Renaissance, see Cassirer, *The Individual and the Cosmos*, pp. 92ff.

43. Needless to say, during the Renaissance magic and astrology were not opposed to the sciences of nature of the day but constituted an essential part of the scientific point of view of the age. The rapport between astrology and the empirical sciences of the Renaissance was not dissolved until the works of Copernicus and Galileo became widely accepted, and even then the astrological perspective continued its life in occultist and esoteric circles and continues to do so to this day.

44. We have dealt extensively with this theme in our book *Knowledge and the Sacred*, Chapter 5, "Man, Pontifical and Promethean," pp. 160ff.

45. "It is not a humble vision; it poured into Renaissance culture an egoism which, though it was often tempered by Christian awareness, contrary evidence, or a sense of

hubris, characterized in some degree the self-consciousness of most artists." Davies, *The Renaissance Views of Man,* p. 64.

46. The Renaissance shared the medieval opposition to Islam on religious grounds without sharing its intellectual respect for Islam and the Islamic intellectual traditions. The Renaissance and not the Middle Ages must be seen as the beginning of the Western tendency to look upon Islamic civilization with the air of superiority and disdain based upon having to deal with something inferior. This is a truth rarely understood by those modern Muslims who take pride in the supposedly Islamic origin of the Renaissance without understanding the metamorphosis everything inherited from Islam underwent in the West during this period.

47. The loss of the distinction between *intellectus* and *ratio,* so characteristic of modern thought, is indicative of the new anthropomorphism with its consequent rationalism.

48. The Chinese scholar Wing Tsit-chan writes, "In short, his [Confucius's] doctrine can be summed up as ethical humanism." *Encyclopedia of Philosophy* (Vol. 1, 1967), p. 189. He adds in another essay, "Humanism had been growing in China for centruies before the time of Confucius, but it was he who brought it to maturity." *Encyclopedia of Religion,* Vol. 4 (New York: Macmillian, 1987), p. 17. For the use of humanism in the Confucian context in more recent discussions, see Tu Wei-ming, Milan Hejtmanek, and Alan Wachman (eds.), *The Confucian World Observed: A Contemporary Discussion of Confucian Humanism in East Asia* (Honolulu: The East-West Center, 1992). See also Ch'u Chai and Winberg Chai (eds. and trans.), *The Humanist Way in Ancient China: Essential Work of Confucianism* (New York: Bantam, 1965).

49. "This dynamic trial underlies the assumption of our interconnectedness to all reality and acts as an overriding goal of self-cultivation. Thus through the deepening of this sense of basic identity the human body may participate fully in the transformative aspects of the universe." May E. Tucker, "The Relevance of Chinese Neo-Confucianism for the Reverence of Nature," *Environmental History Review* (Summer 1991), pp. 64–65.

50. Tu Wei-ming, *Confucian Thought: Selfhood as Creative Transformation* (Albany: State University of New York Press, 1985), p. 75. The Confucian scholar Tu Wei-ming is one of the important authors in recent years who has sought to bring out the religious significance of Confucianism beyond the humanistic-rationalistic image that was created by both Western and Westernized Chinese scholars. For a bibliography of his works, see pages 189–196 of the above work. Among Western scholars there have been also those who have appreciated the authentically religious and traditional character of Confucianism; these include Marcel Granet in France and Huston Smith in America. Such an appreciation is now on the rise.

51. See Herbert Fingerette, *Confucius: The Secular as Sacred* (New York and London: Harper & Row, 1972).

52. Ibid, p. 1.

53. For example, Heexlee G. Creel in *Confucius and the Chinese Way* (New York: Harper, 1960) emphasizes the Confucian accent upon the primary and worth of the individual (pp. 36, 38) disregarding the magical element, while Wing Tsit-chan, "The Story of Chinese Philosophy," in Charles A. Moore (ed.) *Philosophy: East and West* (Princeton, N.J.: Princeton University Press, 1944), p. 27, emphasizes the individual in relation to the social order, but again accentuates only the rationalistic elements to the detriment of the ritual and the magical.

54. Fingerette, *Confucius,* p. 75.

55. Ibid., p. 77.

56. From Confucius, quoted in ibid., pp. 78–79.

57. Makdisi in his already cited work is obviously using humanism strictly in the sense of the *studia humanitatis* without any philosophical connotations. For works that use humanism in the sense of the cultivation of the arts and sciences especially in Abbasid Baghdad, see Arkoun, *L'humanisme arabe,* and Kraemer, *Humanism in the Renaissance of Islam.*

58. On Sa'dī see Henri Massé, *Essai sur le poète Saadi* (Paris: P. Geuthner, 1919); also the Introduction by George M. Wickens to Sa'dī, *Morals Pointed and Tales Adorned: The Bustān of Sa'dī* (Toronto: University of Toronto Press, 1974).

59. It is most important to carry out a detailed study from the traditional point of view of the nature of man following such seminal works as *Man and His Becoming According to the Vedanta* of René Guénon, trans. M. Pallis (London: Luzac, 1945), and *From the Divine to the Human* of Frithjof Schuon, trans. Gustavo Polit and Deborah Lambert (Bloomington, Ind.: World Wisdom Books, 1982). Such a study would accentuate further the remarkable similarity of various traditional doctrines of man, despite obvious theological, juridical, and social differences on the one hand and the view that grew out of humanism in the West and its consequences on the other.

60. There is a description of the step-by-step loss of the image of man as *imago Dei* by Gilbert Durand, the well-known French anthropologist, in his *Science de l'homme et tradition* (Paris: Berg International, L'Ile Verte, 1979). See also Elémire Zolla, *The Uses of Imagination and the Decline of the West* (Ipswich, U.K.: Golgonooza Press, 1978).

61. See Titus Burckhardt, *Sacred Art in East and West,* trans. Lord Northbourne (London: Perennial Books, 1967), p. 148; Hans Sedlmayr, *Verlust der Mitte* or "Loss of the Center" trans. as *Art in Crisis* by Brian Batter Shaw (London: Hollis & Carter, 1958); and Frithjof Schuon, *The Transcendent Unity of Religions* (Wheaton, Ill.: Theosophical Publishing House, 1933), pp. 61ff.

62. See Tage Lindbom, *The Tares and the Good Grain or the Kingdom of Man at the Hour of Reckoning,* trans. Alvin Moore, Jr. (Macon, Ga.: Mercer University Press, 1983).

63. Foremost among this group are, of course, the traditional authors referred to above. For a more extensive discussion of their writings and the traditional view of man, see Nasr, *Knowledge and the Sacred,* Chapter 5.

64. One of the most important works in this category is Gilbert Durand, *Science de l'homme et tradition,* Chapter 3, "Homo proximi orientalis: Science de l'homme et Islam spirituel," p. 91.

6

The Rediscovery of Nature: Religion and the Environmental Crisis

شیرازهٔ دین که در جهان بر پاشید   بنیاد حیات در زمین در پاشید

آلوده هوا و آب و کوه و دریا   ارکان وجود زندگان در پاشید

In the land of the setting sun, religion did the cosmos lose
To sciences and philosophies turned against the Spirit,
And its reflections in these natural forms.
Cut off from its roots, a natural philosophy did arise,
Which could not but suffocate this living planet,
Leading to a near-death state of chaos and destruction,
Which now religion can no longer ignore;
For how can we seek salvation when our very acts
Are destroying God's creation, stifling the prayers
Of countless creatures who shall bear witness on that Day,
Which is the Day of Days, the Hour of reckoning,
Toward which we all journey, and those creatures
Witness against our barbarous acts of the murder of nature?
No! Religion cannot but turn again to that order of nature,
Which still speaks in a silent voice of the Wisdom and
Love,
Of the One whose Mercy alone can save us from us,
From that arrogant ignorance parading as knowledge,
Which in this late hour threatens not only our lives, human,
But the whole web of life to which we are wed by our sinews and bones.

After several centuries of an ever-increasing eclipse of the religious significance of nature in the West and neglect of the order of nature by mainstream Christian religious thought, many Christian theologians have in the past two or three decades become interested once again in nature. It has taken the disastrous consequences of the environmental crisis and the threat to the very fabric of life to arouse religious thought in the West to the *religious* significance of the order of nature and the need to revive a theology concerned with Creation as well as redemption. Diverse paths have been chosen to face this challenge, some seeking to go back to the traditional roots of Christianity, others to turn East to Indian and Far Eastern religions, and yet others to search for the wisdom of the Native Shamanic religions, especially those of the Americas. And there are many who have sought to transform Christianity itself, including some of its most cherished doctrines and symbols in order to create a new religious attitude more conducive to the needs of the environment. Judaism in the West has also responded to the challenge of the environmental crisis mostly in a fashion parallel with that of Christianity, although it has not been willing to sacrifice much of its doctrines and sacred history.

As for the non-Western religions, during the past few centuries they have marshalled all their forces to preserve their identity before the onslaught of a powerful foreign (that is, Western) civilization at once materially and militarily overwhelming and for the most part religiously oppressive within its borders while supporting missionary activity abroad to a large extent for political purposes. Furthermore, until quite recently, the technological oppression against nature has had its origin mostly in the West. Therefore, these religions remained impervious to the full impact of the environmental crisis. Now they are beginning to respond, but in a manner very different from what one observes in the West. This is because, first of all, in contrast to mainstream Western Christianity, these non-Western religions have never lost their interest in the order of nature nor have they surrendered the religious view of nature to a scientific one that would by definition negate their principles. In fact, the views they held about nature, as outlined briefly in Chapter 2, survived until their modern encounter with secularism and materialism and, in most cases, have not been given up to this day.[1]

To understand the role of the religious understanding of the order of nature today and the possibility of the revival of this view, it is necessary to cast a critical glance on at least some of the Christian voices seeking to create what some now call "eco-theology" before turning to other religions. Today, there is also much written by philosophers and scientists concerned with ecology that deals with environmental ethics and that have in fact a religious impact and in some cases a directly religious dimension. But it is not possible to deal with such topics in the present context, for our purpose is to study religion per se in its relation to the order of nature; therefore, we must limit ourselves to those who speak as religious thinkers or theologians. Furthermore, we have selected only a small number of personages among the expanding group of Christians who now devote themselves to this subject, the principle of selection being both the significance and influence of the person considered and the necessity to have as wide a representation as possible from various schools and perspectives within Christianity.

RECENT AND CURRENT CHRISTIAN RESPONSES
TO THE ENVIRONMENTAL CRISIS

A study of the history of Christian concerns with the environmental crisis reveals the great diversity of approaches to the subject based mostly upon responses to the accusations made by such people as Arnold Toynbee and especially Lynn White[2] that Christianity is in a basic way responsible for the attitude of domination over nature by modern man, which has led to the environmental crisis. Reacting mostly from an apologetic position, some have sought to refute the thesis altogether by pointing to the presence of the environmental crisis elsewhere.[3] Others, as already mentioned, have accepted the criticism against the Christian view of nature and pointed out the significance of non-Western religions and philosophies of nature,[4] whereas another group has sought solutions within the Western tradition.[5] Our goal here is not to trace the causes of the environmental crisis, which at the deepest level reflects externally modern man's inner ailment and spiritual crisis,[6] but rather to present current views of Christian thinkers about the religious significance of nature in the light of the environmental problem and their understanding of it.

As early as the 1950s H. Richard Niebuhr, the Protestant theologian, spoke of "loyalty to the community of life,"[7] but few other theologians at that time took the question of the environment seriously.[8] In the 1960s the situation gradually began to change. The Lutheran Joseph Sittler spoke of "a theology for the earth," cosmic redemption and nature's participation in salvation. Rejecting pantheism, he emphasized that the world was not God but God's and considered this attribution to be sufficient to unite theology and ecology in grace.[9] Also during that period Richard Baer, another Protestant thinker, tried to formulate the new "eco-theology" by emphasizing that the world belongs to God, that God loves the world He created, and that He values process, systems and the "web of life."[10]

Even before the appearance of the essay by Lynn White (see note 2), the World Council of Churches had sought to unite theologians interested in ecology and the treatment of nature as God's gift to be used in light of the principle of stewardship and sensitive to the fact that natural forms have a value in themselves and are not to be looked upon from a utilitarian viewpoint. Some influential works were written by this group, called Faith-Man-Nature, before it disbanded in the 1970s.[11] Meanwhile, the White essay had appeared, arousing a great deal of reaction, which was to lead ultimately to the selection by the Catholic Church of St. Francis as the patron saint of ecology and numerous defenses of Christianity in the light of the accusations of White from both Catholic and Protestant quarters.[12]

In the 1970s one of the members of the disbanded group of Protestant theologians, Paul Santmire, produced a number of influential works examining the theology of the environment. In *Brother Earth: Nature, God and Ecology in Time of Crisis*, Santmire sought to provide a theology drawn from Christianity as a response to Lynn White. Santmire emphasized that the Kingdom of God embraces nature as well as man and that social justice must include the natural as well as the human world. Nature, according to Santmire, has its own rights independent of man, and it is the religious duty of people to preserve and protect nature. In his later work, *The Travail of Nature: The Ambiguous Ecological Promise of Christian Theology,* [13] Santmire provided a detailed history and analysis of Christian documents bearing upon nature, ranging from St. Irenaeus and Origen to St. Augustine, to the twelfth-century interest in the cosmos and the rebirth of nature in the Renaissance, to the "subordination of nature" by St. Thomas Aquinas, the embracing of nature by St. Francis, the cosmic visions of St. Bonaventure and Dante, to the Reformation and the secularization of nature, and finally to the triumph of personalism with Karl Barth and Teilhard de Chardin. Few works have succeeded in bringing out the rich tradition of Christian teachings concerning nature as has Santmire's. His popularity indicates in fact the great growth of interest in this field during the 1980s among Christian thinkers despite the as yet feeble response of the churches to the environmental crisis.

Returning to the 1970s, one should also mention John B. Cobb, the most influential of Whiteheadian or process theologians in the domain of the environment. He emphasized that all things participate in a process that is of value to God and must be therefore respected by man. People themselves participate with God in caring for nature and cannot separate themselves from the process of nature. In *Is It Too Late?,* written in 1972, Cobb sought to examine the role of Christianity in what was then called the ecological rather than environmental crisis. He concluded that past forms of Christianity are inadequate to the needs of the moment and also rejected the Oriental and primal religions as possible solutions. He spoke of a "new Christianity" that would expand rights to include nature. Because everything in the Universe is significant to God, it is possible to develop a "theology of ecology." In a later work, *Liberation of Life,* written with Charles Birch in 1981, Cobb applied this "new ethics" to all things including subatomic particles, which also possess a potential for enriching experience, and he spoke of a pyramid of life at whose apex man is situated.

During the 1970s environmentalism itself became a kind of "religion," and in fact nearly all of the so-called "New-Age religions" have emphasized the significance of the Earth and its rediscovery as a sacred reality. While among Christians a number of people turned to the question of the religious significance of the land, [14] the "new religions" often turned to the worship of Earth as a mother-goddess. Numberous other movements, from those that claimed to revive the ancient mystery cults of Isis and Osiris to Druidism to natural magic and sorcery and to the opting of the Shamanic religions in a truncated form, have since come to the fore and fill much of the contemporary religious landscape, especially in America. These phenomena constitute the subject of a separate study and need to be analyzed carefully, but they cannot be dealt with here where our concern is with traditional religions, even if now modernized, and not with recently created religious movements. But the turning of environmentalism into a religion itself and the return of cults of the Earth in the present-day context are themselves significant in that they point to the need in the souls of human beings for the religious understanding of nature eclipsed in the West by modern science and neglected until quite recently by the mainstream religions themselves.

In turning environmentalism into a religious concern some also went further than the question of bestowing rights upon nature and sought to realize the Divine in nature by turning to the Oriental religions, among which Zen played the most important role. Prime examples are the American poet and environmentalist Gary Snyder, who appealed to both Zen and the American Indian traditions to create a new attitude toward nature, and the well-known writer on Oriental religions Alan Watts, who soon became a cult figure.[15] But even among traditional Christians a major thinker such as Thomas Merton turned to the East not only for rediscovering methods of meditation, but also to recapture and integrate into the Christian view the Zen and Taoist attitudes toward nature. And this strand of religious response to the environmental crisis has remained to this day, as seen by the continuing attention paid by Christian thinkers to Oriental attitudes toward nature.[16]

The last two decades built upon these earlier concerns of the few Christian theologians who had turned their attention to the question of the environment, while interest in this subject increased exponentially. Numerous approaches came to be taken from the most liberal Protestant positions to traditional Catholic and Orthodox ones. One of the strands that has sought to combine the concern with the environment with feminism is "eco-feminism," which identifies the subjugation of the Earth in Western civilization with the suppression of women, some of its exponents questioning the very structure of Christianity as it has existed during the past two millennia.[17] Others have left formal Christianity in favor of "earthy" religions, the revival of sorcery and magic, earth-goddess figures and the like, with which, as already mentioned, we are not concerned here.

Among the most often heard voices in Protestant circles, those who combine concerns of feminism with Christian theology, is Sallie McFague, who first developed what she termed "metaphorical theology" and which she has then applied to the problem of the environment.[18] For her the language of revelation is not itself sacred but is only metaphorical to be changed by theologians according to changing circumstances. The description of God in the Bible is finally only a "model" that she sets out to criticize and finally replace by another "model." McFague begins her criticism by attacking the "monarchical model" because it makes God distant from the world and concerns only human beings on the basis of domination, as if the monotheisms did not consider God to be the king of the whole Universe and as if the majesty of God expressed in His role as king excluded His beauty and mercy.[19] She also criticizes this "model" because it is hierarchical, a characteristic to which she is strongly opposed. Only in a world where the majesty of God is forgotten and the hierarchy which is innate to the nature of existence denied could the enfeebled vestiges of the symbol of kingship and its concomitant hierarchy be conceived as the cause of the environmental crisis, and the symbol of God as king, which is far from being limited to Christianity, reduced to a dangerous metaphor.[20] One needs to remember that it is only now, when the very idea of majesty and hierarchy are being obliterated in the modern world, that the environment is being destroyed with an unprecedented fury on the basis of not hierarchy and majesty but egalitarianism, materialism, and greed. Furthermore, it is important to note that in a religion as "matriarchal" as Hinduism, God is spoken of as the king and ruler of the Universe whose majesty is reflected in all legitimate temporal authority.

McFague then turns to the possibility of considering the world as "God's body" and asks,

> What if . . . the "resurrection of the body" were not seen as the resurrection of particular bodies that ascend, beginning with Jesus of Nazareth, into another world, but as God's promise to be with us always in God's body, our world?[21]

She develops this theme in building a new "model of God" that would encourage holistic attitudes toward nature and avoid distancing God from the world.[22] In her use of heuristic and metaphorical theology McFague also speaks of God as mother, lover, and friend of the world. Her compassion for the world of nature and her awareness of the acuteness of the environmental crisis cause her to forgo rather easily the perennial description of God as contained in the Bible and also mentioned explicitly by Christ, as at the beginning of the Lord's Prayer with its patriarchal language. Could one in fact change "Our Father who art in Heaven" to something else such as "Our Mother who art in or on Earth" without destroying the very channels through which Christianity has revealed its message? In Islam the Names al-Rabb (the Lord) and al-Malik (the King) are Names of God, sacred not only in their meaning but also in their form, and it is beyond the power of man to change them even for what might appear to be a worthy purpose. The equating of symbol in its traditional sense as contained in revealed descriptions of God of Himself with metaphor to be changed at will by humans is, to say the least, most problematic from the traditional theological point of view.

McFague remains aware, however, of the reality of evil in contrast to many "creation theologians." She mentions the necessity of stressing Creation rather than simply personal redemption while reminding us that the evil within us manifested in selfishness, greed, etc., is real and a sin in the Christian meaning of the term.[23] The destruction of the environment is in fact the result of sin in the theological sense. Consequently, human beings must first of all admit their role in the despoiling of the planet, and, second, realize their responsibility for preserving the community of life. There must be a general repentance, and the "planetary agenda" must be the top concern of all religions.

In turning to the ethical aspect of the theological concern with the environment, McFague seeks to harmonize liberation theology, eco-theology, and feminism, and she relates the domination over nature to the domination of the poor by the rich and also of women by men.[24] She calls for a more "earthy" theology to help people live rightly on Earth, but a theology that, rather than being based on the religious understanding of the order of nature, accepts fully the current scientific description of that order. She does not provide a theological or metaphysical criticism of modern science but argues for its blind acceptance.[25] There is thus an attempt to combine Christian ethics with a scientific view of nature, which is totally separated from the religious understanding of nature, a trait that, far from being limited to a few theologians like McFague, characterizes most of the current Christian theologians' concern with the environment. While talking of compassion for all creatures and of humans being cousins of stars, such theologians accept completely the theory of the big bang, the explosion of matter and the emergence of life and all its complexities from matter through evolution, as the one and only story of Creation without at all criticizing theologically or metaphysically the foundations of a quantitative science that is the basis of the entire current scientific understanding of nature. Nor do they assert the reality of that symbolic science of nature which is the foundation of all traditional cosmological sciences.

The complete acceptance of the modern scientific view of nature as the basis of theology is modified by the philosopher and historian of religion Langdon Gilkey, who discusses the shortcomings of the modern scientific understanding of order and its philosophical ambiguity. Although accepting the role of mainstream Christian theology in cultivating a certain negative attitude toward nature and failing to consider its theological significance, Gilkey also emphasizes the central role of modern science and technology in the creation of the current environmental crisis.[26]

In contrast to McFague and many other Christian theologians, Gilkey proposes a new understanding of nature that "not only assumes a scientific understanding but also explores other ways in which we humans relate to nature and so can be said to 'know' nature."[27] Interestingly enough, for Gilkey these other ways include not only earlier Western sources, which are being pursued by a number of scholars and tehologians, but also the archaic and primal religions. He is in fact among a small number of academic scholars of religion who not only seek seriously to formulate a new theology of nature, but also to look beyond the Christian tradition for sources of knowledge while remaining aware of the richness of the Christian tradition, so much of which had been relegated to oblivion during the past few centuries, while the reality of cosmic redemption was being replaced almost completely with the redemption of the individual without concern for the sacred quality of the cosmos as "the habitation of the Spirit."[28]

Turning to the Catholic world, it is necessary to first discuss all the "creation spirituality" associated especially with the name of Matthew Fox because of the great influence he has exercised in certain religious circles concerned with the environmental crisis. It needs to be added, however, that Fox formulated views opposed by many in the Catholic hierarchy and that recently he left the Catholic Church for Episcopalianism. His well-known writings were, however, written while he was a Catholic and drew mostly from Catholic tradition despite the unusual and in many cases unorthodox interpretations that he has made of such teachings.[29]

The background of Fox's "creation spirituality" is to be found in the tradition of Christian mysticism to which he has always been attracted, especially the mysticism of Hildegard of Bingen and Meister Eckhart, some of whose writings he even edited but has interpreted in a view alien to the traditional understanding of these personages. Fox distinguishes between true and false mysticism, identifying the former in a manner characteristic of "New-Age spirituality" with the latest findings of modern science.[30] He considers mysticism to be "world-confirming" and embracing a cosmology, and not "world-denying." Also in the manner of mystics everywhere, Fox speaks of "heart knowledge," which he, however, equates more with "awakening the heart, strengthening it, expanding it, watering it, and enabling it to reach its full, cosmic potential for joy."[31] But he does not speak of the heart intellect and that heart knowledge which is distinct from both the fruit of ratiocination and emotional states and which is the instrument of authentic metaphysical knowledge.[32]

Fox considers mysticism to be opposed to the "patriarchal," claiming that "to see the world that is more feminist will include the mystical."[33] He also calls mysticism "panentheistic," by which he means that all things are in God and God is in all things. In this way he seeks to remove the duality between the inward and outward, claiming that atheists are simply against theism and that they would accept panentheism. Likewise, he seeks to remove the duality of light and darkness by associating both with mysticism, which means "being-with-being," the term *being* having also the connotation of suffering beings and victims of hate and oppression.[34]

Fox is also a severe critic of the Christology of the past few centuries that substituted the historical Jesus for the cosmic Christ.[35] Rationalism and what he calls the "patriarchal mind set" destroyed cosmology and banished the cosmic Christ from the seventeenth century onward, substituting for it the historical Jesus and a purely anthropocentric perspective. He calls for a revival of the cosmic role of Christ, stating, "I believe the issue today for the third millennium of Christianity—if the earth is to survive into the next century—is *the quest for the cosmic Christ.*"[36] This means a major paradigm shift and the formulation of a cosmology composed of modern science, mysticism, and art. In fact, Fox believes that the knowledge of the cosmic Christ is not possible without "access to twentieth-century scientific revelations of the radically dynamic and creative nature of the universe."[37] Of course, he also seeks the aid of the Western mystical tradition from Basil of Caesarea and Gregory of Nazianzus, Hildegard of Bingen, St. Francis, and Mechthild of Madgeburg, to Dante, Eckhart, Julian of Norwich, and Nicholas of Cusa, as well as the aid of Eastern sources. And yet these sources are all an adjunct to the knowledge derived from the telescope and the microscope.

According to Fox, the cosmic Christ is the pattern that connects all things, time and space, the microcosm and the macrocosm and is also "Mother Earth, Crucified and Resurrected."[38] The cosmic Christ can help prevent matricide or the killing of Mother Earth and even the paschal mysteries, that is, the passion, resurrection, and ascension of Christ gain new meaning as the passion, resurrection, and ascension of Mother Earth conceived as Jesus Christ. Furthermore, Christ's Second Coming is identified with the renaissance of contemporary culture and the Church, what he calls "the re-invention of the human,"[39] the revival of sexual mysticism, the substitution of Christos for *chronos,* the appreciation of mysticism in its universal unfolding, etc., and not with an actual eschatological event. He even dreamt of a Vatican III to discuss the doctrine of the cosmic Christ; at least he did so while still a Catholic!

In his book *Creation Spirituality*,[40] Fox develops these themes further in direct relation to the environment, calling for theologians to begin with Creation and the cosmos and only later turn to the human story, "which then attracts us like a jewel set in the larger drama of creation itself."[41] Accepting that traditional cosmology was destroyed at the end of the Middle Ages, he proposes four steps for the formulation of a new cosmology and creation spirituality: (1) awe and delight; (2) darkness, suffering, and letting go; (3) creativity and imagination; and (4) justice and celebration, adding up to compassion. God, according to Fox, can be found in our times in the *Via Positiva* or awe in the mystery of nature, the *Via Negativa*, or darkness, emptying and nothingness, the *Via Creativa*, or our power to co-create with God, and the *Via Transformativa* or the relief of suffering in combatting injustice.[42] These are the commandments with the help of which creation spirituality can be established and the Western world liberated and the violation of the mystic fostered in Western culture brought to an end, leading also to the liberation of Earth from the consumerism and greed of modern civilization.[43]

It is interesting to note that despite his different theological background and much greater attention paid to mysticism, Fox, like McFague, accepts fully the modern scientific account of the world of Creation, and while appealing to the words of Christian mystics, he hardly ever seeks to resuscitate the religious understanding of the order of nature about which many of them spoke. Also, like most other Christian theologians faced with the environmental crisis, his main concern is ethical rather than noetic although he keeps referring to Christian mystics and metaphysicians who claimed to have possessed a *knowledge* of the order of nature other than what is reached only through the external senses and limited only to the outward aspect of things, not to speak of a purely quantitative knowledge that does not even embrace the whole of the outward dimension of corporeal realities.

While Fox's unorthodox Christology brought reactions against him from Catholic authorities and he has now left the Catholic Church, other theologians more in the mainstream of Catholicism have also been keenly concerned with the environmental crisis of late. A case in point is John Haught, who refutes the thesis that the environmental crisis has been the fault of religion, but who feels that this crisis is a major challenge to religion and can in fact help to bring about a creative transformation within it.[44] Haught comments pointedly on the difficulty of finding a common moral outlook between materialistic naturalism and followers of religion in ecological issues and the shortcomings of such documents as "Joint Appeal by Science and Religion on the Environment" because it is impossible to have serious environmental ethics without the Universe having meaning in the religious and philosophical sense. Haught therefore criticizes openly such avowed agnostics and opponents of the religious view as Carl Sagan, E. O. Wilson, and Stephen Gould, who seek to draw from religious morality to save the environment while negating the truth of religion, which is the foundation of such a morality.

Haught also speaks of the necessity of a shift in cosmology but asks as to where such a shift can come from since the modern view of nature derives completely from modern science, which he does not find to be sufficient, stating that "though it [modern science] is necessary, science alone is an insufficient basis for an understanding of the Universe."[45] Because most modern cosmologists and astronomers consider the Universe to be "pointless," it is difficult to be seriously interested in saving the environment if one accepts their point of view. Haught therefore rejects the scientific pessimism issuing from modern scientific cosmology and looks for an alternative, which he finds in process theology.[46]

Haught distinguishes between being removed from the world in the religious sense and "cosmic homelessness" in this world, which leads to indifference to the plight of the world of nature and which moreover has been fortified by modern science's abstraction of man from the material world. As depicted by Michael Polanyi, science creates a picture of the Universe from which the creator of this science, that is, man, is absent.[47] Haught claims, however, that this aspect of modern science is now changing since quantum mechanics implies the necessity of consciousness and the boundary conditions of the Universe are conducive to life. In contrast to much of theology, which has emphasized this "cosmic homelessness," religion according to Haught can be thought of as a prolongation of the cosmic adventure so that man can feel at home in the cosmos. As Haught states:

> We and the earth and the universe, all together, still live in "exile" from our universal destiny, but not inevitably from one another. Thus we are not obliged to feel "lost in the cosmos."[48]

Haught argues that we and the Universe are related eschatologically and that our destiny is therefore inseparable from that of the cosmos, not in a material sense but in the ultimate sense of our final end before God. Even our bodily resurrection is connected to the fate of the cosmos. Therefore, in destroying nature we are affecting ourselves adversely not only in this world but even in the ultimate sense that, in Christianity, is related to the resurrection of the body.[49] Although accepting the precepts of modern science and especially evolution, Haught nevertheless seeks the nexus between man and the cosmos in eschatological terms and sees their interconnection and relation to lie even beyond the realm of the material and what can be studied by a science bound only to the physical dimension of reality.

Another facet of the present Christian concern with the environment is related to the revival of elements of Celtic spirituality, which was always intertwined with the world of nature, the Celtic world resisting the modern technological onslaught of nature and the rise of modernism itself more than did the Germanic and Latin components of European civilization. Much of the writings of the Celtic tradition, not available until now, are being made accessible to the larger public,[50] whereas a number of theologians are turning to Celtic sources. For example, Sean McDonagh, influenced by both Thomas Berry and Teilhard de

Chardin, calls for a new theology based on seeing God in nature, the stewardship of the Earth, and Benedictine and Franciscan spirituality. But he also emphasizes the significance of Celtic spirituality, which insists so much upon God's presence in nature.[51] Some of the most notable contemporary British theologians (John Macquarrie, for example), have also turned to Celtic spirituality as a source of inspiration for the formulation of a theology more aware of the religious significance of the cosmos.[52]

The Orthodox (Eastern) Church has also had a rich tradition of dealing with the spiritual reality of nature and has been less influenced by secularistic and scientific philosophies than have the Western churches. Its theologians became gradually interested in the environmental crisis by and large only in the 1970s, but it has formulated some of the most profound religious responses to the environmental crisis in recent years.[53] Of special interest, as far as the response to the environment is concerned, are the writings of the English Orthodox scholar and theologian Philip Sherrard, who in *The Rape of Man and Nature*[54] provided a scathing and in-depth criticism of the role played by a materialistic science in the desecration and ultimate destruction of nature, a criticism based upon tradition and the traditional understanding of Christian metaphysics and theology. Then in *Human Image—World Image,* Sherrard sought to provide a Christian view of the order of nature whose acceptance alone can, according to him, prevent the catastrophe that the environmental crisis is bound to bring about if it continues in its present course.

What distinguishes Sherrard from other contemporary Christian thinkers dealing with the environment is that, in contrast to most of them, he insists that no reconciliation can exist between the Christian or for that matter the religious view of the order of nature in general and the scientific understanding of that order. The first view is based upon certain metaphysical and spiritual principles that the second one denies.[55] Therefore, "a revival of a spiritual understanding of the physical world can come about only on condition that these propositions [of modern science] are rejected, and are replaced by those that underlie the cosmologies of the great sacred religions."[56] Sherrard points to the manner in which the Christian view of nature was destroyed, and he describes how the "other mind of Europe"—exemplified by figures from Paracelsus and Robert Fludd, the Cambridge Platonists and Thomas Traherne, from Jakob Böhme to Claude de Saint Martin, from Bishop Berkeley to William Blake and more recently Oskar Milosz[57]—was eclipsed and removed from the mainstream of Western scientific and philosophical understanding of nature. Furthermore, he believes that it is essential to understand how Christian sacred cosmology was destroyed before it can be reconstituted and restored.[58]

To bring about the restitution of sacred cosmology and the authentic religious understanding of the order of nature, what is required, according to Sherrard, is a mystical and intellectual knowledge of God and the divine realities, a knowledge which is not only personal but one that can be translated into the knowledge of the cosmos that "illumines every object and every form of being."[59] This knowledge exists in the Christian tradition, but early Christian theology was not served well by certain teachings of St. Paul against accepting the presence of God in the world of the natural elements. According to Sherrard, however, some of the early theologians such as St. Justin Martyr, Origen, and Clement of Alexandria did relate the Trinity of Creation and Incarnation. This link was, however, soon broken, and the relationship of Creation to Christ and the Father cast aside and the Incarnation no longer envisaged in relation to Creation as seen in both Latin and Palamite theology. What was lost is what Sherrard calls the theoanthropocosmic vision; henceforth, the sonship of the Divine Logos was envisaged primarily in the historical Jesus and not in the world of Creation, as also asserted by some of the current theologians mentioned above. In reality, however, according to Sherrard, Christ is only one form of the embodiment of the Divine Logos, the cosmos being the other.[60] Creation of the world is linked to the eternal generation of the Son, both of whom are aspects of a single Divine Act.

It was the cosmological vacuum created by the neglect of Christian theology of nature that made possible the non-Christian and profane view of the natural world.[61] As a result, Creation came to be considered as a totally independent order of reality, "a second subject of being," set against God and man. Sherrard criticizes severely any theology that posits Creation as a "second Being" as false and interprets the verse "In Him we live, we move and have our being" (Acts 17:28) in the sense of all creatures having their being in God. Creatures exist "within" God and there is no unbridgeable gap between them, for "of Him, through Him, and to Him, are all things" (Rom. 3:36). He draws from the esoteric doctrine of "creation in God," already mentioned earlier in this book, as existing in the esotericism of all the monotheistic religions, which he interprets to mean that "creation is nothing less than the manifestation of God's hidden Being: the other world is this world, this world is the other world. If the kingdom of God can come to earth, it is because in essence the earth is the kingdom of God."[62] This view of immanence does not, however, deny that of transcendence, and the author does not mean simply to identify God and the world in a substantial and "material" way.

Sherrard identifies a veritable science of nature not with quantitative measurement but with the understanding of the Divine Presence in every form.[63] Every object possesses its own *lógos* and reflects a sophia that must be known. The sensible world is in fact an icon of the spiritual world in which everything has meaning in light of the whole. To isolate and separate a part of this whole and study it in an independent setting is nothing less than to murder it at its roots "in thought if not in deed."[64] But this is precisely what happens in modern science and more generally even in the prevalent religious view of nature, which is based upon a dualism separating God from His Creation, considered as a completely distinct order of reality.

To understand how this dualism has come about, resulting in the world of nature being considered as an independent order of reality to be divided, analyzed, and dissected like a cadaver, Sherrard turns to the causes of this dualism, which he enumerates as four in number. First is the idea of *creatio ex nihilo,* which he interprets not in the usual manner but in the esoteric sense already mentioned in our discussion of "creation in God" and in the manner of a St. Gregory of Nyssa or Erigena, who considered *Nihil* to be another name of God so that *creatio ex nihilo* means Creation from and out of God.[65] St. Gregory of Nyssa even identifies *nihilo* with the supra-essential Essence or Non-Being of God Himself, a view later confirmed by Jakob Böhme.[66] Second is the modern notion of time and space. These concepts have no reality in themselves and exist only when material modalities of Creation are related to other material modalities but which cease to exist when Creation is considered as a whole in relation to the Creator. Third is a one-sided rejection of pantheism, not in its aspect of confounding God and His Creation, a view metaphysically false, but in its insistence that Creation is not a second domain of reality or "subject of Being" independent of God. Finally, by insisting only upon the aspect of the Will of God in bringing Creation about rather than the necessity of Creation flowing from His Nature,[67] the dualism between God and His Creation is only emphasized and Creation is only seen as a movement *ad extra* as far as God is concerned.

In contrast to the dualism caused and projected by these four factors, Sherrard envisages Creation as an expansion of the Divine Life. God is the supreme Lover and cannot not love. He cannot but manifest Himself in Creation, which is the "inner landscape of His own Being, God making Himself visible to Himself and simultaneously making Himself visible to us."[68] This Creation from within the Divine possesses in fact three stages and is not in a "single stroke." First, God reveals Himself to Himself making Himself conscious of the latent possibilities of His own Being. Second, this formless content of Divine Intelligence or Divine Logos is differentiated in individual forms but still in an immaterial state. These are the uncreated spiritual energies, Divine Ideas, or *lógoi* of classical Christian writers such as St. Maximus referred to in Chapter 2. They are the Image-Archetypes that are intermediaries between the world of pure formless and intelligible realities and the visible world. Third, there is the manifestation of these *Image-Archetypes* in the concrete beings of this world.[69] Every existent is therefore the visible form of a Divine Name. "Each created being is also a concretization of divine Being and is embraced by this Being."[70]

Having outlined a metaphysics that is universal and that has its correspondence in other traditions, particularly Islam, Sherrard then turns to the specifically Christian doctrine of the Trinity, which he applies to this scheme. According to him the Holy Spirit transforms the abstract Intelligence-content of the Logos into a world vibrating with the life of God.[71] Through the *fiat* in God indentified in its execution with the Holy Spirit, the life of Truth is bestowed upon the celestial Image-Archetypes and those in turn become the "garment of God" in Heaven and the "divine glory" that, according to the Psalms (19:1), "the heavens declare." These Image-Archetypes are therefore not abstract on their own level; nor are they simply abstract principles for the world of visible realities that are their living manifestations. Through them this world itself becomes a Divine Manifestation.

Just as the Image-Archetypes are the personal being God—rooted in the personal triune Godhead—so the created world, too, is the personal living God, rooted in the same Godhead. The visible universe is the living Body of God. It is the temple of the living God.[72]

As for incarnation, Sherrard considers the very process of Creation thus described as "the eternal process according to which the divine Logos is embodied."[73] The Logos is incarnated not only in the historical Jesus but also in the cosmos, the two being related. Consequently, from the Christian point of view the doctrine of Creation can only be understood in the light of Christology. What Sherrard calls the "theandric mystery consummated in Christ"[74] is therefore the model for the understanding of not only human beings but all creatures. The Logos becomes flesh (sarx), but this sarx is not only the flesh of the human body. Rather, it is that of all matter.

The manifesting Logos contains within itself all Image-Archetypes, and the relation between them is one of union and not identity, and it is this rapport that provides the relationship between the Divine and the creaturely element in every created existent. Repeating St. Maximus, Sherrard asserts, "As all creation is grounded ontologically in the world of Image-Archetypes, and is their manifestation, so all creation is the Body of Christ, the Incarnation of the Logos."[75] In this manner the doctrines of Incarnation, Trinity, and Creation become inalienably united and nature comes to be seen in the light of the Christian understanding of reality.

Finally, there is a subtle point with which Sherrard concludes this discourse, one that, despite its audacious and problematic formulation, contains a profound symbolic truth. The living Image-Archetypes are the self-expressions of the Divine Logos "given birth through the agency of the Holy Spirit. It is through this act that God acquires His Lordship and thus properly speaking becomes God."[76] In reality, God can only be God to those He gives being, and through the birth of the Image-Archetypes in a sense God Himself is given birth. This birth in God of the Image-Archetypes is an act of inner hierarchization, and the means by which this birth occurs is a feminine principle in the Divine, the receptacle in which the Image-Archetypes are given figure, pattern, and body although still in an immaterial state. This Feminine in the Divine discloses "in the transparency and beauty of living forms the Being by whom she herself is disclosed. In this way she establishes that relationship by virtue of which God becomes God. In this way she gives birth to God."[77] And this, according to Sherrard, is the secret of the term "mother of God" (Theotokos) given to the Virgin.[78]

The Theotokos identified in Christianity with the Virgin Mother is the Eternal Sophia (Sophia aeterna) and universal nature (natura naturans) "in which flower all the forms of being . . . from the highest archangels down to the most elementary material organisms."[79] On the highest level the Feminine Principle is the Nihil or Non-Being Itself.[80] She contains within herself the world of Image-Archetypes, the created as well as the uncreated, the visible and the invisible aspects of things. God gives being, whereas the Feminine Principle provides form and body and resides over the process of Creation, being the "artificer of all things."[81] She does not create directly but mediates between the potential and the actual.

The theandric mystery, then, is that through which the sacramental reality of the created world is consummated, and the being through whom this consummation takes place is the "Mother of God" in her universal aspect as well as particular aspect as the Virgin Mary. Sherrard concludes,

> Thus the Mother of God is not simply the foundation of the world of creatures; she is herself this world. While remaining always spiritual, above space and time, she is also the root of what is material, spatial and temporal. She is not only *Natura naturans,* she is also *Natura naturata.* She is Earth as a single immaterial feminine divinity, and she is Earth as a manifold, material reality. She is herself the Body of the cosmic Christ, the created matrix in whom the divine Logos eternally takes flesh. She is the bridge that unites God to the world, the world to God, and it is she that bestows on the world its eternal and sacred value. She is the seal of its sacred identity.[82]

In this work, which is one of the most profound current Christian responses to the environmental crisis and the destruction of Christian cosmology, Sherrard reinstates the Christian view of the order of nature, drawing from traditional Orthodox Christian sources, and he equates the destruction of the natural environment at the deepest level with the violation of the body of the Virgin. But precisely because of its traditional nature, his message is not as widely heard as those who surrender theology to whatever philosophical and scientific tenets happen to be prevalent.

Before concluding our discussion of Christianity, it is necessary to point out that present-day Western Christian responses to the environmental crisis have drawn very little from the Christian esoteric and theosophic tradition with their elaborate doctrines concerning nature, whereas those who have drawn from such sources have usually not identified themselves with contemporary Christian theological concerns. There are, however, a few exceptions, one being Arthur Versluis, who in his book *TheoSophia* seeks to revive the predominantly Protestant theosophical tradition as reflected in such figures as Jakob Böhme, Johann Gichtel, Friedrich Ötinger, Louis Claude de Saint-Martin, Franz von Baader, and others.[83] In a chapter entitled "Hierophanic Nature," he points to the significance of the theosophical movement in creating "a renewed awareness of nature as theophany—as, finally, divine revelation."[84] His concern is also with reinstating the religious view of the order of nature in light of the present environmental crisis. The work of Versluis represents the greater attention being paid gradually, in some circles at least, to the deeper teachings of the Christian tradition as they bear upon the Christian view of nature in contrast to those who would surrender what remains of the Christian tradition in the name of creating an eco-theology in harmony with prevalent scientific theories, often equating sacred doctrines with the most recent scientific findings, which will no longer be most recent tomorrow, considering both as being "stories" about the Universe.

JEWISH RESPONSES IN THE WEST TO THE ENVIRONMENTAL CRISIS

Jewish thinkers in the West have responded to the destruction of the natural environment both as a reaction to Christian concerns with the issue and as an answer to the ever-growing significance of the problem for society at large, but they have drawn mostly from traditional Jewish sources. Only in rare cases have attempts been made to change the tenets of Judaism itself as one sees in certain types of contemporary Christian eco-theology. Moreover, during the past two decades many significant Jewish thinkers have emphasized the necessity for Judaism to confront this issue more fully and provide an authentic Jewish "environmental philosophy."[85]

Most Jewish writers have until now emphasized the ethical dimension of the issue in conjunction with Jewish law. A case in point is Ismar Schorsch, who in his "Learning to Live with Less"[86] underscores traditional Jewish teaching about self-restraint, which is opposed to the current consumerism and materialism that are the immediate causes for the destruction of the environment.[87] Like many other Jewish thinkers, he also emphasizes the significance of Jewish law and its development of injunctions against inflicting pain upon animals, its teachings about the use of land, self-denial, and, of course, the Sabbath as a day of rest from the very types of activities that, in today's context, affect the environment so adversely. The blend of ascetism and love of learning emphasized in Judaism can, according to Schorsch, provide a model for correct action vis-à-vis the natural environment.

Another Jewish author, Eric Katz, also emphasizes the practical and specific teachings of Jewish law and practice.[88] What matters, according to this view, is the observation of commands promulgated by the law rather than specific attitudes. The world of nature is one in which man must exercise responsibility in accordance with God's laws.[89] According to Katz, Talmudic scholars interpreted "subdue the earth" (Genesis 1:28) not in the sense of total domination because man is also the steward of the natural world. Judaism is therefore against destruction and domination of nature and is also opposed to simply the preservation of nature without any interference in it as preached in Jainism. Rather, it favors the conservation of nature while always remembering that the world does not belong to humanity but to God as attested to in Scripture: "The earth is the Lord's and the fulness thereof; the world and they that dwell therein" (Psalms, 24:1). Katz emphasizes the theocentric rather than anthropocentric perspective of Judaism. We are temporary tenants in God's Creation and have no right of possession to it. The Sabbath itself implies stewardship of God's Creation, for it marks a period when nothing is created through human work, nothing destroyed and the bounties of nature are enjoyed.[90]

After discussing various Jewish laws concerning the protection of the land, animals, forests, etc., Katz turns to the important principle of *Bal tashchit* (do not destroy) from Deuteronomy 20:19–20, which means forbidding destroying trees in wartime. He seeks to extend this principle not only to trees but the whole of nature in both war and peace. *Bal tashchit* prohibits *wanton* destruction, but this qualification (that is, *wanton*) has itself changed throughout history. Today it must be considered beyond utilitarian considerations and seen in the light of the principle that the world belongs to God and therefore that natural entities should not be destroyed. *Bal tashchit* is not anthropocentric but has the function of preserving God's Creation. "Destruction is not an evil because it harms human life—we humans should not believe that God sends the rain for us—it is an evil because it harms the realm of God and his creation."[91]

While emphasizing the theocentric character of Judaism, Katz states that Judaism does not confirm the sacredness of natural objects in themselves. Rather, these objects are sacred because of God's creative process. As stated by another Jewish thinker, "Every natural object is the embodiment of the creative power of God and is therefore sacred."[92] In this manner the tension between extreme separation of God from His Creation and worship of natural forms is removed; Katz, like many other Jewish thinkers, presents a Jewish response to the environmental crisis based upon Jewish law and traditional attitudes toward nature without taking recourse to Jewish mystical and esoteric ideas and yet emphasizing the proximity of God to His Creation.

There are, however, many Jewish thinkers who have turned precisely to Jewish esotericism in one form or another to provide a contemporary Jewish view of nature and the cosmos, and this includes even a number of Jewish scientists. An important example of recent Jewish thought on the subject drawn from the more esoteric dimensions of Judaism is Arthur Green's book *Seek My Face, Speak My Name,* dealing with a contemporary vision of Judaism. Green also turns to the discussion of Creation and the world of nature.[93] Green accepts the claims of evolutionary theory (as do most of his Christian counterparts). However, he seeks to interpret this in a religious manner, speaking of the evolution of the One Itself from simpler to more complex forms, the Divine Energy surging to levels of development with ever greater complexity.[94] At this point of the process, human beings are at the apex of existence and "the human is beloved only because we are the mirror-reflection, the portrait, of the divine self."[95]

Green turns to the Jewish concept of *mitsvah* or "togetherness," which means an act that brings God and man together, and mentions that some *mitsvot* bring about a greater presence of the Divinity and hence need to be emphasized. One such *mitsvah* is *Shabbat* or the Sabbath, which is "an extended meditation on the wonders of the created world and the divine presence that fills it,"[96] hence its importance for greater awareness of the spiritual significance of the natural environment. Another such *mitsvah* is "that of acting with concern for the healthy survival of Creation itself."[97] The ethic flowing from it is a strong commitment to *ahavat ha-bri'ot* (the love of all of God's creatures) and a sense of absolute responsibility for their survival. Green emphasizes that no love of God is possible without the love of His Creation.

Green also deals with another set of *mitsvot* called *tsa'ar ba'aley hayyim* (the suffering of living beings), which imply having a sense of the suffering of animals and sympathy for their pains. "We are close to the animal kingdom, and although allowed to rule over it, can only do so as God's viceroy with responsibility before the ultimate Ruler of the universe."[98] Following Cabalistic cosmologies, Green speaks of the world of Creation as the manifestation of the One and locus of Divine Presence. Our commitment to the One must engender, therefore, our commitment to the Earth where His Presence is manifested and "a commitment to preserving the great and wonderous variety of life species in which the One is manifest."[99] For Green, therefore, the solution to the environmental crisis is, on the one hand, a sacralized vision of Creation based on Jewish sources, especially esoteric ones, but interpreted in an evolutionary manner with an attempt at preserving a religious understanding of what he calls the "evolutionary process," and, on the other hand, an ethics again drawn from traditional Jewish sources emphasizing both closeness to the world of nature and responsibility for Earth and its creatures.

NON-WESTERN RELIGIONS IN THE FACE OF THE ENVIRONMENTAL CRISIS

When we turn to non-Western religions, including Islam (the vast majority of whose followers live outside the West), we face a radically different situation despite the interest shown in these faiths in environmental ethics common with Christianity and Judaism. Let it be said at the outset that the treatment of the environment itself has not been better among adherents of these religions than it has been in the West, especially as far as the modernizing elements of their societies are concerned. During the modern period the Chinese have devastated much of their land[100] and the Japanese have not only polluted a good portion of their islands but also been instrumental in the near extinction of the whale and many of the forests of Southeast Asia. India is now becoming rapidly industrialized, and the environmental situation grows from bad to worse not only in Delhi and Calcutta but even in small villages that until now had possessed an economic life in remarkable equilibrium with the environment. Nor is the record of the Islamic world any better, as witnessed by cities such a Cairo and Tehran. Moreover, one observes environmental catastrophe not only in present or former Communist lands such as China or the former Soviet Union, which ignored the environmental crisis as being a disease of capitalism, but even in countries that seem to be apparently free to make decisions concerning the natural environment.

A closer examination reveals, however, that this freedom is more apparent than real, economically and therefore ecologically speaking. Non-Western societies are forced into a global "economic order" within which they have little choice but to follow models of so-called development that are formulated in the West and in which non-Western religions and philosophies hardly play a role. There are also other important political and social considerations, not least of which is overpopulation—a direct consequence of modern medicine—that play a dominant role in environmental decisions taken usually with indifference to religious views, although the question of family planning has direct religious bearings and has triggered a great deal of religious debate and reaction in many places.

Moreover, non-Western religions have spent much of their energy during the past two centuries trying to preserve their very existence against the dual onslaught of secularist and Christian missionary activity and have only of late come to realize the significance of the challenge of the environmental crisis. Their response has therefore been quite feeble until now despite the immense resources they can bring to bear upon a solution to this issue. There have been a number of responses that need to be discussed. It is, however, necessary to emphasize once again that the environmental crisis is a consequence of major transformations that occurred primarily in the West and is a result of the adoption of a secularist view of nature and the creation of a science and technology whose never-ending "innovations" tied to consumerism threaten to devour the entire globe. It is the non-Western world, with the exception of Japan, that is almost always at the receiving end of these innovations and changes. The agenda is always set by the West, and it is that agenda to which others must then respond. Consequently, both the participation and the response of Western religions to the environmental crisis are different in many basic ways from those of non-Western religions. There are, of course, other factors to consider: differences of degrees of strength of faith and religious practice; attachment to the religious view of the order of nature; and the availability of authentic metaphysical and cosmological doctrines in the two worlds.

Turning first of all to the Native American traditions that, although in the West, are non-Western in the sense of being nonmodern, the environmental crisis has been a cause of confirmation of their traditional religion to themselves and the rest of the world. Despite differences among them, Native Americans share a reverence of nature as locus of Divine Presence, a kinship with all forms of life, a vision of the sky or Heaven as their father and Earth as their mother, a respect for the land, a sense of their guardianship of sacred places, a tradition of direct communion with various animals, experienced not only biologically but also as embodiments of celestial archetypes, and the like. These and other teachings, some of which have been mentioned in Chapter 2, have been repeated by numberous Native American leaders,[101] while statements bearing upon the care of the Earth and the land such as that of Chief Seattle have been oft repeated even by non-Native American environmentalists. It can in fact be said that the environmental crisis has provided indirectly, and even amid the ravages brought upon much of the land of the Native Americans, an opportunity for the revival of their religion as well as of primal religions in Hawaii, Polynesia, Australia, Africa, and nearly everywhere else where primal religions survive. Followers of these religions call themselves the guardians of the Earth and have as such attracted to themselves many contemporary environmentalists. The current fashion of neo-Shamanism in America, although opposed quite rightly by authentic representatives of the Native American religions, is caused to some extent by the environmental crisis and the awareness of the significance of nature it has resuscitated in many circles, although this awareness is not always directed through authentic channels.

Although eclipsed in China for several centuries, Confucianism has seen a revival during the past few years, and many now refer to the Confucian world as embracing much of the Pacific rim in Asia, and even to Japanese civilization as possessing a Confucian element. Of late there have been Confucian responses to the environmental crisis by both Confucian scholars and Westerners sympathetic to Confucianism. A Confucian scholar such as Tu Wei-ming emphasizes that in Confucian and especially neo-Confucian philosophy "All modalities of being are organically connected."[102] *Ch'i* is at once matter and energy in a unified cosmological theory, which is opposed to the dualism of mind and matter prevalent in the West. Tu Wei-ming emphasizes the significance of biology rather than physics for Chinese philosophers and their vision of "the Great Harmony,"[103] which can act as a philosophy for man's relation to the natural environment. His response is therefore in a sense the revival in contemporary terms of the holistic philosophies of nature of classical Chinese thought, especially neo-Confucianism and also Taoism, some of whose tenets were mentioned in Chapter 2.

A Western admirer and student of Confucianism, Mary E. Tucker, pursues the same line of thought in seeking an answer to the mechanistic view of the world in the holistic and organic perspective of neo-Confucianism.[104] According to Tucker, such a view avoids the anthropocentricism so much responsible for modern man's irresponsible destruction of nature, and reemphasizes the correspondence between the microcosm and macrocosm by reasserting the elaborate correspondence between man and the elements, the seasons, colors, spatial directions, and so forth.[105] The origin of this type of thought is to be found in the *I-Ching* and is emphasized by others, such as the Han thinker Tung Chung-shu, and was inherited by neo-Confucianism, which, like much of Chinese thought, was not interested in the origin of the cosmos but in its organic wholeness. Human beings form with the natural world a great chain of being united by *ch'i*, which involves a dynamic vitalism. Life is engaged in a constant process of transformation with which human beings should harmonize their actions.

Tucker emphasizes that in neo-Confucianism self-cultivation can only be comprehended in the context of this particular view of nature. The wholeness of the cosmos has a direct bearing upon the moral and spiritual formation of human beings, and moral and cosmic laws are inseparable. Moreover, man forms a single body with Heaven and Earth, a view which Tucker calls *anthropocosmic* rather than anthropocentric, a perspective that is confirmed by the eleventh-century neo-Confucian Chang Tsai's *Western Inscription,* which states:

> Heaven is my father and the Earth is my mother and even such a small creature as I find an intimate place in their midst.
>
> Therefore, that which extends throughout the universe I regard as my body, and that which directs the universe I consider as my nature.
>
> All people are my brothers and sisters and all things are my companions.[106]

Tucker points to the pertinence of the relation between the philosophy of nature and virtue and cosmology and ethics so central to Confucianism and formulated so elaborately in neo-Confucianism as a solution to the present environmental crisis. She also emphasizes the importance of looking seriously at this holistic aspect of Confucianism rather than at the supposed rationalism and humanism that the European Enlightenment saw in this most socially oriented of the Far Eastern traditions.

Turning to China's neighbor India, one sees, during the past few years, the sudden rise in awareness of the environmental crisis as a result of the Bhopal tragedy and the rapid deterioration of the quality of the natural environment in most big cities and even smaller towns. Both Hindus and Muslims, although caught in tragic recent communal conflicts, are unfortunately united in their destruction of the environment, which they share together, but neither side has as yet drawn fully from its spiritual and metaphysical resources to create a viable religious response to this most dangerous of crises.[107] As far as Hinduism is concerned, various writers have sought to turn to the principle of *ahimsa* (literally nonviolence or noninterference), which was used by Gandhi in a political sense but which can also be used to define man's attitude toward the environment. This is in fact the basis of the Jain ideal of not interfering with the processes of nature.[108] *Ahimsa* could not be carried out fully in a country such as India with its vast population, but many emphasize it as an ideal in the Hindu's attitude toward the environment and as the basis of a Hindu environmental ethics. Others have tried to have recourse to the Gandhian understanding of the term in combination with Gandhian economics, which emphasized environmentally sound village economics, and they have opposed modern industries, which are the main source of the devastation of the natural world.

On the theoretical level, attention has been directed to the feminine elements in Hinduism such as *prakṛti* and *śakti* in relation to the material pole of the cosmos and the image of the Earth as mother. In the context of Hinduism such a task entails more a revival of certain dimensions of the tradition than the mutilation of traditional theologies as one finds in certain eco-theologies in Christianity. But some female Hindu writers have also used these terms in combination with Western feminist critiques of the male and "patriarchy."[109] It is interesting to mention in this context the practical Chipko movement by women who since 1977 have revitalized an older movement to save the forest and trees by forming chains around them to prevent them from being cut. This major environmental movement has a number of male members but is constituted primarily of women who consider it their duty to be the primary protectors of nature.[110]

Altogether the response of Hinduism to the environmental crisis has until now been primarily ethical while some have drawn from certain strands of Hindu mythology without the kind of innovation seen in the West. But although the rich resources for the formulation of a Hindu philosophy of the environment have been indicated,[111] the major intellectual figures of orthodox Hinduism have not as yet turned to a comprehensive formulation of an authentic Hindu response. As for modernized Hindus, they have for the most part repeated Western formulations with some local Hindu color and without any emphasis upon the authentic Hindu view of nature as independent of and in many aspects opposed to the prevalent scientific worldview. Too often there has been that superficial so-called harmony with whatever happens to be scientifically fashionable, a trait that has characterized most of modern Hindu thought, in contrast to the traditional view, ever since the end of the nineteenth century.

When we turn to Buddhism, we find a situation similar to Hinduism as far as concentration on ethics is concerned, although many who have written on Buddhism have turned to Buddhist metaphysics based on the idea that form is emptiness and emptiness form to emphasize the traditional Buddhist understanding of reality.[112] For years also Western scholars and students of Buddhism have discussed the Zen view of nature and the Buddhist criticism of modern science,[113] while the implications of Buddhism for a type of economics more friendly to the environment have received much attention in the West.[114] But the heart of the Buddhist response to the environmental crisis has been an emphasis upon Buddhist ethics. Even the Dalai Lama, while mentioning the interrelatedness of all things in the Buddhist perspective, speaks of the ethics of preserving the environment as taking care of one's own house. "Taking care of the planet," he writes, "is nothing special, nothing sacred or holy. It's just like taking care of our own house. We have no other planet, no other house, except this one."[115] Like many other Buddhist authorities he also emphasizes the importance of the traditional Buddhist virtue of compassion, associated with the Bodhisattvas, applied to all beings and the importance of gaining greater discernment and knowledge.

Various authors have sought to point to those aspects of Buddhism that do not shun cosmology but contain a view of nature appropriate for the present situation. Most of these schools are to be found in Mahāyāna, especially *Tathāgatagarbha* and *Ālayavijñāna,* which complement each other, and insist on the possibility of all beings attaining the supreme enlightenment of Buddhahood.[116] They also emphasize the challenge of Buddhism to human arrogance and the humanistic conception of man that developed in the West from the Renaissance onward, both of which prevent man from realizing the interdependence of all things. Buddhist awareness also implies a realization of not only the emptiness of things, but also the integration of all things in one universal body identified with the *Dharmakāya.*[117]

The traditional Buddhist doctrine of *dharma,* mentioned in Chapter 2 in connection with the order of nature, has also been resuscitated as a central concept in formulating a Buddhist philosophy of the natural environment. Some have also combined this traditional concept with modern ideas concerned with the environment such as *Gaia.*[118] *Dharma* has been discussed at once as the law or principle of things of which we must be aware in relation to them and as our duty to show compassion toward all beings and to act as stewards and caretakers of the natural world. Here again the ethical dimension has been especially emphasized by most Buddhist authors.

In the Buddhist countries as in Hindu India attempts have been made to create greater consciousness of the environmental crisis and to help ordinary people harbor a less belligerent attitude toward nature.[119] Most of the local religious authorities have emphasized the reverence for life that is so much a part of the traditional Buddhist concept of human life in relation to all other sentient beings.[120] Of course, the question of knowledge and ignorance and discernment also remains central, and many have emphasized the importance of being able to detect the elements of greed and false assertions of the ego, which are a basic part of the spiritual crisis that is itself the root of the environment crisis.[121]

Turning finally to Islam, we find, on the one hand, a situation similar to those of Hinduism and Buddhism in that the traditional authorities had not turned their attention to the environmental crisis until recently and now do so mostly from an ethical point of view. On the other hand, there is a different situation in that in Islam the whole question of an Islamic science different from Western science is considered seriously. It is in fact one of the central issues in the present-day intellectual world of Islam and is of more concern to Muslims than, let us say, Hindu science or Confucian science, as still pertinent bodies of knowledge which would be an alternative to the view of nature issuing from modern science, are to Hindus and Confucians. Of course such a concern is far from being absent in Hinduism, Confucianism, and, in fact, other non-Western traditions but the degree of concern is perceptibly different. In the Islamic world, since the challenge posed to the Western manner of studying Islamic science and the necessity of considering Islamic science from its own point of view were stated in the 1960s,[122] the question of an alternative science of nature has been kept alive, and its consequences for the environmental crisis have become more significant over the years.[123] There has also been much interest in the reformulation of traditional cosmologies especially by Islamic metaphysicians, philosophers, and Sufis who have provided the intellectual dimension of the Islamic view of the order of nature.[124]

Despite this intellectual interest, however, much of the Islamic response to the environmental crisis has been ethical and concerned with immediate issues faced in a similar manner by most other non-Western countries on the receiving end of modern technology and the products of a global economy moving ever more toward consumerism.[125] Religious scholars have referred to Quranic verses pertaining to the preservation of water, earth and forests and appealed to Islamic Sacred Law (al-Sharī'ah) as source for an environmental ethics in a manner that resembles in certain ways the appeal of Jewish thinkers to the halakhah or Jewish Sacred Law. A thorough study of the Sharī'ah and substantial law (al-fiqh) bearing upon the environment was made over a decade ago by S. Waqar Ahmad Husaini and has influenced many later attempts to provide an Islamic response to the environmental crisis on the basis of the Sharī'ah, especially in Saudi Arabia as well as in other areas where the Sharī'ah is still widely used as the law of the land.[126] But Husaini also dealt with the complexity of the issue caused by the constant emulation and imitation of Western science and technology and the problem which that poses for the rejuvenation of Islamic culture and the possibility of applying its own teachings to the solution of the environmental crisis.

The theme of responsibility based on our being the vicegerent of God on Earth (khalīfat Allāh fi'l-arḍ) in a world created by Him, reflecting His signs (āyāt), and praising Him everywhere,[127] is also used widely[128] as we see in contemporary Christianity and Judaism. The few Islamic 'ulamā' or official authorities of the Divine Law and the Islamic sciences who have spoken on the subject, such as the Grand Mufti of Syria, Shaykh Aḥmad Kiftaru, have also emphasized the question of human responsibility in a world that does not belong to us but to God and over which we have a right only as His vicegerents and not as independent beings. [129]

A number of Muslim scholars have also been fully aware of the relation between the "values" underlying modern science and the technology, which as its application is responsible directly for the environmental crisis, and have written critically on this issue with the aim of substituting Islamic values in Muslims' encounters with the natural environment. An example is Parvez Manzoor, who recognizes that "ecology is part and parcel of religious *Weltanschauung*"[130] and is confident that Islamic values can provide a remedy for the crisis at hand.

Manzoor complains quite rightly that in the current discussion on religion and the environment Islam is usually left out. One does not know whether it is as a result of ignorance or arrogance that in discussions taking place in the West on monotheism and the environmental crisis, during which monotheism is usually criticized for reasons already mentioned, practically no account is taken of Islam except when it is criticized as part of the monotheistic family. Little is said otherwise of a billion Muslims worldwide and a religion that, while believing in the transcendence of the Divine Principle, has lived traditionally in a world peopled by angels and *jinn,* or psychic forces where everything is alive and under the command of God, where men's right of domination over nature have been limited, and where the purpose of the study of nature has always been to gain knowledge of God's Wisdom and not simply power and domination over the natural world.

Moreover, Islam has developed what some feminists refer to pejoratively as "patriarchy" without losing harmony with the natural environment, at least before the advent of modernism, and in fact creating a balance with nature that is comparable to that of any religion based on matriarchy or any other principle. The case of Islam, in its traditional and not modernistic or puritanical form, is a most important one in the current debate between traditional formulations of Christianity and Judaism and alternatives being proposed in so many quarters. Manzoor is correct in pointing out how unfortunate is the singular absence in the West of the Islamic tradition in recent and current discussions on religion and the environment.

Manzoor examines the link between Islamic ethics and the world of nature, asserting that "To infuse the natural world with transcendent (revealed) ethics is the main purpose of man according to the Quran,"[131] and that Islam possesses "monotheistic solutions" to the environmental crisis. He points to a number of Islamic principles he considers necessary for providing an Islamic response to the crisis at hand. These include *al-tawḥīd* (unity that also implies interrelatedness), *khilāfah* (vicegerency of man), *amānah* (trust and stewardship), *al-Sharī'ah* (which he translates as ethics rather than law), *'adl* (justice), and *i'tidāl* (moderation). They constitute, according to Manzoor, the principles of the Islamic understanding of the environment. Moreover, nature is replete with the signs (*āyāt*) of God, and to decipher them constitutes an act of worship (*'ibādah*). [132]

Unlike many other modern Muslim thinkers whose minds are replete with scientism and who seek to combine their scientism with such a view of transcendence as to leave the world free for a complete secularist approach to its study, Manzoor insists on the centrality of the sacred view of nature in Islam. He distinguishes between sacralization and divinization and asserts that, whereas Islam supports the *de-divinization* of nature, only God being the Divine as such, it certainly opposes its *desacralization*. He is in fact quite aware that to desacralize nature is also to desacralize and ultimately to debase man.

In the Islamic world, then, while the environment continues to deteriorate and not enough attention is paid by religious authorities to the subject, notable efforts have been made to provide an Islamic response to the crisis. While some have sought to revive the traditional Islamic cosmologies and understanding of the order of nature, combined with a criticism of the modern scientific understanding of nature as the only valid one, most others have turned to ethics and more specifically the Divine Law. Also, many key Quranic concepts, such as those mentioned above, have been resuscitated. But in responding to the challenge of the environmental crisis, no notable Muslim thinker has sought to change the nature of God or our understanding of Him. For the contemporary Muslim, Allah "sits" securely on His "Throne" (*al-'arsh*) and rules over the Universe. In this respect the situation of Islam is very different from that of present-day Christianity. It resembles more the other non-Western religions where religious authorities have sought to resuscitate and revive certain aspects of the tradition that had previously been less emphasized, rahter than to mold a whole new theology including the image of God on the basis of the findings of a quantitative and horizontal science whose applications have brought such devastation upon the environment.

COMPARISONS AND CONTRASTS

The response of Western religions in comparison to those elsewhere represents both contrasts and similarities that need to be brought out clearly in order to understand better the possibility of resuscitating the religious understanding of the order of nature on a global scale. Western responses, as exemplified by most but not all of the cases discussed previously, accept by and large the very scientific view of nature and the secularization of the cosmos that, along with the inner spiritual poverty of the modern world, have been responsible, more than all other factors, for the current environmental crisis. Most Western religious thinkers have accepted the Enlightenment definition of reason and evolutionism as the veritable "story of the cosmos,"[133] such figures as Milosz and Sherrard notwithstanding. The higher states of being, the corporealization of higher realities into material form, which is universal in traditional cosmologies, have hardly been reconfirmed, and most of the attempt has consisted in warding off the criticisms of an Arnold Toynbee or a Lynn White by seeking to unravel the traditional formulations of Christianity not from "above" by taking recourse to Christian esoteric teachings, but for the most part from "below." Those who have questioned Darwinian evolution have usually been "fundamentalists"—who are not taken seriously by the intellectual mainstream—still interested in religion, whereas the metaphysical, logical, and even scientific absurdities of evolution, now discussed by many a scientist, have been hardly used by the popular theological writers on the environment. [134]

It is difficult to understand why the destruction of the environment is at all significant if it is itself part of the evolutionary process and we who are destroying nature are nothing but products of that very process. How can there be ultimate value to anything without finality? In the religious view of the order of nature all species in this world and, in fact, all forms are manifestations of Divine Creativity and represent something of ultimate value precisely because they have their root in the Immutable and reflect the Immutable in the world of becoming.

For modern man it is easy to understand why if all the paintings of Rembrandt were to be destroyed it would mean an irreparable loss to the artistic heritage of the West even if there were still Raphaels and El-Grecos in various museums. The reason for such an attitude is that a finality is accorded to these great works. Now on an unimaginably higher level of reality, each species is like a perfect work of art, complete and perfect as it issues from the Hand of the Great Artisan. And despite mental acquiescence to evolutionism, even modern man still has an almost "instinctive" appreciation of each species as a form of art with its own perfection, and beyond ecological considerations human beings are saddened by the disappearance of a species. But if evolutionism is taken seriously any species is simply an element in the flowing river of process with no ultimate value whatsoever. It is difficult in fact to defend the rights of creatures to life, if one accepts the prevailing evolutionist view, save by appealing either to sentimentality or biological expediency, neither of which are theologically pertinent.

Furthermore, many current eco-theologians, as well as philosophers of ecology, remain rabid followers of Teilhard de Chardin, who sought to create a religion out of evolution. [135] This is even more difficult to understand, for not only does Teilhard make a religion out of evolution, but he is also the great champion of modern technology and by implication condones all the havoc brought about by that technology upon the environment. For him smokestacks polluting the air of a valley are signs of the progress and evolution toward the "noo-sphere." No wonder that defenders of such types of eco-theology have had so little impact on the ever-accelerated march of modern technology toward the destruction of the planet!

Several current theological responses to the environmental crisis have also sought to change what has remained of traditional Christianity to accomodate modern beliefs or have sought refuge in forgotten elements of Christianity, seeking to revive them not within the framework of traditional Christianity but in opposition to it—there being, of course, notable exceptions such as Philip Sherrard, who has sought to revive forgotten teachings within, and not in spite of, Orthodox Christianity. Christianity has come to be criticized not because of its theological neglect of nature during the past centuries and for surrendering the order of nature to a purely secularist science, but because of its fundamental tenets that in some cases include criticizing its understanding of the nature of God and denying the reality of evil in the world.[136] Carrying a political and social agenda for which the environmental crisis has been found as an ally, some have begun first to demonize certain terms such as "patriarchy" and then to attack Christianity for being patriarchal, some even going so far as to refer to Christ as *Christa* without there being any proof that a matriarchal religion or society would be more successful in avoiding the environment crisis if this were to be the only or most important factor. Such individuals should take a stroll at noon in Delhi before being so categorical about that "culprit" called "patriarchy," which they consider to be the chief cause of Western humanity's aggressive attitudes toward nature.

During the whole Scientific Revolution and its aftermath, modern science brought about much agnosticism but said nothing of the nature of the Divinity. We had to wait for the environmental crisis to seek to change the nature of God Himself as He has revealed Himself in Judaism, Christianity, Islam, as well as elsewhere. Again, one must ask how can one destroy through purely human agency the vessel, the form in which the Sacred has manifested itself, without further destroying access to the Sacred? As all traditions have taught over the millennia, it is not only the content or Spirit of sacred teachings that is sacred but also the form in which the Sacred has revealed Itself. One cannot break the chalice in the hope of gaining greater access to the sacred nectar contained therein.

Another feature of much of eco-theology especially creation spirituality is its opposition to otherworldliness and the distinction between world-confirming and world-negating mysticism. Many Muslim authors also have criticized Christianity for being otherworldly. But in the context of the environmental crisis, nothing would help the natural world more than if the predominantly Christian West and Buddhist Japan would become much more otherworldly and make less use of the products of their natural environment. One can only imagine what positive changes might come about in America's national parks if more visitors stayed home and concentrated on ascetic practices rather than bringing the consumerist lifestyle to the very islands of virgin nature, now threatened, not to speak of the rest of America. And how improved would be the plight of the forests of Malaysia if Japanese lived like Tibetan Buddhists before the destruction of that venerable civilization. How can one forget that the recently anointed patron saint of ecology, St. Francis, was an ascetic if there ever was one. That did not prevent him from addressing the birds and considering the Sun and the Moon as his kin. The modern world needs nothing more than that so-called world-denying mysticism that is nothing other than its ascetic aspect that seeks to control the passions and to slay the dragon within, without which the greed that drives the current destruction of nature cannot be controlled.

Moreover, world-denial is simply one aspect of a single reality whose other dimension is "world-confirmation," but the soul cannot confirm the world as sacred without first of all denying the "world" that disperses the soul from within and makes it ever more reliant upon the material environment for the satiation of an ever-increasing thirst. One wonders how, in the light of the crucial nature of the problem at hand, a deeper distinction is not made by often well-intentioned eco-theologians between the world as enticement toward passion, greed, and aggression and the world as God's Creation and ultimately theophany.

At no time in history has there been greater need than now to confirm the teachings of religions about withdrawal from "the world" in the sense of disciplining one's passionate soul and domineering oneself in relation with the world rather than denying its beauty and spiritual quality, of contemplating it rather than considering it only for one's "needs." It is in awareness of this fact that certain Christian theologians such as Jurgen Moltman have made the concrete proposal to practice the Sabbath in the original sense of abstaining for one day a week from all commercial, productive, and industrial activities. In practice, of course, the reverse is recurring, with the laws left from older Christian days prohibiting Sunday trade being diluted and abrogated in one country after another in the Western world in the name of economic development to which human convenience is of course always added without hardly any regard for environmental consequences.

And yet another feature of much of Christian eco-theology that tries to deal with "deep ecology" is to criticize Christianity and other monotheistic religions for considering man to be the crown of Creation, or what Islam calls *ashraf al-makhlūqāt,* and pleading for the equality of man and other creatures and an eco- or bio-centrism to replace what the followers of such views consider to be Christian anthropomorphism. It is of course true that anthropomorphism, which in the West certainly did not issue from Christianity alone, is at the heart of that worldview which has helped to disrupt the order of nature as we have already discussed in earlier chapters. The danger of anthropomorphism lies, however, in the fact that it is false not because it is substituted for bio-centrism but because it takes the place of theocentrism, which accords with the true nature of things and which is also found in traditional Christianity as in other theistic religions with corresponding doctrines to be found in nontheistic religions. God *is* the center of our bring as well as the Origin and End of all Creation. Our center is not in the biological world, certainly not if we view man from a spiritual and theological point of view. To introduce simply the prevalent and fashionable idea of democracy into the whole of Creation is to overlook both biological and cosmological realities and the hierarchy of existence. If we were equal to other creatures, there would in fact be no environmental crisis. Moreover, to propose such a view of equating man with the biological world in a quantitative sense and of seeking our center in a world perceived solely through the external senses is to remove from man his great responsibility as not only the custodian of the Earth but also the channel of grace for all beings. Moreover, it is to destroy further man's true center within himself, the center that is ultimately *the* Center, the Center of us and of all brings. It would thus bring about even further disequilibrium in a chaotic world already suffering from the loss of the Center.

To accord rights to other creatures and not to absolutize the rights of man over nature does not mean an egalitarian conformity and biological uniformity that would destroy for us the Divine Center and the role we have in protecting other beings in a way that they do not have vis-à-vis us. To have the possibility of even speaking of such an issue means that we occupy a special position on Earth as what Islam calls God's vicegerent or *khalīfah*. We cannot destroy our theomorphic nature but only forget or distort it. And the answer to the consequence of the present forgetfulness of who we really are, which is at the heart of our greedy aggression against nature, does not lie in seeking a bio-centrism that would simply not succeed because it is not true despite its fashionable espousal as what appears as the extension of democracy. Rather, it lies in returning to that the centrality of the Divine Principle, which in the theistic climate is called theocentrism—or for Christians what Sherrard calls theoandrocosmism—that lies at the heart of the religious message in general and the Christian one in particular.

What is notable in the current Christian response to the environmental crisis is a tendency in the opposite direction. On the one hand, there are those seeking to delve more deeply into theologies of nature long forgotten and even Christian esoteric doctrines, and on the other hand, there are those who take elements from the Christian mystical tradition and also other religions, such as the Native American or Buddhist, in the direction of creating a radically different Christian theology. And there are yet others who seek to modernize Christianity even more than before with the hope of creating a widely acceptable Christian response but without much sign of success. There are also contrasts between the periphery and central or mainstream churches, contrasts that are sometimes extreme. Moreover, many have moved away from formal Christianity toward various "New-Age" movements while still making use of certain Christian ideas.

What is most common among the majority of Western religious thinkers is their approach to the environmental crisis from the point of view of ethics rather than knowledge. Few question the complete validity and also monopoly of the scientific understanding of the world or confirm the value of the religious view of the order of nature beyond the realm of the emotional and poetic.[137] They are even willing to wed Christian ethics to a worldview totally opposed to the metaphysical principles of all religion without discussing how a set of ethical principles can be correlated with a worldview that denies ultimately the significance of those principles. From the opposite side the secularist world, which has "ghettoized" religion in the modern world and cut off its hands from nearly every public domain from economics to politics, now welcomes cooperation between religious ethics and modern science to ameliorate the consequences of its view of nature without permitting religion to leave the ever more marginalized mode of existence that is has had both intellectually and practically in the West during the past few centuries.

As far as Judaism in the West is concerned, its response shares with Christianity two important traits—an emphasis upon ethics and an attempt in many circles to draw from the Cabala and other esoteric Jewish doctrines to formulate a view of the cosmos that could serve as the background for a contemporary Jewish theology of nature. But, as already mentioned, in contrast to Christianity, few Jewish thinkers have sought to change their understanding of the nature of God or to destroy traditional and sacred forms that have dominated Judaism over the millennia. If there have been a few voices here and there seeking to change

Judaism itself, they have not been heard as loudly nor have been as consequential as the voices of those who have followed such a path in contemporary Christian circles. If anything, the environmental crisis has drawn many Jewish thinkers back to the significance of the *halakhah* with its care for animals and in fact the rest of Creation, this being true even among some Jews who do not hold on to *halakhah* rulings fully in their everyday lives. Herein is also to be found a feature that distinguishes not only Judaism but also Islam with its *al-Sharī'ah*, or Sacred Law, from Christianity where a comparative set of laws understood as immutable divine laws as they pertain to nonhuman parts of Creation does not exist, at least not in the same way as in the other two members of the Abrahamic family.

Outside of the West the response from various religions to the environmental crisis generally came somewhat later than in Europe and America[138] and also with less awareness of the forces and ideas that have brought this crisis about, since naturally non-Western religions have been removed from those centers in Western civilization where the forces now destroying the natural environment originated before spreading to other parts of the globe. Most non-Western religions have therefore more or less followed the religious trends in the West concerning the environment and have concentrated upon the ethical dimension of the problem, as one can see in the Assisi Declaration concerning the care of the Earth. However, they have refrained from seeking to "reinvent" man or religion or change the image of God as we find in certain Western circles. On the contrary, they have found an opportunity to reassert the tenets of their religion and blame the Western religious traditions' neglect of such truths as the cause of the crisis. This is quite evident in the case of the Native American traditions that it hardly needs to be mentioned. But even in Buddhism, Confucianism, Hinduism, and Islam, one observes the same trend of reemphasizing their own traditional teachings, attacked by the West during the past two centuries, rather than inventing new religious views. This crisis has also helped to give a sense of self-assurance to many non-Western religious people who have been under constant pressure from both Christian missionaries and Western secularism ever since the colonial period. This self-assurance comes from the realization of an inner weakness with lethal possibilities within the civilization and worldview that, they feel, has been trying to destroy their identity and convert them to another perspective with all the worldly power in its possession.

It is important to note once again here, as far as contrasts are concerned, that putting Communist China, consumerist Japan, and a few other Communist nations in Asia aside, religion is a much stronger force in the non-Western world than in the West, and even in the above-mentioned lands the people still possess a strong attachment to the religious understanding of the natural order. Despite a century of rationalism followed by Marxism in China and neo-Kantian philosophy in Japan, where philosophy departments are like branches of those in Western universities, the masses of the people are much closer to the older prescientific view of nature than are people in the West, with the exception of out-of-the-way places such as Italian and Irish villages.

As for India, the Islamic world, and Buddhist countries not dominated by

Communism, this attachment to religion and its worldview is even stronger. Despite the fact that the bullet train from Tokyo to Osaka passes by the foot of Mt. Fuji, for the vast majority of Japanese people Mt. Fuji has not as yet become simply Pike's Peak—just another mountain to be climbed and "enjoyed." Something of the sacredness of Mt. Fuji still survives in the consciousness of the Japanese population. Even in Communist North Korea and the People's Republic of China certain mountains are still held to be sacred, not to mention those of Hindu India.

As for the Islamic world, within the context of Abrahamic monotheism, both the awareness of nature as God's handiwork and the nexus between moral laws and cosmic laws remain very strong. Most Islamic cities still have a *muṣallā* (literally place of prayer) where people gather to offer special prayers for rain or the avoidance of calamities. Of course, this attitude has not died out completely in the West as one can observe in a Spanish or Sicilian town. But the survival of this attitude is very different in the two worlds. The response of the citizens of Los Angeles during the earthquake of 1993 was very different from those of Tabas in Iran in the 1978 earthquake where nearly everyone was praying hard after the devastating event and connecting the earthquake not only to God's Will but also to the consequences of negative human action. Or consider the recent earthquake in Egypt, which was followed by the call to prayer (*al-adhān*) throughout Cairo, resulting in the reestablishment of remarkable peace and serenity in the face of a major natural disaster. The mentality that considers this way of viewing nature as simply superstition has a far greater hold upon the Western public than in other parts of the globe, and this affects deeply the religious response to the environmental crisis in the two different parts of the world under consideration.

Likewise, the traditional science of nature or what we have called sacred science[139] survives in non-Western societies in a very different manner from that in the West. In the West those who deal with such subjects do so for the most part as occult sciences torn away from their metaphysical and traditional roots and rejected not only by the modern scientific establishment but also by mainstream religions. In contrast, in the East these sacred sciences still survive in a living manner and are practiced and taught by traditional authorities who, far from being at the margin of the religious establishment, are often among leading religious authorities. There is no accepted category of "sacred science" in the modern West, whereas such a category is part of the still widely accepted traditional religious landscape of most other faiths. The religious response to the environmental crisis is therefore bound to be very different as far as certain basic issues are concerned. A contemporary Christian thinker, were he to wish to rediscover Christian sacred cosmology and the authentically Christian view of the order of nature, would have to unpeel many layers of a mind-set marked by humanism, scientism, rationalism, and all the other factors mentioned in the earlier chapters, layers that separate the consciousness of most present-day Westerners from the traditional vision of the world and that have in fact created the modern mind. The vast majority of non-Westerners, even if modernized, would have only to remember their grandparents to return to their traditional roots.

The presence of this secular element even within modern Christianity is seen clearly in the case of Orientals and Africans converted to Christianity. As a result, they become usually much more comfortable in fitting into modern consumerist society and begin to disregard even more than before their traditional attitude toward nature. For most of them this conversion does not familiarize them with a St. Iranaeus or a St. Maximus the Confessor, but with a modernized version of Christianity in which the concepts of domination over nature and self-redemption rather than redemption of the cosmos and even the accruing of wealth and material possessions are extolled. The role of such groups in the rapid modernization of certain parts of Asia and Africa can hardly be denied, and this phenomenon itself is indicative of the differences in the relationship of Western Christianity and other religions toward the secularist and scientistic worldview and also the differences in degree to which this worldview has succeeded in replacing the religious understanding of the order of nature in both the Western and non-Western worlds.

Despite these distinctions, however, important similarities exist between religious reactions in these two worlds, the most important of which is the common approach to the crisis as an ethical one despite some exceptions alluded to above. As already seen, the response of Christianity and Judaism has been primarily ethical, and the other religions have for the most part followed suit. Also, most responses in both worlds have remained enfeebled because of their refusal to combat openly the worldview that has reduced the order of nature to a purely quantitative entity to be exploited at will. If anything, at least in the West, where there is a greater degree of political freedom, some religious bodies have opposed government actions that have a direct bearing upon the destruction of the environment, whereas this has been rarer in the non-Western world.

The crucial issue of resuscitating the religious understanding of the order of nature remains, however, an unfinished task, one that is more difficult to achieve for Western Christianity—long tied to modern civilization with its secularizing worldview—than for other religions that for the most part have preserved their traditional teachings more intact until now. Furthermore, as already pointed out, the sacred sciences and the sacred view of nature are still much more central to the non-Western traditions than to Western Christianity where, as a result of historical events partly outlined in earlier chapters, they have become much more marginalized. In any case, the task at hand in both East and West is the revival of the religious view of the order of nature, derived not from modern science—which is, to be sure, a particular and consequential mode of knowing nature yet not derived from metaphysical principles—but from the traditional sources of these religions and the twin foundations of revelation and intellection[140] upon which the traditional and sacred sciences are based.

The environmental crisis affords a great challenge to all religions. It provides them with the opportunity to express anew their own vision of the order of nature, eclipsed in the West ever since the advent of modern science. It also places the responsibility upon them to expound the sacred nature of Creation without falling into the error, seen in certain Christian responses today, of making the condition of saving the Earth forgoing the hope of Heaven, as if having destroyed much of the planet we can only save the rest by forgetting our ultimate end and Heaven itself, which would need to be consumed by the Earth rather than being the Spiritual Empyrean of which Earth is the consort and to which is must be wed in order to bring about harmony.

What is needed, first of all, is to reassert the metaphysical reality of Heaven and Earth, and then provide a vision of the sacredness of Earth in the light of Heaven and ultimately the Supreme Principle, which is the Sacred as such. There is need of ethical action toward all natural beings on the basis of a knowledge of the order of nature corresponding to an objective reality, a knowledge that is itself ultimately a sacred science, a *scientia sacra*. There is need to rediscover those laws and principles governing human ethics as well as the cosmos, to bring out the interconnectedness between man and nature in the light of the Divine, an interconnection not based on sentimentality or even ethical concern related to the realm of action alone, but one founded upon a knowledge whose forgetting has now brought human beings to the edge of the precipice of annihilation of both the natural order and themselves.

Finally, what religions must provide at this late moment is not only an ethics expanded to include the nonhuman, but also with the aid of their inner teachings, a sacred science that provides knowledge as to why other creatures must also be treated ethically, how they are related to us not only physically and biologically but also psychologically and spiritually. Such a science would also reveal how creatures share our final end and affect our spiritual destiny by virtue of our inner and outer correspondences with them and as a result of our role as God's vicegerent and channel of the light of the supernal world for the natural order as well as of their role as a revelation of God's Wisdom and Power and therefore object of a knowledge that is ultimately salvific.

NOTES

1. There are, of course, exceptions such as in nineteenth-century Confucian China where a number of thinkers began to interpret Confucianism in a rationalistic manner under the influence of Western thought leading to the Marxist interpretation of the Confucian view of nature by a number of twentieth-century Chinese thinkers. See the many works of Tu Wei-ming, including his "Confucianism," Chapter 3 in Arvind Sharma (ed.), *Our Religions* (New York: HarperCollins, 1993), pp. 139ff.

2. See the well-known essay of Lynn White, Jr., "The Historical Roots of Our Ecological Crisis," *Science* (No. 155, 1967), pp. 1203–1207. As for Toynbee, he once wrote, "The remedy [of the environmental crisis] lies in reverting from the *Weltanschauung* of monotheism to the *Weltanschauung* of pantheism, which is older and was once more universal." David and Eileen Spring (eds.), *Ecology and Religion in History* (New York: Harper & Row, 1974), p. 147. For our part we do not believe that any of the primal religions were pantheistic in the modern philosophical sense of the term and that such assertions are especially outrageous when they refuse to consider Islam with its billion followers and pure monotheism, which has had a very different history in its treatment of

the natural environment from that of the West. We shall turn to this question later in this chapter.

For a Christian response to the claims of White, Toynbee, and others with similar views, see Stephen R. L. Clark, *How to Think about the Earth: Philosophical and Theological Models for Ecology* (London: Mowbray, 1993).

3. An author such as Arthur Peacocke, who has devoted much of his work to the relation between Christian theology and science, defends Christianity strongly against those who blame it for the environment crisis by pointing to the presence of the environmental crisis elsewhere. See his book *Theology for a Scientific Age* (London: SCM Press, 1993), *passim*.

4. For example, Eliot Deutsch, while rejecting the views of hard-headed pragmatists who wish to create a new environmental ethics based solely on pragmatism and scientific knowledge, writes, "By turning to Asian thought . . . for inspiration we might yet find a way to bring our scientific understanding of nature's organic complexity into an integral harmony with a spiritual understanding of reality's simplicity." In J. Baird Callicott and Roger T. Ames, *Nature in Asian Traditions of Thought: Essays in Environmental Philosophy* (Albany: State University of New York Press, 1989), p. 265. We have also dealt with this issue and defended the necessity to turn to non-Western traditions, including Islam, for the recovery of a spiritualized vision of nature. See S. H. Nasr, *Man and Nature* (London: HarperCollins, 1989), Chapter 3.

5. In the same volume in which Eliot Deutsch's article appears, David Kalupahana takes the opposite view and appeals to nonabsolutist American pragmatism to claim that "such answers [concerning the environmental crisis] are already available to him [the Westerner] at his doorstep." Callicott and Ames, *Nature in Asian Traditions*, p. 256. There are those who have turned to much more traditional Western sources such as medieval mystics, Celtic Christianity, or the Church Fathers, some of whom we shall discuss in this chapter.

6. See Nasr, *Man and Nature*, Chapter 1.

7. See Niebuhr's *The Purpose of the Church and Its Ministry* (New York: Harper & Row, 1956), p. 38. On Niebuhr and the early history of Christian theological concern with the environment see Ian Barbour, *Ethics in an Age of Technology* (San Francisco: Harper, 1993), pp. 57–82.

8. We recall vividly how, upon delivering the Rockefeller Lectures at the University of Chicago in 1966 and the subsequent appearance of them as *Man and Nature: The Spiritual Crisis of Modern Man*, we were taken to task by many Christian theologians on both sides of the Atlantic for pointing to the Christian theological neglect of nature as being a cause of the environmental crisis and for considering this crisis to be essentially spiritual and religious rather than simply a matter of misguided technological planning. Needless to say, much has changed in this domain during the last generation.

9. See Joseph Sittler, *The Care of the Earth and Other University Sermons* (Philadelphia: Fortress Press, 1964).

10. See Roderick F. Nash, *The Rights of Nature: A History of Environmental Ethics* (Madison: University of Wisconsin Press, 1989), pp. 100–101. This work contains a scholarly account of the environmental movement among Christian thinkers, particularly in America.

11. Especially Faith-Man-Nature Group, *Christians and the Good Earth* (New York: Friendship Press, 1972) and *idem. A New Ethics for a New Earth* (New York: Friendship Press, 1971).

12. See Ian Barbour, *Western Man and Environmental Ethics: Attitudes Toward Nature*

and Technology (Reading, Mass.: Addison-Wesley, 1973), which exposes the debate engendered by Lynn White's provocative essay, some of whose ideas we had discussed in our Rockefeller Lectures at the University of Chicago many months before White, but with whose main thesis, which blames Abrahamic monotheism in general and Christianity in particular for the environmental crisis without paying enough attention to the secularization of the cosmos by modern science and philosophy, we do not agree.

13. Published in Philadelphia by the Fortress Press in 1985, Santmire's book contains a wealth of information about Christian attitudes toward nature drawn from nearly the whole of Christian history. On the Western Christian tradition's views in general toward nature with emphasis upon St. Francis, see also Roger D. Sorrell, *St. Francis of Assisi and Nature: Tradition and Innovation in Western Christian Attitudes toward the Environment* (New York: Oxford University Press, 1988).

14. See, for example, Wendell Berry, *The Unsettling of America: Culture and Agriculture* (San Francisco: Sierra Club Books, 1986), and his *The Gift of Good Land: Further Essays, Cultural and Agricultural* (San Francisco: North Point Press, 1981). On the Catholic side, see John Hart, *The Spirit of the Earth: A Theology of the Land* (New York: Paulist Press, 1984), where he speaks of God being the owner of the land over which we only have a trust and custodianship that we must fulfill responsibly.

15. Snyder advocated including all creatures and not only man in American democracy in the same way that the American Indians spoke of various creatures as peoples and included them in their religious cosmos. He expressed these ideas in poetry in his 1975 opus *Turtle Island* (New York: New Directions), which became quite popular. Likewise, Theodore Roszak, who coined the word "counter-culture" in his book *The Making of a Counter-Culture* (Garden City, N.Y.: Doubleday, 1969), spoke of both Oriental doctrines and the "Shamanistic worldview," which needed to be revitalized. In Roszak's celebrated *Where the Wasteland Ends: Politics and Transcendence in Postindustrial Society* (Garden City, N.Y.: Anchor Books / Doubleday, 1973), he provided a scathing criticism of the scientistic worldview, rare among those in academic circles concerned with the environment, and he appealed to the revival of ancient wisdom concerning nature contained in the sapiental and gnostic dimensions of various religions. See also Roszak's *The Voice of the Earth* (New York: Simon & Schuster, 1992), where he speaks especially of "ecopsychology."

16. As a recent example see John B. Butcher, *The Tao of Jesus* (San Francisco: Harper, 1954), written by an Episcopalian priest but using Taoist and other non-Christian themes and sources.

17. One of the most influential figures among this group is Rosemary R. Ruether. See her *Gaia & God: An Ecofemenist Theology of Earth Healing* (San Francisco: Harper 1992). See also Elizabeth Johnson, *Women, Earth, and Creator Spirit* (New York: Paulist Press, 1993), for a Catholic view on the subject.

18. See Sallie McFague, *Metaphorical Theology: Models of God in Religious Language* (Philadelphia: Fortress Press, 1982). It should be added that McFague is not the only proponent of metaphorical theology in Protestantism. One of the best known of contemporary German Protestant theologians, Eberhard Jüngel, has also claimed that all theological language is metaphorical, although his understanding of this term is not quite the same as McFague's. See Roland D. Zimany, *Vehicle for God: The Metaphorical Theology of Eberhard Jüngel* (Macon, Ga.: Mercer University Press, 1994).

It must also be remembered that some themes treated by McFague, including the significance of the Earth as mother, are also of concern to male Christian theologians and have been taken up by no less a figure than Jürgen Moltmann. See his important work on the theology of nature, *God in Creation: An Ecological Doctrine of Creation* (London: SCM Press, 1985).

19. Concerning the "monarchical model" McFague writes, "It has three major flaws: in the monarchical world, God is distant from the world, relates only to the human world, and controls that world through domination and benevolence." Sallie McFague, *Models of God: Theology for an Ecological, Nuclear Age* (Philadelphia: Fortress Press, 1987), p. 65.

20. McFague concludes her discussion of the "monarchical model" by stating, "The monarchical model is dangerous in our time; it encourages a sense of distance from the world; it attends only to the human dimension of the world; and it supports attitudes of either domination of the world or passivity toward it." Ibid., p. 69.

21. Ibid., p. 70.

22. McFague has developed this theme further in *The Body of God: An Ecological Theology* (Minneapolis: Augsburg Fortress Press, 1993), where she emphasizes the organic view of the cosmos by certain interpreters of modern sciences (the diversifiers) as against the group that reduces the world to a mechanism and whom she calls the unifiers (p. 91). She considers a holistic metaphysic as one that would include both the reductionist view of nature and the holistic one, or both the mechanistic and the organic. In emphasizing the significance of the body she relies upon such a perspective and also seeks to preserve both the "agential model," which preserves transcendence, and the organic one, which empha-sizes immanence (p. 141).

The whole question of the significance of the body has come to the fore in the West in the past few decades in both Christian theology and Western culture in general. In the next chapter we shall deal with its significance in the rediscovery of the order of nature.

23. "It is, as he [St. Augustine] said in a term that may sound quaint and anachronis-tic but which is ecologically up-to-date 'concupiscence,' an insatiable appetite which causes one to want 'to have it all' for oneself." Sallie McFague, "A Square in the Quilt," in Stephen C. Rockefeller and John C. Elder (eds.), *Spirit and Nature* (Boston: Beacon Press, 1992), p. 43.

24. "The states of women and nature have been historically parallel: as one goes, so goes the other." Ibid., p. 45. This is a highly questionable assertion, to say the least, if the matter is considered globally.

25. "Probably the single most important thing that theologians can do for the planetary agenda is to insist that the 'world' in question, the world in which to understand both God and human beings, is the contemporary scientific picture of the earth, its history, and our place in it that is emerging from astrophysics and biology." Ibid., p. 50. It seems that having surrendered the world of nature to modern science, religion is now asked, in the name of the environment, to also surrender God to this science and allow a quantitative science of nature to determine for us who have created such a science the way to under-stand God.

26. "It can probably be agreed that our modern relations to nature, and behind them our attitudes toward and understanding of nature, have disclosed themselves as disasters. Also it can be said that at fault are at once our Western religious traditions as they have been interpreted and the modern understanding of nature. Both together made possible, even resulted in, our industrial and technological use of nature and so, in the end, the exploitation and despolitation of nature." Langdon Gilkey, *Nature, Reality and the Sacred: The Nexus of Science and Religion* (Minneapolis: Augsburg Fortress Press, 1993), p. 79. See also Chapter 8, "Nature, Order, and Value," pp. 109–130, for a discussion of the history of the idea of order from the Greeks to the present, touching relatively briefly upon some of the points we have also dealt with earlier in this book.

27. Ibid., p. 79.

28. To see how this idea is now returning in diverse Christian circles, it is sufficient to quote both a Protestant and an Orthodox source. James A. Nash writes, "As the habitation of the Spirit and the context of sacramental presence, the cosmos is a sacred place. We are created to live together in the fullest possible accord with God's justice and peace, as valued parts of God's beloved habitat, and ours. The diversity, vitality, and beauty of this habitat must be protected, certainly for its own sake, but also for the sake of humanity's physical *and* spiritual well-being." Nash, *Loving Nature: Ecological Integrity and Christian Responsibility* (Nashville, Tenn.: Abingdon Press, 1991).

The Orthodox Archimandrite Timothy Kallistos Ware writes, basing himself on Patristic sources, "This idea of *cosmic redemption* is based, like the Orthodox doctrine of icons, upon a right understanding of the Incarnation. Christ took flesh—something from the material order—and so he made possible the redemption and metamorphosis of all creation—not merely the immaterial but the physical." Ware, *The Orthodox Church* (Harmondsworth, U.K.: Penguin Books, 1981), p. 240.

On the attitude of different Christian churches toward the order of nature and theologies of Creation, see Per Lonning, *Creation: An Ecumenical Challenge?* (Macon, Ga.: Mercer University Press, 1989). See especially Section 5, p. 165, which deals with different churches, including the Orthodox, Catholic, and Protestant, separately.

29. For Fox's reasons for converting to Episcopalianism see "The Episcopal Decision," *Creation Spirituality* (Vol. 10, no. 11, Summer 1994), p. 3, where he writes, "My decision to embrace the Anglican tradition is about including some Anglo-Saxon (and Celtic) common sense into twenty-first-century Catholicism," p. 3.

30. "Just as modern science effectively denied mysticism to our culture for three hundred years, so too the post-Einsteinean scientific era is launching an era of mystical awareness." Matthew Fox, *The Coming of the Cosmic Christ: The Healing of Mother Earth and the Birth of a Global Rennaissance* (San Francisco: Harper & Row, 1988), p. 47.

31. Ibid., p. 54.

32. On the heart-intellect as understood traditionally, see Frithjof Schuon, *L'Oeil du coeur* (Paris: Dervy Livres, 1974), pp. 13ff.

33. Fox, *Cosmic Christ*, p. 56.

34. It is interesting that Fox considers mysticism to be the only possible way to "deep ecumenism" and understanding of other religions, reasserting in another language, at least as far as this point is concerned, the thesis of F. Schuon and other traditional authors that the only possible ecumenism is esoteric ecumenism and the only possible unity among religions, the "transcendent unity of religions," to use Schuon's well-known formulation. We have already dealt with this subject in Chapter 1 of this text.

35. In Part 3 of *The Coming of the Cosmic Christ*, pp. 75ff., Fox confirms the notion of Jeroslav Pelikan that "Enlightenment philosophy deposed the cosmic Christ." Pelikan, *Jesus Through the Centuries* (New Haven, Conn: Yale University Press, 1985), p. 63.

36. Fox, *Cosmic Christ*, p. 78.

37. Ibid., p. 79.

38. "I believe the appropriate symbol of the Cosmic Christ who becomes incarnate in Jesus is that of Jesus as Mother Earth Crucified yet rising daily." Ibid., p. 145.

39. It is difficult to understand from a theological and even logical point of view how man who is the "image of God" can be reinvented without "reinventing" God or how a being can re-invent himself. Who is then doing the re-inventing if not a being who is now being re-invented? This call common to Fox, Wendell Berry, and others can be answered

by saying that all that modern man needs to do is to remember what it means to be really human as this state has been understood perennially in various traditions.

40. Matthew Fox, *Creation Spirituality: Liberating Gifts for the Peoples of the Earth* (San Francisco: Harper 1991).

41. Ibid., p. 13, One wonders why a theologian should not begin with *theos* rather than either Creation or man and study both the latter two catergories of reality in the light of their common ontological principles!

42. Ibid., p. 18.

43. Fox also states a set of concrete proposals for the spiritual revival of America based upon creation spirituality.

44. See John F. Haught, *The Promise of Nature: Ecology and Cosmic Purpose* (New York: Paulist Press, 1993), Introduction.

45. Ibid., p. 12.

46. Accepting the evolutionary theory, Haught writes, "As I look at the theological alternatives I see none that comes closer to giving us a framework within which to pull together the insights of science and religion into a cosmology that encourages in us an evolutionary adventurousness as well as preserving care that might inspire appropriate ethical attitudes toward nature." Ibid, p. 38.

47. Michael Polanyi, *Personal Knowledge* (New York: Harper Torchbooks, 1964), p. 142.

48. Haught, *Promise of Nature*, p. 65.

49. "Our personal immortality could be understood as the deepening through death of our relatedness to the cosmos. . . . Our own personal destiny cannot be separated from that of the entire cosmic story. Thinking of our own bodily resurrection as inseperable from the fate of the entire universe might make us less indifferent toward the natural world to which we will forever be related." Ibid., p. 142.

It is interesting to note that the seventeenth-century Islamic philosopher Mullā Ṣadrā wrote extensively on the resurrection on the Day of Judgment of not only man but also all creatures and that this theme is to be formed in many Islamic writings of eschatology. See, for example, Mullā Ṣadrā, *Risālat al-ḥashr*, ed. Muḥammad Khwājawī (Tehran: Mawlā Publications, 1363 A.H. / 1984).

50. Thomas Merton was one of the first contemporary religious thinkers to concern himself with medieval Irish poetry written by monks in celebration of the spiritual signifi- cance of nature. In recent years his early and isolated interest has become the concern of a much more extensive circle. See, for example, Caitlin Matthews, *The Elements of the Celtic Tradition* (Rockport, Mass., and Shaftesbury, U.K.: Element Books, 1989; contains an extensive bibliography); and Christopher Bamford and William P. Marsh, *Celtic Chris- tianity, Ecology & Holiness* (Hudson, N.Y.: Lindisfarne Press, 1987).

51. See Sean McDonagh, *To Care for the Earth* (London: Geoffrey Chapman, 1986); also see his *The Greening of the Church* (Maryknoll, N.Y.: Orbis Books, and London: Geoffrey Chapman, 1990).

52. See Macquarrie's "Paths of Spirituality," in Michael Maher (ed.), *Irish Spiritu- ality* (Dublin: Veritas, 1981), pp. 7ff.

53. See, for example, Paulos MacGregorios, *The Human Presence: An Orthodox View of Nature* (Geneva: World Council of Churches, 1978), and *Cosmic Man: The Divine Presence* (Geneva: World Council of Churches, 1980), pp. 210ff.

54. Ipswich, Suffolk, Golgonooza Press, 1987. This book has been published in America as *The Eclipse of Man and Nature* (Hudson, N.Y.: Lindisfarne Press, 1987).

55. "There can be, in the nature of things, no reconciliation between the Christian or

any other sacred cosmology and the modern scientific worldview for the simple reason that the metaphysical presuppositions on which this worldview is based are themselves totally nonspiritual." Philip Sherrard, *Human Image—World Image* (Ipswich: Golgonooza Press, 1992), p. 131.

56. Ibid., p. 131.

57. Ibid., p. 132.

58. In Chapter 6 of *Human Image,* Sherrard deals with the destruction of the Christian view of nature according to Oskar Milosz. For the thought of Milosz see Christopher Bamford (ed.), *The Noble Traveller: The Life and Writings of O.V. de L. Milosz* (West Stockbridge, Mass.: Lindisfarne Press, 1985).

59. Sherrard, *Human Image,* p. 147.

60. "The historical appearance of Christ is only one form of embodiment; the Universe of matter is another form, and in this form the cosmic Christ is from the beginning and always showing forth images of God in nature, for nature is the Body of God." Ibid., p. 149.

61. This is a theme we dealt with several decades ago in our book *Man and Nature,* which, as already mentioned, was criticized by many Christian theologicans at that time when Christian theology showed little interest in the natural environment.

62. Sherrard, *Human Image,* p. 152.

63. "The only science of nature worthy of the title is one that induces an understanding of the reality of this divine presence of which each sensible form is the revelation or ephiphany." Ibid., p. 152. It is of interest to note here that in Ibn ʿArabian cosmology the levels of reality, including the physical one (*ʿālam al-mulk*), are called Divine Presences (*al-ḥaḍarāt al-ilāhiyyah*) and that the consideration of each sensible form as epiphany is identical with the well-known Quranic doctrine that all things are the *āyāt Allāh,* which means signs of God, and ultimately theophanies or epiphanies to which the Sufis refer as *tajalliyyāt,* the singular *tajallī* meaning precisely theophany, because *tajallī* is always the *tajallī* of a Divine Name or Quality.

64. Ibid., p. 153.

65. See Dermot Moran, *The Philosophy of John Scottus Erigena* (Cambridge and New York: Cambridge University Press, 1989), pp. 236, 238ff; and Harry A. Wolfson, "The Indentification of *ex-nihilo* with Emanation in Gregory of Nyssa," in Wolfson, *Studies in the History of Philosphy and Religion* (Cambridge, Mass.: Harvard University Press, 1973), pp. 199–221.

66. According to Böhme, "God created the world out of nothing because He Himself dwells in nothing—that is, He dwells in Himself." *Psychologia Verum,* Question 7–23, quoted by Sherrard, *Human Image,* p. 155.

67. This debate also had a long history in Islam not only between the theologians and the philosophers but also between the Sufis and both groups. Islamic metaphysics on the highest level has always sought to reveal the mystery of cosmogenesis as being related to both the freedom and the necessity within and issuing from the Divine Principle.

68. Sherrard, *Human Image,* p. 157. Again, one is reminded here of the famous "sacred saying" of the Prophet (*al-ḥadīth al-qudsī*), "I was a hidden treasure. I wanted to be known and therefore I created the world so that I would be known."

69. These stages of Creation or "descent" from the Divine Principle are elucidated in an elaborate fashion in Islam by both Sufis such as Ibn ʿArabī and ʿAbd-al-Karīm al-Jīlī and later Islamic philosophers such as Mullā Ṣadrā. See Jīlī, *Universal Man,* trans. Titus Burckhardt; English trans. Angela Culme-Seymour (Sherborne, U.K.: Beshara Publica-

tions, 1983); and Mullā Ṣadrā, *al-Asfār al-arba'ah* (Qumm: Dār al-ma'ārif al-islāmiyyah, Vols. I and II, 1387 (A.H.)/ 1968).

70. Sherrard, *Human Image,* p. 161.

71. "There is an Annunciation in the Trinity as well as terrestrial Annunciation—a divine *fiat* in God Himself in relation to His own Being—and this is executed by the Holy Spirit." Ibid., p. 162.

72. Ibid., p. 163.

73. Ibid., p. 163.

74. This is explained more fully in Sherrard's *The Rape of Man and Nature,* pp. 24ff.

75. Sherrard, *Human Image,* p. 165.

76. Ibid., p. 176.

77. Ibid., p. 176.

78. Islam also accepts Mary, the mother of Jesus, as the Virgin Mother, but being based on the aspect of God as the Absolute cannot of course accept the idea of *Theodokos,* for God as the Absolute cannot have a progenitor.

79. Sherrard, *Human Image,* p. 177.

80. To which Sufis also refer in the feminine form, the Divine Essence (*al-Dhāt*), which is the Beyond-Being, possessing feminine gender in Arabic.

81. Sherrard, *Human Image,* p. 180.

82. Ibid., p. 181.

83. See Arthur Versluis, *TheoSophia: Hidden Dimensions of Christianity* (Hudson, N.Y.: Lindisfarne Press, 1994).

84. Ibid., p. 96, Chapter 6.

85. As an example of recent Jewish concern with the environment see *Conservative Judaism* (Vol. 44, no. 1, Fall 1991) and *The Melton Journal* (no. 24, Spring 1991; and no. 25, Spring 1992), all devoted to the question of Judaism and ecology.

86. Ismar Schorsch, "Learning to Live with Less," in Stephen Rockefeller and John Elder (eds.), *Spirit and Nature* (Boston: Beacon Press, 1992), pp. 24ff.

87. "In a society that has made of extravagance a commonplace and distraction a fiendish art, Judaism at its best holds out one model—often dismissed or abused in reality—for reining in the appetites of human consciousness—a strain of asceticism blended with a love of learning." Ibid., pp. 36–37.

88. See Katz's "Judaism and the Ecological Crisis," in Mary E. Tucker and John A. Grim (eds.), *Worldviews and Ecology* (Lewisburg, Pa.: Bucknell University Press, and London: Associated University Presses, 1993), pp. 55–70. This view is also confirmed by Robert Gordis in "Judaism and the Environment," *Congress Monthly* (vol. 57, no. 6, September–October 1990), p. 8; and also by Jeanne Kay in "Concepts of Nature in the Hebrew Bible," *Environmental Ethics* (Vol. 10, 1988), pp. 326–327.

89. "Nature is envisaged as one of the spheres in which God meets man personally and in which he is called upon to exercise responsibility." E. L. Allen, "The Hebrew View of Nature," *The Journal of Jewish Studies* (Vol. 2, no. 2, 1951), p. 100.

90. The theme of stewardship has been developed among many Jewish thinkers parallel to Christian ones. See, for example, David Ehrenfeld and Philip J. Bentley, "Judaism and the Practice of Stewardship," in Marc Swetliz (ed.), *Judaism and Ecology: A Sourcebook of Readings* (Wyncote, Pa.: Shomrei Adamah, 1990), p. 97. It is also interesting to note the interest among some Christian theologians to develop the theme of the sabbath as possessing significance for the preservation of the environment. See, for example, Moltmann, *God in Creation,* pp. 276ff.

91. Eric Katz, "Judaism and the Ecological Crisis," in Tucker and Grim (eds.), *Worldviews and Ecology*, p. 66.

92. Gordis, "Judaism and the Environment," p. 10.

93. Arthur Green, *Seek My Face, Speak My Name: A Contemporary Jewish Theology* (Northvale, N.J.: Jason Aronson, 1992).

94. "The One strives to evolve itself into ever more complex, advanced, and conscious forms of existence, whether these exist only here, or in another manner in other worlds as well. Our religious understanding of evolution means that the divine energy is ever reaching forward and upward . . . toward more sophisticated and complex levels of development." Green, *Seek My Face*, p. 71.

95. Ibid., p. 72.

96. Ibid., p. 82.

97. Ibid., p. 84.

98. Ibid., p. 86.

99. Ibid., p. 86.

100. Concerning China's far from positive environmental record, see Vaclav Smil, *The Bad Earth* (Armonk, N.Y.: Sharpe, 1984); and Lester Ross, *Environmental Policy in China* (Bloomington: Indiana University Press, 1988).

101. For example, Chief Oren Lyons of Onondaga Nations has stated:

> In the perception of my people, the *Houdenosaunee,* whom you call Iroquois, all life is equal, and that includes the birds, animals, things that grow, things that swim. It is the Creator who presents that reality. As you read this by yourself in your sovereignty and in your being, you are a manifestation of the creation. You are sovereign by the fact that you exist. This relationship demands respect for the equality of all life.

From a public address quoted by John Grim, "Native American Worldviews and Ecology," in Tucker and Grim (eds.), *Worldviews and Ecology*, p. 51.
See also Audrey Shanandoah, "A Tradition of Thanksgiving," in *Spirit and Nature*, p. 15.

102. Tu Wei-ming, "The Continuity of Being: Chinese Visions of Nature," in his *Confucian Thought: Selfhood as Creative Transformation* (Albany: State University of New York Press, 1985), p. 35. On Chinese views of nature and their contemporary signficance, see also Tu Wei-ming, *Centrality and Commonality: An Essay in the Chung-yung* (Honolulu: University of Hawaii Press, 1976).

103. Tu Wei-ming, "The Continuity of Being," p. 41.

104. See Mary E. Tucker, "The Relevance of Chinese neo-Confucianism for the Reverence of Nature," *Environmental History Review* (Summer 1991), pp. 55–69.

105. See also Theodore de Bary et al. (compilers), *Sources of Chinese Tradition*, Vol. 1 (New York: Columbia University Press, 1960), Chapter 8, pp. 510ff.

106. Quoted by Tucker, "Relevance of Chinese neo-Confucianism," p. 66. Tu Wei-ming draws contemporary lessons from this very text by pointing out that, according to it, the least of us has a place in the Universe and we are its guardians. According to this view "there is no post-lapsarian state to encounter and . . . alienation as a deep-rooted feeling of estrangement from one's primordial origin is nonexistent. Furthermore, the idea of man as a manipulator and conqueror of nature would also seem to be ruled out." Tu Wei-ming, *Confucian Thought*, p. 158.

107. See Seyyed Hossein Nasr, *Religion and the Environmental Crisis* (New Delhi: Indira Gandhi National Center for the Arts, 1993).

108. See Michael Tobias, "Jainism and Ecology: Views of Nature, Nonviolence, and Vegetarianism," in Tucker and Grim (eds.), *Worldviews and Ecology,* pp. 138–149.

109. See, for example, Vandana Shiva, *Staying Alive: Women, Ecology and Development* (London: Zed Books, 1988).

110. Vandana Shiva says in reference to Hinduism, "All the nature deities are always female, by and large, because all of them are considered *prakṛti,* the female principle in Hindu cosmology. Also, all of them are nurturing mothers—the trees feed you, the streams feed you, the land feeds you, and everything that nurtures you is a mother." From an interview quoted by Christopher K. Chapple in his "Hindu Environmentalism: Traditional and Contemporary Resources," in Tucker and Grim (eds.), *Worldviews and Ecology,* p. 120.

111. See ibid., pp. 113ff, as well as Chapter 2 of the present text. On contemporary Hindu responses to the environmental crisis, see also Ranchor Prime (ed.), *Hinduism and Ecology: Seeds of Truth* (London and New York: Cassell, 1992). The author deals in the first section (pp. 8ff) with the traditional Hindu teachings about nature; in Part 2 (pp. 58ff), entitled "India in the Balance," with current India and the attempt to implement on behalf of certain groups and despite government opposition, Gandhian economics based on self-sufficiency, village economics, and self-sacrifice; and in Part 3 (pp. 80ff) with current ecological movements as well as catastrophes that will affect India's future. The author speaks of both the Chippko movement to save trees and the environmental thought of A.C. Bhaktivedanta Swami Prabhupada and the self-sufficient and environmentally sound communities he established in the West at the end of his life. There is also a frank and moving discussion of environmentally catastrophic events taking place in India today, including the unbelievable pollution of the water of Vrindavan, the sacred precinct of Krishna.

112. The Dalai Lama in referring to this basic reality asserts that "form is emptiness, and emptiness is form." See his essay "A Tibetan Buddhist Perspective on Spirit in Nature," in *Spirit and Nature,* p. 114.

113. Among the most acute treatments of the criticism of modern science from a Buddhist point of view is to be found in Frithjof Schuon, "A Buddhist Eye on Science," in his book *In the Tracks of Buddhism,* trans. Marco Pallis (London: Allen & Unwin, 1968), pp. 39ff.

114. The essay of E. F. Schumacher, "Buddhist Economics," in his book *Small Is Beautiful: Economics as if People Mattered* (New York: Harper & Row, 1975), has been particularly influential.

115. The Dalai Lama, "A Tibetan Buddhist Perspective," p. 117.

116. See Brian Brown, "Toward a Buddhist Ecological Cosmology," in Tucker and Grim (eds.), *Worldviews and Ecology,* pp. 124ff.

117. "This movement of the wind from ignorance to wisdom, from cross materialism to the universe as a sacred body, is the very movement of Absolute Consciousness from an implicit to an explicit self-awareness. . . . Such a cosmology, grounded in universal Emptiness, would reinvigorate the human in an ethic of reflection upon and care for life in its entirety, as the species which can identify the integrity of the whole in the richness of its diverse particularities." Ibid., p. 136.

118. See Allan Hunt Badiver (ed.), *Dharma Gaia* (Berkeley, Calif.: Parallaz Press, 1990).

119. See Martine Bachelor and Kerry Brown (eds.), *Buddhism and Ecology* (London: Cassell, 1992), much of which is devoted to case studies of Ladakh (India), Japan, Sri

Lanka, and Thailand and how attempts are being made in awakening these lands to a greater sense of harmony with the natural environment.

120. One can mention in this context the works of the Vietnamese monk Thich Nhat Hanh.

121. "The ecological crisis is at root a spiritual crisis of self-centered greed, aided and abetted by ingenious technologies run amok." Stephen Bachelor, "The Sand of the Ganges: Notes Toward a Buddhist Ecological Philosophy," in Bachelor and Brown (eds.), *Buddhism and Ecology*, p. 33.

122. It was our own works such as *Science and Civilization in Islam* and *An Introduction to Islamic Cosmological Doctrines*, both published in the 1960s, that first brought this challenge of viewing Islamic science from the Islamic point of view and as an alternative way of studying nature to the forefront of attention in the Islamic world. Since then many other studies have followed suit. See, for example, Osman Bakar, *Tawḥīd and Science* (Kuala Lumpur: Secretariat for Islamic Philosophy and Science, 1991).

123. We ourselves were the first to draw the consequences for the environment of taking Islamic science seriously. See our *Man and Nature* and "The Ecological Problem in the Light of Sufism: The Conquest of Nature and the Teachings of Eastern Science," in Nasr, *Sufi Essays* (Albany: State University of New York Press, 1991), Chapter 10, p. 152. This link has also been followed by a number of other scholars. See, for example, Glyn Ford, "Rebirth of Islamic Science," in Ziauddin Sardar (ed.), *The Touch of Midas: Science, Values and Environment in Islam and the West* (Manchester, U.K.: Manchester University Press, 1984), Chapter 2, p. 26, where the author discusses both the question of considering Islamic science as an alternative science of nature and its consequences for the environment.

124. See Nasr, *An Introduction to Islamic Cosmological Doctrines; idem.* "Islamic Cosmology," in UNESCO, *Islamic Civilization* (in press); also the two-part study by William Chittick, *The Disclosure of God: Ibn al 'Arabī's Cosmology, Part I,* and *The Breath of the All-Merciful: Ibnal 'Arabī's Cosmology, Part II* (both in press), which deal in an elaborate fashion with Ibn 'Arabī's complex cosmology.

125. The environmental plight in Islamic countries is discussed in Fazlun Khalid and Jeanne O'Brien (eds.), *Islam and Ecology* (London: Cassell, 1992).

126. See Husaini's *Islamic Environmental Systems Engineering* (London: Macmillan, 1980).

127. See Chapter 2, the section on Islam.

128. See Iqtidar Zaidi, "On the Ethics of Man's Interaction with the Environment: an Islamic Approach," in Eugene C. Hargrove (ed.), *Religion and Environmental Crisis* (Athens: University of Georgia Press, 1986), pp. 13–16.

129. We have also dealt many times with this subject. See "Sacred Science and the Environmental Crisis: An Islamic Perspective," in Nasr, *The Need for a Sacred Science* (Albany: State University of New York Press, 1993), pp. 129ff.

130. Parvez Manzoor, "Environment and Values: The Islamic Perspective," in Sardar (ed), *Touch of Midas*, p. 151.

131. Ibid., p. 154.

132. Ibid., pp. 155–161.

133. See, for example, the writings of the influential writer on the environment Thomas Berry, such as his work with Brian Swimme, *The Universe Story: From the Primordial Flaring Forth to the Ecozoic Era—A Celebration of the Unfolding of the Cosmos* (San Francisco: Harper, 1992). In Chapter 12, "The Modern Revelation" (pp. 223ff), the information provided by modern science is equated with revelation in the religious sense, and the modern "story of the Universe" is equated with traditional myths (p. 268).

Berry also writes, "It's all a question of story. We are in trouble just now because we do not have a good story. We are in between stories. The old story, the account of how the world came to be and how we fit into it, is no longer effective. Yet we have not learned the new story." Berry, *The Dream of the Earth* (San Francisco: Sierra Club Books, 1990), p. 123.

Berry has the noble aim to create not a *Pax humana* but a *Pax gaia* embracing the whole of nature (p. 220), and yet he globalizes the current Western outlook on both modern science and sacred myth in such a way that they do not at all accord with the views of the vast majority of the followers of religions other than those of the West.

134. We do not wish to deal here with criticisms of the theory of evolution, which we have discussed in our *Knowledge and the Sacred,* Chapter 7; see also Osman Bakar (ed.), *Critiques of the Theory of Evolution* (Kuala Lumpur: The Islamic Academy of Science, 1987).

135. See Wolfgang Smith, *Teilhardism and the New Religion* (Rockford, Ill.: Tan Books, 1988).

136. Matthew Fox, in fact, proposes to submit the doctrine of Original Sin with that of "original blessing." See his *Original Blessing: A Primer in Creation Spirituality* (Santa Fe, N.M.: Bear, 1983).

137. The case of Sherrard, mentioned above, is exceptional indeed, although at the level of criticizing modern technology and its devastation of the environment as well as man's normal life there have been other notable voices, especially Jacques Ellul. See, for example, Ellul's *The Technological Society* (New York: Vintage Books, 1964), and *Perspectives on Our Age: Jacques Ellul Speaks on His Life and Work* (New York: Seabury Press, 1981), where he also speaks of the devastation brought about by modern technology upon non-Western socities; *The Betrayal of the West* (New York: Seabury Press, 1978); and the 1985 special issue of *CrossCurrents* devoted to the critique of technological society by Ellul.

138. When in the early 1960s we spoke in the Islamic world of the impending environmental crisis even before writing *Man and Nature,* the few who were interested were not among the *'ulamā'* or class of religious scholars, many of whom even today are not fully aware of the scope and significance of this crisis. The same attitude could be seen among most Hindu and Buddhist religious figures until the 1980s.

139. See Nasr, *The Need for a Sacred Science.*

140. By intellection here we do not of course mean the use of reason but of *intellectus* or *noüs,* of which the rational faculty is but a mental reflection. On the traditional understanding of intellection, see S. H. Nasr (ed.), *The Essential Writings of Frithjof Schuon* (Rockport, Mass., and Shaftesbury, U.K.: Element Books, 1986), pp. 344ff.

7

The Wisdom of
the Body

حکمت صُنع پادشاه جهان   هست در جسم رازهای نهان

بر تن و جان و بر زمان و مکان   رو بخوان آیه های حکمت او

This body at once dust and worthy of resurrection before the Lord,
Prison of the soul, yet its earthly companion,
The steed upon which she rides through the journey of life,
Veil before our inner senses, still tabernacle of God and His City.
Hindrance, yet aid in the realization of the One,
Our own self, but the skin to shed at death's final call.
Abandoned to a science of motion and matter,
No longer seen as locus of the Spirit, depository of Wisdom Divine,
Religion must now reclaim it as its own, to discover again
That mystery of the body so easily forgotten,
And through it regain that knowledge of nature,
Whose order reflected in our bodies,
We experience from within, in this our only place of encounter,
With that greater cosmic order, the macrocosm,
Of which we are a small replica and our bodies,
A mirror of that world, bridge to God's Creation,
In essence worthy of transmutation into the body of Glory,
Resplendent with the light of the Spirit,
For which, even here and now, it is a sacred temple.

It is only in our physical body that we experience directly the order of nature from within, and it is obviously through the body that we are able to encounter the world of nature about us. Our body—and it is with the human body that we are concerned in this chapter—is at once an extension of the world of nature and part of our "self," which we are able to know directly and of which we have an immediate consciousness, in contrast to what surrounds us and what we distinguish from "us" or that which we grasp immediately and intuitively as our "self" in our ordinary consciousness.[1] We identify ourselves with our body and yet distinguish ourselves from it; and while we know our body and experience it directly, we do not *really* know it, at least not all of us. Furthermore, there are those whose consciousness of the body is developed in such a way that they gain a new relation with it and even exercise certain controls over the body that are literally extraordinary, because most people do not possess such powers nor seek such a state of consciousness.

Religions have spoken of the body as a barrier to spiritual advancement and at the same time as a sacred precinct. But in all cases religion has been traditionally most acutely interested in the physical body whereas in the modern world the secularization of the understanding of the order of nature has become increasingly reflected in modern men and women's understanding of their own bodies resulting in an ever greater conflict with the religious view, a conflict that has now exploded upon the public stage in the West with the progressive penetration of modern technologies into the very processes of life. It is now a major public issue to decide where family planning stops and murder begins and even wherein lies the sanctity of life that modern civilization insists upon on the one hand—at least as far as human life is concerned—and destroys with such impunity on the other.

The great drama concerning the origin of human life and the enormous questions posed by bioengineering and related problems of bioethics all point to the truth that the religious understanding of the order of nature, as far as the human body is concerned, is now faced with a final challenge by the scientistic and secularist view. With the acquiescence to a large extent of Western religion, this view succeeded in secularizing the cosmos and extending its mechanistic view—or for that matter the agnostic, vitalistic one—of the order of nature to an ever greater degree to the human body. Consequently, the human body has come to be seen by many as no more than a part of that purely quantitative order of nature governed by the laws of physics and chemistry to which many seek to reduce biology itself. For that very reason the recovery of the religious view of nature must turn to the central issue of the body where the spiritual, psychic, and physical elements combine in a unity, the whole of which is of necessity of significance to religion. That is also why the greatest resistance has been shown even in the modern West to the exclusive claims of a materialistic understanding of the body and a purely materialistic medicine. Both the environmental crisis and the rediscovery of the significance of nature by religious thinkers, as discussed in the preceding chapter, have therefore been accompanied during the past few decades with a remarkable rise of interest in the physical body and its religious significance. And it is here that the greatest struggle is now taking place in the West between the claims of diametrically opposed views concerning the meaning of life and death and the significance of the human body.

Let it be said at the outset that in all traditional religions the human body is considered sacred. This is true not only of the primal religions or a religion such as Hinduism but also of the Abrahamic ones, despite the eclipse of this aspect of religion in many of the mainstream circles of Western Christianity during the past few centuries and its relegation to occultist circles associated with such figures as

Mme. Blavatsky and Alice Bailey. In the Bible it is stated "Our bodies are the
temple of the Holy Spirit which is in us" (I Cor. 6:19). And in the Quran God
says, "I breathe into him [Adam] My Spirit" (XXXVIII:72). The body is thus the
locus of the presence of the Spirit, and by virtue of that presence it is as sacred as a
temple.

The body has also been compared to a city belonging to God and is therefore
His domain; although given to us and made obedient to our will, the body is ultimately responsible to God.[2] Furthermore, we are also responsible to God for its
preservation and well-being.[3] In any case, the sacredness of the human body, with
its correspondences to the macrocosm and even its metacosmic significance, symbolically speaking, is so evident in the various religions of the world that it hardly
needs to be debated or demonstrated. It is sufficient to view the sacred architecture of places as different as Luxor and Chartres, all related to the body of what the
Sufis call the Universal Man, to realize the universality of the doctrine of the
sacredness of the body of the prophet and *avatāra* and by extension of all human
beings, a doctrine that still survives to a large extent in many parts of the world.

It was this central truth of religion that was challenged in the West starting
in the Renaissance, as reflected in the drawings of the physical body by Leonardo
da Vinci, which already reveal an almost mechanical conception of various organs
and parts. From the interest in the anatomy of a dead cadaver identified as "the
body" at that time, it was a short step to the mechanical view of the body and even
the conception of the body as a machine, proposed by Descartes and especially
Julien de La Mettrie and accepted by many philosophers and physicians, if not the
public at large.[4] From that period to this day there has been a continuous destruction of the mystery of the human body and its transformation from an inner space,
private, and belonging to God, to a public space from which all sense of mystery is
removed.[5] The consequence has been the creation of a medicine at once marvelous
in its achievements and horrendous in its failures and in the final dehumanization
of the human patient, which has now become such a major moral issue and which
along with the excessive commercialization and "technologization" of medicine
has drawn many people, even in the West, to alternative forms of medicine based
on the holistic view of the human being that embraces body, soul, as well as
spirit.

The change in the conception of the body resulting in the image that has now
become prevalent was a gradual one. Even a century ago people in the West had a
different understanding of their bodies than they do now, as reflected in part in
their views about sexuality. The change inaugurated by Descartes and William
Harvey about the human body did not begin to have a broader impact until the
end of the eighteenth and beginning of the nineteenth centuries.[6] The idea of the
body as "constant" biological reality is a recent one triggered by a clinical view
that saw the patient's body as though it were dead.[7] The reality of the soul was
cast aside, and the relation between it or the self and the body, if not totally
denied, was made much less central from what one finds in traditional schools of
medicine.[8] Henceforth the body became a concrete object as one would find in a
chemistry or physics laboratory and no longer a living psycho-biological entity.[9]

The human body became a public and social entity parallel with the new definition of man as *homo aeconomicus* shorn of his mystery, and the body lost its sacred
character and "magic" with which followers of all religions had associated it.
Today, as asserted by Barbara Duden, the process has reached its limit, at least in
the mainstream scientific understanding of the body, which has now lost all its
mystery and become "public space."[10]

It is in the light of this historical process, whose details we cannot examine
here, that the present crisis in the understanding of the significance of the body
must be considered. Today, there is the general tendency in the West to seek to
rediscover the significance of the body both religiously and otherwise.[11] This
tendency ranges from the glorification of sports and athletics beyond all proportions and the desacralization of sexuality peddled ever more commercially, to the
reintroduction of spiritual techniques dealing with the body in Christian monasti-
cism and the attempt to rediscover the sacred character of sexuality. It ranges from
the emphasis upon bodily movements, loud sounds, bright colors, etc., that
characterize so much of popular culture today, a culture that has rebelled through
emphasis upon bodily reality against the excessively cerebral civilization of the
modern world and its dualism of mind and body, to reappraising the relation
between body and soul in various forms of holistic medicine.

In the West two opposing forces seem to be interacting and confronting each
other, sometimes in an explosive manner, in the realm concerned with the meaning of the human body. On the one hand there is the movement toward the
rediscovery of the sacred nature of the body within mainstream churches as well as
in so-called New-Age religions. This is seen in the much greater interest shown
today in the study of the subtle (that is, non-material) body in earlier Western
sources; in non-Western traditions dealing with the body as demonstrated in the
spread of *Haṭha Yoga;* in alternative schools of medicine such as acupuncture and
Ayurvedic medicine, which are holistic in nature; and many other kinds of treatments of the body based on the concept of the wholeness of the body, in natural
foods, in what is now called "body theology" and even faith healing and prayer to
cure illnesses.

On the other hand there is an ever greater scientific penetration into the
workings of the body considered as a complicated machine and even on the basis of
a scientific understanding of the physical world no longer in vogue among many
contemporary physicists. The result is a crisis of major proportions with ethical,
economic, and social repercussions that are evident for everyone to see, although
few have turned to the central issue, which is the diversity of views held as to what
constitutes the human body.

It is true that the Christian view of the human body, as far as its sanctity is
concerned, despite being attacked, has never been completely abandoned in the
West. Still, it is an enigma for someone studying the West from the outside to
understand how a religion based upon the Incarnation, upon the penetration of
the Logos into the very body of Christ, and which believes in the resurrection of
the body as a central element of its teaching should allow so easily having the
physical body be taken out of its domain of intellectual concern and concentrating

for so long on theologies that no longer take the spiritual significance of the body seriously. Nor is it easy to understand how mainstream Western Christianity, in contrast to other religions and even Orthodox Christianity, lost for the most part its spiritual techniques involving the body as well as the mind. In any case, as part of the effort to rediscover the religious order of nature, and in fact at the heart of this effort, stands the necessity to realize anew that the body is the temple of God; not only in a metaphorical sense but also in a symbolic and therefore real sense, the human body is the theater for the manifestation of God's Wisdom, the microcosm possessing a cosmic significance and a reality having a role in spiritual realization. It is also essential to realize the significance of the corporeal body in recovering the traditional and hence normal rapport of man with the world of nature.[12] To achieve these ends, however, it is first necessary to remember the traditional teachings of various religions concerning the human body.[13]

VIEWS OF RELIGIONS IN THE NON-WESTERN WORLD

The Primal Religions

The significance of the human body as a replica of the cosmos—in constant direct communion with the world of nature and possessor of its own wisdom independent of human ratiocination—is an obvious feature of the life of the followers of primal religions. The body paintings seen among the Maori, the Australian Aborigines, Africans, Native Americans, and others are related directly to the awareness of the cosmic significance of the physical body. It must not be forgotten that *ornament* in the original sense meant embellishment with cosmic and divine qualities,[14] and that cosmetics, so trivialized today, derives from the Greek *kosmetikos*, which means "to adorn" while also being related to the term *cosmos* and therefore implies being adorned with cosmic qualities, to become "cosmic-like."

Not only do primal people have a sense of the body different from modern men, but they also "live" in the body in a manner very different from the way those who are the products of an excessively cerebral civilization experience their bodies. If the primal people have not produced a Plotinus, Śankara, or Dante, they have nevertheless produced sacred dances which reveal with equal depth the same metaphysical truths but in the language of the body rather than of the mind. It is enough to hear a traditional African drumbeat and the swaying of human bodies to its rhythms in the forests of Senegal or Nigeria or observe Native American dances to realize directly the meaning of living according to a wisdom incarnated in the body rather than embedded in the mind.

Furthermore, the primal religions all emphasize the direct contact between the body of man and the elements of nature, not in a "naturalistic manner" but in the sense that the body possesses a subtle link to the web of life beyond our ordinary mental understanding. Also, man becomes identified in his body and not only his mind with this or that animal, plant, or mountain considered not simply as a "physical object" in the modern scientific sense, but as the embodiment of a celestial archetype. The headgear worn by various primal peoples and belonging to different animals, as well as names given to certain hero seers such as Sitting Bull, refer to the same reality. The body is seen in the light of a holistic vision of nature that emphasizes at once the link between all beings and the "essential" identification of the symbol and the symbolized, the earthly form and its celestial archetype.

The extended use in primal religions of the body in religious acts and rituals must also be emphasized. In this domain such religions display a philosophy of the body that is central to their perspective but that is also to be found in other religions including Christianity, where despite the ever greater separation of the mind or soul from the body from the seventeenth century onward, the body still continues to play a certain role in rituals. In Islam, which is in a sense a return to the primordial religion, this role is even more central as seen in the five daily prayers (ṣalāh) where the movements of the body are an integral part of the rites complementing the enunciation of verses from the Quran. Thus, as far as religious rites are concerned, the significance of the human bodily form in them, as seen especially in the primal religions, is a constant of human history, appearing in different guises in various religions, but remaining a basic element in rites that aim to integrate the human being and assist him or her in the realization of one's final end, which is salvation, perfection, and ultimately union and deliverance, an end that also includes the reality of the body.

The Egyptian Tradition

The whole of Egyptian cosmology can be said to revolve around the cosmic role of man and the symbolism of his body reflecting various divine qualities. The sacred character of the body was emphasized constantly in the Egyptian religion where the relation of life, death, and resurrection always involved the entire being, including body and soul. Egyptian temples were at once the locus of the presence of the Divinity and the body of cosmic man, as revealed in the brilliant studies of R. A. Schwaller de Lubicz.[15] Careful measurements of the Temple of Luxor permitted him to assert that "The Temple of Luxor is indisputably devoted to the Human Microcosm."[16] Moreover, he showed that the temple corresponded to the human body minus the crown of the skull, which symbolizes the rational faculty as against direct intelligence whose seat is the heart.

> In their temples the ancient Egyptians speak only of the Principles of the World and of the Cosmic Man within terrestrial man (Microcosm). Thus in detaching the crown when the intention so requires, they separate the organ, which is the symbol of the fall from the divine, direct Intelligence into transitory nature.[17]

Schwaller de Lubicz points out the subtle but principal difference between man envisaged as the Perfect Man before what Christianity calls the Fall and Fallen Man who has lost the direct intuitive knowledge possessed by Adam but potentially accessible to all who are willing to undergo the necessary spiritual discipline to open once again the "eye of the heart" within them. He underscores the difference between Egyptian and Greek thought of the classical period, the latter being primarily rationalistic, by pointing precisely to proportions of the body used in the architecture of the two civilizations based upon excluding the crown of the skull (Egyptian) and its inclusion (Greek). He reminds us that "Man without this crown of the skull represents the prenatural Adamic Man as well as Man having surpassed Nature. Between the two is located terrestrial man, undergoing birth and death."[18]

Thus, the Egyptian tradition provides an important but now forgotten lesson of the symbolism of the body of the Perfect or Universal Man (the *al-insān al-kāmil* of Islam), a reality we all carry within ourselves and which we *are* potentially, as it is related to the temple. The human body is itself the temple of the spirit and therefore the model of the sacred architecture of various traditions from Christianity to Hinduism. The importance of this aspect of the body from the religious point of view can hardly be overemphasized. The very experience of the spaces of such edifices of sacred architecture as Chartres, Luxor, or any classical Hindu temple, symbolizing the body of the Perfect Man or in the case of Christianity "God-man" in contrast to "profane space," reveals even today how much of the religious significance of the body has been lost in the modern world thanks to a large extent to its mechanization on the one hand and on the other to the belief in its derivation, not from the Hands of the Divine Artisan, but from some unknown species resembling the chimpanzee.

Hinduism

Of all the surviving religions of the world, none deals so extensively with the human body as far as spiritual practices are concerned as does Hinduism. When one thinks of India what immediately comes to mind are yogis controlling their bodily movements in an extraordinary fashion and performing unbelievable bodily feats even if yoga in its integral meaning is far from being concerned only with the body. One envisages the cosmic dance of Śiva, and naked *sadhus* for whom the whole of space is their garment and who consciously associate their bodies with the cosmos.

And then there is Tantrism and sacred sexuality, which have been especially misunderstood in the West and whose distortion stands out particularly in the sea of erroneous interpretations associated with the pseudo-Hinduism that has become a part of the present-day religious landscape in the West and especially in America. But despite misinterpretations, the common perception that the body is treated in a particularly significant manner in Hinduism, especially as far as techniques of realization are concerned, is true. Both in its theoretical treatises and living practices, Hinduism represents a source of immense richness for the understanding of the religious and spiritual significance of the body even if some of its tenets are specific to itself and cannot be transplanted to other religious climates.

Already in the Chāndogya Upanishad there is reference to the subtle centers of both the heart and the head or *cakras,* which were developed so extensively later in *Kuṇḍalini Yoga.* One reads in this basic sacred text of Hinduism,

One hundred and one are the channels of the heart.
Of these but one extends right up to the head;
Ascend thereby to immortality!
The rest, at thy departing,
Everywhere get lost. [19]

It was in the eighth century A.D. that these teachings became fully elucidated in that form of yoga known as Tantrism. [20] In this well-known school the body is considered to be the manifestation of the Divine. Within Tantrism, in the *Siddha* movement, which dates back to the sixth century A.D., the teaching concerned mostly the *siddha* or spiritually adept who has attained perfection (*siddhi*) through a transubstantiated body. There thus developed probably in the tenth century A.D. schools of "body cultivation" (*kāya-sādhana*) from which grew "forceful yoga" (*Haṭha Yoga*), so popular in the West today. [21] All of these schools concerned themselves especially with the life-force (*prāṇa*), which unites body and soul in a single whole and which is also central to the holistic perspective of Ayurvedic medicine. [22] The tradition of *Kuṇḍalini* was summarized in the sixteenth century in *Satcakranirupana* and made available in the West through the remarkable works of Sir John Woodroffe such as his *Serpent Power, Principles of Tantra, The World as Power,* and *Śakti and Śakta-Essays and Addresses.*

Woodroffe emphasizes the basic tenet of Tantrism, which is that matter, and therefore the body, is also a manifestation of *Śakti* power, that is, the power emanating from the feminine aspect of the Divine Reality. Hence, the body must not be opposed or despised. [23] *Māyā* itself, often translated as "illusion," is in fact the creative, feminine power of the Divine and is related etymologically to the root *mā,* meaning to measure. Far from being mere illusion, it is the power that through "measurement," in the Pythagorean sense of the term, generates this world and constitutes its "substance." Far from being unreal, it is in a sense consciousness veiling itself. [24] "Spirit, Mind and Matter (hence the body) are ultimately one, the two latter being the twin aspects of the Fundamental Substance or Brahman and Its Power or Śakti." [25] The body itself is a form of consciousness "so greatly veiled and the life force is so restrained that we get the appearance of insensibility, inertia, and mere mechanical energy." [26] But this is only an appearance. One can contemplate even in the gross body the aspects of consciousness that underly its reality. [27]

The gross body is only the lowest level of our "bodily reality" that, according to Hinduism, as in other traditions, includes other bodies commencing with the "sutble body," which is the immediate principle of the physical body. It is this body that is realized in *Kuṇḍalini Yoga* through access to the energy centers or *cakras,* which correspond to different points on the physical body, and that possess numerous channels (*nāḍī*) spread over the whole of it. The *cakras* are usually described in symbolic language and are related to various cosmic and divine powers, each possessing a "presiding deity." Through the practice of *Kuṇḍalini* these centers are activated, the goal being the highest *cakra* where the "thousand-petalled lotus" opens and the feminine force of *Kuṇḍalini,* itself the individu-alized form of the cosmic *Śakti,* meets the masculine force of Śiva in a cosmic embrace.[28]

In yoga a distinction is made between *Dhyāna Yoga*—in which ecstasy is attained through mental processes (*kriya-jñāna*) of meditation, the invocation of a *mantra,* and detachment from the world—and *Kuṇḍalini.* "The second stands apart as that portion of *Haṭha Yoga* in which, though intellective processes are not neglected, the creating and sustaining Śakti of the whole body is actually and truly united with the Lord Consciousness. The yogi makes Her introduce him to Her Lord, and enjoys the bliss of union through her."[29] In *Kuṇḍalini* through the very pulse of life in his body, man realizes Universal Life. Therefore, the body is to be respected and revered. To deny it is to deny the Universal or Divine Life that flows through it; it is to deny the unity of spirit, soul, and body and to forget that it is the manifestation of the Divine Feminine Power or Śakti.[30] From the perspec-tive of Tantrism, because the spiritual, the mental, and the physical cannot be separated, all being aspects of the one "all-pervading consciousness," the body must also be considered in spiritual realization and has therefore profound reli-gious significance.[31]

One also finds in the Hindu tradition extensive teachings about the relation between the mind and body, a relation that is itself transformed through spiritual practice. The underlying basis of such practices is the set of correspondences between the body and various cosmic realities and divine beings, these correspon-dences and relations pertaining to various dimensions and aspects of the specifi-cally religious doctrine of the rapport of the body to the order of nature on the one hand and the world of the Spirit on the other.

Here we have had to confine ourselves to only a sample of Hindu teachings about the use of the body and its significance in spiritual realization by way of bringing about recollection of the meaning of the body as "the temple of God." In the context of our present concern it is not necessary to discuss here the operative processes whereby the body is transubstantiated and brought into union with the subtle and cosmic bodies, although, of course, this subject is of great importance from a practical point of view.[32]

Japanese Buddhism

In turning to Buddhism we limit our discussion to Japan because of the emphasis of Japanese Buddhism—at least many of its most important schools—upon the religious significance of the human body, and not because such teachings are absent elsewhere, especially in Tibet and China. Moreover, the religious meaning of the body has permeated much of general Japanese culture with its highly refined and formalized conception of the human form, its movements, and its significance in inner cultivation. But the case of Japan also reflects some of the ideas that characterize the Far East and in fact the Orient in general. These doctrines include the conceptual distinction but ontological unity of mind and body and the fact that this unity must be cultivated through spiritual practice and not be taken simply for granted as a fact of the human condition. There is also the doctrine central to Japanese Buddhism and again found elsewhere in the Orient that wisdom must be developed in both body and mind and that wisdom is "physical" as well as intellectual; hence the significance of meditation involving the body.[33]

Although influenced by Jungian psychology, the Japanese scholar Yasuo Yuasa continues to emphasize the traditional interpretation of such a perspective in which intellectual insights are tested by the bodily actions and deeds of those who claim to possess such insights.[34] In Zen, for example, *satori,* or sudden illumination, is verified by the action of the person who has had such an experience rather than by mental propositions. Modern Western schools of thought concerned with the body, and even those that are interested in the unity of body and mind, study conditions they consider to be general to human beings, without pointing out the need for spiritual development, and fail to consider exceptional cases of realized beings where this unity has been actualized through spiritual practices. In the East, in contrast, it is precisely only the case of the realized beings or spiritual teachers, in whom the unity of mind and body is achieved, that is of central interest. That is why Japanese thought emphasizes so much "achieved body-mind unity," a concept alien for the most part to the Western intellectual tradition, especially to modern thought, which avoids discussing perfected human beings. Today in the West what is of interest is the relation between mental and somatic states in general, whereas Oriental and especially Japanese thought is concerned with how disciplined spiritual practice can lead to body-mind unity in which form and aesthetic elements also play a major role.

This is even seen in medicine. In modern Western medicine the relation between body and mind is taken to be a constant, in contrast to Oriental medicine where the truth that this relation is always changing is fully considered. The most obvious case is that of yogis whose mind can control certain parts of the body over which others have no power and which modern medicine considers to be beyond the control of our conscious will. The body-mind relation is in fact different in different individuals, and therefore the power of healing is not available to all people in the same way. The body is not simply a pure object, biologically defined as claimed by modern medicine; rather, it can be transformed in the process of the realization of unity of spirit, mind, and body, which is the fruit of spiritual effort and disciplined practice.

Yuasa analyzes the thought of two of the leading thinkers of modern Japan who have been concerned with the physical body: Tetsurō Watsuji and Nishida Kitarō. Although these individuals were deeply influenced by modern Western thought, they still held a view of the body more in accord with the traditional Japanese perspective than with the modern one. Watsuji dealt with both ordinary and extraordinary human beings, but even his treatment of the general human types differed from that of Western thinkers.[35] According to him the West emphasizes the mind's temporality against the body's spatiality, whereas the fundamental mode of human existence is spatial in an "in-betweenness" (*aidagara*) that is the "spatial field" (*basho*) in which "we find the interconnected meanings of the life world."[36] Human existence means to exist with the life-*basho* and that implies to exist by virtue of one's body. To exist within the world, therefore, implies the spatial dimension of the body, which bestows a significance upon spatial experience very different from that which issues from the modern idea of a disembodied mind coexisting in a dualistic context with the body.

Nishida Kitarō turns from ordinary to exceptional individuals.[37] He asserts that in ordinary cases of "*basho* vis-à-vis being," intuition is passive and only acting active. Through intuition the mind-body receives data from the outside world and internalizes it. In the case of the realized person, however, the situation becomes reversed. Intellectual intuition is active and integrates experience in such a way that the mind-body acts spontaneously (which Nishida Kitarō calls "passively"). The person simply reacts to the active and creative thrust of the intuition. As to what this intuition is, it corresponds to what traditional doctrines term "superconsciousness," which Yuasa, influenced by modern Western psychology, refers to as "dark consciousness" that acts in "*basho* vis-à-vis nothing." The term "nothing" must, however, be understood here in its traditional Buddhist sense of *śunyāta*.

To clarify this assertion, more needs to be said about dark and bright consciousness. As the latter is identified with ordinary consciousness, the former must be identified with the supernal consciousness and not the unconscious of Freudian and Jungian psychology if it is to conform to the Buddhist perspective. The bright layer of consciousness penetrates the dark layer through the practice of meditation in which breathing plays a central role as the one physiological function that can be controlled willfully. Through breathing, the newly transformed consciousness penetrates into the body, and other routes of interaction are opened that also transform the body and bring about the unity alluded to above. It is this transformation from one mode of consciousness to another that changes the space or *basho* of human existence from one in "being" in the sense of ordinary existing things for the ordinary person to one in nothingness, which means the realization of the void and the attainment of illumination.

In dark consciousness, which, if understood traditionally, is dark because of its intensity of luminosity, the ego of bright consciousness corresponding to the self of Descartes' *cogito* disappears, and the unity of one's being including both mind and body is realized. As to how this is achieved, it comes through personal religious cultivation (*shugyō*) and artistic training (*keiko*). Cultivation is essential to living in such a manner that the bright consciousness imposes a form upon mind-body in such a way that ultimately the dark consciousness can take over. As for artistic training, it derives ultimately from religious cultivation.

All of these teachings expressed by contemporary Japanese thinkers, despite being influenced by modern categories of thought, have their roots in the classical Buddhist tradition of Japan, many of whose masters emphasized the significance of the body from the earliest period. The first great expositor of Buddhism in Japan, Kūkai (A.D. 774–835) had already provided a detailed ten-stage explanation of how dark consciousness replaces bright consciousness and claimed that *Dharmakāya*, or Divine Body of the Buddha, communicates directly with the body of the practitioner of Shingon, which Kūkai founded. Shingon had an erotic dimension resembling *Kuṇḍalini Yoga*, and it is summarized in the famous saying *Sokushinjōbutsu*—that is, "attaining enlightenment in and through this very body."[38] Kūkai described illumination thus:

> If you direct your *mind* to the Exoteric teaching, it will take three *Kalpas* [eons], [but] if you keep your *body* in the Esoteric treasury [of teachings], the lives of the sixteen [the sixteen boddhisattvas in the mandala] is [attainable] instantaneously.[39]

For Kūkai the elements constituting the Universe and including conscious-ness are elements of the Buddha-body. "Mahāvairocana [Budda-body] is the *essentia* of the universe itself, not in the material sense, but in the metaphysical dimension."[40] The six elements, (earth, water, fire, wind, space, and conscious-ness) of Buddhist cosmology are the *samaya* body of Tathāgata, *samaya* meaning the state in which metaphysical reality appears in phenomenal form, so that from the religious point of view the visible universe is the phenomenal form of the Buddha-body itself. In man's ascending the ladder of perfection, the Buddha-nature descends to an ever greater degree into his soul and even his body. In fact, ultimately all beings are interrelated, and the human body *is* the Buddha's body.[41]

It was this early doctrine of the spiritual significance of the body that was to be emphasized by so many later masters such as the thirteenth-century teacher Dōgen, who insisted upon the significance of the role of the body in *zazen* and molting the body-mind in a unity in such a way that self-consciousness would disappear, the deeper unity of mind and body would be achieved, and man would experience in his seated meditation the *satori* of the Buddha. For Dōgen, cultiva-tion is in fact achieved through the body, and he goes so far as to say that in order to become rid of the illusion of self-centeredness, one must realize that the body does not belong to the rational consciousness. The body must be allowed to dominate over the mind so that man can forget himself and become authenticated by all things.[42]

The teachings of Kūkai flowered most of all in the Shingon school of esoteric Buddhism, which continues as an important branch of Buddhism in Japan to this day.[43] According to this school, knowledge of the self results from "the mutual empowerment of the practitioner's microcosmic and macrocosmic activities. This is said to require use of body, speech, and mind, with faith."[44] The secret activity of the body is emphasized as it manifests itself in the *mudras*,[45] or hand gestures, which identify the individual secretly with the Universe. "In this way the human body functions as a living symbol of the macrocosm."[46] It was in allusion to this doctrine that Kūkai wrote, "If the Buddhas are the Dharma Realm, they exist within my body. If I myself am also the Dharma Realm, then I exist within the Buddhas."[47] The *mudra* is considered as a symbol of the Dharma Realm—that is, the Universe—with the help of which one points the body toward Dharma

Realm. The entire body's posture can also be used as symbol of union with the deity.[48]

Likewise in Shingon practice, the *mantras* are related to the body as well as the mind, as one also finds in Sufism. As far as Shingon is concerned,

> In the "worldly practice" the meditator contemplates a Buddha-image placed before him, and visualizes a lotus within the deity on which appears a moon disk. Within this disk appear the syllables of the mantra, emitting light. The practitioner visualizes the syllables individually, seeing their radiance grow stronger, and then visualizes them entering through the crown of the head to circulate throughout his own body, removing all impurities and obscurities.[49]

The exposition of the actual practice of the *mantra* continues by describing the sounds of the *mantra* and then mentions that "the practitioner visualizes mantric phrases moving with his own breath in and out of his body."[50] These phrases leave his mouth to enter the abdomen of the deity, circulate through the breast of the deity, leave by its mouth, and enter the practitioner again through the crown of his head, the movement continuing in an unbroken circle. One hardly needs to add anything to this description to evoke the central role played by the body in Shingon Buddhism dating back to the early teachings of Kūkai.

Before leaving the Japanese world, a word must be said about the "overflow" of the religious significance of the body into Japanese culture in general, as reflected in the key Japanese concept of *hara*. By *hara* "the Japanese understand an all-inclusive general attitude that enables a man to open himself to the power and wholeness of the original life-force and to testify to it by the fulfillment, the meaningfulness, and the mastery displayed in his own life."[51] This mastery involves especially the body whose movements and postures even in everyday life of traditional Japanese culture are controlled and conformed to spiritual principles in a sense similar to what one finds in Islamic *adab,* meaning at once culture, literature, courtesy, *and* bodily comportment, in which how one carries oneself about physically and the discipline of the body in sitting or other positions reflects likewise spiritual principles.[52] In spiritual realization *hara* gains ever-greater significance, and various regions of the body change their meaning and participate in man's transformation. As one observer noted:

> In the new vision the symbolism of the body also takes on a different meaning. The head and the space above it symbolize the mind and its realm as the totality of the Divine Order. The heart and its beating symbolize the soul and its world—the realm where man testifies in love and freedom to Being. The lower body symbolizes Nature working in secret—the realm of the Divine Source. Here, everything concerned with the Greater life is conceived, carried, and born. Here all renewal has its beginning and from here alone it ascends.[53]

The journey of man must begin from where he is here on Earth. It is from Earth and this body and with their aid that mankind must commence the path of spiritual realization. *Hara* is what makes this possible. It integrates the body into the mold of the spiritual life and, being everywhere prevalent in traditional Japanese culture, bestows a sense of the sacredness of the body and its religious significance upon the whole of the traditional culture beyond the confines of the circles actually undergoing spiritual training involving the body. Respect for both the body and its intimate link with the soul, as reflected in the life of the members of traditional societies such as that of Japan, indicates the significance of the religious understanding of the meaning of the body for various traditional collectivities and also by implication and extension the living reality of the religious understanding of the order of nature for ordinary members of traditional societies and those who still live within the matrix of a traditional worldview, even if no longer in a completely traditional society.

CHRISTIANITY

Despite the elipse of the significance of the human body in Western Christian thougbt, and even to a large extent practice, ever since the Renaissance and the Reformation, the Christian tradition itself is very rich in teachings concerning the body to which many recent works by both Catholic and Protestant theologians have been turning. In the Eastern Church, however, this tradition has never been eclipsed; it also continued strongly in Christian Hermeticism as long as the tradition itself was active and is now being resurrected as a consequence of renewal of interest in Christian esotericism including what can broadly be called Christian Hermeticism. It is therefore to these two dimensions of the Christian tradition that we now turn in our attempt to deal briefly with the traditional Christian understanding of the religious and spiritual significance of the physical body.

The use of the body in spiritual practice and its positive significance are both emphasized especially in the mystical school within Orthodoxy called Hesychasm, the name originating from the Greek *hesychia* meaning "quiet."[54] This venerable tradition of contemplative prayer and invocation, which has survived to this day in such centers of Orthodox spirituality as Mt. Athos and other places in Greece and in other Orthodox countries, dates back to the earliest centuries of Christian history. Although some of the early masters such as Evagrius of Ponticum and Origen wrote of prayer as being essentially concerned with the mind and the soul, in the *Macarian Homilies,* attributed traditionally to St. Macarius of Egypt, the body is emphasized along with the mind, and the heart is spoken of as the center of the body. From these beginnings there developed the method of "the prayer of the heart" which became tied to physical exercises, breathing, and particular bodily postures, "head bowed, chin resting on the chest, eyes fixed on the place of the heart."[55] The culmination of these prayers was the mystical experience of the vision of the Uncreated Light of God for which perhaps the greatest of the Byzantine mystics, the eleventh-century St. Symeon, is particularly famous.

The use of the body in prayers was, however, criticized by Barlaam the Calabrian, perhaps influenced by the nominalism prevalent in Europe in the late

Middle Ages. In a manner similar to many later Western Christian theologians he went as far as to consider the use of the body in prayer as being materialistic and compromising the utter transcendence and unknowability of God. It was the great Orthodox theologian St. Gregory of Palamas who arose to respond to Barlaam and to defend Hesychasm and the use of the body in prayer, a question that was, of course, related to the theology of icons and the meaning of the body in the Incarnation itself.

St. Gregory of Palamas, who lived in the fourteenth century, established firmly the Hesychast tradition within the theology of Orthodoxy, and his works became authoritative in later centuries. In *The Triads* Gregory turned directly to the Hesychast method of prayer and the transformation of the body.[56] After quoting biblical verses about the human form being the temple of God, he distinguished clearly between the body itself and fleshly thoughts and sinful desires. Gregory noted:

> This is why we set ourselves against this "law of sin" and drive it out of the body, installing in its place the oversight of the mind, and in this way establishing a law appropriate for each power of the soul, and for every member of the body. . . . He who has purified his body by temperance, who by divine love has made an occasion of virtue from his wishes and desires, who has presented to God a mind purified by prayer, acquires and sees in himself the grace promised to those whose hearts have been purified. . . . So we carry the Father's light in the face of Jesus Christ in earthen vessels, that is, in our bodies, in order to know the glory of the Holy Spirit.[57]

The body then, far from a distraction to the mind, can become the vessel that contains God's presence. Spiritual practice means in fact keeping the mind within the body rather than leaving it in its dispersed state. St. Gregory asked: "Can you not see, then, how essential it is that those who have determined to pay attention to themselves in inner quiet should gather together the mind and enclose it in the body, and especially in that 'body' most interior to the body, which we call the heart?"[58] Only in placing the mind in the body can one in fact attain virtue. That is why one of the masters of Hesychasm was to say, "The hesychast is one who seeks to circumscribe the incorporeal in his body."[59]

Gregory also speaks of the significance of the control of the breath as a means of controlling the mind and preventing it from becoming distracted, leading thereby to "recollection,"[60] concentration of the eye on the breast or navel, and the significance of the postures of the body—all pointing to similarities with techniques of spiritual realization found in yoga and elsewhere but forgotten in the West until quite recently. At the same time St. Gregory of Palamas emphasizes the importance of overcoming the passion of the body, which "has been attached to us as a fellow-worker by God."[61] When the passions are overcome and the mind is full of spiritual joy, it can penetrate into the body, transforming it and making it spiritual so that the body no longer drags the mind downwards but is elevated itself. "Thus it is that the whole man becomes spirit."[62] The spirit thus transmitted to the body "grants to the body also the experience of things divine, and allows it the same blessed experiences as the soul undergoes."[63] The spirit is therefore transmitted not only to the soul but also the body, and the body participates with the soul in the quintessential prayer that transforms the whole being of man.[64] And like the soul the body obeys the Commandments of God, the eye conveying the Mercy of God, the ear attentive to His Commandments, and the tongues, hands, and feet at the service of His Will.

It is of great significance that the teachings of St. Gregory and other masters of Orthodox theology who have dealt with Hesychasm have remained as a living part of Orthodoxy to this day as has the path of Hesychast practice. Such was not to be the case in the West where, despite the presence of certain Catholic and Protestant practices that also emphasize the importance of the body, the mainstream of religious thought not only surrendered the world of nature but also the body to the quantitative science of matter and motion and later evolutionist biology. No wonder then that in the current revival of interest in the spiritual significance of the body in the West, not only are many people turning to yoga, Shingon, and other practices, but also to Orthodoxy and especially the Hesychast tradition. Yet, as already mentioned, the Western tradition is also very rich in sources dealing with the religious and spiritual significance of the body, this being especially true of Christian Hermeticism, both Jewish and Christian Cabala, alchemy, and other major esoteric schools cast aside from the seventeenth century onward.

One of the figures who appeared at the very moment of the demise of the older cosmological perspective and the rise of modern science and who was very much concerned with the esoteric significance of the body was Robert Fludd, the seventeenth-century English scientist, physician, alchemist, astrologer, musician, and also Christian Hermeticist and philosopher. Although not taken seriously by later positivistic scientists and rationalistic philosophers, Fludd's views are a worthy example of Christian Hermetic doctrines concerning the human body in its relation to the macrocosm and its spiritual significance, and they also reveal the type of thinking prevalent among a number of Renaissance thinkers, having roots in the Hermetic tradition, which was integrated into certain dimensions of Christianity earlier and which made possible the "spiritualization of matter" as far as both the human body and the materials of the objects of sacred art were concerned.[65] Fludd considered himself a follower of the "perennial philosophy" in the sense that it was understood in the Renaissance. He presents ideas concerning the human body and its cosmic correspondences that are to be found in many other traditions including, of course, the Jewish and Islamic. At the same time he operated in a still Christian universe and must be understood within the context of Christian esotericism. It is especially in his *Utriusque Cosmi Maioris Scilicet et Minoris Metaphysica, Physica Atque Technica Historia* printed in Oppenheim (Germany) in 1617 that Fludd deals with the human being including the body as a microcosm whose correspondences with the macrocosm he discusses extensively with the aid of a number of illustrations typical of many Renaissance Hermetical works.[66]

Man corresponds to both the ethereal and elemental parts of the macrocosm. The signs of the zodiac corresponding to the fixed stars rule over his whole body, Aries over his head to Pisces over his feet. The world of the elements is also shared by him in the sense that the four humours of his body correspond to the four elements of which everything in the sublunar region was composed according to Aristotelian cosmology. Man's higher faculties, moreover, correspond to the realms above the zodiac, his reason and intellect corresponding to the angelic and archangelic worlds and carrying man to God Himself.

Fludd also analyzed parts of the brain in their relation to the three higher human faculties of reason, mind, and intellect as well as the faculties of memory and motion. Being a physician, he was well acquainted with human anatomy, probably mostly via Andreas Vesalius, and he spoke of the wonders of the body and the function of the various organs. He was also deeply interested in the subtle body of which Paracelsus had also spoken and distinguished it from the gross body, which most people consider as their only body. Fludd saw the gross body as the lowest part of the human being and yet an integral part of it and made in such a way by God as to reflect the cosmos in its details and particulars, including its numerical symbolism. He discussed correspondences not only between the signs of the zodiac and the various organs of the body, but also between the planets and the organs in a manner well known to astrologers.[67]

In discussing the cosmic significance of the human body and its intricacies, Fludd was torn between the concept of the body as a prison and its positive role as the manifestation of Divine Wisdom. In speaking of the biblical story of Jacob's Ladder, which he understood as the symbol of the hierarchy of being, he wrote,

> How amazing it is that things so disparate as the vile body and the immortal spirit should be joined together in man! No less miraculous it is, that God himself should have contracted into corporeality; and that man should be so made that he can participate in eternal beatitude. What joy there is in this world comes alone from the presence of the spirit in the corruptible body.[68]

What one observes in Fludd is the tension between two different understandings of the body that characterizes most of Western religious thought and that was certainly instrumental in allowing the body to be turned so easily to an object of scientific investigation without consideration of the religious understanding of the body as the "temple of God" and the forgetting of the Pauline dictum, "Know ye not that ye are the Temple of the living God?" And yet Fludd represented that dimension of Christian religious thought in the West which displayed great interest in the religious significance of the body, its cosmic correspondences and even metacosmic significance. In contrast to other traditions, however, in the West a thinker such as Fludd was soon expelled from the arena of serious discourse, either scientific or religious, and the way was opened for a rapid demystification of the body and the reduction of its religious significance until the recent revival of interest in its theological importance.

THE CASE OF ISLAM AT ONCE "WESTERN RELIGION" AND BELONGING TO THE NON-WESTERN WORLD

Islam, which is both non-Western and Western in the sense of belonging to the same family of religions as Judaism and Christianity, contains teachings within the matrix of Abrahamic monotheism that are of the utmost importance for the current search in the West to rediscover the religious significance of the human body. In Islam, as in Christianity, there is a firm belief in bodily Resurrection and therefore the participation of the body in our ultimate destiny. The Quranic descriptions of paradise, so often misunderstood in the West as being sensuous and unspiritual, present spiritual realities through sensuous descriptions and emphasize the positive aspect of the body in its relation to the Spirit. Moreover, while rejecting incarnation, Islam constantly emphasizes the unity of the spiritual and the corporeal, and much of Islamic art, especially Sufi poetry, returns constantly to the theme of the spiritualization of the bodily and the sensuous and the corporealization of the spiritual in total opposition to the Cartesian dualism that has pitted the mind or spirit against the body in the West during the past four centuries.[69] The esoteric saying of the Shi'ite Imams *arwāḥunā ajsādunā wa ajsādunā arwāḥunā*, "Our spirits are our bodies and our bodies our spirits"[70] besides having eschatological and alchemical meanings, also points to the ultimate unity of the spirit, soul, and body in accordance with the unitary perspective of Islam.[71]

Throughout Islamic history numerous spiritual authorities have expounded the spiritual meaning of the body on the basis of the Quranic teachings complemented by the *Ḥadīth* and, in the case of Shi'ism, the sayings of the Imams in addition to those of the Prophet. As a first step, they have warned about identifying ourselves with the body considered simply as the seat of passion. Second, they have sought to distinguish the body as locus of God's Wisdom and Presence and as aid in the spiritual life from the veil woven of concupiscense and passion in a manner similar to St. Gregory of Palamas. Third, they have drawn attention to the fact that we are not composed only of body and soul but also of spirit, which transcends their dichotomy and finally integrates them into an ultimate unity. It is in this sense that one must understand the opening verse of the famous *qaṣīdah* of the celebrated twelfth-century Persian Sufi poet Sanā'ī:

مکن در جسم و جان منزل که این دون است وآن والا

قدم زین هر دو بیرون نه، نه اینجا باش و نه آنجا

Do not reside in body or soul, for that is debased and this elevated,
Take a step beyond both, be neither here nor there.[72]

Finally, the Islamic traditional authorities have expounded in various languages the spiritual significance of the body, its role in spiritual realization, its relation to our awareness of ourselves, its symbolism, its rapport with the macrocosmic reality, the hierarchy of bodies including the subtle, the spiritual significance of sexuality,[73] and numerous other doctrines whose full exposition would require many volumes.[74] Both the Sufis and Islamic philosophers have been especially concerned with this issue. Among the Sufis, the Kubrawiyyah of Central Asia are known particularly for their expositions of the physiognomy of the "body of the man of light" and 'Alā' al-Dawlah Simnānī for his identification of various levels of the inner man and his subtle bodies with the "prophets of one's being."[75] Those Sufis who have written about the techniques of *dhikr* or invocation and Sufi sacred dance or *samā'* have also dealt of necessity with the body as an integral part of the being of the person who participates in the work of spiritual transformation.[76]

As for the philosophers, it is especially the later figures such as Mullā Ṣadrā and his followers such as Ḥājjī Mullā Hādī Sabziwārī who have written on the spiritualized body, the subtle body, the body of resurrection, and similar subjects. But these teachings possess earlier precedents. As far as Sufism is concerned, the most elaborate expositions of this theme are to be found in Ibn 'Arabī upon whom in fact later philosophers relied greatly. And among the earlier thinkers of Islam who influenced both the philosophers and certain Sufis, it was the Ikhwān al-Ṣafā' who devoted a great deal of discussion to the various aspects of the body. It is, therefore to the Ikhwān and Ibn 'Arabī that we turn in order to provide some concrete examples of Islamic doctrines concerning the human body.

There are three epistles (*rasā'il*) among the fifty-one comprising the *Rasā'il* ("Epistles") of the Ikhwān al-Ṣafā', or the Brethren of Purity, that deal with the body directly.[77] These include the thirteenth (9th Epistle of Vol. 2) entitled "Concerning the Composition of the Body," the twenty-sixth (12th Epistle of the same volume) "Concerning the Saying of the Sages That Man Is a Microcosm," and the thirty-fourth (3rd Epistle of Vol. 3) "On the Saying of the Sages That the World Is a Macrocosm."[78] The first treatise develops the theme of the body as a house in which the soul dwells, going into great detail in comparing the two. But it is emphasized that the human microcosm is comprised of the house as well as its dweller. Because man must know himself in depth, he must look upon himself from three different perspectives: the body in itself, including its parts and composition; the soul in itself independent of the body; and finally their union together, which comprises the whole of man. The body is therefore included in the understanding of the totality of the human state.[79]

In describing the structure of the body by comparing it to a house with the different materials of which it is made, the function of its parts, and so forth, the Ikhwān also rely extensively upon numerical symbolism, in the Pythagorean sense, and see in this mathematical order the basis of the unity of the body, its link with the macrocosm, and its reflection of the archetypal realities that these numbers symbolize.[80] They also extend the comparison of the body to a city with its separate quarters, spaces allotted for different functions, the various powers dominating it, and the like. Of course, what they have in mind is the traditional city built on the basis of metaphysical and cosmological principles and not the chaotic urban sprawls that go by the name of cities in many parts of the world today.[81] Detailed comparisons are made to evoke the intricate workings of the body made more evident by the realization of their similarities with the complex yet ordered functioning of a traditional city.[82] This type of comparison is of great importance not only in underscoring the religious significance of the body as a result of the symbolic character of traditional cities, but also in revealing the living nexus between humans and their environment in the traditional setting. The neglect of the body as an integral part of the human microcosm, rather than just a machine, is certainly not unconnected to the reduction of the modern urban environment to an inhuman mechanical ambience in which the spirit suffocates and about which even some of the defenders of the secularized view of the body and the cosmos have come to complain of late.

Finally, the Ikhwān extend the circle of analogy and correspondences by comparing the body and the world of nature itself. Thus they write,

> The body itself is like the earth, its bones like mountains, its marrow like mines, the abdomen like the sea, the intestine like rivers, the veins like brooks, the flesh like dust and mud. The hair on the body is like plants, the places where hair grows like fertile soil and where there is no growth like saline earth. From its face to its feet, the body is like a populated city, its back like desolate regions, its front like the east, back west, right the south, left the north. Its breathing is like the wind, words like thunder, shouts like lightening. Its laughter is like the light of noon, its weeping like rain, its sadness like the darkness of night, and its sleep like death as its wakefulness is like life. The days of its childhood are like spring, youth like summer, maturity like autumn, and old age like winter. Its movements and acts are like the movements of the stars and their rotation. Its birth and presence are like ascending constellations and its death and absence like their setting.[83]

In the 3rd Epistle of Volume 3 on the world being a macrocosm (*insān kabīr*, literally "great man" in Arabic), the analogy between man and the cosmos is reversed to show the correspondences between the cosmos and the human microcosm constituted of spirit, soul, and body. In a number of poetic comparisons, the Ikhwān make the reader aware that in a sense we contain the whole of the cosmos within ourselves, and what we find within is also to be found in the world of nature, not only in the materialistic sense mentioned by many modern writers, but most of all in a qualitative sense. Our inner understanding of our bodies is therefore a key for the understanding of the world of nature, as is our comprehension of the rapport between our soul and body, their complementarity and integration into a whole. The Ikhwān bring out the truth that we are related to the stars, as asserted also by many modern eco-theologians, but they insist that this relationship is not only material or, in modern terminology, the simple sharing of chemical elements. Rather, it is a relation based upon the reflection of the same archetypal realities in both the macrocosm and microcosm, demonstrated by the Ikhwān through numerical symbolism, and also through the fact that our total human being, consisting of spirit, soul, and body, is comprised of the same substances that together comprise the macrocosm. We are linked to the world of nature not only through body but also soul and spirit, and the relation among spirit, soul, and body within ourselves is a key for the understanding of the spiritual and religious significance of the order of nature.

In conformity with the Islamic perspective based upon the Quran, which insists so much upon the Wisdom of God reflected in His Creation, especially the human body, the Ikhwān emphasize that the aim of their discussion of the body is precisely to evoke the significance of "the signs of God and His secrets" (*āyāt Allāh wa asrāruh"*),[84] which are to be found in the human body. Throughout the ages, in fact, the sense of wonder in God's Wisdom has been central to the study of the body in the sapiental dimensions of Islamic thought. Likewise, the study of the body has been considered as a key for the understanding of the mysteries contained within it by the Creator, especially the mystery of the heart where the corporeal level of the human state meets the higher levels of man's being. It is to this truth that the eleventh-century religious thinker and Sufi al-Ghazzālī, perhaps the most famous among Islamic theologians, was referring when he wrote:

> The science of the structure of the body is called anatomy: It is a great science, but most men are heedless of it. If any study it, it is only for the purpose of acquiring skill in medicine, and not for the sake of becoming acquainted with the perfection of the power of God. The knowledge of anatomy is the means by which we become acquainted with the animal life: By means of knowledge of animal life, we may acquire a knowledge of the heart, and the knowledge of the heart is a key to the knowledge of God.[85]

Ibn 'Arabī was to develop many of these and other themes dealing with the body, including sexuality, on the deepest level of their significance in several of his writings, especially the monumental *al-Futūhāt al-makkiyyah* ("The Meccan Illuminations"),[86] where allusion to the body and its wisdom including the significance of the body being kneaded of clay (*al-tīn*) by God, as asserted in the Quran, is to be found in various chapters. He also wrote a work entitled *al-Tadbīrāt al-ilāhiyyah fī iṣlāḥ al-mamlakat al-insāniyyah* ("Divine Governings Concerning the Reform of the Human Kingdom") dealing directly with the subject of the spiritual significance of the body.[87] The first chapter of this work is titled "Concerning the Existence of the Vicegerent (*khalīfah*) Who Is the King of the Body," whereas the third chapter is titled "Concerning the Establishment of the City of the Body and Its Elaboration from the Point of View of It Being the Dominion of This Vicegerent."[88] As borne out by their titles, these chapters contain a discussion of both the *khalīfah* who resides in the body and the body as his "residence."[89] Ibn 'Arabī interprets the *khalīfah* as the Evident Guide (*al-imām al-mubīn*), the Throne (*al-'arsh*), and the Mirror of the Truth (*mir'āt al-*

Ḥaqq) as well as the point at the center of the circle of existence. He says "the first being God created was a simple, spiritual substance,"[90] which he identifies with the *khalīfah* residing in the body. The body is therefore the seat of the highest reality created by God in the whole Universe, the *rūḥ* or the Spirit of God Himself which He blew into Adam's body.

Ibn 'Arabī states that once God created the *khalīfah*—that is, man—He built for him a city to reside therein with workers, masters, and government, the totality of which He called the body. This city consists of four pillars corresponding to the four elements and a center that God chose as the residence of the *khalīfah*, this being the heart. The corporeal is itself the locus of that real heart to which the Quran refers in so many varses such as "It is He who sent down the Divine Peace into the hearts of believers" (XLVIII:4) and "Whosoever believes in God, He will guide his heart" (LXIV:11).

Then God created in the highest point of the city, which is the brain, an abode from which the *khalīfah* rules over the entire city, which includes the organs of the body, the senses, and the imagination. In the middle of this elevated realm He built a treasury, which is that of thought, and at the end of it the treasury of memory. He also made the brain the domicile of the vizier of the *khalīfah*, which is none other than reason. Then he created the soul (*nafs*), which derives from the Pedestal (*al-kursī*) just as the Spirit (*al-rūḥ*) has its abode around the Throne (*al-'arsh*), the Throne and the Pedestal, derived from Quranic cosmology, representing levels of the boundary between the Divine and cosmic orders.[91] Ibn 'Arabī also discusses the rapport between the spirit and the soul in man as well as their relation to the body. He mentions the saying of al-Ghazzālī that the body is born of the wedding of the spirit and the soul, thus underlining another basic esoteric doctrine concerning the body, a doctrine according to which the body is an extension of the soul and the soul even has the potential to regenerate its body, although at this juncture of cosmic history God has blocked this creative power of the soul, thus preventing it from manifesting such a power.

Altogether the Islamic teachings about the body emphasize its Divine Origin—that is, being created by God and possessing as finality of the greatest significance for the understanding of the human state. We see in the marvelous functioning of the body the manifestation of God's Wisdom and associate the body with mankind's final end. On the one hand the body is part of that totality, which is man, and must therefore be integrated into the final reality of the human state in eschatological terms. On the other hand the body is a creation of God and has its own rights so that man is responsible for it and cannot claim it as his own independent of the rights of the Creator. As already mentioned, according to a *hadīth* on the Day of Judgment each organ of the human body has its own independence and will bear witness before God concerning the action of the soul of the body in question, while in this world each part of the body praises God separately and in its own way. The relation between the soul and the body is an integral one beyond all external dualities and is so profound as to transcend the accident of death.

THE PRESENT REDISCOVERY OF THE BODY

As mentioned at the beginning of this chapter, the rediscovery of the human body is a major component of the present-day cultural scene in general and religious movements in particular in the West and especially America. One observes the worship of the body as an expression of human animality, as seen in the role played by sports idols, and even the reduction of the body to pure quantity and simply a machine, as exemplified by the constant quest for the breaking of records and the increase of statistics in sports and ever-greater use of machines in body-building. There is also the new "discovery" of the sexuality of the body, resulting in both the glorification of the human form independent of the soul and desacralization of sexuality and its reduction to a purely biological activity divorced from its mystery and sacred character.

Parallel with these developments, which along with the ever-greater gratification of the senses and the hedonism characterizing both the West and also to an ever greater extent the modernized parts of the rest of the globe, there is the religious quest for the rediscovery of the body, which manifests itself in mainstream Christianity, as already mentioned, as well as in so-called New-Age religions that have until now existed mostly in America and northern European countries but are now spreading also into the Catholic nations of Europe such as Spain and France where they are meeting strong opposition from Christian groups.[92] Almost all "New-Age" religions emphasize the significance of the body, the cosmic correspondences between the microcosm and the macrocosm, the holistic attitude toward the mind-body bi-unity with strong interest in holistic medicine, and many other features that are often fragments of traditional teachings. But these are taken out of context and outside a traditional framework. They are therefore deprived of an integral metaphysics and cosmology that alone can provide the light necessary to understand fully such teachings and offer the essential protection from the danger of forces of dispersion and even dissolution accompanying any attempt to deal with doctrines and practices of a sacred origin out of context and in a fragmented fashion. Despite the often nebulous, insubstantial, and even devious and demonic character of much that goes under the name "New-Age spirituality or religion," what is of interest in the present context is that this is the path chosen by many people who often possess good intentions but who lack the discernment necessary to rediscover wholeness and the spiritual significance of the body.

As for mainstream Christianity, this quest to rediscover the religious significance of the body has taken many forms, including the attempt to introduce methods of meditation involving the body and often drawing from Oriental sources so that many devout Christians now speak of Christian Yoga and Christian Zen.[93]

Another current trend is the development of what is now called "body theology," which according to one of its exponents "is nothing more, nothing less than our attempts to reflect on body experience as revelatory of God,"[94] the task of this theology being "critical reflection on our bodily experience as a fundamental realm of the experience of God."[95] But when we inquire further as to what is meant by bodily experience, we discover that it is not the experience of Christ at Calvary nor of a Padre Pio receiving the stigmata nor even a mystic having a vision of God in sensible theophanies, but such ordinary experiences as "the smell of coffee," "the scent of a honeysuckle," or "bodies violated and torn in war." This type of body theology is therefore very different from the type of religious understanding of the body concerned with realized beings as understood in the Orient including Japanese Buddhism, which we have already discussed. And yet the attempt is precisely to rediscover the religious significance of the body in a world that has forgotten the integral metaphysics and the traditional cosmologies within whose context alone can the full religious significance of the body be understood.

Some Christian authors have been aware of the lost tradition of the theology of the body, which they now seek to resuscitate. An example is the Catholic author Benedict Ashley, who has devoted a vast work to both Christian and non-Christian Western traditions of dealing with the theological significance of the body.[96] Although Ashley deals critically with the scientific and modern philosophical understanding of the body, including those of Kant and Marx, the author spends most of his effort in bringing out the salient features of various Christian theologies of the body, especially Christian Platonism and Christian Aristotelianism and their confrontation with seventeenth-century humanism and later schools of thought such as process philosophy. It is in the light of this long tradition, resulting in the eclipse of the traditional Christian teaching, that Ashley speaks of the Christian view of the spiritual body, the glorified body, and the questions of immortality, ending with a discussion of the "Godliness of matter." He states that "the dignity of matter is in its *humility,* its openness to God's creative love, his *agape* of generous giving love, to which it responds with *eros,* love that needs and receives the gift."[97] Circumventing the modern scientific understanding of matter as quantity or "measurable event," Ashley reasserts the older doctrine of matter as the mirror reflecting God's creativity, a doctrine of great importance for a reevaluation of the meaning of the body and its religious significance.

> If matter of the universe "mirrors" God and the human body sums up the universe in this mirroring of God, and if the human intelligence uses this body to know the universe in which it begins to see God, and in seeing its own body as part of the universe begins to know its inner self, then indeed in its inner self it finds the image of God.[98]

The contemporary scene is witness to various attempts to rediscover the religious significance of the body, attempts that have led to results ranging from the sublime to the ridiculous. But whether one considers the rediscovery of authentic Christian traditional doctrines, the recourse taken to veritable Oriental teachings, the amalgamation of residues of esoteric doctrines whose foundations have been forgotten, the resuscitation of elements of religions long dead, or the invention of new cults with the greatest spiritual and psychological dangers for its

followers, one observes everywhere the attempt to rediscover the deeper significance of the human body, of this bridge to the world of enchanted nature and link
to our inner being from which modern man became alienated through the same
process that alienated him from the external world of nature.

THE WISDOM OF THE BODY REDISCOVERED

In summary, what then is the religious significance of the body as understood in
various traditions, some of which we have alluded to above? Before answering this
question, it must first of all be emphasized that there *is* such a thing as a religious
and spiritual knowledge of the body that is independent of whatever scientific
knowledge may be gained of it. The former derives from revelation, intellection,
direct experience, and intimacy, and the latter, as far as modern science is concerned, from the external senses dealing with the body as a purely objective
"thing" to be studied and analyzed as any other "thing." The scientific study of
the human body has taught mankind a great deal about its functioning but has
also veiled much of its reality. It has created a science and a medicine with
amazing achievements and also dangerous shortcomings and has led indirectly to
the blurring of the very significance of life, not to say its sanctity, and the line
separating social engineering, family planning, and the destruction of life. It has
saved many lives while precipitating social and demographic disorders that have
the gravest consequence for the world of nature as well as the moral order that has
ruled over human societies until now, not to speak of economic problems related
to medicine, which have become major issues in highly industrialized societies.

It is not our task here to provide a critique of the truncated understanding of
the body in modern medicine based on reductionism, which finally sees the
human body as a complicated machine and nothing more than that[99] and which is
driving many people to search for alternative forms of healing. We only wish to
state that, although the modern scientific and medical understanding of the body
certainly corresponds to an aspect of its reality, it does not by any means exhaust
its reality. Our bodies, which are the temple of God and participate in the
Resurrection, are not fully revealed on screens used for MRI tests and in X-rays.
The religious and spiritual knowledge of the body is a direct and veritable knowledge, also possible to authenticate "experientially," which remains valid independent of whatever medical or scientific knowledge we gain of the body and which
cannot be repudiated by any totalitarian claims of modern science. Moreover, the
monopolistic claims of a positivistic science (and not the legitimate finding of
modern medical sciences) of the body must be repudiated to provide "a space" for
the reestablishment of the authentic religious and spiritual view of the significance
of the body and the reassertion of elements of various forms of traditional medicine
without apologetics of any kind.[100]

According to the religious understanding of the body, it *is*, to use the
language of theism, the House of God wherein resides the Spirit and in fact, as
Islam states, God's Spirit. It is therefore sacred and participates mysteriously in

the Divine Presence associated with the Spirit. It is also the depository of His Wisdom revealing even on a purely phenomenal and quantitative level the incredible intelligence that makes its functioning possible. The body, in fact, has its own intelligence and speaks its own "mind," reflecting a wisdom before which the response of any human intelligence not dulled by pseudo-knowledge or veiled by pride and the passions can only be wonder and awe at the Wisdom of the Creator. It needs a much greater leap of faith to believe that such a wonder as the body could be the result of simple chance and so-called evolutionary processes than belief in God as its creator or the Tao or *Dharma* as principles that in a nonpersonal way determine the laws of the cosmos and make possible the incredible workings of the body.

The human body also corresponds to the cosmos, not only in the sense of sharing with it the same constituent elements, but in containing in miniature form the whole cosmos. It is by virtue of this correspondence between us as living bodies, soul, and spirit and the cosmos as a whole, which is also alive—having its own "soul" and dominated by the Spirit—that we are able to know the cosmos. We also occupy a special and central position in it because of our being the cosmic totality in miniature form, a replica of the Universe, so that in the deepest sense the body of the cosmos is *our* body. Our intimate contact with the forms of nature around us as well as attraction to the beauty of the stars issues not from simple sentimentality but from an inner *sympatheia,* which relates us to all things, a union of essences or "inner breath" to which Rūmī refers as *hamdamī* and which joins us, in our mind and body bi-unity, to the world about us and finally to the entire cosmos. This link is, however, much greater than simply the presence of iron in our blood and in rocks. It involves the Spirit, which inbreathes our body, and the cosmos and the Divine Archetype, which our bodies reflect, the same supernal realities that are also reflected in the mineral realm but delimited according to the particular level of existence associated with that kingdom, the same holding true also for the plant and animal worlds.

The body is at once a separate reality from the soul and in unity with it. As already mentioned, the total human microcosm is in fact comprised of *spiritus, anima,* and *corpus,* as asserted by the Western tradition and not only the mind and body of the prevailing dualism of modern thought. Moreover, the body is an integral part of our being, not only in this world but also in our ultimate destiny. Herein lies the significance of the doctrine of the Resurrection of the body emphasized especially in Christianity and Islam. The material body conceived by modern science as consisting of molecules and atoms is not only a physical and independent reality. Rather, the body is the result of a descent from above and is reintegrated ultimately into its principle.[101]

Being the locus for the manifestation of the Spirit, the body is also a most important instrument for spiritual practice. The rapport between "mind" and body in fact depends on our spiritual state of awareness and is not constant among all human beings. The body can be experienced as the "crystallization" of the spirit, as in spiritual alchemy where the goal is the spiritualization of the body and corporealization of the spirit.[102] It is the inner rapport between body and spirit and the transformation brought about in the former by the latter that underlies the vast spectrum of phenomena dealing with the incorruptibility of the bodies of saints, as noted by both Christianity and Islam, the special characteristics of the body of the *jivān-mukti* in Hinduism, the attraction of the bodily remains of saints for the faithful, the illumination of the countenance of saintly people, the presence of halos that appear also in the iconography of the sacred art of many religions, even faith healing and many other phenomena too diverse to describe here.

The human body, seen from the point of view of traditional religions, is not the result of accidents or evolutionary changes brought about by chance. Rather, it is a divine creation reflecting certain archetypal realities through its symbolism. Man's erect position, his gait, the separation of the head from the shoulders, the breast, the genital parts representing divine procreativity and, of course, the face all symbolize divine realities. Moreover, the male and female bodies each reflect an aspect of a whole and a divine prototype that causes each sex to view the other as a pole of "divine attraction" and find in bodily union a source of liberation, albeit momentarily, from the confines of our everyday, worldly consciousness.[103] It is enough to understand the symbolism of the human body to comprehend its spiritual origin, why it participates in the Resurrection, and why it constitutes an integral part of our reality as beings living in time but destined for immortality. It also becomes easy to comprehend why in such religions as Christianity, Hinduism, and Buddhism the body of the God-man or *avatāra* in human form plays such a central role not only in everyday religious rites and in sacred art but also esoterically and why it is able to reflect not only cosmic but also metacosmic realities.

Although many traditional schools of thought speak of the hierarchy of spirit, soul, and body within man, there is also a hierarchy of the body itself. Not only are we endowed with a physical body, but also a subtle body, an imaginal body, and even "bodies" on higher planes reaching the Divine Order itself in which it is possible to speak of the Divine Body.[104] We possess *bodies* situated in a hierarchic fashion and corresponding to the various level of the cosmic and metacosmic hierarchy. Through these "bodies" we are connected to all the cosmic realms as, of course, our own existence is stretched into realms beyond the physical body, realms in which we participate not only with our intelligence, mind, and imagination (understood in the traditional sense of *imaginatio* and not as fantasy) but also with our "bodies." And it is these "bodies" that participate along with their lowest projection on the physical plane in our ultimate reintegration *in divinis*.

Finally, the rediscovery of the wisdom of the body and its assertion as authentic knowledge is the key to the reestablishment of the correct rapport with the world of nature and the rediscovery of its sacred quality. As long as we consider the body as a mere machine, it is not possible to take seriously the religious understanding of the order of nature nor to live in harmony with it. To rediscover the body as the theater of Divine Presence and manifestation of Divine Wisdom as well as an aspect of reality that is at once an intimate part of our being and a part of the natural order is to reestablish a bridge between ourselves and the world of nature beyond the merely physical and utilitarian. To rediscover the body as the abode of the Spirit, worthy of Resurrection before the Lord, and intimate companion in the soul's journey in this world, sacred in itself and in the life which permeates it, is to rediscover at the same time the sacredness of nature. It is to reestablish our link with the plants and animals, with the streams, mountains, and the stars. It is to experience the presence of the Spirit in the physical dimension of our existence as well as in the world of nature to which we are linked both physically and spiritually, through our bodies as well as our souls and the Spirit which is reflected in both our bodies as the temples of God and the world of nature as the theater of theophanies and mirror of Divine Creativity.

NOTES

1. In Islamic philosophy this immediate knowledge is called knowledge through presence (al-'ilm al-ḥuḍūrī) in contrast to the knowledge we gain indirectly through concepts, which is called acquired knowledge (al-'ilm al-ḥuṣūlī). This direct knowledge obviously has profound epistemological and philosophical implications that cannot be treated here. See Mehdi Ha'iri Yazdi, *The Principles of Epistemology in Islamic Philosophy: Knowledge by Presence* (Albany: State University of New York Press, 1992).

2. It is interesting to note here that according to Islamic eschatological teachings, on the Day of Judgment each organ of our body will bear witness before God, independent of our will, concerning our good and evil actions.

3. This is the theological basis of the prohibition of suicide, which is considered a major sin in Islam. Not having created our bodies and given it life, we have no right to take life away from it.

4. See especially de La Mettrie's *L'Homme machine,* which wielded much influence in Europe during the eighteenth century.

5. It needs to be mentioned that religion did not give up the body as rapidly as it gave up the cosmos to a science of matter and motion. Opposition to dissection, based on the idea of the sacredness of the human body, continued as did faith healing, prayer as a means of healing, and emphasis upon the role played by a healthy soul in the health of the body. One need only recall that Christian Science belongs to nineteenth-century New England and that even today religious views of the health and sickness of the body, either in opposition or complementary to mainstream medical views, are very much alive in both America and Europe. If anything, they are on the rise.

6. See Barbara Duden, *The Woman Beneath the Skin: A Doctor's Patients in Eighteenth-Century Germany,* trans. Thomas Dunlap (Cambridge, Mass.: Harvard University Press, 1991), which contains a detailed discussion of how the concept of the human body has changed in the West since the eighteenth century. The author is an associate of Ivan Illich, who has led the research during the past two decades on this central issue.

7. Ibid., pp. 1–3.

8. "It involved a degradation of the notion of the self extended into a unique and involuable corporeal volume, to one in which the self only loosely possessed a body." Karl Figlio, "The Historiography of Scientific Medicine: An Invitation to the Human Sciences," *Comparative Studies in Society and History* (Vol. 19, 1977), p. 277.

9. "This [the new medical] gaze turned the body, and with it the patient who possessed it, into a new kind of discrete object." Duden, *Woman Beneath the Skin,* p. 4.

10. This is to a large extent the theme of Duden's book, *Disembodying Women: Perspectives on Pregnancy and the Unborn,* trans. Lee Hoinacki (Cambridge, Mass.: Harvard University Press, 1993).

11. See, for example, David V. Tansley, *Subtle Body: Essence and Shadow* (London: Thames & Hudson, 1977), a popular work that is nevertheless indicative of interest in the subject.

12. The profound link between our conception of our body and the world has been realized by several contemporary thinkers concerned with "the theology of the body." For example, the theologian James B. Nelson writes, "Descartes, whose philosophy so profoundly influenced the body understandings of modern medicine, taught us that the body is essentially a machine. . . . One of the invidious results of this social construction of body meanings is our disconnection from nature. If my body is essentially a complex machine, I am also strongly inclined to view the earth's body mechanistically. I see neither its organic wholeness nor my deep connection to it. I feel essentially 'other than' the earth." Nelson, *Body Theology* (Louisville, Ky.: Westminster, John Knox, 1992), p. 49.

13. This is such a vast subject that one could not do justice to it even in making a judicious summary of each tradition. We have therefore selected certain elements from a number of religions to bring out complementary aspects of the understanding of the body in such a way that together they present at least many of the major aspects of this question and facilitate a better comprehension of the traditional view of the body. It needs to be mentioned that each integral tradition possesses all of the major teachings about the significance of the body despite great formal differences and that within a single tradition there can be various views about the body, some in opposition to others. But here it is always the question of understanding the perspective under consideration and also remembering the ambiguity and ambivalence of the "body" itself as at once veil and receptacle of the spirit.

14. On the traditional meaning of *ornament* see Ananda K. Coomaraswamy, "Ornament," in Roger Lipsey (ed.), *Coomaraswamy, I: Selected Papers: Traditional Art and Symbolism* (Princeton, N.J.: Princeton University Press, 1977), pp. 241ff.

16. See his monumental work *Le Temple de l'homme.* The summary of Schwaller de Lubicz's research in this domain is to be found in *The Temple in Man: Sacred Architecture and the Perfect Man,* trans. Robert and Deborah Lawlor (New York: Inner Traditions International, 1977).

16. Ibid., p. 24.

17. Ibid., p. 52.

18. Ibid., pp. 53–54.

19. R. C. Zaehner, *Hindu Scriptures* (London: Dent & Sons, 1977), p. 126.

20. For the history of the development of the doctrine of the subtle body in Hinduism as well as Buddhism and Tantrism, see John Mann and Lar Short, *The Body of Light,* illustrated by Juan Li (Boston and Tokyo: Charles Tuttle, 1990); for Hinduism see pp. 39ff.

21. On different terms involved in yoga see Georg Feuerstein, *Encyclopedic Dictionary of Yoga* (New York: Paragon House, 1990).

22. It is this doctrine, popularized, that is at the basis of the many works of Deepak Chopra, which are making Ayurvedic medicine popular in America today. See, for example, his *Ageless Body, Timeless Mind: The Quantum Alternative to Growing Old* (New York: Harmony Books, 1993).

23. John Woodroffe, *The World as Power* (Madras: Ganesh, 1974), pp. 161ff, "Power as Matter" (*Bhūta-śakti*).

24. John Woodroffe, *Śakti and Śakta: Essays and Addresses* (Madras: Ganesh, 1975), p. 178.

25. Ibid., p. 186.

26. Ibid., p. 206.

27. "In the four Ātmās which are contemplated in the Citkuṇḍa in the Mūlādhāra Cakra, Ātmā prāṇarūpī represents the vital aspect, Jñānātma the Intelligence aspect, and Antarātmā is that spark of the Paramātmā which inheres in all bodies, and which when spread (Vyāpta) appears as the Bhuta or five forms of sensible matter which go to the making of the gross body. These are all aspects of the one Paramātmā." Ibid., p. 186.

28. For the position of the *cakras* on the gross body and the activation of the *chakras*, see Mann and Short, *The Body of Light*, pp. 50ff. On the *cakras* and *nāḍīs* see also Mircea Eliade, *Yoga: Immortality and Freedom*, trans. Willard Trask (Princeton: Princeton University Press, 1969), pp. 236ff.

29. Woodroffe, *Śakti and Śakta*, p. 438.

30. "To neglect or to deny the needs of the body, to think of it as something not divine, is to neglect and deny the greater life of which it is a part; and to falsify that great doctrine of the unity of all and of the ultimate identity of Matter and Spirit. Governed by such a concept, even the lowliest physical needs take on a cosmic significance. The body is Śakti. Its needs are Śakti's needs; when man enjoys, it is Śakti who enjoys through him. In all he sees and does, it is the Mother who looks and acts. His eyes and hands are Hers. The whole body and all its functions are Her manifestation." Ibid., p. 440.

31. On the Tantric tradition, see also Agehananda Bharati, *The Tantric Tradition* (Westport, Conn.: Greenwood Press, 1965).

32. There are today many practical manuals in various European languages on this subject. But it needs to be added that the actual practice of any spiritual technique, including those making use of the body, must be under the direction of an authentic master. The "do-it-yourself" or "self-realization" kits so easily available on today's commercialized scene can be of great harm and can even lead to psychological imbalance. This is true of all traditional teachings among which Hindu ones seem to suffer perhaps from the greatest degree of illegitimate exploitation and distortion.

33. "Truth is not only a way of thinking about the world; it is a mode of being in the world, part of which includes one's own bodily existence." Yasuo Yuasa, *The Body: Toward an Eastern Mind-Body Theory*, ed. Thomas P. Kasulis; trans. Nagatomo Shigenori and T. P. Kasulis (Albany: State University of New York Press, 1987), p. 2 of the editor's introduction.

34. Ibid., pp. 21ff. The analysis that follows is based upon his exposition, which, however, also includes comparisons with modern Western psychology and philosophy that are not of concern in the present discussion.

35. Ibid., pp. 37ff.

36. Ibid., p. 38.

37. On the analysis of Nishida's thought see ibid., pp. 49ff.

38. Ibid., p. 82. For a detailed account of Kūkai's teachings concerning the body, see pp. 125ff. On Kūkai see also Yoshito S. Hakeda, *Kūkai—Major Works: Translated with an Account of His Life and a Study of His Thought* (New York: Columbia University Press, 1972).

39. From his *Goshōrai mokuroku*, quoted by Yuasa, *The Body*, p. 148.

40, Ibid., p. 150.

41. "This body is my body, the Buddha body, and the bodies of all sentient beings. They are all named the 'body'. . . . *This* body is, no doubt, *that* body. *That* body is, no

doubt, *this* body. The Buddha body is no doubt the bodies of all sentient beings, and the bodies of all sentient beings are no doubt the Buddha body. They are different, but yet identical. They are not different, but yet different." From Kūkai, *Sokushinjōbutsugi,* quoted in Yuasa, *The Body,* p. 156.

42. "To cultivate-authenticate all things by conveying the self [to them] is delusion; for all things to come forward and cultivate-authenticate the self is *satori.* . . . To model yourself after the way of the Buddhas is to model yourself after yourself. To model yourself after yourself is to forget yourself. To forget yourself is to be authenticated by all things. To be authenticated by all things is to effect the molting of body-mind, both yours and others." From *Doge I in Nihon shisō taikei* quoted in Yuasa, *The Body,* p. 116.

43. On the Shingon school see Minoru Kiyota, *Shingon Buddhism: Theory and Practice* (Los Angeles and Tokyo: Buddhist Books International, 1978); and Taikō Yamasaki, *Shingon: Japanese Esoteric Buddhism,* trans. and adapted by Richard and Cynthia Peterson; eds. Yosuyoshi Morimoto and David Kidd (Boston and London: Shambhala, 1988), which discusses the history of the Shingon school as well as its doctrines and practices.

44. Yamasaki, *Shingon,* p. 112.

45. The term *mudra* probably entered Sanskrit from Avestan and originally meant "seal" and entered Japanese from Sanskrit. In Buddhism it came to be used as early as the Gandharan period and signified the hand gestures of the Buddha, each of which possessed a specific meaning. The use of the *mudra* is, of course, also to be found in Hinduism, and its significance is primordial. Many consider it to be the origin of the arts and the alphabet. On the significance of hand gestures in India, see Ananda K. Coomaraswamy, *The Mirror of Gesture: Abhinaya Darpana of Nandi-Kesvara* (New Delhi: Munshiram Manoharlal, 1987).

On Kūkai's theory of *mudras* see David Shaner, *The Body-Mind Experience in Japanese Buddhism: A Phenomenological Study of Kūkai and Dogen* (Albany: State University of New York Press, 1985), especially Chapter 2, "A Phenomenological Description of Bodymind," p. 37.

46. Yamasaki, *Shingon,* p. 112.

47. From his *Discourse on the Visualization of Truth by Mindful Recitation of Mantra,* quoted in Yamasaki, *Shingon,* p. 112.

48. For the description of various *mudras* used in Shingon, see Yamasaki, *Shingon,* pp. 114ff.

49. Ibid., p. 118.

50. Ibid., pp. 118–119.

51. Karlfried Graf von Durkheim, *Hara: The Vital Centre of Man,* trans. Sylvia-Monica von Kospoth in collaboration with Estelle R. Healey (London: Unwin Paperbacks, 1977), p. 12.

52. It is interesting to note that in the modern world and especially in America, while the body is extolled beyond measure, it does not participate in a meaningful way in everyday life in any way resembling the discipline found in the Japanese *Hara* or Islamic *adab.* No greater contrast exists between the body language of a classroom of American students, with notable exceptions, and what one finds in a circle of students in al-Azhar University not to mention adepts in a Zen monastery.

53. von Durkheim, *Hara,* p. 119.

54. On this school and its history see Timothy Ware, *The Orthodox Church* (Hammersmith: Penguin, 1981 and Baltimore: Penguin, 1963), pp. 72ff.

55. Ibid., p. 75.

56. See Gregory of Palamas, *The Triads,* trans. Nicholas Gendle (New York and Toronto: Paulist Press, 1983), p. 41.

57. Ibid., p. 42.

58. Ibid., p. 43.

59. John in his *Ladder of Divine Ascent* quoted by St. Gregory, *The Triads*, p. 45.

60. Much of Hesychasm, including the prayer of the heart, invocation, and recollection resemble Sufism and the practice of *dhikr*, indicating remarkable morphological similarities and not historical influences. See S. H. Nasr, "The Prayer of the Heart in Hesychasm and Sufism," *Greek Orthodox Theological Review* (Vol. 31, nos. 1 and 2, 1986), pp. 195ff.

61. St. Gregory, *The Triads*, p. 48.

62. Ibid., p. 51.

63. Ibid., p. 51.

64. On the participation of the body in quintessential prayer in Hesychasm, see also Timothy Kallistos Ware, *The Power of the Name* (London: Marshall Pickering, 1989). On the whole question of the prayer of the heart in Hesychasm, see Vladimir Lossky, *Theologie mystique de l'église d'Orient* (Paris: Aubier, 1944), especially Chapter 10, pp. 193ff.

65. On Robert Fludd, see Joscelyn Godwin, *Robert Fludd: Hermetic Philosopher and Surveyor of Two Worlds* (Boulder, Colo.: Shambhala, 1979); Allen Debus, *The Chemical Dream of the Renaissance* (Cambridge, Mass.: Harvard University Press, 1969), pp. 20ff; *The English Paracelsians* (London: Oldbourne, 1965; New York: F. Watts, 1966, pp. 104ff; "Robert Fludd," in the *Dictionary of Scientific Biography* (New York: Scribner's 1972), Vol. 5, pp. 47–49; Serge Hutin, *Robert Fludd (1574–1637), alchimiste et philosophe rosicrucien* (Paris: Edition de l'Omnium littéraire, 1971); and Frances A. Yates, *The Rosicrucian Englightenment* (London and Boston: Routledge and Kegan Paul, 1972), pp. 70ff.

66. Many of these illustrations have been reproduced by Godwin in *Robert Fludd,* pp. 68ff.

67. Ibid., pp. 72–73.

68. Quoted by Godwin in *Robert Fludd,* p. 71.

69. The Persian poet Ḥāfiẓ is a supreme example of this principle, his poetry being at once highly spiritual and sensuous. For a more general discussion of this theme see our essay in Rolof Beny and Seyyed Hossein Nasr, *Persia: Bridge of Turquoise* (London: Thames & Hudson; New York: Time and Life, 1975), pp. 23–44.

70. Corbin's, *Spiritual Body and Celestial Earth* (Princeton: Princeton University Press, 1977), Part II, p. 108, deals basically with this issue. Many of the later Islamic philosophers such as Mullā Ṣadrā have also dealt with this saying as a foundation for their exposition of the doctrine of the imaginal world, the subtle body, and many basic features of Islamic eschatology. Islamic sources have also spoken often of the body taking the form of the spirit. See Sachiko Murata, *The Tao of Islam* (Albany: State University of New York Press, 1992), p. 191.

71. Needless to say, traditional Islamic thought, like traditional Christian thought as reflected in so many Christian sources and especially Christian Hermeticism, believes in the tripartite division of the human microcosm into *rūḥ* (*Spiritus*), *nafs* (*anima*), and *jism* (*corpus*) in opposition to the later dualism of body and soul or mind and body.

72. Sanā'ī, *Dīwān*, ed. Mudarris Raḍawī (Tehran: Ibn Sīnā Press, 1341 A. H. Solar/1963), p. 51.

73. As far as sexuality is concerned, the attitudes of Islam and mainstream Western Christianity are quite different. In Christianity sexuality has been traditionally imbued with the sin that has been the consequence of the Fall; hence, the necessity of the sacrament of marriage. In Islam sexuality is itself sacred although strictly governed by the Divine Law

(*al-Sharī'ah*); consequently, Islamic marriage is a contract between the husband and wife on the basis of the law rather than a sacrament. On the differences see Frithjof Schuon, *Christianity/Islam: Essays on Esoteric Ecumenism,* trans. Gustavo Polit (Bloomington, Ind.: World Wisdom Books, 1985), pp. 112–113.

74. Unfortunately, no such work exists as yet in English although Sachiko Murata, *Tao of Islam* (Albany: State University of New York Press, 1992); William Chittick, *The Sufi Path of Knowledge* (Albany: State University of New York Press, 1989); Henry Corbin, *The Man of Light in Iranian Sufism,* (trans. Nancy Pearson (London: Shambala, 1978); and a few other works deal with certain aspects of this vast issue.

75. His views as well as those of Najm al-Dīn Kubrā, Najm al-Dīn Rāzī, and others are treated amply by Corbin in *The Man of Light.*

76. In the Shādhiliyyah Order the works of Ibn 'Atā' Allāh al-Iskandarī are especially significant from this point of view. See, for example, his *Traité sur le nom Allāh,* trans. Maurice Gloton (Paris: Les Deux Océans, 1981). As for the Qādiriyyah, Chishtiyyah, and Naqshbandiyyah Orders, see Mir Valiuddin, *Contemplative Disciplines in Sufism* (London and The Hague: East-West Publications, 1980).

The Sufi dance emphasizes creating harmony between the body and the cosmos in a unitary adoration of God, as seen in the case of the Mawlawī *samā',* and of bringing the Divine Presence right into the body, as seen in the *hadrah* of the Shādhiliyyah Order. On Sufi dance see Jean-Louis Michon, "Sacred Music and Dance," in S. H. Nasr (ed.), *Islamic Spirituality: Manifestations* (New York: Crossroad Publications, 1991), pp. 469ff.

77. On the Ikhwān, a tenth-century group probably of Ismā'īlī background who influenced the Islamic world greatly and their epistles, see Nasr, *An Introduction to Islamic Cosmological Doctrines* (Albany: The State University of New York Press, 1948), pp. 25ff. There is as yet no translation of the whole of the *Rasā'il* into English, the closest in a European language being the translation/cum paraphrasing of F. Dieterici, *Die Philosophie der Araber,* 16 vols. (Leipzig and Berlin: J. C. Heinrichs'sche and Nicolai'schen, 1858–1891). For recent studies of the Ikhwān and partial translations see the bibliography and supplementary bibliography of Nasr, *Introduction to Islamic Doctrines,* pp. 291–293, 306–307.

78. See the *Rasā'il* of Ikhwān al-Safā' (Beirut: Dār Sādir, 1957). The three epistles are to be found in the following pages: Vol. II, pp. 378–395; Vol. II, pp. 456–479; and Vol. III, pp. 212–231.

79. Ibid., p. 379.

80. On the Ikhwān's understanding of numbers, see Nasr, *Introduction to Islamic Doctrines,* pp. 47ff.

81. On the traditional Islamic city see Titus Burckhardt, *Fez-City of Islam* (Cambridge: Islamic Text Society, 1992); and Nadjmoud-Dine Bammate, *Cités d'Islam* (Paris: Arthaud, 1987).

82. "Know then and may God give thee aid, that the body of man was constructed by the Creator like a city. Its anatomical elements resemble stones, bricks, trunks of trees, and metals which enter in the construction of the city. The body is composed of different parts and consists of several biological systems like the quarters of the city and its buildings. The members and organs are connected by diverse joints like the boulevards with respect to the quarters." From Vol. III of the *Rasā'il,* trans. by S. H. Nasr, *Introduction to Islamic Doctrines,* p. 99 (with modification). See also Murata, *The Tao of Islam,* p. 30. We have summarized the views of the Ikhwān concerning the human body in Chapter 4 of our above-cited work entitled "The Microcosm and Its Relation to the Universe," pp. 96ff.

83. Ibid., pp. 101–102.

84. *Rasā'il,* Vol. II, p. 394.

85. Al-Ghazzālī, *Alchemy of Happiness* (Albany: J. Munsell, 1873), pp. 38–39.

86. In Nasr, *Three Muslim Sages* (Delmar, N.Y.: Caravan Books, 1979), Chapter 3, where we have dealt with Ibn 'Arabī, we translated this work as *The Meccan Revelations.* Recently, however, the first partial translation of it has appeared as *Meccan Illuminations.* See Michel Chodkiewicz, (ed.), *Les Illuminations de la Mecque, The Meccan Illuminations* (Paris: Sindbad, 1988). To avoid confusion, we are therefore using here the same title as the one chosen by the translators.

87. Published by Henrik S. Nyberg, *Kleinere Schriffen des Ibn al-'Arabī* (Leiden: E. J. Brill, 1919). For Ibn 'Arabī's view of the body, see also Souad Hakim, "Invocation and Illumination according to Ibn 'Arabī," in Stephen Hirtenstein (ed.), *Foundations of the Spiritual Life according to Ibn 'Arabī—Prayer & Contemplation* (Oxford and San Francisco: Muhyiddin Ibn 'Arabī Society, 1993), pp. 33ff.

88. Nyberg, *Kleinere Schriffen,* pp. 120–128, 131–138, respectively.

89. The content of these chapters has been summarized by Nyberg, *Kleinere Schriffen,* in his German introduction to the work in the section entitled "Der Mensch," pp. 90ff.

90. Ibid., p. 121, of the Arabic text.

91. On the symbolism of the *'arsh* and *kursī* in Islamic cosmology see S. H. Nasr, "The Islamic View of the Universe," in the UNESCO series *Islamic Civilization* (in press).

92. This tension is particularly observable in France. See Jean-luc Porquet, *La France des mutants, Voyage an coeur du Nouvel Age* (Paris: Frammarion, 1994).

93. See, for example, Aelred Graham, *Zen Catholicism: A Suggestion* (New York: Horcourt, Brace, and World, 1963); and the works of Bede Griffiths such as *River of Compassion: A Christian Commentary on the Bhagavad-Gita* (Rockport, Mass.: Element Books, 1990); and William Johnston, *Still Point: Reflections on Zen and Christian Mysticism* (Bronx, N.Y.: Fordham University Press, 1986).

94. Nelson, *Body Theology,* p. 50.

95. Ibid., p. 43.

96. See Benedict Ashley, *Theologies of the Body: Humanist and Christian* (Braintree, Mass.: The Pope John XXIII Medical-Moral Research and Educational Center, 1985).

97. Ibid., p. 697.

98. Ibid., p. 697.

99. It is strange that, in the modern world, man first invents something then identifies himself with his own invention. The Renaissance invented the mechanical clock and developed other kinds of machines, and then philosophers and scientists come along to call man himself a machine as if he had not existed before his invention. During this century the computer has been invented and has invaded modern life. Now, many call the brain a computer, again equating it with man's creation, as if before the invention of the computer the brain was other than what it is now.

100. The works of Ivan Illich have provided ample criticism on the basis of careful scientific investigation of the totalitarian claims of modern medicine. See especially his *Medical Nemesis: The Exploration of Health* (New York: Pantheon Books, 1982).

101. For a masterly explanation of this doctrine in Hinduism, which despite its differences in eschatological doctrines from the Abrahamic religions presents similar teachings concerning the total state of man and the role of the body in the human state, see René Guénon, *Man and His Becoming According to the Vedanta,* trans. Richard C. Nicholson (London: Luzac, 1945).

102. We have not dealt in this work with the doctrines of alchemy and their direct

bearing upon the study of the spiritual significance of the body. We wish only to emphasize here that alchemy as spiritually understood does in fact contain some of the profoundest teachings on the spiritual significance of the body and its transformation into the "body of immortality," to use the imagery of Taoist alchemy, which identified the transformation of metal into gold with the gaining of "bodily immortality." On this subject see Titus Burckhardt, *Alchemy: Science of the Cosmos, Science of the Soul,* trans. William Stoddart (Longmead, U. K.: Shaftesbury, 1981), especially pp. 57ff; also see Joseph Needham (with the collaboration of Lu Gwei-Djen), *Science and Civilization in China,* Vol. 5 (Cambridge: Cambridge University Press, 1974).

103. On the symbolism of the body, see Frithjof Schuon, "The Message of the Human Body," in Schuon, *From the Divine to the Human,* trans. Gustavo Polit and Deborah Lambert (Bloomington, Ind.: World Wisdom Books, 1982), pp. 87ff.

104. This is not only true of Buddhism, which speaks of the *Dharmakāya,* but even Islam where a figure such as Mullā Ṣadrā, while confirming the transcendence of the Divine Essence, states why the Quran speaks of the "Eyes" or "Hands" God and that these refer to the concept of the body in the highest sense of the term in the Divine Order Itself. If the supreme principle of the body had not existed in that Order, God would not have spoken of certain of His Attributes in terms referring to various parts of the body. Mullā Ṣadrā, of course, insisted upon the doctrine of transcendence or *tanzīh* while also emphasizing *tashbīh* or symbolic comparison without which the various parts of the body referred to in the Quran would not possess any meaning. Moreover, Mullā Ṣadrā refuted completely the views of those early sects that identified parts of the body literally with God, thereby attributing anthropomorphic traits to Him against orthodox Islamic teachings. This aspect of Mullā Ṣadrā's teachings is to be found especially in his *Sharḥ uṣūl al-kāfī.*

8

Religion and the Resacralization of Nature

حسن گیتی از جمال حق بود   هستی عالم از او صادر شود
کنه این سرّ را کند ایمان عیان   در پیام لبّ دین افشا شود

Let us cast aside this veil,
Veil of forgetfulness and ignorance.
Let us remember again who we were, are, and shall be,
And what is this world of Nature,
Our complement, our companion, our abode,
Like us the fruit of the fiat lux,
Still bearing within her that morning light,
Light of the dawn of Creation,
And still witness to that wisdom Supreme,
Locus of the Presence of the Realm Divine.
Let us honor her in her sacralized reality,
And not rend her asunder with that voracious aggression,
Which will but erase our life here on Earth,
Divinely ordained as our home of which we are a part.
To honor Nature we must first recall the Source of all,
And seek within, that reality now hidden.
Let us then cast aside the veil,
And remember who we are and what Nature is,
Nature which will have the last word on that final day.
Let us remember and not forget,
Lest we lose the occasion to recollect,
And in destroying Nature our perdition quicken.

We have journeyed long and far through diverse worlds and over many centuries to come to this point of affirmation of the sacred quality of nature, now forgotten and in need of reassertion. Nature needs to be resacralized not by man who has no power to bestow the quality of sacredness upon anything, but through the remembrance of what nature is as theater of Divine Creativity and Presence. Nature has been already sacralized by the Sacred Itself, and its resacralization means more than anything else a transformation within man, who has himself lost his Sacred Center, so as to be able to rediscover the Sacred and consequently to behold again nature's sacred quality. And this remembrance and rediscovery can only be achieved through religion in its traditional forms as the repositories of the Sacred and the means of access to it. Furthermore, such a transformation can only come about through the revival of the religious knowledge of the order of nature, which itself means the undoing of the negative effects of all those processes of transformation of man's image of himself, his thought, and the world about him that have characterized the history of the West during the past five centuries and to which we have alluded in the earlier chapters of this work.

The history of the modern world is witness to the fact that the type of man who negates the Sacred or Heaven in the name of being a purely earthly creature cannot live in equilibrium with the Earth. It is true that the remaining traditional peoples of the world also contribute to the destruction of their environment, but their actions are usually local and most often the consequence of modern inventions and techniques of foreign origin,[1] whereas the modernized regions of the globe are almost totally responsible for the technologies that make the destruction of nature possible on a vast scale, reaching as far as the higher layers of the atmosphere. It is the secularized worldview that reduces nature to a purely material domain cut off from the world of the Spirit to be plundered at will for what is usually called human welfare, but which really means the illusory satisfaction of a never-ending greed without which consumer society would not exist. There is no escaping the fact that the destruction of the natural order on the scale observable around us today was made possible by a worldview that either had denied or marginalized religion as well as weakened and penetrated it from within, as one sees in the West during the past few centuries and most forcefully in recent decades.

There are those individuals who take recourse to a new philosophy in the current sense to save the natural environment,[2] but such philosophies are not sufficiently powerful to sway the human community on a global scale at this moment of acute crisis. Nor do they have access to the Sacred, which alone can enable us to reassert the sacred quality of nature and therefore realize its ultimate value beyond the merely utilitarian. They can certainly help in changing the mental landscape cluttered by so many forms of philosophical agnosticism and nihilism, but they cannot bring about the change in the human condition necessary for even the physical survival of human beings. Only religion and philosophies rooted in religion and intellection are capable of such an undertaking. It might, in fact, be said that, while man lived according to traditional teachings, he was not only at peace with Heaven, but also by virtue of that peace, he lived in harmony with Earth. Modern man, who has eclipsed the religious view of the order of nature and "ghettoized" religion itself, has not only caused the disappearance of numerous plant and animal species and endangered many others, but has nearly caused humans themselves to become an endangered species.

Many people point to the practical and ethical issues involved in the environmental crisis—such as the unbridled greed of present-day society—that have increased by a thousandfold the destruction of the environment, and they have sought solutions only on the practical level. Even if we limit ourselves to the realm of *praxis,* however, one must question what power save external brute force can bring about control over the passionate elements within the souls of human beings so that they will not demand so much materially from the world of nature. There might be a few philosophers for whom such a power might be reason, but for the vast majority of human beings it cannot but be religion. The passions within us are like a dragon now unleashed by modern psychological perspectives for which evil has no meaning. Only the lance of a St. George, the lance symbolizing the power of the Spirit, can slay the dragon. How tragic is the world in which the dragon has slain St. George.[3] The passions thus let loose cannot but destroy the world.

Man is created to seek the Absolute and the Infinite. When the Divine Principle, which is at once absolute and infinite, is denied, the yearning and the search within the human soul nevertheless continue. The result is that, on the one hand, man absolutizes himself or his knowledge of the world in the form of science, and on the other hand he seeks the Infinite in the natural world, which is finite by definition. Rather than contemplating the Infinite in the endless mirrors of the world of Creation that reflect the Divine Attributes and Qualities, man turns to the material world for his infinite thirst, never satisfied with what he has on the material plane, directing an unending source of energy to the natural world, with the result that it transforms the order of nature into the chaos and ugliness we observe so painfully today in so many parts of the globe and which bear the mark of modern man's activities. Spiritual creativity is replaced by inventive genius, which leaves upon the environment the traces of its unending tinkering with nature and production of gadgets and products in the form of ever-increasing refuse and waste and of the creation of ever-growing wastelands with which the natural environment can barely cope.

Furthermore, this misdirecting of the yearning of the soul for the Infinite to the material world, and the change of the direction of the arrow of progress from that of the soul journeying to God to purely material progress, is made so much more lethal by the absolutization of terrestrial man with its consequent anthropomorphism; man and only man is now the measure of all things.[4] In such a situation it is only traditional religions, with their roots sunk in the Divine and their means of directing the soul to its ultimate goal, that can provide a real cure for the illusion of a centerless soul seeking the Infinite in the multiplicity of nature and the Absolute in its circumferential mode of existence. Only religion can discipline the soul to live more ascetically, to accept the virtue of simple living and frugality as ornaments of the soul, and to see such sins as greed for exactly what they are. And only religion, or traditional philosophies drawn from spiritual, metaphysical, and religious sources, can reveal the relativity of man in light of the Divine Principle and not according to that type of relativism so prevalent in

the modern world, which seeks to make relative the Absolute and Its manifestations in religion in the name of the theory that all is relative, except of course that
human judgment which claims that all is relative. Unless man realizes his relativity in light of the Absolute, he is bound to absolutize himself and his opinions
no matter how hard he tries to demonstrate an unintelligent humility vis-à-vis the
animals and plants or nebulae and molecules.

Religion thus is essential on the practical plane to redirect and transform the
activities of man and bestow spiritual significance to the rapport between man and
the natural order. This is why so many contemporary religious thinkers concerned
with the environmental crisis have turned to the issue of environmental ethics, as
we discussed earlier in this work.[5] Yet religious ethics, although necessary, is not
sufficient. What is needed in addition is the reassertion of the religious understanding of the order of nature, which involves knowledge and not only ethics. A
religious ethics cannot cohabit with a view of the order of nature that radically
denies the very premises of religion and that claims for itself a monopoly of the
knowledge of the order of nature, at least any knowledge that is significant and is
accepted by society as "science." The ground must be cleared and a space created
for the reassertion of the religious understanding of the order of nature as authentic knowledge, without denying other modes of knowing nature as long as the
latter are kept within the confines imposed upon them by the limitations inherent
in their premises, epistemologies, and what one would call their boundary conditions, all of which are encompassed in their paradigms.

To use a contemporary term, somewhat overused and maligned, there is need
of a paradigm shift, but in the Platonic and not Kuhnian sense of paradigm. Such
a shift would make available a worldview where the religious understanding of the
order of nature in the traditional sense would be accepted as authentic along with
sciences based on particular dimensions of nature, such as the quantitative, all
within a metaphysical whole where in fact each mode of knowledge would be
accepted as part of a hierarchy leading to the highest science, which is the science
of the Real as such, or *scientia sacra*.[6] It is not for us here to talk of the constituents
of such a paradigm, which could not but come from the resuscitation of traditional doctrines, nor of the integration of modern science into a universal metaphysical framework, nor even of the future rapport between religion and science.
Our aim here is to assert categorically the necessity of the acceptance of the
religious view of the order of nature on the level of knowledge, and hence a sacred
science rooted in the metaphysical perspective, if a religious ethics involving
nature is to have any efficacy. It is also to emphasize the necessity of clearing the
ground and opening up an intellectual "space" within the contemporary
worldview for the religious knowledge in question to find an abode and to begin to
be taken as real and as serious knowledge corresponding to an objective reality
rather than being relegated to the subjective, the marginal, and even the occult,
with all the dangers that such a situation involves.

UNDOING THE EFFECTS OF THE FALL OF MAN

In the sacred rite of pilgrimage (al-ḥajj) to the house of God in Makkah, Muslim pilgrims circumambulate around the Kaaba seven times in a counterclockwise direction opposed to the movement of the arrow of time. The deepest meaning of this aspect of the rite is the undoing of the effects of the Fall of Man and his reintegration into the Edenic state by virtue of which his imperfections and sins are overcome and he regains his state of original purity.[7] One might say figuratively that a similar process has to be undertaken intellectually, mentally, and psychologically in order to reassert seriously the religious knowledge of the order of nature. The processes, both philosophical and scientific, that led not only to the secularization of the cosmos, but also the monopoly of such a view in the mainstream of modern thought in the West, have to be reversed. Contemporary man must be able to reabsorb whatever is positive in the later phases of his mental development, such as certain types of empirical knowledge of nature, back to the origin or to the metaphysical dimension of the traditional religious universe in which the domain of nature still possesses a sacred meaning.

Man must have the negative elements of his immediate past, which are veritable sins, in the theological sense, against the Spirit expiated through the very process of return and reintegration similar to the case of the pilgrim. Moreover, in the same way that the reintegration of the pilgrim into the Edenic state does not imply the loss of his memory or personality, such a return by contemporary thought certainly does not mean forgetting what has been learned, as long as it is real knowledge and not conjecture parading as science. The question is one of integration of the sciences into a metaphysical perspective and, furthermore, the reestablishment of a knowledge of nature rooted in traditional religions, as discussed in Chapter 2, as well as the rediscovery of an aspect of nature as reality to which this knowledge corresponds. Only in this way can the religious understanding of the order of nature be reasserted seriously and a reality to which religious ethics corresponds be rediscovered. Anything short of that goal fails to do justice to the meaning of the religious understanding of nature and overlooks the dichotomy between pious assertions of religious ethics such as the sanctity of life and a completely dominant "science of life" for which the very term "sanctity" is meaningless. It also fails to come face-to-face with what underlies the environmental crisis and the forces threatening human existence on Earth.

Even if such a "space" were to be opened up and the religious view of the order of nature reasserted, it would of course have to be of necessity on a scale global in its intellectual outlook, although local in its practical applications. The integral teachings of the Western religious tradition must be rediscovered and reformulated beyond the distortions and limitations imposed upon them by five centuries of secularist sciences and philosophies. Moreover, the view of other traditions must also be expounded both for the followers of each tradition and for a global religious perspective on the order of nature that would be able to confront in a united voice those who deny any meaning, purpose, or sacred quality to nature. One might say that the formulation of such a global religious perspective on nature, to which this present study is itself devoted, complements the formulation of the doctrine of the Divine Principle in a universal perspective and across religious frontiers to which those who have spoken of "the transcendent unity of religions" or "global theology" have devoted their efforts.[8]

In the same way that there are many heavens, each belonging to a particular religious cosmos, and yet a single Heaven of which each of the particular heavens is a reflection and yet in essence that Heaven Itself, so are there many earths and forms of religious knowledge of these earths. But there is a perspective that encompasses many salient features of those diverse forms of religious knowledge, despite their differences, leading to a knowledge of *the* Earth that would be recognizable by the various religious traditions at least in their sapiental dimensions if not in their theological, social, and juridical formulations. It is in the light of this knowledge, drawn from various traditions—which can in fact enrich other traditions in many ways today—that we must seek to reassert the sacred quality of nature and to speak of its resacralization.

It is also in the light of this knowledge that we must appraise whatever significance a particular discovery in physics or some other science might have beyond itself. Modern science *qua* modern science cannot deal with the philosophical and metaphysical implications of its discoveries. And if individual scientists do so, they make such interpretations as philosophers, metaphysicians, and theologians. This assertion remains true as long as modern science functions within its present paradigm. What will happen if there is a change of paradigm is another matter. In any case, such remarkable discoveries as Bell's theorem cannot themselves lead to metaphysical and theological truths but have metaphysical implications that could only be comprehended if the religious knowledge of the cosmos and the order of nature as understood in this text were to be accepted as a legitimate mode of knowledge of nature.[9] In any case such a knowledge is of the utmost significance for the rediscovery of the sacred quality of nature and the reestablishment of a rapport based on harmony between man and nature. It is also crucial for creating a new understanding between religion and science, and, with the help of traditional metaphysics, for integrating modern science into a hierarchy of knowledge wherein it could function without claims of exclusivity and without disrupting the essential relation between man and the cosmos, which possesses a reality beyond the realm of pure quantity and even beyond the empirical and the rational.[10]

THE RELIGIOUS COSMOS

Beyond the diverse cosmologies and understandings of the order of nature in various traditional religions there stands, as already mentioned, a religious view of the cosmos that reveals remarkable universality if one goes beyond the world of forms and the external to seek the inner meaning of myths and symbols in different religious universes. First, it needs to be remembered that a religion not only addresses a human collectivity; it also creates a cosmic ambience, a sector of the Universe that shares in the religious realities in question. When a devout Muslim sees the crescent moon at the beginning of the lunar month, he closes his eyes and offers a prayer to God and sees in the moon the symbol of the Islamic revelation and, more specifically, the Prophet, who might be said to possess a "lunar" nature. [11] Buddhists hear the *dharma* in the flow of rivers, and for Hindus the Ganges *is* the river flowing from paradise, the river which, being holy, purifies those who bathe in it. For Judaism and Christianity there is such a thing as the Holy Land, and Jerusalem is cosmically significant precisely because of its nexus to religious events of crucial importance associated with it. Moreover, for traditional Jews and Christians this significance is not only historical or imposed by human memory, but cosmic. Mt. Sinai is not just any mountain that some human being considers to be important because of the Mosaic revelation. It is important in itself within the universe of Abrahamic monotheisms. Likewise, Spider Rock in Canyon de Chelly, in Arizona, is not only considered to be sacred by the Navajos; it *is* sacred within their religious cosmos.

This truth is brought out in the cosmological schemes of many traditions, from the Tibetan Buddhist, to the Christian, to the Islamic. The various Buddhas *do* perform many functions within the Buddhist cosmos. Christ and the angels *are* real within the Christian universe, not only subjectively but also objectively. And the *Mi'rāj* or Nocturnal ascent of the Prophet, during which he ascended to Heaven from Jerusalem not only in spirit or soul but also bodily (*jismānī*), *did* take place objectively within a cosmos that is Islamic for those who participate in the Islamic revelation. One could multiply examples a thousandfold, especially among primal peoples such as the Australian Aborigines, the tribes of the American Plains, or Meso-Americans, but there is no need to do so here. What is important is to become aware of the universality of this principle and its *reality* from the point of view of the religious understanding of the order of nature. It is precisely this reality that is now denied in that sector of humanity affected by secularism, scientism, and modernism because in that world the religious knowledge of the order has been deprived of any legitimacy, and the realities forming the object of this knowledge have been either denied or subjectivized and psychologized. A purely quantitative science of nature could obviously not do otherwise. Nor could those philosophers and even theologians who accept that kind of science as the only legitimate knowledge of nature. And yet the religious view is based upon a truth that cannot be denied once its metaphysical significance is fully understood.

According to the metaphysical teachings of various traditions and the cosmologies which are their applications to the cosmic sector, the Divine Principle is not only the Origin of the cosmos but also the Source of the religion that links humanity to both the Divine Principle and the order of nature. Some religious traditions such as Confucianism, Taoism, and Buddhism do not concern themselves with the creative and generating function of the Divine Principle as do the Abrahamic monotheisms and Hinduism. But in both types of faiths, there is the Supreme Principle that is the Origin of both man and the cosmos, even if "Origin" is not understood in a cosmogonic sense in some cases. More particularly, each religion is the manifestation of a Divine Word, a Logos, or demiurgic principle that, within the religious cosmos created by a particular revelation or "heavenly dispensation," is the direct source of the religion in question as well as the immediate "ruler" of the cosmos within which that religion functions.

To use the terminology of the Divine Word or Logos common to the Abrahamic religions, it can be stated on the one hand that God said "Be (*kun*) [Quran; XXXVI: 81] and there was" or "All things were made by him [the Word or Logos]; and without him was not any thing made that was made" (John 1:3). On the other hand this Word through which God created the world is in Islam the Quran, one of whose names is *Kalām Allāh,* the Word of God, and in Christianity Christ. The source of the very existence of the cosmos and the origin of revelation are therefore the same in each religion. And it is through revelation that the inward nexus between the follower of a particular faith and the "cosmic sector" in which that faith dominates is revealed.

Within each religious universe, the Logos manifests the Divine Reality as well as God's Will and His Grace to the realm of Creation along with the world of men and enables human beings to gain an inner understanding of and a sympathy (in the original Latin sense of *sympatheia*) for the realm of nature. As mentioned in the previous chapter, human beings are composed of spirit, soul, and body, all of which are permeated by the grace of the religion in question, and they participate in the divine laws promulgated by that religion. The cosmos is also composed of corresponding levels of existence of which only the most outward, corresponding to our bodies, is discoverable by relying solely upon the external senses. Moreover, in the same way that our body is related to our psyche and soul and our soul to the spirit at the center of our being, even if most of us remain unaware of this link, the external body of the cosmos, permeated like the microcosm by the light and grace of God emanating through the Logos, is also linked to the higher levels of cosmic existence, to what traditional cosmologies describe as "souls of the spheres," "nature spirits," angels, the World Soul, the cosmic intelligences, and so forth.

Of course, as a result of man's present spiritual imperfection and fall from an original state of purity, he has lost direct access to the Spirit within, to the inner kingdom that Christ asks his followers to seek before everything else. Likewise, the world of nature has been darkened and in a sense participates in man's fall and what Christian theology calls Original Sin. But not having committed the sin of man, nature is more innocent and therefore still preserves more than fallen and imperfect man something of its original and paradisal perfection now finally being destroyed by a humanity that does not even show interest in the meaning of sin, much less man's committing of it and responsibility for the consequences of his actions.

In any case the reality of the levels of both macrocosmic and microcosmic reality remains, and it is this reality that provides the ontological structure for the religious understanding of the order of nature. Within the religious universe, man is related to the world of nature not only through physical elements or even psychological resonances but through the Logos and ultimately God. Each plant has a significance not only in its physical appearance but in its subtle reality and ultimately in reflecting and being a symbol of a divine archetype, residing immutbly in the Divine Intellect, with which it is identified essentially here and now.[12] A person who has reached the center of his own being sees in every phenomenon of nature, in the crystals, plants, and animals, in the mountains and skies and the seas, realities that are not exhausted by the "merely" physical but that reveal themselves through the physical, realities that also reside within the being of man and come from the Logos and ultimately God. Man is thus united with nature in body, soul, and spirit and, in the final end, in God. On a more concrete and immediate plane he is united to the cosmos around him by the Logos who is the immediate origin of the rites and symbols governing his life and the source of the life of the world about him as well as its laws and its ultimate meaning.

Furthermore, precisely because man possesses a consciousness and intelligence capable of knowing the Absolute and reflects the Divine in a central manner as a theomorphic being, he is also the channel of grace, or what Islam calls *barakah*, for the world of nature. Nature is governed not by man, despite his claims, but by God. And yet it is given to man to act as the bridge (*pontifex*) between Heaven and Earth and as channel of grace and light for the natural order. That is why his responsibility is so grave. He is given the power to rule over nature but also the capability to destroy it or bring corruption upon the face of the Earth, against which the Quran speaks in many passages.[13] His actions have a cosmic consequence whether he desires it or not, and his abdication from the role of pontifical man to accept the role of Promethean man, in the sense discussed in Chapter 5, cannot but affect the order of nature in the most negative way. The denial of the role of the Logos in the cosmos and rejection of a knowledge derived ultimately from the Logos but concerning the cosmos cannot but have the direst consequences for the order of nature and, of course, for man himself, as contemporary history demonstrates so clearly.

RELIGIOUS RITES AND COSMIC HARMONY

One of the consequences of the metaphysical doctrine of the meaning of the cosmos and man's role in the religious universe in which he lives is confirmation of the rapport between sacred rites and harmony of the order of nature. As a result of the eclipse of the religious view of nature in the modern world, the very idea that sacred rites might be related to cosmic and natural events is considered preposterous or at best quaint, to be studied by cultural anthropologists as relics of an "animistic" past or made the subject of jokes and caricatures, as in the case of the Native American rain dance. That prayers might actually affect weather conditions, or religious rites influence the course of some natural calamity, are simply not a part of the modernist and scientific worldview even if many individuals today, who still possess faith, continue to pray for a sunny day when they want to plant the fields or climb a mountain. What is denied in the prevalent modern perspective is in fact one of the essential elements of the religious view of the order of nature that is worthy of the most serious consideration and that has been and remains crucial in many different religious universes.

One can draw from numerous religious worlds to illustrate this link between sacred rites and the harmony and functioning of nature, a link that is the logical consequence of the religious view based on the instrumentality of the Logos in the genesis and ordering of the world of nature on the one hand and revelation from which sacred rites, as divinely ordained institutions, originate on the other. In fact, all the religious traditions, whose teachings concerning nature were mentioned to some extent in Chapter 2, as well as those not discussed in this book, provide many illustrations of the principle under discussion, namely the link between sacred rites and the order of nature, based on the effect that such rites have on the traditional element ether, which is the principle of the elements constituting the physical realm.

By way of example let us limit ourselves to the Native American religions, to Confucianism, and to Islam without ever losing sight of the universality of the principle involved. Nearly all the Native American rites include elements of the natural order and are based on an inner link with the very processes of nature, from rain dances to sand paintings used to cure illnesses, to the supreme rite of the sun dance. In the latter rite practiced mostly by the Native Americans of the Great Plains, a pole that is a sacred tree is chosen to which the individual ties himself by means of a rope and then performs a grueling three-day rite of fasting, prayer, and dance to and from the pole, which symbolizes the cosmic axis above which stands the Sun, the center and pole of our natural world and at the same time itself the symbol of the Divine Principle.[14] This ritual creates an "inner identity" between the performer of the rite and the center, which is also *the* Center as a result of which the whole ambience is blessed and the grace of the Center emanates throughout the periphery rejuvenating the natural order, as emphasized especially by the Cheyenne. In fact, during the third and last day of the sun dance the power issuing forth from the sacred tree as a result of the sacred rite brings about many healings.

According to an eyewitness account of a sun dance directed by a Crow medicine man, Thomas Yellowtail, who died in 1993, "The third day is the day of cures. From morning onwards, a crowd of people, including entire families of white farmers, come to the Sun Dance site and patiently wait for Yellowtail to let them share in the healing power with which the sacred tree is as it were filled as a result of the rite of which it has been a center."[15] Such a rite having at once microcosmic and macrocosmic consequences, affecting at the deepest level both man and the world of nature about him, is typical of those sacred rites of the primal religious that have been preserved intact and have not decayed into sorcery, which must be strictly distinguished from sacred rituals of authentic religions, whatever might be the "efficacy" of such deviant practices.

In Confucianism one observes the same rapport between human rituals and the cosmic order, as can be observed in so many aspects of the life of traditional China, such as the cosmological symbolism of the *Ming-Tang* and the movement of the emperor, the link between Heaven and Earth, through various parts of this replica of the cosmos, which was the *Ming-Tang,* in conformity with the order of the seasons and the harmony of nature. The structure of the *Ming-Tang* itself recapitulated that of the empire, which was divided into nine provinces just as the *Ming-Tang* was divided into nine units.[16] In the Chinese perspective, including Taoism, which emphasizes even more than Confucianism the inner link between man and nature, man is considered as the teleological completion of the natural order, and his actions, especially rituals, help to bring about cosmic perfection. "Man is Nature's complement in the creation of a perfect universe. It is in this sense that the artifice of ritual society can be viewed as an extension of natural principle."[17] According to Wang Chih, "Heaven and earth are the source of life. Ritual and propriety are the source of order, the *Chun-Tzu* [famous Confucian source] is the source of ritual and propriety. To practice these, pene-trate their unity, multiply them, and love them to the full is the source of becoming a *Chun-tzu,* and *Chun-tzu* orders (*li*) heaven and earth."[18] *Hsün-tzu* asserts that the sage, by penetrating the spiritual world, forms a trinity with Heaven and Earth and therefore affects the natural world around him. Ritual is an extension of the principles of the natural world and a cause for its inner transfor-mation. Confucian rituals not only bring order to society but also create harmony with the order of nature and also man to both contribute to and benefit from the cosmic order.

Turning to the very different world of Islam, we see that, according to a saying of the Prophet or *ḥadīth,* God placed the Earth for Muslims as a mosque.[19] That is why a Muslim can pray anywhere in virgin nature as long as it is not ritually defiled, and that is why the space of the mosque, built in urban settings already removed from nature, is an extension of the space of virgin nature.[20] The rite of the daily prayers (*ṣalāh*) is therefore closely bound to the Earth, which has been designated by God as the ground upon which the most sacred rite of the religion is performed. As for the times of the prayers, they are astronomically determined and correspond to cosmic moments. The prayers not only rejuvenate the body and soul of man but also emphasize the harmony of human life with the rhythms of nature and fortify and complement nature's harmony.

It is very significant that the central part of the daily prayers is the recitation of the opening chapter of the Quran or *al-Fātiḥah,* which is comprised of verses whose verb is in the plural rather than the singular form. Men and women stand before God directly on the Earth sanctified specifically for Muslim prayers and utter such verses as "Thee do *we* worship," "In Thee do *we* take refuge," and "Lead *us* unto the Straight Path." They are therefore praying not only for themselves but for the whole of Creation. On the deepest level in the daily prayers man prays as the *khalīfat Allāh* or the vicegerent of God on behalf of not only humanity but the whole of the natural order for which he was placed by God on Earth as vicegerent. There is definitely a dimension of the prayers involving the natural ambience around man and which one "feels" concretely upon performing the prayers.

The same cosmic rapport is to be seen in the rite of the pilgrimage or *ḥajj* to Makkah, the center of the Islamic world, the city that is also the earthly intersec-tion of the *axis mundi,* and those circumambulating around the Kaaba emulate the circumambulation of the angels around the Divine Throne (al-'arsh).[21] There is definitely a cosmic dimension to this rite, which has been elaborated in many traditional sources. Furthermore, the rapport between sacred rites and the harmony and order of nature is so much emphasized in Islam that, according to a ḥadīth, the world will not come to an end as long as there are people on Earth who remember the Name of God and continue to invoke "Allah, Allah," a practice central to the rituals of Sufism. In Islamic esoteric teachings there are also elaborations concerning the spiritual hierarchy that sustains the visible Universe and the power of walāyah, usually translated an "sanctity" in Sufism, which governs the world invisibly, a power without which the order of nature would turn into chaos and the world would flounder.[22] Even on the popular level, throughout the Islamic world is the belief that God places on the Earth at all times saintly men who through their presence and the rituals and prayers that they perform preserve the order of nature, and that the rites of Islam, which such beings perform at the highest level, and with the greatest perfection, are necessary not only to uphold social order but also to enable human beings to live in harmony with nature and to preserve the harmony of nature itself.

According to the text of the Quran, all creatures in fact share in man's prayers and praise God, for it states, "The seven Heavens and Earth and all beings therein celebrate His praise, and there is not a thing but hymneth His praise" (XVII:44, Pickthall translation slightly modified). This means that man's prayers, celebration of God's praise and other ritual practices, whose final goal is the remembrance of God, form parts of the chorus of the praise of God by the whole of Creation and a melody in the harmony of "voices" celebrating the Divine, a celebration which on the deepest level is the very substance of all beings.[23] The saint hears the invocation of nature wherever he turns. As the Turkish Sufi poet Yunus Emre sings in one of the most famous poems of the Turkish language about the paradisal reality which virgin nature sill reflects and manifests,

> The rivers all in Paradise
> Flow with the word Allah, Allah,
> And ev'ry longing nightingale
> He sings and sings Allah, Allah.[24]

Rites and rituals performed by human beings, therefore, fulfill part of the rites of the whole of Creation, and the refusal by human beings to perform rites destroys the harmony of the natural order. Moreover, to destroy nature and cause the extinction of plants and animals as a result of human ignorance is to murder God's worshippers and silence the voice of the prayer of creatures to the Divine Throne. It is to seek to negate the purpose for which the world of nature was created, for, according to a famous ḥadīth, God created the world so that He would be known, and the prayers of natural creatures are none other than their knowing God. It means ultimately that, to destroy nature, is to destroy both the humanity committing such a sin and the natural ambience of such a humanity.

In the religious view of nature in general there is an economy of the cosmic as well as human orders comprising the spiritual, psychic, and physical realms.

Rituals are part and parcel of this economy, making possible the flow of grace, the reestablishment of correspondences, and the revival of preestablished harmonies. Human rites play a central role in the preserving of this harmony on the terrestrial realm where men occupy a central position without being allowed to usurp the right of absoluteness, which belongs to God or the Absolute alone. When human beings refuse to perform sacred rites, a central element of the terrestrial harmony is destroyed and human beings become "worthless" and "useless" as far as the ultimate purpose of Creation is concerned, which is to bear witness to God, to love Him, and ultimately to know Him.

The traditional respect for the human state "so difficult to attain," as the Buddhists assert, and the encouragement to have a family and bring new human beings into the world, as emphasized by other faiths such as Judaism and Islam, are both based on the central thesis that, through the human state, the ultimate purpose of Creation, in which Creation itself plays a central role, can be attained. And this ultimate purpose is itself made possible through the following of religious laws and injunctions, at the heart of which is ritual. That is why in the Islamic world there is a folk saying that the virtue of having a child is to add another person to the world who asserts "There is no divinity but God" (*Lā ilāha illa'Llāh*) and that the value of human life is precisely in being able to fulfill this end for which man was created. To rebel against this purpose is not only to become "useless" from the religious point of view but also to become a negative agent of destruction running havoc upon the Earth and corrupting it, as the Quran asserts.

In Islamic terms, once man refuses to follow the *Sharī'ah* and perform the rites promulgated by it, he can no longer fulfill his function as God's vicegerent on Earth. Rather, he begins to usurp the role of the Divinity for himself. The pertinence of this doctrine to the current environmental crisis is too obvious to require elaboration. Moreover, such a view possesses a profound truth no matter how much a secularized world finds the performance of sacred rites to be irrelevant to the processes and activities of the order of nature and the cosmic ambience within the framework of a worldview that has severed all ties between moral laws and cosmic laws. In fact, it can be asserted that the significance of religion is not only to discipline the passions and provide the lance for St. George to slay the dragon of selfishness, greed, and callousness within the soul—which provides the psychic energy for much of the destruction of the environment—but also to provide rites that, in addition to saving the soul of the individual, play a vital role in the preservation of the invisible harmony of the order of nature and the economy of the cosmos.

THE GAIA HYPOTHESIS AND THE UNITY OF EXISTENCE

The traditional religious views of the order of nature were based on the interrelation of all things, or what one might call the unity of existence, without confusing this term in the present context with such metaphysical doctrines as the *waḥdat al-wujūd* of the Sufis,[25] which assert that there is only one Reality in the ultimate sense, that is God, and which we usually translate as "the transcendent unity of being" in order to avoid confusion with the unity and interrelation of all things on the level of cosmic existence. It might in fact be asserted that this latter principle is basic to traditional cosmologies that emphasize the aspect of unity and interrelation and refuse to consider objects only in their aspect of separateness and multiplicity, as has been done by modern science until recently.[26]

During the past few years the *Gaia* hypothesis has been proposed by certain scientists to explain the behavior of Earth as an interrelated whole, a kind of organism in which parts are related together in unforseen ways rather than simply as a vast conglomerate of mass in motion to be studied by separating and analyzing each part.[27] The hypothesis, which has now been extended by some to the visible Universe as a whole, has been opposed by many scientists while being enthusiastically embraced by a number of occultists, as well as a wing of the camp of eco-theologians. But the hypothesis is also receiving serious attention from some scientists, environmentalists, and mainstream religious thinkers. It is significant in that it marks a departure from most of the older scientific endeavors based on analysis, segmentation, and division rather than synthesis and integration.

The *Gaia* hypothesis can be viewed from the perspective of the traditional knowledge of the order of nature as a step in the right direction but still confined to the purely physical aspect of things. It is, of course, remarkable to discover the web of relations between forests in the Amazon and droughts in the Sahara or the use of refrigerants and the hole created in the ozone layer of the upper atmosphere. It forms a powerful framework for ecological and environmental studies carried out on the basis of modern science. But the hypothesis still views the physical domain as a closed system unto itself even if it extends to the galaxies and if one speaks of the infinite Universe. The whole of the physical level of reality is, however, only one level of reality that, despite its vastness, is like a pebble before the Sun when compared to the psychic and beyond it the spiritual worlds.

The religious understanding of the order of nature could expand the horizon of the *Gaia* hypothesis to reveal not only the relation of the blood content of polar bears to the pollution of the Hudson River, but also the vaster economy of the Universe dominated by the Logos and the various manifestations of the Divine Principle in different religious universes with their spiritual and angelic hierarchies and intermediate and psychic worlds. *Gaia* could be envisaged again as the Earth (which in fact *Gaia* means in Greek) understood in the context of religious cosmology without doing injustice to the physical component of it. The unity sought could then embrace man in all his levels of reality, including the spiritual as well as the cosmos, extending beyond the physical order but including the physical and its laws. In a sense the religious understanding of nature could provide a vertical dimension for the *Gaia* hypothesis whose search for the unity of the Earth as a living and organic whole has remained until now confined to the horizontal level. A paradigm could be created on the basis of traditional cosmologies, which could serve all the needs of those seeking to solve the environmental crisis while remaining faithful to the nature of reality, all of whose levels are interconnected, whether a particular humanity remains conscious of the higher levels of existence or not. A religious understanding of the order of nature makes evident the veritable "unity of existence" of which the *Gaia* hypothesis, as understood by most of its contemporary defenders, is a horizontal and two-dimensional projection and reflection. Only traditional religion makes possible the third and vertical dimension and access to the higher levels of existence that play a dominate role in the life of the cosmos as well as of man whether one chooses to be aware of them or not.

THE QUESTION OF EVIL AND THE NATURAL ORDER

It is hardly possible to speak of the resacralization of nature and the reestablishment of the religious understanding of the order of nature without dealing with the question of evil and sin. These religious concepts have had diverse meanings among various religions anad sometimes among theological schools within the same religion. Thus one cannot overlook these differences in journeying from one traditional world to another. Certainly both the participation of nature in the Fall of Man and Original Sin as understood in Christianity do not have any meaning in the context of Confucianism and not even the same significance in Islam, which accepts the doctrine of the Fall of Man but not Original Sin. Despite serious differences on this issue, however, certain metaphysical principles have a universal import as far as the relation between nature and evil is concerned and they need to be mentioned here. First, nature is a reflection and even remnant of a paradisal reality that is both transcendent and immanent vis-à-vis it. Second, in its present state nature no longer manifests that reality in its fullness. Third, evil in the theological sense exists in the world of Creation by virtue of its separation from the Divine Principle, which alone is "good" as asserted by Christ in reference to the Father. But this doctrine does not mean that nature is not sacred or that it has ceased completely to contain and reflect something of the paradisal reality.

The separation of Creation from its source is the metaphysical origin of what theologically is called evil. The world is a series of veils (*al-ḥijāb* in Islam) before the Divine Reality or of *Māyā* veiling *Ātman,*[28] but *Māyā* is also Divine Creativity so that the world of nature both reveals and veils the Divine. This separation or evil is manifested in the element of strife and death, which exists in nature, an element that is, however, always overcome by life and harmony. It is enough to contemplate the natural world as yet unspoiled by man to realize how beauty overwhelmingly dominates over ugliness, and harmony dominates over discord. Nevertheless, it is true that the lion and the lamb do not lie together in peace now and will not do so until the complete reintergration of nature into its spiritual principle associated with eschatological events.

What is considered in Christianity and Islam as well as Judaism as the fall of nature from its original perfection, which means its nascent state in Divine Proximity, is seen in non-Abrahamic religions such as Hinduism as the darkening of the cosmic ambience in its outward aspect through the downward movement of the cosmic cycles, especially in the *Kali Yuga* or Age of Darkness, which characterizes the current period of history. In such an age the transparency of the cosmic ambience before the reality of the spiritual world is dimmed to an ever-greater degree as a result of the ever-increasing consolidation, externalization, opacity, and quantification of the cosmos through a process that upon reaching its final point, results in the present cosmic cycle coming to an end.[29] And yet the cosmos never loses its sacred quality and will continue as a locus of Divine Presence to the end of the world.

Here it is necessary also to mention the role of man in the terrestrial and cosmic ambience. It is the darkening of the soul of man that also reflects upon the natural ambience and leads to its destruction. The environmental crisis is before anything else a spiritual crisis. In this sense nature participates in man's Fall but not all of nature's is corrupted by this Fall. If men of the Adamic age were to walk on Earth today, they would still see the face of nature as theophany. As many Christian mystics (such as Jakob Böhme) have said, nature as paradise is still here but it is we who are absent from it. And even today a sage still sees the trees of paradise in beholding a forest and contemplates in the vision of a sublime mountain peak the sacred mountain at the center of the cosmos itself.

In a deeper sense, the nature that was the terrestrial paradise is still here, only she is hiding her face from the gaze of Promethean man, who, cut off from his own center as well as the spiritual principles governing the cosmos, has no interest in nature other than its subjugation and dominion.[30] Evil and sin are realities in the human soul, and they must also be considered in the domain of nature both in relation to the effect of human beings acting upon nature and the "exterioirization" or fall of nature in her external aspects from that perfection which characterized her origin.

Strangely enough, however, nature has preserved that original spiritual reality better than human beings, whose participation in what is theologically called sin is active and willful and not passive as in the world of nature. The Fall of Man is more complete than the fall of the world of nature although man still contains within himself the kingdom of God, to use the famous saying of Christ. The macrocosm is less removed from her achetype and more perfect than man, even in its outward aspect, which veils to some extent the paradisal reality it still bears within itself. It is not, however, correct to assert, as do some current eco-theologians, that the question of evil has no significance in the domain of nature. For the realized sage it is clear that nature both reflects its original paradisal beauty and veils that perfection to the extent of its fall from its original state, a fall that means an externalization that does not destroy but veils the inner reality of nature analogous in many ways to the situation of man. His Fall also means a veiling of his heart, but we still carry the perfection of our Edenic state within the center of our being, and all we have to do is to melt the hardened crust of our heart with the help of the Sacred to gain access to the ever-gushing spring of the Spirit, which still flows at the center of our being, even if we have no direct access to it in our present condition of exteriorization and dispersion.

The resacralization of nature must be carried out with full awareness of the significance of the meaning of evil. the Fall of Man, removal from original perfection, the loss of paradise, as well as the spiritual revival of the cosomos and other relevant teachings seen according to different views of cosmic history by various traditions but accepted in one form or another by religions ranging from Hinduism to Islam. What is significant in the context of the present study is the realization that it is possible to reassert the doctrine of the sacred quality of nature across religious frontiers despite differences of understanding in various religions of the meaning of mankind's Fall, evil, and sin.

Furthermore, it is not necessary to deny these traditional doctrines in order to exalt the world of nature, as is done by current propagators of what has come to be known as "creation spirituality." Nature is sacred even if removed from her paradisal origin, analogous to the way that human life is sacred although most men commit sins and participate in evil acts. It could be argued that nature has even more rights than does contemporary man in being considered as sacred because nature has not fallen as much from its archetype as has man. The order of nature, to use the language of Islam, is still perfectly surrendered to the Will of God; hence, it is *muslim* (meaning in Arabic literally one who has surrendered to God) in a perfect but passive way. Nature has her own prayer and invocation and reflects more directly than most human beings the Divine Qualities or the *lógoi*, which are the principles of all things. The very fact that modrn man does not accept this thesis is itself proof of this assertion. The presence of evil in the world should not therefore in any way detract from the undertanding of the sacred quality of nature and the re-assertion of the religious understanding of the natural order, which has itself taken this element into consideration in most of its sapiental and metaphysical dimensions.

If anything, awareness of the traditional teachings concerning the presence of evil or imperfection in both the cosmic order and in man should make it clear that the realization of the sacred quality of nature implies self-discipline and inner spiritual realization. People who see the light of God within themselves also see it reflected in the realm of nature. The resacralization of nature is not possible without an awakening by us human beings as to who we are and what we are doing in this world. Conversely, nature can also teach man and remind him of that inner spiritual reality which he carries deeply within himself. Thus, it is not possible to cast the veil of opacity and transience of natural forms aside to contemplate their sacred and paradisal qualities without the rediscovery of the sacred within ourselves, an act that is possible only through religion, the rare exceptions only proving the rule.

TO BEHOLD THE SACRED QUALITY OF NATURE: CONCLUDING COMMENTS

The Earth is bleeding and the natural enviroment suffering in an unprecedented manner from the onslaught of man. The problem is now too evident to deny, and the solutions proposed are many but for the most part insufficient. Earth will not be healed by some kind of social engineering or changes in a technology that cannot but treat the world of nature as pure quantity to be manipulated for human needs whether they be real or imaginary. All such actions are no more than cosmetics with an effect that is of necessity only skin deep.

What is needed is a rediscovery of nature as sacred reality and the rebirth of man as the guardian of the sacred, which implies the death of the image of man and nature that has given birth to modernism and its subsequent developments. It does not mean the "invention of a new man" as some have claimed, but rather the resurfacing of the true man, the pontifical man whose reality we still bear within ourselves. Nor does it mean the invention of a sacred view of nature, as if man could ever invent the sacred, but rather the reformulation of the traditional cosmologies and views of nature held by various religions throughout history. It means most of all taking seriously the religious understanding of the order of nature as knowledge corresponding to a vital aspect of cosmic reality and not only subjective conjectures or historical constructs. There must be a radical restructuring of the intellectual landscape to enable us to take this type of knowledge of nature seriously, which means to accept the findings of modern science only within the confines of the limitations that its philosophical suppositions, epistemologies, and historical development have imposed upon it, while rejecting completely its totalitarian claims as *the* science of the natural order. It means to rediscover a science of nature that deals with the *existence* of natural objects in their relation to Being, with their subtle as well as gross aspects, with their interrelatedness to the rest of the cosmos and to us, with their symbolic significance and with their nexus to higher levels of existence leading to the Divine Origin of all things.

Furthermore, in speaking of the religious view of the order of nature we must now do so in a global context reflecting the global character of the problem at hand. It is necessary to delve into religions as different as the Shamanic and Hindu, Buddhist and Abrahamic, without a relativization that would destroy the sense of the sacred in each tradition. There are perspectives and schools within most religions that have not paid much attention to the domain of nature, as seen especially in Western Christianity, but within every integral tradition there *are* those schools that have dealt with the domain of nature both in its spiritual and cosmic reality. It is those schools that must be sought and studied across religious frontiers in a manner so as to preserve the authenticity of each tradition while bringing out the spiritual significance of nature in a universal fashion.

In the same way that during the past decades much effort has been extended in bringing out in a meaningful manner the relation of various religions as far as the meaning of God, revelation, sacred scripture, spiritual practice, and other aspects of religion are concerned, it is necessary to carry out such types of study for the order of nature. In fact, this book has been written as a humble step in the carrying out of this task, which requires both the understanding of the views of different religions and the acceptance of the religious view as such as authentic knowledge of the cosmic and natural domains with all that such an assertion implies vis-à-vis secularist philosophies and sciences.

On a more practical level, it is necessary to create respect on behalf of the followers of a particular religion for what is held to be sacred in another religion not only in the domain, say, of sacred art and architecture but also in the world of nature. A Muslim in Benares does not consider the Ganges to be sacred for himself but must accept its sacredness for the Hindus and respect it, as was done for Hindu holy places by traditional Muslims of Benares for centuries and vice versa as far as Muslim holy places were concerned; this mutual respect has continued for the most part and still survives to some extent despite recent communal tragedies. The respect accorded to manmade sites possessing religious significance must also be extended to natural ones despite difficulties that come about when two or three religions claim the same site or land as holy, as we find in Palestine and Israel, or when the economic considerations of a more powerful people confront the belief system of others who consider a particular forest, river, or mountain to be sacred. The despicable record of the modern world in overlooking the claims of others to the sacred not only in an abstract manner but also concretely, such as land, rivers, forests, etc.—as seen in the destruction of much of the habitat of the Native American peoples—has been itself a major cause of the present environmental crisis and cannot any longer act as a model for future dealings among peoples. In evoking the religious understanding of the order of nature, this sense of respect for the religious teachings concerning nature of religions other than our own must be strengthened in the same way that respect for other human beings or houses of worship of other faiths is encouraged, at least by the majority of those concerned with religion and spirituality on a global scale today.

Religions serve as the source of both an ethics involving the environment and a knowledge of the order of nature. They can abet and strengthen one another in both domains if authentic religious teachings are not compromised and diluted in the face of secularism. This is particularly true of Western Christianity, which for so long has tried to identify itself with a civilization that has grown more secular every day. Traditional Christian teachings even in the domain of nature are in fact much closer to those of other religions than to the modern secularist philosophies of the West, as witnessed by questions concerning the sanctity of life and abortion.

A study of the religious understanding of nature across religious frontiers also affords the possibility of religions enriching each other or certain religions recollecting aspects of their own heritage (now forgotten) through contact with a living tradition. This is certainly as true for sacred sciences and sacred cosmologies as it is for metaphysics, which survive as central realities in certain traditions in contrast to Christianity where they have been for the most part marginalized or forgotten. Conversely, Christianity and to some extent Western Judaism provide valuable knowledge for non-Western religions concerning the confrontation of religion with secularism and the real nature of modern ideas and modes of thought.

Thus, at this moment in human history the revival of a sacred view of nature, which can only issue from authentic religion, requires a drawing together of various religions in providing a religious response on both the ethical and intellectual level. It means not only the formulation of a religious ethics toward nature, which would be comprehensible and compelling for the vast majority of the inhabitants of the globe who still live in a religious universe. It also means the formulation of the knowledge of the order of nature and ultimately sacred sciences that can shine like jewels in the light of each particular religious cosmos, which, possessing a light of a color specifically its own, causes the jewels also to glitter in a particular manner unique to its conditions.

Finally, every being in the world of nature not only issues from the Divine Principle or the One, but also reflects Its Wisdom and, to use theistic language, sings the praises of the Lord. The religious understanding of the order of nature, which we can share only on the condition of conforming ourselves to the world of the Spirit, enables us to read the signatures of God upon the face of things and hear their prayers. It thereby re-creates a link between us and the world of nature that involves not only our bodies and psyches but also the Spirit within us and our final end. It enables us to see the sacred in nature and therefore to treat it not only with respect but also as part of our greater self. It reminds us how precious is each being created by God and how great a sin to destroy wantonly any creature that by virtue of its existence bears the imprint of the Divine and is witness to the One who is our Origin and End, for as the Arab poet has said:

تدلّ على انّه واحدٌ   و في كلّ شئ له آيةٌ

In all things there exists a sign from Him:
Which bears proof that He is One.

wa'Llāhu a'lam

NOTES

1. This includes the queston of overpopulation, which in of course a direct consequence of modern medical practices with their great successes combined with catastrophic consequences.

2. See for example, Henryk Skolimowski, *A Sacred Place to Dwell* (Rockport; Maine: Element Books, 1993), where he speaks of his "ecological philosophy," which contains, nevertheless, important religious elements.

3. See Whitall N. Perry, "The Dragon That Swallowed St. George," in Perry, *Challenges to a Secularist Society* (in press).

4. See Martin Lings, *Ancient Beliefs and Modern Superstitions* (Cambridge: Quinta Essentia, 1991); and Lord Northbourne, *Looking Back on Progress* (Pates Manor, U.K.: Perennial Books), 1970.

5. See especially Chapter 6.

6. We have dealt with these issues in our book *Knowledge and the Sacred* (Albany: State University of New York Press, 1989), Chapter 4. We have also dealt with the heirarchy of the sciences fron the natural to the metaphysical in the context of the Islamic

tradition in *Science and Civilization in Islam* (Cambridge: The Islamic Texts Society, 1987) and *Islamic Science: An Illustrated Study* (London: World of Islam Festival Publishing Co., 1976).

7. According to Islamic law, when a pilgrim performs the *hajj* with sincerity, God forgives his or her sins and in a sense the person begins life anew. That is one of the reasons why many people hope to die on pilgrimage so that they will depart this world in a state of purity. To this is added a second reason, which concerns the act of pilgrimage itself. According to a *hadīth*, a person who dies on pilgrimage dies the death of a martyr *(al-shahīd)* and so enters paradise. But the two reasons are obviously interrelated, for it is because the *hajj* integrates man in his state of original purity that dying on the way to the *hajj* has such a consequence upon the soul.

8. See Nasr, *Knowledge and the Sacred*, pp. 100ff, where we have dealt with some of these figures.

9. Bell's theorm in a sense sets a limit upon what we can know about subparticles quantitatively and points to an underlying unity that would explain the observable relation between two phenomena themselves in space and time but with a relation that cannot be logically explained in terms of objects existing in the ordinary sense in space and time but which imply "nonlocal" connections and the presence of another order of reality. But this other order or reality and unity itself lie beyond the realm of physics as understood today. That is why Böhm's theory of the implicate order is rejected by so many physicists as having no basis in the science of physics. The metaphysical explanations given of Bell's theorem by such figures as Wolfgang Smith (see his essay "Bell's Theorem and the Perennial Ontology") show precisely how metaphysical and theological knowledge can interpret the significance of a physical discovery and not how modern physics can lead by itself to the religious view of the order of nature, as claimed by so many proponents of "cosmic consciousness" and "New Age" spirituality.

10. The whole question of the rapport between religion as it makes claims upon the cosmos and modern science is, of course, of great significance but is not the subject of the present study whose aim is to underscore the significance of the religious understanding of nature.

11. In the same way that in astrology the Moon, as the lowest heavenly body, synthesizes the celestial influences of the planets above, so does the Prophet as the last in the chain of prophecy synthesize the prophetic message of the whole prophetic cycle. That is why in many Islamic cosmological schemes in which each prophet corresponds to a planet, the Prophet of Islam occupies the heaven of the Moon. See Nasr, *Islamic Science*, p. 33. From another point of view the Moon, in intergrating all the celestial influences above it and transmitting it to Earth, symbolizes the heart of Adam, the "primordial man," who is the prototype of man as the bridge between Heaven and Earth. See Titus Burckhardt, *Mystical Astrology According to Ibn'Arabi*, trans. Bulent Rauf (Gloucestershire: Beshara Publications, 1977), pp. 31–34.

12. On the veritable meaning of symbols understood traditionally, see René Guénon, *Fundamental Symbols: The Universal Language of Sacred Science*, trans. Alvin Moore (Cambridge: Quinta Essentia, 1994); and Martin Lings, *Symbol and Achetype: A Study of the Meaning of Existence* (Cambridge: Quinta Essenta, 1991).

13. For example, when the Quran asserts, "Do not do mischief in the Earth, working corruption" (XXIX:36). The Quranic idea of "corrupting the earth" or being "corrupter of the Earth" *(al-mufsid fi'l-ard)*, which has a legal status in Islamic law and has been discussed by classical Muslim jurists as far as obeying God's Law and being just in human society are concerned, certainly possesses a natural and cosmic dimension and can be easily

applied to the corruption of the Earth from the point of view of the destruction of the natural environment today.

14. On the description of the sun dance and its spiritual signifiance see Joseph E. Brown, *The Spiritual Legacy of the American Indians* (New York: Crossroad Publications, 1982), Chapter 7, "Sun Dance: Sacrifice, Renewal, Identity," pp. 101–105; Frithjof Schuon, "The Sun Dance," in Schuon, *The Feathered Sun* (Bloomington, Ind.: World Wisdom Books, 1990), pp. 90–100; and Titus Burckhardt, "The Sun Dance," in Burckhardt, *Mirror of the Intellect*, trans. William Stoddart (Albany: State University of New York Press, 1987), pp. 164–170. Brown writes, "The Sun Dance is thus not a celebration by humans for humans; it is an honoring of all life and the source of all life that life may continue." Brown, *Spiritual Legacy*, p. 105.

15. Burckhardt, *Mirror of the Intellect*, p. 168.

16. For the symbolic significance of the magic square connected with the *Ming-Tang* and its cosmic correspondences, see René Guénon, *The Great Triad*, trans. Peter Kingsley (Cambridge: Quinta Essentia, 1991), Chapter 16, pp. 110ff.

17. Robert Eno, *The Confucian Creation of Heaven: Philosophy and the Defense of Ritual Mastery* (Albany: State University of New York Press, 1990), p. 153.

18. Ibid., p. 153.

19. According to the *ḥadīth*, "The Earth was placed for me as a mosque and purifier."

20. See Seyyed Hossein Nasr, *Islamic Art and Spirituality* (Albany: State University of New York Press, 1987), pp. 37ff.

21. On the esoteric symbolism of the Kaaba and the *ḥajj*, see Henry Corbin, *Temple and Contemplation*, trans. Philip and Liadain Sherrard (London: KPI, 1986), Chapter 4, pp. 183ff; and Charles-Andre Gilis, *La Doctrine initiatique du pèlerinage à la Maison d'Allâh* (Paris: Les Éditions de l'Oeuvre, 1982).

22. See Michel Chodkiewicz, *Seal of the Saints: Prophethood and Sainthood in the Doctrine of Ibn 'Arabī*, trans. Liadain Sherrard (Cambridge: Islamic Texts Society, 1993).

23. According to Sufi doctrine the very "stuff" of which the Universe is made is the "Breath of the Compassionate" (*nafas al-Raḥmān* or *al-nafas al-raḥmānī*) and the existence of all things is nothing but their invocation and praise of God. That is why the sage hears the *dhikr*, or invocation of God, in the sound of the running streams and the cry of the eagle, in the rustling of the trees, in the wind, and the sound of the waves breaking upon the shore. For a summary of this view see Nasr, *Science and Civilization in Islam*, Chapter 13.

24. Translated by Annemarie Schimmel, *Mystical Dimensions of Islam* (Chapel Hill: University of North Carolina Press, 1975), p. 332; see also Yunus Emre, *The Drop That Became the Sea*, trans. Kabir Helminski and Refik Algan (Putney, Vt.: Threshold Books, 1989), pp. 72–73, where the entire poem is translated, although somewhat differently. It might be added that the contemplative person hears the sound "Allah, Allah" here and now in the rivers that flow in virgin nature precisely because nature is not even now separated from the paradisal reality that it manifests for those who have the eye to behold the reality behind and beyond the merely phenomenal and sensual.

25. On the meaning of *waḥdat al-wujūd* also translated as "Oneness of Being" see Martin Lings, *A Sufi Saint of the Twentieth Century* (Cambridge: Islamic Text Society, 1993), chapter V; and S.H. Nasr, *Three Muslim Sages* (Delmar, N.Y.: Caravan Books, 1975), pp. 104ff.

26. We have dealt with this issue extensively as far as Islamic cosmology is concerned in our book *An Introduction to Islamic Cosmological Doctrines* (Albany: State University of New York Press, 1993).

27. See James Lovelock *Gaia: A New Look at Life on Earth* (Oxford: Oxford University Press, 1979); and Lovelock, *The Ages of Gaia* (New York: W.W. Norton, 1988).

28. See Frithjof Schuon, "*Ātmā—Māyā*," in his book *In the Face of the Absolute* (Bloomington, Ind.: World Wisdom Books, 1989), pp. 53ff.; and Schuon, *Esoterism as Principle and as Way* (Pates Manor, U.K.: Perennial Books, 1990), "The Mystery of the Veil," pp. 47ff.

29. See René Guénon, *The Region of Quantity and the Signs of the Times*, trans. Lord Northbourne (London: Luzac, 1953).

30. We recall many years ago walking one early morning with 'Allāmah Ṭabāṭabā'ī— one of the great traditional philosophers, spritual figures, and saintly men of Persia—in a beautiful high valley in the Alborz Mountains outside Tehran. We had all just prayed the morning prayers and there was a strong sense of spiritual presence in the whole idyllic natural ambience. The master said that if only one or two "profane" people from the city, individuals who not pray and have no inner communion with nature, were to appear, the entire ambience would change and nature would suddenly hide her spiritual aspect. In a few minutes this is exactly what happened. Two city people with a nontraditional outlook and presence appeared around the bend of the river beside which we were walking. Suddenly the ambience changed and something became eclipsed. It was as if in a traditional Muslim household a strange man would suddenly enter the home and the women would quickly put on veils to hide their beauty from the gaze of the stranger. The master smiled and said that is what happens when those who are strangers (*nā maḥram* in Persian, that is, literally not part of the intimate family) enter into the inner precinct of nature. Nature hides her most intimate beauty from them.

Index

293